What Has This Got to Do
with the Liberation of Black People?

SUNY SERIES IN AFRICAN AMERICAN STUDIES
John R. Howard and Robert C. Smith, editors

What Has This Got to Do with the Liberation of Black People?

*The Impact of Ronald W. Walters
on African American Thought and Leadership*

Edited by
Robert C. Smith,
Cedric Johnson, and
Robert G. Newby

Published by State University of New York Press, Albany

For information, contact State University of New York Press, Albany, NY
www.sunypress.edu

Production by Jenn Bennett
Marketing by Michael Campochiaro

Library of Congress Cataloging-in-Publication Data

What has this got to do with the liberation of Black people? : the impact of Ronald W. Walters on African American thought and leadership / edited by Robert C. Smith, Cedric Johnson, and Robert G. Newby.
    pages cm. — (SUNY series in African American studies)
    Includes bibliographical references and index.
    ISBN 978-1-4384-5091-9 (hardcover : alk. paper) 1. African Americans—Politics and government—20th century. 2. African Americans—Politics and government—21st century. 3. African American leadership—History—20th century. 4. African American leadership—History—21st century. 5. Walters, Ronald W. 6. Political scientists—United States—Biography. 7. African American political scientists—Biography. I. Smith, Robert C. (Robert Charles), 1947- author, editor of compilation. II. Johnson, Cedric, 1971- author, editor of compilation. III. Newby, Robert G., author, editor of compilation.
    E185.615.W436 2014
    323.1196'073—dc23

2013019518

10 9 8 7 6 5 4 3 2 1

For Pat

Contents

Part III

Part IV

Part V

Part VI

Part VII

Tables and Figures

xi

Acknowledgments

We should first like to acknowledge the work of Scottie Smith in editing the papers and preparing the volume for publication. Michael Rinella, State University of New York Press' senior acquisitions editor, early on recognized the significance of a collection of essays on Walters and expeditiously facilitated the review and production processes. The anonymous reviewers also recognized the significance of the volume and provided generous and discerning commentary. We appreciate the consideration of Transaction Publishers and the University Press of Florida in granting permissions, without costs, to include previously published essays by Walters in this volume.

The volume is dedicated to Patricia "Pat" Walters, Ron's wife of forty-seven years. Without Pat's support—emotional, intellectual, and financial—Ron Walters could not have done his work.

Shortly before the book was accepted for publication, Hanes Walton Jr. died. Like Walters, Walton was an architect of the modern study of African American politics. His contribution to this volume is among his last publications. But over four decades of prodigious research and conceptual refinement he helped to make the study of African American politics a major field of study in American political science. His death, like Walters', leaves a large void in the field. His passing as this book went to press is melancholy, but his intellectual legacy is an abiding source of comfort and inspiration.

Introduction

ROBERT C. SMITH

For more than a decade I tried to persuade Walters to write his memoirs. Indeed, in my last email communication with him days before he entered the hospital for the last time I raised the issue. I was writing in response to his "Reflections" essay published in this volume and wrote that the essay "gets me to thinking of the perhaps not so dead horse I've been beating for lo these many years—you need to write the MEMOIR man—you owe it to the young, and to the intellectual and political understanding of one of the most critical periods of our history."[1] In trying to persuade him to write the memoir, I would occasionally compare him with Arthur Schlesinger Jr., the distinguished liberal historian and political activist who in 2000 published the first volume of his memoirs.[2] Although he did not particularly care for the comparison, I would say, "Through Schlesinger's writings and career one can trace the history of postwar liberalism in the United States, and through your writings and career we can trace the history of post–civil rights era black politics in America."[3]

Walters would always respond by saying something like "no one is interested in reading about me," or "I am not interested in writing about me," or "maybe I will get to it when I finish my book on" whatever he was working on at the time. Unfortunately, he died before he could "get to it" if indeed he ever would have gotten to it. This is unfortunate, because as uncomfortable as he might have been with the comparison to Schlesinger, his memoir would have been to black politics what Schlesinger's was to American liberalism.

1

That is, his-story was not about him but about history; a history that, like Schlesinger, he not only chronicled but shaped. Indeed, Walters' history goes back to the civil rights era itself, for in 1958 at the age of twenty when he was president of the NAACP Youth Council in his hometown of Wichita, Kansas, he helped to organize the first modern lunch counter sit-in.[4] This was almost two years before the more famous Greensboro, North Carolina, sit-in, which historians view as a pivotal event in the development of the protest phase of the civil rights movement and the eventual passage of the landmark civil rights laws of the 1960s.[5] At the time of his death in September 2011 at the age of seventy-three, Walters was internationally recognized as the foremost scholar of race politics in the United States and as the most influential strategist in black politics since Bayard Rustin.[6]

From Wichita to Washington

Ronald William Walters was born in Wichita on July 20, 1938. The eldest son in a family of seven children, his father was Gilmar "Butler" Walters, a "Buffalo Soldier," Tuskegee airman and a professional musician. His mother, Maxine, was a civil rights investigator for the state of Kansas. Walters' parents were racially conscious and socially active, which as Robert Newby discusses in his chapter in this volume, undoubtedly influenced his engagement with politics and civil rights.

After graduating from Fisk University, Walters earned a PhD in political science from American University. In the late 1960s he established and became founding chair of the first African American Studies program at Brandeis. In the early 1970s he became chairman of Howard University's Political Science Department, helping to turn it into one of the two leading academic centers for the study of African American politics.

A prolific writer, he authored more than one hundred articles and seven books, including important studies on the theory and practice of Pan Africanism, on African American leadership, on strategies for black participation in presidential elections, on reparations, and on the resurgence of conservatism as an expression of white ethnic nationalism. In addition to his scholarly writings, Walters was the leading interpreter of African American politics in the national media. He wrote articles in most of the leading newspapers and appeared on virtually all of the national television and radio news and commentary programs (appearing a record ninety-one times on C-SPAN). His column on black politics was syndicated by the National Newspaper Publishers Association (NNPA). He also worked as a roving correspondent for NNPA, covering major national and international events. He was also a principal commentator on black politics for *BET News*. From these numerous media activities, he helped to shape popular understanding of race politics in America.

Walters was among a handful of black scholars able and willing to bridge the divide between scholarship and politics. This is a divide that many scholars do not wish to bridge because they think scholarship should be detached from politics, while others cannot bridge it because of the esoteric nature of their work and still others cannot because of their critical perspectives. While maintaining a critical perspective, Walters throughout the post–civil rights era was an advisor and strategist for the black leadership establishment. Vernon Jordan, the former head of the Urban League, described him as "an indispensable part of the brain trust of the movement."[7] He was a top advisor to Charles Diggs, the founding chair of the Congressional Black Caucus, where Walters helped to shape the group's philosophy and early strategies. He also advised caucuses of local and state black elected officials—the black caucuses of both the Democratic and Republican parties—and was an influential force at the National Black Political Conventions of the 1970s. In 1984 he was a principal strategist in Jesse Jackson's presidential campaign. And he participated in the writing of every post–civil rights era "black agenda" from the 1972 Gary Convention to the Million Man March.

In addition to his work in domestic politics and policy, he had an extensive background and experience in international affairs (his doctoral dissertation was on U.S. foreign policy toward Africa, and one of his books was on South Africa's development of nuclear weapons). At Howard he organized conferences on Pan Africanism, was a leader in several antiapartheid organizations, and was among the founders of TransAfrica and chairman of the board of its affiliate organization TransAfrica Forum. He was also a consultant to the United Nations on racism and discrimination.

As a professor, Walters taught and mentored some of the nation's leading black political scientists. From 1969 to 1996 he was on the faculty at Howard; then he was recruited by the University of Maryland, College Park as professor of Government and African American Studies, Distinguished Leadership Scholar, and director of the African American Leadership Academy. He retired in 2009, but at the time of his death he had been persuaded to return to Howard as the senior scholar in residence in African American politics.

In his "Reflections" essay completed weeks before his death, Walters reflected on his career:

> For over forty years, my research has sought to address the political condition of African American peoples. I came of age during the civil rights era and, like many of my colleagues, inherited the progressive values of the age with respect to how to utilize my profession. The pressures were also substantial because it was the dawn of black studies, and the thirst of those who had inherited new political rights in 1964 and 1965 pushed many of us to engage the aspirations of our communities for empowerment tactics and strategies. I remember a friend of mine and I would talk on the phone and one question we would ask each other at odd intervals was, "What does this have to do with the liberation of black people?" This question has guided my selection of research topics since that time.

We believe Walters' work of the last forty years represents an important lens through which one can assess the political aspirations and struggles of African Americans since the death of Dr. King in 1968. We believe further that his legacy of the successful blending of theory and practice is important to this and future generations of scholars and practitioners.

Black Activism Encounters American Political Science

Political science, like most of the sciences, natural and social, in the United States was at its origins a racist and white supremacist profession. Rogers Smith, among others, has shown that an overt ideology of white supremacy and racism dominated political science research from the founding of the discipline in the 1880s until the

1920s.[8] From the 1920s until the 1970s political science scholarship ignored the glaring contradiction of the racial oppression of blacks in the midst of one of the world's leading democratic states.[9] Even after Gunnar Myrdal laid bare this contradiction in his monumental 1944 work, most political scientists remained oblivious to what Myrdal called the "dilemma" of the "Negro problem" in American democracy.[10] In this regard political science lagged behind history, sociology, and anthropology, which as early as the 1940s began to pay some attention to what the black political scientist Martin Kilson called "the edifice of white supremacist pariahization, marginalization, torment and oppression of black people in American life."[11]

The civil rights revolution of the early 1960s, the black power revolt, and the ghetto rebellions of the mid-1960s finally forced the issue of race onto the agenda of American political science and its professional associations. White mainstream political science in its "race relations" approach to the study of race politics tended to focus on the concerns of whites about stability and social peace rather than the concerns of blacks about freedom and equality.[12] As a result of the tumultuous system-destabilizing events of the 1960s and the implementation of affirmative action, the profession in the 1970s began to open its doors to a relatively larger number of African Americans.

In small, token numbers blacks began to enter the profession in the 1930s and 1940s, when scholars like Ralph Bunche, Merze Tate, Robert Martin, Samuel DuBois Cook, Robert Brisbane, and Vincent Brown earned PhDs from the nation's prestigious universities.[13] This first wave of black political scientists, although trained at some of the nation's leading universities, usually could only find employment at the nation's historically black colleges and universities. Working in obscurity in these small, resource-poor institutions without financial support or grants and with large numbers of classes and students, these first-generation black political scientists in a limited way launched an alternative to the mainstream race relations approach. As Walton and Smith write, "They published in obscure and poorly diffused journals and little-known presses, which resulted, in many instances, in their work being overlooked and undervalued. Racism's manifestations in academia allowed much valuable work to remain unseen. Not only was the results of their research made invisible, but these scholars themselves became invisible in the profession."[14]

Walters was a part of the second wave or generation of political scientists, entering graduate school and the profession in the late 1960s and early 1970s. They entered in relatively larger numbers and were influenced by the civil rights and black power movements. Walters and his cohort offered a different perspective, one Katherine Tate in her chapter in this volume describes as a "black science." This perspective focuses less on system stability and social peace and more on trying to empower blacks as a group as a means to provide solutions to long-standing social and economic problems in the black community, even if this means challenging the status-quo, upsetting whites, and disrupting system stability.[15]

This new perspective resulted in the creation of African American Studies programs and the strengthening and restructuring of the graduate political science curriculums at Howard and Atlanta universities. As I indicated earlier, Walters began his career as the founding chair of the first African American Studies program at Brandeis. Although his graduate specialization was international relations, at Brandeis he shifted to domestic U.S. politics, developing courses in African American politics. In 1970 Samuel DuBois Cook, the first African American appointed to the political science faculty at Duke University (in 1971), while a program officer at the Ford Foundation persuaded the foundation to award major grants to Howard and Atlanta to strengthen and expand their doctoral programs in political science. In 1972 Walters was recruited to head Howard's Political Science Department. With the resources of the Ford grant, Walters expanded the department's faculty, recruited a larger number of graduate students, reshaped the curriculum to include a full-fledged black politics field while at the same time attempting to infuse the traditional fields (American politics, international relations, public administration, comparative politics) with the new black science perspective.[16]

Also, at this time new, autonomous disciplines challenging black professional associations were organized in the social sciences. Walters played important roles in organizing and leading two of these associations, the National Conference of Black Political Scientists (NCOBPS) and the African Heritage Studies Association.[17]

In 1973 Howard University sociologist Joyce Ladner edited *The Death of White Sociology*. This was the earliest effort of black scholars to render a systematic critique of mainstream "white bourgeois" social science and think through what a black alternative, a black science, might look like. Walters was one of two political scientists contributing to the volume; the other was Charles Hamilton the coauthor with Stokely Carmichael of the influential black power manifesto *Black Power: Politics of Liberation in America.* In his chapter "Toward a Definition of a Black Social Science," Walters wrote, "one of the clearest duties of the black social scientists is to challenge the very foundations of white social science and its effects on the black community. . . . Each social scientist must recognize the need to bend his efforts toward the creation of some form of community power."[18]

In addition to challenging the epistemological, theoretical, and to some extent methodological foundations of the social sciences, activist-oriented scholars seeking to empower the black community also had to challenge the discipline's apolitical, disengaged norm of neutrality and objectivity in social research. In general, graduate students in the social sciences in the 1960s and 1970s were socialized to adhere to the Weberian canon of objectivity. This canon eschews normative concerns by focusing on describing, explaining, and theorizing the world, leaving changing it to the "politicians."[19] As an activist scholar Walters was more inclined toward the Marxian view of the role of the social scientist. "The philosophers have only interpreted the world," Marx wrote in his famous *Theses on Feuerbach,* "the point, however, is to change it."[20] Walters was not a Marxist; he was a Du Boisian and drew his professional inspiration from Du Bois' view of the duty of the black scholar to use knowledge to uplift the race.

The kind of activist, change-oriented research and publishing Walters wished to pursue was antithetical to the norms of professional political science. In his forty years Walters published more than one hundred articles; not a single one of them was in a traditional, mainstream political science journal. As he wrote in the "Reflections" essay:

My work is and has been interdisciplinary, since as a young scholar attempting to break through the rejection slips of the major journals, I came to understand the standards by which I was being evaluated for publication and decided that many of them, while useful to the discipline, were not useful to the truth I was attempting to discover, consistent with my larger objectives. So, I came to be somewhat suspicious of

the disciplinary narrowness, not only with respect to subject
matter but methodologies, and came to believe that what was
needed more than anything was the correct interpretation
of the studies that were done on African American political
life. The sum total of that concern was that I was not led to
produce much original data from self-initiated studies but to
test the studies that were being produced against what I knew
from deep involvement in community politics to arrive at the
black truth as I understood it.

Thus, most of his work was published in specialized journals, in journals of black studies and in journals of thought and opinion, most
notably *Black World.*

Political Strategist and Public Intellectual

This activist approach to research and writing also informed Walters' book-length manuscripts. They were change-oriented or what
he referred to in his *Death of White Sociology* essay as "liberation oriented social science."[21] Often his writings emerged directly out of or
were informed by his work as a political strategist, as, for example, in
his book *Black Presidential Politics: A Strategic Approach,* which flowed
partly from his work as Jesse Jackson's principal strategist in his 1984
presidential campaign. Similarly, he published a series of articles in
Black World written in the midst of the ideologically divisive National
Black Political Convention of the 1970s, essays deliberately crafted to
bridge the ideological conflicts he observed as a leading convention
strategist.[22] Finally, out of his many years of advising the Congressional Black Caucus and other black elected officials was forged his
thought that the post–civil rights era system–oriented electoral politics and processes were not enough to extract policy benefits from
the system. Instead, he urged black leaders to simultaneously employ
an "insider strategy" of electoral politics and an "outsider strategy"
of protests and mass mobilization. This dual strategy he explains in
detail in his contribution to *African American Leadership* and in *Freedom Is Not Enough: Black Voters, Black Candidates and American Presidential Elections.* Again, these studies are informed as much by his

"deep involvement in community politics" as they are by traditional academic research and theorizing.

Finally, Walters believed that black scholars, to the extent they were able, should be public intellectuals. They should be public intellectuals in the sense of translating their sometimes esoteric academic knowledge into information that could be shared with the general public in lectures, newspaper interviews, radio and television appearances, and in regular columns and occasional op-eds in both black and mainstream outlets. The most frequently quoted black political scientist—and one of the most frequently quoted scholars of any color—Walters saw this time-consuming and often tedious engagement with the media as an integral part of his work. In a 1990 *Washington Post* profile, Jacqueline Trescott suggested Walters' effectiveness with the media, his "media savvy," was based in part on his activism. Describing him as the "peripatetic protester" and the "griot of black politics," she concluded that his engagement with the events, issues, and personalities he wrote about enabled him to "edit years of expounding into an electronic sound bite."[23] Aspects of this part of Walters' work are treated in Cedric Johnson's chapter in this volume.

Major Themes in Walters' Writings and Work

Although it is not easy given forty years of work encompassing the broadest array of writings and activism, five major themes may be distilled to constitute the core themes or concerns of Walters' life and career.

The first is scholarship in the production of knowledge; knowledge relevant to, what he often referred to as, the liberation of black people. Although the dignity, freedom, and equality of people of African descent were the principal focus of his work, he believed that the black freedom struggle would inevitably contribute to the freedom struggles of all people. This knowledge acquisition, however, must be integrally linked to activism. This idea of activism is a second theme of Walters' work.

A third theme of Walters' work was African American leadership; a leadership that emanated from the black community in the sense that the individuals who present themselves for leadership have their origins in the community and its culture and reflect its needs and aspirations. The study, development, and nurturing of this kind of leadership was an abiding concern.

A fourth theme is public policy, the development and implementation of public policies to achieve for African Americans equal access to and the equal allocation of societal resources. This required, in his view, policies sensitive to the historical legacies of racism as well as racism's manifestations in contemporary institutional practices.

A final theme is unity, the bringing together collectively of African Americans of different ideologies, parties, and institutional affiliations to develop common agendas and strategies around serious programs devoted to bettering the spiritual and material conditions of African people.

Overview of Chapters

In a single volume we cannot claim to cover all of these themes or any one of them with the greatest of depth. However, within the limitations of space, and the availability, resources, and time of the contributors, we endeavored to be as representative, comprehensive, and detailed as possible. We have assembled a distinguished, diverse, multigenerational group of scholars to provide this assessment of Walters' work and its impact and influence on African American thought and politics. All of the contributors are admirers of Walters and several are his former students. We honor his life and legacy in this book. But in the letter of invitation we made it clear that the "best way to honor him is to subject his work to rigorous, critical assessment. . . . We honor him best with that degree of admiration and detachment that great thought deserves."

All except three of the essays were especially prepared for this volume.[24] The essays by Cory Cook and Errol Henderson were originally prepared for presentation at the 2005 annual meeting of the National Conference of Black Political Scientists at a special plenary on Walters' work. The essay by Katherine Tate was originally prepared for the 2012 annual meeting of the National Conference of Black Political Scientists.

The volume is divided into seven sections. The first section begins with an essay by Robert Newby. Newby is Walters' oldest and dearest friend, having grown up with him in Wichita. His chapter is a personal, somewhat idiosyncratic biographical essay that places Walters' career in the context of his growing up in the semi-segregated "wheatlands" of Kansas. A strong, close-knit race-conscious family in a vibrant black community and his study at Fisk University are among the forces that shaped Walters into one of the "tallest trees" of the last half century in the struggle for the liberation of African peoples. Aldon Morris' chapter recounts the history of the Wichita drugstore sit-in in 1958 and the role played by Walters in organizing this first modern sit-in. Morris also discusses the significance of this "low visibility" protest in the emergence of the lunch counter sit-in movement. He writes that "It is rare that a major leader of a pioneering protest movement also becomes an accomplished social scientist who provides a scholarly account of the movement in which he participated." This is exactly what Walters did. Morris draws on Walters, other studies of Wichita, and his own seminal research to present a nuanced and learned history of this "groundbreaking model" of civil rights protest.

The final essay in this section is by Walters himself. In fact, it is the last thing that he completed days before he entered the hospital for the last time. We have titled the essay "Reflections." It was written in response to a series of questions asked by the editors of the *National Political Science Review*. In his response he reflects on the difficulties he faced in the discipline in trying to do political science research as an activist scholar committed to making his work relevant to the liberation of black people. Often, he writes, as he attempted to navigate the norms and ethos of the discipline he would find himself asking, "What has this got to do with the liberation of black people?" As he often did with his writings, he sent me a copy of the essay, writing, "Bob, you have heard some of this before. But in print, is it too candid?" My response: "No, the candor makes the essay all the more alluring. It is poignant and will make our older colleagues reflect and should be of inspiration for some of the young."[25]

In the next section the chapter by Tate serves to foreground the rest of the chapters in the volume. She compares Walters' work with the works of Linda Williams and Derrick Bell, two other recently deceased black scholars who practiced what she calls "black science." Rejecting the "assumptions that the politics and personal attributes of researchers are irrelevant to the science they practice," black science "competes with values rooted in white nationalism that generally dominates mainstream work." Black science scholars' values she avers are rooted in the "bias" of black liberation, concerned with the development of knowledge that exposes and explains "the inherent inequality in the status of African Americans" and work in the "tradition of advocating group empowerment." In locating Walters' work within this tradition, she analyzes his books on black presidential politics, white nationalism, African American leadership and reparations, highlighting the "often subversive" nature of his scholarship and its "unyielding pessimism." Tate, like other contributors to this volume and other scholars of black politics generally, is critical of Walters' tendency to view the black community as possessing "an organically grown set of unified black interests" and his downplaying of the significance of black conservatives, which she claims Walters "surgically" remove from black politics.

Cedric Johnson's chapter describes his experiences working with Walters as a graduate student at the University of Maryland and at the African American Leadership Institute, which Walters founded. He then situates Walters work in what he calls the "wider new Democratic political milieu" of Clinton era neoliberalism, focusing on Walters' critique of the Africa Growth and Opportunity Act as an example of his oppositional public intellectual work.

The third section begins with Andra Gillespie's analysis of Walters' contribution to the coauthored *African American Leadership*, highlighting his advocacy of a dual "insider-outsider" strategy where black leaders link routine electoral-institutional politics with mass mobilization and protests. Like Tate, Gillespie too is critical of what she sees as Walters' failure to see the "increasing diversity of interests within the black community." Rejecting what she calls Walters' "unity imperative" or his "big tent" philosophy, Gillespie offers a "modest proposal" for the recognition of differences in the black community and a new leadership "model of organized factions." She also calls on scholars and journalists to employ "fact-based empirical" assessments and other "metrics" to evaluate black individuals' claim to leadership and the effectiveness of their strategies and programs.

Errol Henderson brings together or attempts to synthesize two of the most important—perhaps the two most important—themes of Walters' work—black leadership and black nationalism or the imperative of black unity in spite of ideological diversity. Walters believed black unity was imperative because, in spite of all the talk of the declining significance of racism and a post-racist, colorblind society, racism—dynamic and evolving for sure—remains the decisive determinant of the well-being of the black community. While Henderson acknowledges the significance of racism and the importance of black nationalism in combatting it, he, with Tate and Gillespie, too believes Walters often in his activism and scholarship "succumb[ed] to the siren call of the black unity thesis." Henderson contends that the enormous ideological diversity in the black community renders Walters' "big tent" black nationalism a "chimera." This prominent "lacuna" in black politics was unresolved by Walters and continues to be unresolved. Thus, Henderson calls for further research and reflection because, "simply put, we need to understand the motive forces driving the adoption of diverse ideologies and the dynamic factors that lead to changes in the ideological outlook of black peoples with respect to which leaders they support and follow, utilizing whatever means and toward whatever ends."

The two chapters in the next section use Walters' *White Nationalism, Black Interests: Conservative Public Policy and the Black Community* as theoretical and hypothesis-generating frameworks for the conduct of innovative and important empirical research. In this most provocative of his books, Walter argues that a "substantial component" of the ascendant conservative movement in the United States should be theorized as akin to other ethnic nationalist movements observed historically and comparatively as, for example, in the former republics of Yugoslavia. In other words, a part of the conservative movement is not just principled opposition to "big government" and high taxes but is also a manifestation of a long-standing white nationalist movement committed to reinstituting and strengthening racialized hierarchies of power and privilege. This theorizing of conservatism, white nationalist interests, and public policy opens fascinating new possibilities for research on race politics, which are explored in the Belk and Cook chapters.[26]

In a penetrating, data-rich analysis of the Tea Party movement that emerged during the Obama presidency, Belk argues that it emerged precisely out of the "very conditions that Walters predicted would produce a radical conservative uprising." With the election of the first nonwhite president and the economic dislocations caused by the Great Recession, some whites experienced what Walters called a sense of "power deflation" that made them more receptive to appeals of radical conservatives. Consequently, white nationalism animates the Tea Party movement and some of the more virulent opposition to the president and his policies. Belk's is a fine study of the Tea Party movement in its own right, but its theoretic and analytic powers are enhanced by his skillful application of Walters' theory of white nationalism.

Cook is equally skillful in his use of the theory. His work focuses on "identity politics" research on Congress. Cook notes that this fairly extensive body of research has ignored the representation of whites and males, the dominant groups in the society, while concentrating on the representation of subordinate minority groups: blacks, Latinos, and women. Using Walters' work as a frame of reference, Cook's chapter addresses this gap in the literature on congressional representation by focusing on how Congress represents the interest of whites. Cook acknowledges that it is more difficult to identify "white interests" than black, Latino, or female interests, but he finds Walters' suggestion that legislation designed to produce "racially disparate outcomes" that favor whites or males is a useful empirical indicator. Using this indicator, Cook coded over twenty thousand bills introduced in the House between 1991 and 1999 to determine whether they had racially disparate impacts.

Analyzing bill sponsorship, co-sponsorship, and roll call voting, his preliminary findings lend support to Walters' theory: white legislators do promote white racial group interests although less consistently so than blacks promote black interests. He also found that white, conservative Republican representatives are more likely to advance white racial group interests. Cook concludes that Walters was correct that the 1994 Republican takeover of Congress "resulted in white legislators pursuing an agenda committed to maintaining racial hierarchies of prestige and power." Cook's research suggests the need to broaden the boundaries of research on identity politics in Congress, and he expands the analysis of white nationalism in national politics to study the emergence of the Tea Party as a nationalistic response to the election of President Obama.

In the fifth section Hanes Walton and Lenneal Henderson focus specifically on Walters' activist scholarship, with Walton looking at his work as a strategist in presidential elections and Henderson looking at his work on the District of Columbia.

Henderson locates Walters' District activism in the action research tradition of sociologist Kurt Lewin.[27] Action research, in Lewin's view, does not "separate the investigation from the action needed to solve the problem." District problem solving was the focus of Walters' last book, *Democratic Destiny and the District of Columbia,* where he brought together a group of young scholars to address the multifaceted problem of democratic governance or lack thereof in the nation's capital. Walters was a resident of suburban Maryland, but his political soul and mind was in the majority black city of Washington, which Henderson avers was his "laboratory" for understanding and working to achieve African American empowerment. Although *Democratic Destiny* was Walters' first book-length examination of District politics, Henderson writes it was "the culmination of nearly thirty years of work by Walters on the political dynamics of Washington, D.C."

Walters was involved in multiple areas of advocacy and activism in the District, including writing dozens of articles in Washington area newspapers and as many interviews on local television and radio advancing the cause of home rule and self-determination. He appeared frequently before congressional committees and used Howard faculty, students, and other university resources to advance District interests. As a pro bono consultant he played an important role in drafting the 1979 constitution for statehood for the District. As the other chapters in this volume show the major foci of Walters' work were national and global; Henderson's chapter serves to remind us that he was a local as well as a cosmopolitan.

Walton's chapter addresses the abiding concern of Walters in national politics, which was the development of "leverage" strategies to empower the black electorate in presidential elections. He wrote dozens of academic papers, strategy memos, and newspaper columns in addition to two books on black strategies in presidential elections. Walton locates Walters' work in a tradition pioneered by Du Bois, Ralph Bunche, and the NAACP's Henry Lee Moon, who in 1948 wrote *Balance of Power: The Negro Vote.* Walters' *Black Presidential Politics: A Strategic Approach* was a theoretical reformulation of the work of Du Bois, Bunche, and Moon in light of the nationalization of the black electorate as a result of the 1965 Voting Rights Act. Walters' work in the 1984 Jesse Jackson presidential campaign was yet another of his laboratories to test theories he was developing against what he learned from his engagement with the seamy realities of two-party politics in the United States. Walton shows Walters' willingness to reflect on and reevaluate his theories in light of the failures of the Jackson campaigns and especially the campaigns of Al Sharpton and Carol Moseley Braun. At the time of his death he was engaged in further reflection and critical reevaluation of those theories in light of the election, with near-unanimous black voter support, of the first African American president.

In evaluating Walters' work on presidential strategies in the contexts of mainstream political science, Walton concludes that the mainstream's narrow behavioral focus on the individual voter rather than group concerns or interests meant that Walters' work was "undervalued" except in the African American community.

The next part of the book includes three chapters on Walters' internationalism. Karin Stanford, a doctoral student under Walters, presents a panoramic overview of his entire career in foreign affairs, beginning with his doctoral dissertation and his early interest in a career in the U.S. Foreign Service. Stanford shows Walters' concept of "race justice," which animated his domestic concerns, as the animating concern of his internationalism as well. Horace Campbell focuses on Walters' Pan Africanist work, including his activities with the Congressional Black Caucus, the African Liberation Support Committee, TransAfrica, and the United Nations, in which he worked to build a movement to oppose global apartheid. Campbell suggests Walters' scholarship on Pan Africanism, including his 1993 book *Pan Africanism: An Analysis of Modern Afrocentric Movements,* was an attempt to take a fresh look at the phenomenon in the context of his black nationalist conception of the imperative of the unity of all African peoples in a collective struggle on a global scale against racism and white supremacy. Like the domestic critics of Walters' unity imperative, Campbell is skeptical of its utility given the "kinds of feuds, splits and vendettas that plagued black liberation struggles in the United States." Campbell foregrounds his examination of Walters' Pan Africanism with a discussion of the Arab Spring or what he refers to as the African "Awakening" or "Nile revolution."

This awakening, he suggests, opens up possibilities of a redefinition of Pan Africanism toward a more "people-centered" perspective, a perspective, for example, that would focus Pan Africanism on the neglected "work of radical African women," a category for the most part scholars of Pan Africanism including Walters ignore.

Finally, Charles Henry's chapter focuses on reparations for the crimes of slavery and the Atlantic slave trade, which is a subject Walters took up in his 2008 book *The Price of Racial Reconciliation.* Henry, himself the author of a major text on reparations, like Walters, views reparations as primarily a moral issue not subject to the traditional politics of interest group bargaining. Like Walters, Henry also views the issue of domestic reparations as having international implications, comparing, as Walters does, the South African and United States experiences.

The final part of the book gives Walters the last word, followed by an afterword.

In February 2009 Walters was invited to deliver a paper on the Obama election and the prospects for his presidency on issues of concern to African Americans at the Alan B. Larkin Symposium on the American Presidency at Florida Atlantic University. The proceedings of the symposium were prepared for publication by the University Press of Florida.[28] Walters died before he could undertake revisions of his paper. Since I also delivered a paper at the symposium and the editors were familiar with our long association, I was asked and quickly agreed to prepare Walters' draft for final publication. In revising the essay, I used the comments and suggestions from the anonymous reviewers, material from Walters' subsequent writings on Obama (mainly from his weekly columns), and recollections from our frequent conversations. In style, language, and substance I attempted to adhere as closely as possible to Walters' original presentation.[29]

In the essay, he discusses the multiple dimensions of civil rights in the post–civil rights era, the terribly disproportionate impact of the "Great Recession" on the black community, and the pivotal role of the black vote in Obama's nomination and election. Consistent with his long-held leverage theories of black voting in presidential elections, he argued that the black community, given the disparate impact of the Great Recession and the strategic value of its vote, deserved commensurate policy benefits from the first black president. Reflecting on the administration after nearly two years, he concluded those policy benefits (especially with respect to the double-digit black unemployment rate) had not been forthcoming. And black leaders and the black community generally, he concluded, instead of using their leverage to extract those benefits, were giving the president a pass. This he viewed as a strategic error, writing,

> Blacks have a right to demand a useful product from the political system in exchange for their participation and to evaluate the worthiness of politics on that basis. That is, it is valid for them to ask what difference it makes to the satisfaction of their interests that a black is elected president. To give him a pass is to ask for a loss. Because if a black president can ignore those interests, little can be expected from his white successors.

I conclude the volume with an afterword, in which I discuss changes in the political science profession with respect to blacks, black science, and activism since Walters became a political scientist forty years ago. I also engage the arguments in this volume and elsewhere that are skeptical or critical of Walters' argument about the continuing viability and integrity of a black community with collective group interests.

Notes

1. E-mail, Robert C. Smith to Ronald Walters, Subject: *NPSR,* August 18, 2010.
2. Arthur Schlesinger Jr., *A Life in the Twentieth Century: Beginnings, 1917–1950* (Boston: Houghton Mifflin, 2000).
3. On Schlesinger's role in understanding postwar liberalism in the United States, see Stephen Depoe, *Arthur Schlesinger, Jr., and the Ideological History of American Liberalism* (Tuscaloosa: University of Alabama Press, 1994).
4. Aldon Morris, "Black Southern Sit-in Movement: An Analysis of Internal Organization," *American Sociological Review* 48 (1981): 744–67, and Gretchen Cassel Eick, *Dissent in Wichita: The Civil Rights Movement in the Midwest, 1954–72* (Urbana: University of

Illinois Press, 2001). The local public television station in Wichita, KPTS, in conjunction with the Wichita-Sedgwick County Historical Museum and the Kansas Humanities Council produced a documentary of the sit-in. see *The Dockum Sit-in: A Legacy of Courage*, KPTS/PBS, n.d.

5. See Aldon Morris, *The Origins of the Civil Rights Movement* (New York: Free Press, 1984).

6. On the significance of Rustin as a civil rights–era strategist, see Jervis Anderson, *The Troubles I've Seen* (New York: Harper Collins, 1997) and Bayard Rustin, *Down the Line: The Collected Writings of Bayard Rustin* (Chicago: Quadrangle Books, 1971).

7. Dennis Hevesi, "Ronald Walters, Rights Leader and Scholar Dies at 72," *New York Times*, September 14, 2010.

8. Rogers M. Smith, "The Puzzling Place of Race in American Political Science," *PS* 37 (2004): 43–47.

9. Ibid.

10. Gunnar Myrdal, *An American Dilemma: The Negro Problem and Modern Democracy*, 2 vols. (New York: Harper & Row, [1944] 1962).

11. Martin Kilson, "Political Scientists and the Activist-Technocrat Dichotomy: The Case of John Aubrey Davis," in *African American Perspectives in Political Science*, ed. Wilbur Rich (Philadelphia: Temple University Press, 2007), 187. Kilson's profile of Davis is a study in activism by a first-generation black political scientist. On the relative attention of historians and sociologists to race, see Ernest Wilson, "Why Political Scientists Don't Study Race but Historians and Sociologists Do," *PS* 18 (1985): 600–07.

12. Hanes Walton, Jr., Cheryl Miller, and Joseph McCormick, "Race and Political Science: The Dual Tradition of Race Relations Politics and Research," in *Political Science and Its History: Research Programs and Political Traditions*, ed. J. Dryzek et al. (New York: Cambridge University Press, 1994).

13. Kilson, "Political Scientists and the Activist-Technocrat Dichotomy."

14. Hanes Walton, Jr., and Robert C. Smith, *American Politics and African American Quest for Universal Freedom*, 6th ed. (New York: Longman, 2012), xiv.

15. Hanes Walton, Jr., and Joseph McCormick, "The Study of African American Politics as Social Danger," *National Political Science Review* 6 (1997): 229–44.

16. After graduating from the University of California, Berkeley, I enrolled in the graduate program at UCLA. After a year, my major advisor (Harry Scoble) and I independently came to the conclusion that I should leave UCLA and go to Howard to study black politics in the new program Walters was then developing. In my first year at Howard, I became Walters' research assistant, which eventually resulted in the publication of my first article in a scholarly journal that we coauthored. See Ronald Walters and Robert C. Smith, "The Black Education Strategy in the Seventies," *Journal of Negro Education* 48 (1979): 156–73.

17. Walters was also the principal organizer and founding president of the little-known and short-lived National Congress of Black Faculty, an almost impossible effort to organize and sustain a cross-disciplinary organization of all black college and university faculty in the United States. See Ronald Walters and Robert C. Smith, "Black Faculty: Organizing for Survival, Excellence and Service," *The Journal,* published by the Illinois Committee on Black Concerns in Higher Education, Southern Illinois University, Carbondale, 2003. Although engaged throughout his career in organizing and leading black scholarly organizations, he was also active in the discipline's mainstream associations; in 1995, for example, he was elected to the governing council of the American Political Science Association.

18. Ronald Walters, "Toward a Definition of Black Social Science," in *The Death of White Sociology,* ed. Joyce Ladner (New York: The Free Press, 1973), 212.

19. Max Weber, *The Methodology of the Social Sciences* (New York: The Free Press, 1949).

20. Karl Marx, "Theses on Feuerbach," in *Karl Marx and Frederick Engels: Selected Works* (New York: International Publishers, 1969), 30.

21. Walters, "Toward a Definition of Black Social Science," 201.

22. Ronald Walters, "The New Black Political Culture," *Black World* 21 (1972): 4–17 and Walters, "African American Nationalism: A Unifying Ideology," *Black World* 22 (1973): 9–21.

23. Jacqueline Trescott, "Howard University's Participatory Pundit: Political Scientist and Activist Ronald Walters," *Washington Post,* November 8, 1990.

24. We also commissioned papers on Walters' work in the founding of the African Heritage Studies Association and the discipline of black studies by Professor James Turner and on his work with the Congressional Black Caucus in its formative years by Dr. Elsie Scott. Unfortunately, in both cases the lack of access to documents and interviews made preparation of their papers impossible. Professor Manning Marable consented to do a paper on Walters' work with the National Black Political Conventions. Unfortunately, he died shortly after he commenced work on the paper. In his e-mail of acceptance Marable wrote Walters' "scholarship and engagement with public affairs had a profound impact on me as a young scholar." E-mail, Manning Marable to Robert Smith, Subject: Essays in Honor of Ron Walters, February 21, 2011.

25. E-mail, Smith to Walters, Subject: *NPSR*, August 18, 2010.

26. Walters analysis of the relationship between white nationalism and conservatism got me to thinking about the relationship in general between conservatism and racism and America, which ultimately resulted in my book *Conservatism and Racism and Why in America They Are the Same* (Albany: State University of New York Press, 2010).

27. Kurt Lewin, *Resolving Social Conflicts* (New York: Harper & Row, 1948).

28. Kenneth Osgood and Derrick White, eds., *Civil Rights, the Conservative Movement and the Presidency: From Nixon to Obama* (Gainesville: University Press of Florida, 2013).

29. A video recording of the original presentation is at "Ronald Walters on Civil Rights," Florida Atlantic University, http://www.C-span/.org/program284017.2.

Part I

1

Our Tallest Tree

An Essay toward a Biography of Ronald Walters

ROBERT G. NEWBY

On Dr. Martin Luther King Jr.'s birthday, January 16, in 2012, the *CBS Evening News* ran a story on the Dockum Drugstore sit-in. Essentially, the story involved interviews with two participants, Carol Parks Hahn and Dr. Galyn Vesey, both of whom remain Wichita residents. James Axelrod was the reporter. Axelrod, Hahn, and Vesey revisited the site of the drugstore, which is now a landmark. Carol Parks Hahn related that the waitress on that fateful day in July of 1958 actually took her order but then leaned forward and inquired, "You are not colored, are you dear?" When Parks Hahn responded, "Yes, I am," the waitress informed her that she could not serve her. Parks Hahn was in the company of a number of other sit-in participants from Wichita's NAACP Youth Council. This was the beginning of a three-week campaign by the Youth Council.

For CBS the importance of the story was that the beginnings of the civil rights movement were not limited to the South. Axelrod said the importance of this report for CBS was: "The story of what happened here challenges an assumption about racism in this country that it was limited to the South." Here in America's heartland was an important challenge to racism that many Americans thought was a southern phenomenon.

The major event that kicked off the movement was the bus boycott that took place in 1955 in Montgomery, Alabama. Rosa Parks' bold action of refusing to give up her seat to a white passenger sent a shock throughout the nation. It was a bold act of defiance and resistance to white supremacist rule. Her action caught fire among largely black female domestic workers in that city. The interesting thing about this is that the power was in the hands of the black community because the major patrons of the busses in Montgomery were black. The jubilation among blacks in America in December of 1955 cannot be overstated. It was this event that launched a movement and provided the movement with its titular head, Martin Luther King Jr. This protest and cause for jubilation on the part of America's black community occurred just a few months following one of the black community's saddest days. In August of 1955, blacks, as a people, had to endure one of the most degrading events, the lynching of fourteen-year-old Emmett Till in Money, Mississippi. By contrast, the Montgomery Bus Boycott brought to blacks all over the nation a sense of dignity.

The bus boycott was a protest against white supremacist Jim Crow. The thing that interested CBS on King's birthday in 2012 was a protest in Kansas, a state that did not formally practice Jim Crow but did practice systematic racial discrimination. In that sense Kansas was different. Kansas was a mixed bag. This mixed bag was a reflection of Kansas' sort of schizoid history when it came to race. Many have heard of John Brown and "bleeding Kansas." It was John Brown who led the unsuccessful slave rebellion at Harper's Ferry, Virginia. His revolutionary acts had their genesis in Kansas.

The purpose of this essay is to contextualize the development of Walters as a scholar-activist in this history of Kansas and Wichita. Like the question raised by CBS, What made Wichita distinct in the Dockum sit-in? Wichitans often claim this to be the first sit-in of the civil rights movement. Even though it preceded the Greensboro sit-in by a year and a half, to claim to be the first is fraught with problems. In fact, in his leadership, Ron was influenced by many acts of civil disobedience. The bus boycott in Montgomery and CORE's (Congress of Racial Equality) long history of civil disobedience provided models for our actions, as did the bravery of the "Little Rock Nine" in desegregating Central High School in Little Rock Arkansas. These and other acts of resistance provided a context for our protest. Ron Walters and Carol Parks Hahn provided the leadership.

The history of Kansas varied considerably from that of the largely plantation South. While blacks in Kansas suffered from a systematic white superiority in terms of social organization, white supremacy, as an ideology, was not overt. Whereas blacks in the South suffered the daily degradation of what Charles Johnson conceptualized as a "racial etiquette," there was no expectation on the parts of whites in Kansas that blacks should refer to them in terms of "Yes sir" or "No sir" (Johnson 1943, 117–55). There was no expectation that blacks tip their hats to whites or get off the sidewalk to let a white woman pass. In Kansas, blacks were citizens—second-class citizens but citizens nonetheless. In short, Kansas was a northern city with southern ways.

For those not familiar with Kansas history, it is important to know that Kansas' statehood was a lynchpin to the Civil War. There were fierce battles taking place in Kansas. For the most part these battles were over the issue of slavery. The Kansas and Nebraska Act was passed in 1854. One of the main points of contention was whether the territory and subsequently the states of Kansas and Nebraska would permit slavery. For purposes of political balance, the Missouri Compromise of 1820 had allowed Missouri to enter the union as a slave state, along with Maine as a free state. With Missouri as its neighbor, this posed a problem for those who wanted Kansas to be a free state. To promote slavery, the pro-slavery forces from Missouri began to populate the state. There were mini wars in northeast Kansas between these forces and antislavery forces associated with John Brown. It is interesting how John Brown has been treated in history. White history often portrays him as a mad man, while black history tends to treat him as a revolutionary. It was this struggle against slavery that made blacks proud of Kansas history.

There is an interesting twist to this story, however. In reading a history of the Kansas-Nebraska Act in a book by James Rawley (1969) titled *Race and Politics*, it should be noted that the "Free Soilers" were also an antislavery force during this period. Their position, however, was not so much that they did not want black people in Kansas as slaves; they did not want black people in Kansas at all. It was this background that led to Kansas' ambivalent history. On the one hand, Jim Crow was not the law of the state but widespread discrimination was.

The Walters' Roots: Kansas, Wichita, and the "American Dilemma"

To understand the social context that shaped Ron, it will be necessary to root him and his family into what it meant to be black in Kansas following the Civil War. From his research in the late 1930s and early 1940s Gunnar Myrdal (1944), with the able assistance of a number of African American social scientists, particularly Ralph Bunche, produced a two-volume work titled *An American Dilemma: The Negro Problem and Modern Democracy*. Myrdal titled the work based upon what he saw as a major contradiction or "dilemma" between America's espoused democratic principles and its "treatment of the Negro." Kansas produced a similar dilemma—a commitment to no segregation on the one hand and exclusionist whites-only policies on the other. To get around this contradiction, the race policy became a matter of hiding its segregationist policies.

Kansas was admitted to the Union as a "free state" in 1861. Much of the legacy of Kansas was its history as "bleeding Kansas." This reputation for bloodshed was based upon the gruesome battles fought by John Brown against attempts to introduce slavery into the territory. As one black Louisianan who was planning his migration from Louisiana after the Civil War stated in his letter to the governor, the Kansas "soil [was] washed by the blood of humanitarians for the cause of freedom." In the decade from 1870 to 1880, with its eighteen thousand migrants from the South, Kansas was the most popular destination for black migrants (Johnson and Campbell 1981, 60). As Nell Painter noted in her book *Exodusters: Black Migration to Kansas after Reconstruction*:

> . . . Kansas made no special appeal to attract Black migrants; it offered no special inducements. But old abolitionist, temperance Republicans ruled the state, and they held out precisely the same welcome to Black settlers as to white. This even-handed sense of fair play amounted to an open-armed welcome, in comparison to much of the rest of the country at the time. (159)

No doubt this same welcome mat attracted the Walters family in their migration from the white supremacy of Texas after the turn of the century.

Wichita provided a new promise for the Walters clan in their move from Texas. Married in 1895, Lewis William Walters and Julia Melissa Rucker, Ron's great-grandparents, moved from Granbury, Texas to Oklahoma in 1900 and then later to Wichita, Kansas. Of their eleven children, Issac, the second eldest child of Lewis and

Julia, and his wife were the first to move to Wichita from Muskogee, Oklahoma in 1918. The other children were Arthur, Talmadge, Alma, Paulyne, Cleo, Earl, Garfield, and Rufus. By 1920 the entire Walters clan, including Lewis and Julia, had moved to Wichita.

Before leaving Granbury, Texas for the family transition from Texas to Oklahoma and later on to Kansas, Lewis Walters, Ron's great-grandfather, had been a school teacher and preacher. Even though there was considerable resistance to educating blacks following the war, during Reconstruction the Freedmen's Bureau began to stress the need for the education of blacks. With the vast number of newly freed but illiterate blacks, the question, of course, became, "Who will educate the blacks?" (Smallwood 1981, 78). Lewis attended Prairie View College, which had opened with eight boys in 1876. While it is not clear when or if he graduated, according to family history he took on the responsibility and role of filling the void of the desperate need for teachers during this postwar period. Lewis and Julia valued education and became a part of the black self-help movement, which they imbued in their own children and carried with them to Oklahoma and ultimately Wichita. We can only assume that a major impetus for these moves from Texas was the search for an environment where the hostile antiblack attitudes of whites were more muted.

Racial Tensions of the 1910s and 1920s in America and Texas

While the undoing of Reconstruction no doubt played a role in the Walters leaving Texas for a "freer" Oklahoma and Kansas, during this period the quality of black life was tenuous at best. Chief Justice Roger B. Taney had written in his majority opinion for the *Dred Scott* case in 1857 "the black man has no rights which whites are bound to respect." The treatment of blacks following the war in reality shows Taney's opinion continued as law even after emancipation. The following description of what it meant to be black in Texas after Reconstruction is best understood as what the Freedmen's Bureau termed "outrages." In 1981 Smallwood states:

> Whites killed blacks for making a display of their emancipation, for refusing to remove their hats when Anglos passed, for refusing to be whipped, for improperly addressing a

white man, and "to see them kick." The sheriff of DeWitt
County shot a black man for whistling "Yankee Doodle."
Outlaws like John Wesley Hardin and Sam Grant established
reputations for being indiscriminate "nigger" killers, whom
other whites respected or condoned. . . . In Red River County
a bureau maintained that Anglos killed blacks for the "pure
love of killing" and officials confirmed that similar incidents
occurred throughout Texas. (126)

As property during slavery black lives had value to whites. As freedmen, following the Civil War, blacks in Texas and throughout the
South had no monetary value and were resented. Blacks were often
violently attacked based upon the capriciousness of whites. These
acts including murders were widespread with no consequence for
white assailants. As described by the Freedmen's Bureau, these were
"outrages."

Though not as hostile as the post-Reconstruction South, during this period around the turn of the century racial tensions were
quite high in Kansas. Rather than the openness that had attracted
the post-Reconstruction black migration, a vacillation on its policy
prohibiting segregation was beginning in Kansas. Kansas law, following the Civil War and through the turn of the century, presents the
state's back-and-forth policies when it came to Jim Crow. The following is a list of the laws regarding race policy:

1868: Education [Statute]
In cities of more than 150,000 persons, separate schools for
black or mulatto persons were to be established.

1874: Barred public accommodations segregation [Statute]
Prohibited state universities, or other public schools, inns,
hotels, boarding houses, places of public amusement, and
public transportation from discriminating based on race, or
previous condition of servitude. Penalty: Misdemeanor.
Fines between $10 and $1,000; liable for damages to be paid
to the injured person. Fines would be allocated to the public
school fund.

1879: Barred school segregation [Statute]
Cities larger than 150,000 could separate students by race, except in the high schools where no discrimination would be allowed on the basis of color.

1889: Barred school segregation [Statute]
Prohibited discrimination in Wichita's public high school based on race or color.

1905: Education [Statute]
Schools in Kansas City, Kansas, may organize and maintain separate schools for education of white and colored children, including high schools; "but no discrimination on account of color shall be made in high schools except as provided herein."

1923: Civil rights protection [Statute]
Outlawed racial discrimination, including racial discrimination in any state university, college or other school of public instruction. Penalty: Criminal prosecution and damages.

1949: Education [Statute]
Upheld 1862 and 1868 statutes providing for separate schools for black or mulatto students.

1949: Barred public accommodations segregation [Statute]
Prohibited discrimination within state universities, hotels, public entertainments, public carriers. Penalties: $10 to $1,000 and liable to pay damages to injured persons. (http://www.jimcrowhistory)

In reviewing these statutes, note that school segregation was to be the case only in cities of 150,000 or more in 1868. At that time, only Kansas City had a population of 150,000. Wichita's population at the time was less than seven hundred persons. It would be almost seventy years before Wichita would reach that size. In 1910, Wichita's total population was 52,450 of which 2,457 or 4.5 percent was black.

Even with a less than 5 percent black population, white animus led to segregation being instituted in the Wichita schools beginning in 1912. At a Board of Education meeting on September 9, 1912, the school board president announced to mixed feelings on the part of both blacks and whites that a separate school for "colored" would be established. In response to the objection of Mrs. Grant Ewing, a black parent, the school board president asked her: "Would you rather have your boy attend a white school and allow him to be subjected to the indignities and discourtesies which he would be bound to meet at such a school, than to have him walk a little further to a colored school?" To which Mrs. Ewing replied, "I don't think the board, or the superintendent, or the principal of the school would allow him to be ill-treated on account of his color." In reply the board president stated: "But these things are bound to happen without the knowledge of the authorities." "Well if it comes to that," Mrs. Ewing said with a toss of her head, "my little boy is a colored Jack Johnson and he can take care of himself" (Van Meter 1977, 149).

This policy was a change since in the 1890s black children in Wichita attended schools on a nondiscriminatory basis. This new move reinforces the state's ambivalence on the "race question." On the one hand, from its beginning Kansas was a free state. On the other hand, with white supremacy being endemic throughout America, it was just a matter of time before Kansas enacted its own exclusionist policies. But, unlike the South's Jim Crow, white supremacy was not the centerpiece of race politics in Kansas.

The Twenties and the Walters Clan Move to Wichita

It was in this period following the Civil War and the early twentieth century in which Kansas race policies were being "negotiated" that the Walters clan made their move to Wichita. As stated earlier, Isaac, the eldest of Lewis and Julia's offspring, moved to Wichita in 1918. He was followed by his brother, Arthur and wife, Maudine, Ron's grandparents in 1919. It was after this move that Ron's father, Gilmar, was born in 1921. Unfortunately, Maudine died shortly following Gilmar's birth. As a consequence, Julia, Ron's great-grandmother, took the place of the grandmother and played a large role in Ron's upbringing.

The Walters' transition to Kansas and the birth of Ron's dad occurred in a period of considerable racial strife nationally. Lynchings at this time were commonplace. The year 1919 was known as "Red Summer" because of all of the blood that was spilled that year in lynchings and race riots. The violence of whites reached its peak in this period. Kansas was, in some ways, an exception. Even though there were some blacks lynched in Kansas, the record of lynchings in Kansas between the years 1882 and 1968 shows that there were fifty-four lynchings over the course of this eighty-year period. However, of that number thirty-five were whites primarily for horse stealing, and only nineteen were black.

The white nationalist mayhem from which the Walters family was fleeing was not restricted to Texas. An extension of that violence in Texas against blacks reached its peak with a horrific event in Oklahoma, the destruction of Tulsa's "Black Wall Street" and what today would be considered "ethnic cleansing." White jealousy and envy of black success led to the Tulsa Race Riot of 1921. Many thousands of blacks were arrested, hundreds killed, and the Greenwood District was destroyed by fire. John Hope Franklin described this period as "the greatest period of inter-racial strife the nation ever witnessed" (quoted in Ellsworth 1982, 17). While the exact number is not known, *The Wichita Protest*, a black newspaper, reported on June 24, 1921 that many blacks who had to leave Tulsa as a result of that assault on their community migrated to Wichita (Bettis 1921).

While the Tulsa Race Riot of 1921 was one of the more horrific cases of whites attacking blacks on a large-scale basis, such violence by whites against blacks was not uncommon during this period. Beginning in 1917 and reaching its height in 1919, the United States experienced about twenty-five race riots. D. W. Griffith's technologically advanced movie *Birth of a Nation* (1915), based on the novel *The Clansman*, glorified the Ku Klux Klan and served as a recruiting tool. A common practice at the time was to have recruiting ads next to advertisements for the movie. During this period it was often the case that to be an elected official one had to be a member of the Klan or at least approved by it. More directly, in the 1920s the Wichita Board of Education had Klansmen among its members.

Though there was seemingly no similar violent attacks on the black community in Wichita, the animus on the part of whites toward blacks manifested itself in terms of more rigid segregation and exclusion of blacks. As with Wichita's black community more generally, the Walters family experienced growing restrictions on black life. To avoid such a conflagration in Wichita, the Council of Churches sponsored a study and conference to examine race relations in the city. The black church in Wichita provided the leadership for the conference. Wichita pastors R. L. Pope of St. Paul's African Methodist Episcopal (A.M.E.) and John Wesley Hayes of Calvary Baptist authored the working papers for the Conference. The report said of these two ministers, "These men represent the highest and best in the Negro life of Wichita, and their opinions are worthy of careful consideration" (1).

The 1924 report on *The Conference on Race Relations* paints a picture of blacks appealing to a white majority for services to improve their quality of life in Wichita at that time. With regard to employment, the report says:

> Several public utilities do not employ Negroes. In some instances white labor has taken the place of former Negro employees. Lack of employment, while not an excuse for vagrancy and crime, is often an occasion for it. The Negro who will not even act as a strike-breaker, is sometimes willing to steal coal and food for the sake of his family. The question raised by this survey is: Must the Negro fight his way into an honest economic status, or will a wise community policy accord him his chance as a matter of industrial and social wisdom? (Hayes 1924, 4)

These conditions were a call for the citizenship rights of blacks to be upheld. Without the right to a job on a nondiscriminatory basis, blacks were relegated to desperation when it came to survival.

The report went on to express needs when it came to help and specifically to address issues such the risk of childbirth as well as other statistics of Negro births. The report also called for enhancements of the YMCA, including more staff, new buildings, and services for both boys and girls. The report addressed as well services that would improve the general welfare of the black community. As opposed to the tragic events of Tulsa, they saw this approach as a model for the rest of America to adopt. Outlined was not only a report about the

Table 1.1. Wichita's Population, Size, and Percent Black, 1900–1963

Year	Total	Black Population	Percentage
1900	24,671	1,389	5.6
1910	52,450	2,457	4.7
1920	72,217	3,545	4.9
1930	111,110	5,623	5
1940	114,966	5,686	5.9
1950	168,279	8,802	4.8
1960	254,698	19,861	7.8

Source: U.S. Census.

dire conditions and needs of the black community but a five-year plan with a commitment to execute its recommendations.

A central theme of the report was the growing needs of the black community. As the population of blacks grew, segregation became an issue. In 1900, the black population was little more than one thousand. Between 1900 and 1910, the black population doubled to over 2,300. Between 1910 and 1930, Wichita's total population grew from 52,000 to 110,000. The black population grew similarly. It more than doubled from 2,500 to about 5,300 between 1910 and 1930; the percentage of blacks grew from 4.7 percent to 5 percent. These growing numbers were perceived by whites as a threat to their supremacy, spurring the establishment and maintenance of segregated institutions for blacks and whites. As early as 1906, the Board of Education had begun to discuss the "necessity" of separate schools for "colored" children (Van Meter 1977).

When it came to the high school, there were not enough blacks to support having a separate high school. Even so, the participation of blacks in all school activities had its restrictions. Early on blacks were not allowed to swim in the pool at the Wichita High School. After considerable protests on the part of the black community, this policy was relaxed somewhat in February 1924. The Board of Education passed a policy permitting blacks to use the pool on Friday afternoon after the white students had finished swimming and before the pool was filled with "fresh water" for the following week (*Wichita Daily Eagle* 1924, 1). In the mid-1940s this practice was overturned.

Black Schooling in Wichita:
Growing Up Black in Wichita Kansas in the 1940s and 1950s

The black community in Wichita had its beginnings on the city's West Side. Though not all resided on the West Side, the black population in Wichita in 1920 was about 3,500. The first home of the Walters was at 937 N. Wichita Street. According to family history, at that location there were two houses, one of which was the main house where the cooking was done. The smaller house on the property had four rooms, a sitting room and three bedrooms. In the 1920s until the early 1940s, this westside area served as the center of the black community. St. Paul's African Methodist Episcopal church, with a congregation whose family members were among the city's black founders, and its Baptist counterpart, Calvary Baptist, were located across the street from one another. These leading churches and denominations were not only important; central to the identity of each of these churches is the fact that they were the churches of Wichita's black founders. The black community's only hotel, the Water Street Hotel, with its own restaurant was nearby, as was the city's black funeral homes.

Frederick Douglass Elementary School, located next to Calvary Baptist Church, was established to serve this black community as it grew. When the numbers were smaller, black students attended school with whites at Emerson Elementary. As Sondra Van Meter (1977) in *Our Common School Heritage: A History of the Wichita Public Schools* points out, when it came to school attendance policy on race "legal acceptance of blacks did not eliminate social rejection" (56). She goes on to point out that a resolution passed by the Board of Education in September of 1889 required double desks to be replaced by single desks when it came to the mixed attendance at the Park and Emerson schools.

Even though the state's history seemed ambivalent about making segregation the law, as the black population in Wichita grew, white hostility toward blacks began to shape school policy. The exchange between Mrs. Grant Ewing and the superintendent described earlier at a school board meeting was indicative of this growing hostility as were the policies to end the purchase of double desks and the swimming pool policy at the high school. Before the critical mass that made segregation viable, black students attended schools near their residences, which were somewhat dispersed.

Prior to the reassignment to the "colored" schools in 1912, one can only imagine what the school experience must have been like for those few students of African descent around the turn of the century *before* segregation. The fact that segregation became the policy is full testament to the hostility that these students had to endure. In a sense, segregation had two faces. On the one hand in situations where blacks and whites were together, blacks often had to endure white hostility. On the other hand, having their own institutions, blacks were somewhat insulated from that day-to-day white animus with a level of protection and at the same time an opportunity for black self-improvement. In these years, black Kansans fought the stigma of segregation while at the same time promoting their own dignity with their own institutions. It was this dilemma that caused W. E. B. Du Bois to rail against segregation as a form of discrimination in 1934 (Du Bois 1970a, 276), then in the very next year, 1935, raise the question: "Does the Negro need separate schools?" (Du Bois 1970b, 278). That was the duality, the contradiction, faced by Wichita's black community. By having their own black schools and not having to face white animus and a hostile school environment, blacks were more likely to attend school longer. Knowing that literacy and knowledge were keys to self-improvement and improved status, the attendance rates for blacks were higher than those of whites. For the 1918–1919 school year, the average daily attendance rates for blacks was 59 percent of total enrollment but only 47 percent of whites of total enrollment (Van Meter 1977, 150). In all likelihood, the desire for literacy and education on the part of blacks was the driving force behind these numbers.

Ron's Wichita Public School Years: 1943–1955

Born in 1938, Ron entered this world during the Great Depression. These years were not promising for blacks in Wichita. For each decade between 1900 to 1910, the population grew by over one thousand. For the decade between 1920 and 1930 the black population grew by almost two thousand. For the 1930s until 1940, the decade in which Ron and I were both born, the net growth of the black population was only sixty-eight! During these years of the Great Depression, Kansas was not an attractive destination. That stagnation came to an end with the attack on Pearl Harbor and the U.S. entry into World War II. Second only to San Diego in defense spending, the role of Wichita in airplane production was a major attraction for both blacks and whites from the bordering states of Oklahoma, Arkansas, and Texas. Black population in the 1940s grew by over three thousand and by another nineteen thousand in the 1950s to almost twenty thousand by 1960. The percentage of growth increased considerably as well from 5 percent to about 8 percent. This growth, along with the changing racial climate following WWII and heading into the Civil Rights era, placed new stress on issues of discrimination and racism.

Ron's family had its beginnings on Wichita's West Side in 1921. One year after their move to Wichita, the family moved to the East Side at 1203 Cleveland and later to an address on Indiana. In 1938, at the time of Ron's birth, the family moved to their final home at 1050 Ohio. It was this home in which Ron spent most of his child-hood. All of the eastside addresses were within about a four-block radius. This last home became known as "Granny's house." It was where major family gatherings took place. As a consequence of the family's move to the East Side, Ron attended Dunbar Elementary beginning in kindergarten.

Dunbar had a storied history in the black community. First, it was located at the center of the black community, the intersection of 9th and Cleveland, or as it was better known, "the corner." Ron's home was about three blocks from this center. On the northeast corner was the community's major grocery store, Shadid's. The Shadids were "reported" to be Syrians. (By coincidence, this was the family of Ed Shadid, the Pulitzer Award–winning reporter who died in Syria in 2012.) Shadid's brother-in-law owned the drugstore on the north-west corner. These were the major "white" businesses in the black community. At some point in the late 1940s, the drugstore was sold to a black pharmacist, Robert Turner. What is now Turner's Drug-store, as opposed Salome's, with its soda fountain, the pharmacy was a major hangout for young people.

Turner's Drugstore: The Corner

Dunbar with its large playground was the center of athletic competition and other games. Dunbar had *the* major basketball court. Wichita's only black movie theater, the Dunbar, was just north of the drugstore on Cleveland. Further north on Cleveland was a black-owned grocery store. The McClintons, father and son, had two grocery stores. Curtis McClinton Sr. was the first African American to be elected to the Kansas State Senate in 1960. He had served in the Kansas House of Representatives beginning in 1956. In this heavily Republican state, McClinton was a Democrat, as was most of Wichita's black community. Curtis McClinton Jr. played football for the University of Kansas and later the Kansas City Chiefs.

The Walters' strong sense of family helped shape Ron. As stated earlier, the family of Julia and Lewis Walters was large, with eleven children. Most of the siblings had several children, and their children (Gilmar's generation) had a number of children (Ron's generation). The size of the Walters' extended family and their longevity as Wichitans made the family a prominent name in the community. In this period, most blacks in Wichita were restricted to what were then known as "Negro jobs" or faced the "job ceiling" (Drake 1962). As contractors, this restriction was a problem for the Walters brothers who were entrepreneurs. Being a paper-hanger, Ron's grandfather had as his clientele the whole black community. His brothers were plumbers, carpenters, brick masons, and a radio and later TV repairman. They were independent, not relying on whites for their livelihood. Ron's grandfather was a member of the Frederick Douglass Masonic Lodge and his grandmother a member of the Order of Eastern Star. The Masons, as they are commonly known, have a long history of black self-improvement. This provided them an independence from whites, which was a major source of pride for the Walters family. No doubt, family and racial pride were well-entrenched social norms. Though not among the community's professional class or Wichita's black elite, they had two characteristics that made the family prominent—they were among Wichita's black pioneers and they were entrepreneurs.

As an early Wichita family, they could be counted among the founders. When they arrived in 1920, the black population in Wichita was about 3,500. Gilmar, Ron's father, was known in Wichita for being a "race man." His experience in the military service exposed him to blacks from around the nation and varied backgrounds that helped shape his worldview. During his service, he served in units that had a history of both the Buffalo Soldiers and later, when he was in the air force, the Tuskegee Airmen. Gilmar's major organization was the "colored" musician's local union. No doubt this "independence" on the Walters side of his family contributed to Ron's self-confidence. This large extended family had high expectations for Ron, as did Maxine's family. Gilmar and Maxine had been high school sweethearts. With Maxine having grown up in Saint Augustine Episcopal Church, it can be assumed that her family held high status in the black community.

While in the service, Gilmar was often relocated. As much as possible, Maxine traveled with him, leaving Ron and Gerald with their great-grandmother back in Wichita. Ron and Gerald were born in 1938 and 1940, respectively. Later on in the 1950s, the family moved to a new home at 1650 N. Madison into a modern bungalow. Ron's other brothers and sisters, Duane, Terry, Marcia, Sharon, and Kevin, are more or less children of the 1950s. With Gilmar no longer in the service, the family settled and grew at this address.

Dunbar Elementary School: The Black Community's Center

As stated earlier, Dunbar Elementary School was at the center of Wichita's black community. From kindergarten through grade six Ron attended Dunbar. He was one of the school's most notable alums. This institution was so important that in 2007 a local activist historian, Gerald Norwood, organized a Dunbar Elementary School Reunion (1927–1971). The theme of the reunion centered on the importance of Dunbar as a part of the core of Wichita's black community. Dunbar was the result of the policy to establish segregated schools in the early 1900s. Even though this policy was largely opposed by the black community at the time, Norwood, in addressing those in attendance at the 2007 reunion, said that the establishment of the school was of profound importance when it came to the development of the black community. He labeled the decision to establish the "colored schools" as a "bold" step. Of the importance of that policy for the black community, Norwood (2007) states:

If you were an African American elementary school student in Wichita prior to 1912, you would have had to go to an all-white school. . . . Your teachers and your principals would be white. That was the law of Kansas. But a bold new move occurred in 1912. The unified school district of Wichita decided to have separate schools for its African American students. There were four schools initially. They were Douglass Elementary named after the famous black abolitionist and statesman Frederick Douglass located at 617 North Water. L'Ouverture Elementary named after the Santo Domingo hero revolutionary Toussaint L'Ouverture. [There were two other one-room schools, as well, one located in the south end of the city, the other located in the north end.]

There are two points to be made here: 1) this policy was imposed upon the black community, and 2) though there were mixed feelings in the black community on the new policy, one could view the decision as Booker T. Washington's "accommodationism." Washington's influence at this time among whites was unassailable, to the extent that he had convinced whites that blacks and whites could be as "separate as the fingers." His self-help philosophy did hold some sway in Wichita's race relations. Since Dunbar was an all-black school with a black principal and teachers, the school was on a mission to make sure its students excelled.

Dunbar's first principal was Dr. Ferdinand L. Barnett. Barnett was a black Canadian who had been recommended by Booker T. Washington. He was succeeded by Chester Johnson for about five years. The longest-standing principal, however, was native Wichitan James Anderson from 1942 to 1971. Ron would have attended Dunbar beginning in 1943 with James Anderson as his principal. Anderson's longevity speaks for itself. James Anderson was a true leader in the black community and was highly regarded throughout the community. Anderson earned his undergraduate degree at the University of Wichita and his master's at Columbia Teacher's College. Under his leadership, Dunbar maintained its reputation as the best "colored school."

Even though I preceded Ron by two years at Dunbar, we would have had the same teachers. Particularly during World War II, there was a dedicated set of mainly female teachers who believed in the motto of the Colored Women's Clubs, "lifting as we climb." They made sure that the school was represented in citywide activities. In some cases, the teachers would select the student most likely to "represent the race" well at these functions.

Annually, the Junior Red Cross had its promotion by having a fifth grader represent each of the city's forty or so schools. Ron was Dunbar's representative along with two other black representatives from Douglass and L'Ouverture, respectively. These teachers took considerable pride in who they selected to be competitive with Wichita's white students. With Wichita's heavy dependence on defense contractors, Red Cross campaigns were an important part of the propaganda efforts of the Chamber of Commerce. At Dunbar, Ron was selected to provide leadership on their annual campaign. This selection was an indication of what the teachers at Dunbar thought of Ron's leadership. He was usually the smartest pupil in the class.

While not taught the horrors of what it meant to be black in America, we were introduced to blacks of notable achievement. Ron would have learned the writings of Langston Hughes and Paul Lawrence Dunbar. He would have been introduced to the importance of Mary McLeod Bethune, W. E. B. Du Bois, Booker T. Washington, and the scientific achievements of George Washington Carver. As a consequence, our black teachers pointed us toward success and racial pride. During World War II, following the Japanese bombing of Pearl Harbor, the teachers introduced us to Dorie Miller with a poster on almost every classroom door. Even though blacks had been relegated to mess hall duty in the navy, in response to the attack, Dorie Miller became a hero for manning a machine gun to shoot down the attacking Japanese airplanes. For his effort he was awarded the Navy Cross. This knowledge of black people and racial pride was lost immediately upon entering the "white" intermediate schools.

Wichita High School East: "The Corner"

As with almost all teenagers, the high school years were pivotal. That was no less true for Ron. As with all aspects of life in a segregated society, how "race" is lived shapes worldviews for both blacks and whites. For blacks in Wichita in the 1940s and 1950s, the "color line" was well established. That there was segregation "just was." Not that it was acceptable, it "just was." Those were the norms and that was the world. Even so, the local chapter of the NAACP waged its struggle to end these policies (Van Meter 1977, 258). As profound as the Montgomery Bus Boycott became, it is important to recall that the boycotters' first demands were not an end to segregation but a more humane and less insulting form of segregation. Like the reaction of Rosa Parks who had protested bus segregation numerous times, it was the demeaning way in which they enforced the policy that really mattered. In East High School, by the 1950s, the color line was more blurred. Blacks were elected class officers. Blacks were among the highest achievers. Though their numbers were limited, blacks were certainly stars on the football, basketball, and track teams. This was not the case with baseball, swimming, or wrestling, however. With these exceptions, all extra-curricular activities were open to all students, including the drama club with access to roles that were not stereotypical. Even so, there was very little interaction between blacks and whites. Teammates and members of school organizations like band and orchestra did produce some friendships across racial lines. In addition to band and orchestra, Ron was also on the debate team.

Ron entered East High in the fall of 1952. He lived on the border line so had a choice of attending either North or East. Knowing that Ron was finishing his ninth-grade year at Horace Mann and that East needed a good drummer, the band director, Kenneth Thompson, knowing that I knew Ron personally, asked me to recruit Ron to attend East. Ron's experience at East was very successful. He was a leader in so many ways. When Ron became a senior he followed me as head drummer and director of the student pep band. At that time the major audiovisual tool was the movie projector. Ron was one of about twelve students who ran the movie projector. He was also a member of the Hi-Y Club. This affiliation was a carryover from his grade school days in which the YMCA played a major role in our development in the grade school version the Gra-Y. Apart from his mechanical skill, Ron was on the school's debate team. At East, though there were exceptions, opportunities for black students in many ways were the same as those for white students.

Given the small percentage of blacks attending East, being the only black in his classes would have been the norm rather than the exception. Except for members of schoolwide organizations (e.g., team sports, band orchestra, etc.) the interactions between blacks and whites were limited. Given this, blacks were a close-knit group in the school. The isolation in the classroom was compensated for with a meeting at our own "9th and Cleveland" in between classes. East High was a three-story building with separate buildings for a gymnasium and vocational education. The student body was in excess three thousand, with a black student body of less than one hundred. Black students maintained their sense of community by congregating at the intersecting north and west hallways on the first floor, otherwise known as "the corner." The black students also sat together in the cafeteria. The interactions between black and white students tended to be the exception. Being in band and orchestra, this cross-racial barrier for Ron was more relaxed. He was able to negotiate the boundaries between black and white students successfully. His black classmates did not resent his interactions with whites.

Boys State and Boys Nation: A Meeting with the President

One of the highlights of Ron's high school experience was attending the American Legion's Sunflower Boys State. From East, he attended Boys State with a close friend and the head of his class, Pat Little. Ron and Pat had become friends on East's debate team. Essentially, their job at the American Legion's Boys State was to pass laws as if they were the state legislature. In that assembly, Ron served as the assistant state auditor and coeditor of the newspaper at Kansas Boys State. Out of 150 boys from all over the state, Pat and Ron were elected to go to Boys Nation in Washington, D.C. Ron felt that he was elected as a result of what he termed a "fire and brimstone" speech on the need for integration. This speech would have been delivered shortly following the May 17, 1954 ruling in *Brown v. Board of Education, Topeka.* While there as a member of the Kansas delegation, he was able to meet President Dwight D. Eisenhower, a native Kansan. The president requested an audience with the Kansas delegation, and he shook the hands of all of the delegates. The president reminded the delegation of the example they should set given that they were representing the state of Kansas. Ron was very impressed by this occasion. He took a liking to the capital and he came to understand that Washington, D.C. was at the center of the political universe.

One aspect of our bonding was the fact that our respective identities were often blurred, since we were the only two blacks in a band of about eighty musicians and we both played the drums. About the second football game of the season I was injured in a freak accident, which meant to all those white students in the stands that Ron became "Newby." To many of them he remained Newby for the next two years after I had graduated. I must say that our band director was very much ahead of his time, for not only was I the head drummer, but the band director broke precedent to appoint me the first student, black or white, to be director of the pep band.

Away from the school, discrimination was the order of the day. Public accommodations all practiced racial discrimination. When a place did serve blacks, the word would be spread. When The Forum, a downtown cafeteria, opened to blacks in the early to mid-fifties, the word spread fast. When it came to the city's major theaters, blacks were consigned to the balconies. If a theater had only one floor, blacks were not permitted attendance.

These segregated conditions applied to the lunch counters at what were called the "five and dime stores" in downtown Wichita. In addition to Dockum Drugstore, there were lunch counters McClellan's, S. H. Kress, and Woolworths. When it came to service at the counter, there was one exception. W. T. Grant's did serve blacks at the counter, standing room only at the east end of the counter. Otherwise, Dockum of the Rexall chain was just being consistent with the other "five and dimes." The sign that signaled that blacks would not be served read: "We reserve the right to refuse service to anyone."

There were no signs designating "white" and "colored" water fountains, restrooms, or a "colored upstairs." There was no overt segregation. There was no back of the bus or separate railroad cars. Even so, exclusionist policies were ubiquitous. There was an "understanding" that African Americans could be refused service at any and all white establishments. Though restricted to the balcony in movie theaters, there was no crow's nest, a separate wired off section of the balcony, as was the case in the Jim Crow South. Again, these were the contradictory race policies in Kansas.

Entering the University of Wichita

When Ron graduated from East in 1955, it was a foregone conclusion that he would attend the University of Wichita like many of his friends. By this time he had decided that he wanted to be a lawyer. His major was political science. Coming from a working-class family, Ron did not have the luxury of being a full-time student exclusively. He was a full-time student with a full-time job.

Not only was Ron Walters to become a star in school achievement, he was a star socially as well. While the stereotypic academic tends to be a nerd, Ron was not "a square" in the vernacular of the day. He was popular on the dance floor. While at the university our weekends were spent at the Esquire Club, Wichita's most popular nightclub for its black middle class. Even though we were students, we were very much accepted by this professional class. Since his dad, Gilmar, was usually the bassist in the band at the club, Ron often had the opportunity to serenade the women in the audience. His voice was well suited for ballads like "Tenderly," "Blue Moon," "Night and Day," among others.

Continuing to show Ron's social side, Ron, Syd Dobson, and I formed our own brotherhood. We had the audacity to refer to ourselves as "Le Clique." To display this bond, we often wore matching blazers with a patch with overlays of a compass, a double eighth note, and a gavel. The patch was indicative of our professional ambitions. Syd at that time envisioned himself as being an engineer; his career aspiration was represented by the compass. Ron's aspiration at the moment to be a lawyer was represented by the gavel. The musical notes of course represented my interest in music.

Moving on from "Le Clique," Ron was the founding polemarch of the University of Wichita (now Wichita State University) Kappa Alpha Psi chapter in 1958. Like the NAACP and the Gra-Y before that, the founding of the Delta Upsilon Chapter of Kappa Alpha Psi came about as a result of Ron's leadership. When asked of his fraternity brothers how he became the founding polemarch, the answer was simple: he was willing to provide the leadership.

Consistent with his leadership in other areas, those same qualities became important when it came to the sit-in. As president of NAACP Youth Council, Ron always had the confidence that things should and could be changed. Under the leadership of Vivian Parks, the president of Wichita's NAACP branch began aggressive programs to speed up change. Similarly, along with Vivian Parks' daughter, Carol, Ron, began to explore direct action. At the request of Parks, the national office provided advice and resources. Franklin Williams shared the history of various tactics in trying to reshape race policies. Williams shared the notion of direct action and civil disobedience of organizations like CORE

The sit-in was a success because the membership of the NAACP Youth Group believed in Ron Walters. They believed in his integrity, his commitment, his leadership. Ron was well liked and popular. Even though there were apprehensions, Ron convinced us that we were not only right, but we had an obligation when it came to carrying out the sit-in. Whenever he was honored for his leadership of the sit-in, he quickly made sure that the praise would go to all of the participants. It is this characteristic, sharing the credit, sharing the glory, that Ron routinely spread to all of the participants. His leadership was shared with both Vivian and Carol Parks. He also had the essential support of attorney Chester Lewis. Ron and this leadership proceeded with this breakthrough even in the face of opposition by the NAACP national office. Recognizing fellow participants and the role of his cousin, Carol, for her leadership is indicative of why he is so appreciated.

The plan of the sit-in was to fill up the stools in the Dockum Drugstore on Thursday evening, a late shopping night in downtown Wichita and Saturday until we were served. After three weeks, the management relented and told the workers to "serve them, we are losing too much money." This change was not limited to Wichita but a change in policy for the whole Rexall chain, nationally. The story of the sit-in has been documented by some excellent research by Gretchen Eick, a historian at Friends University in Wichita. Eick's *Dissent in Wichita: The Civil Rights Movement, 1954–1972* has provided the documentation on the movement in Wichita. Needless to say, the 1958 sit-in was significant. Of course, the leadership of Ron Walters is central to that story. Soon after the Dockum victory, exclusionist barriers all over the city began to come down.

The Transition from "Student" to Scholar: Pursuing a Black Intellectual Tradition

Ron's leaving Wichita for Fisk was clearly a case of racism having done us and the nation a big favor. Ron's grades in high school were among those of the higher achievers at East. He introduced us all to

Du Bois and E. Franklin Frazier. While I am not knowledgeable about his grades at Wichita, I am reminded of one incident. When he was a sophomore at Wichita, he received an "F" on a paper for a government class. In response to Ron challenging his grade, the professor's explanation was that the paper was really an outstanding paper, but he knew no "colored boy could write a paper of that quality." Ron went to the library and took all of the references he had made in the paper to his office. Upon being confronted with this challenge, the professor conceded that Ron had written the paper and gave him a "C." When asked if the paper was so good why he did not get an "A," the professor responded by saying he had already raised the grade two levels and he was not going to raise it any more. Shortly after this incident Ron left for Fisk, where he thrived to become the student and scholar he became. Going to black America's academic roots and legacy helped shape him in a way he never would have developed at Wichita State.

By contrast, Ron's intellect was respected at Fisk. He graduated from Fisk cum laude. By this time he had taken a scholarly and diplomatic interest in Africa. Ron's majors at Fisk were history and political science. Even though one of the school's top professors dismissed the importance of his interest in Africa, his interest persisted. Obviously, Ron excelled in his studies. He had one goal at Fisk that he did not make, being invited to be a member of Phi Beta Kappa, the honorary fraternity. In response to Ron expressing an interest in Africa and writing his senior thesis on African history, the professor alluded to earlier responded to Ron, "I didn't know Africa had a history." This same professor, a white professor holding the John Hope Franklin endowed chair, was the faculty adviser for Phi Beta Kappa. It was Ron's suspicion that this connection was likely to have been the obstacle to him becoming a member of the prestigious honorary fraternity. While he was denied that honor at the time, for commencement in 2010, Dr. Ronald W. Walters was honored by Fisk as its distinguished alum.

During his student years, Ron served as president of Fisk's chapter of Kappa Alpha Psi, Inc. In that leadership capacity he was able to engage the fraternity with the civil rights movement, even though he did not participate in the Nashville sit-ins. John Lewis was one of his classmates; he knew Diane Nash and James Bevel as well. In his role as president of the fraternity, he was supportive of the goals of the movement. There were, no doubt, two things that kept him on the sidelines when it came to the Nashville sit-ins. First, at the University of Wichita much of his student life had been a divided commitment—organizations such as the NAACP Youth Council, Kappa Alpha Psi, and working full-time as an inhalation therapist at Wesley Hospital. His promise to his family was that at Fisk he would be a dedicated student. Second, much of Ron's childhood was spent under the thumb of the religious fundamentalism of his great-grand-mother, who had left Calvary for the Church of Christ. That religiosity was central to the Nashville movement was a turnoff for him. He was by this time rejecting fundamentalism, even when it was about civil rights. In fact, while in Wichita he had joined St. Paul's A.M.E. as many of the black students at the university had done. This would have been when Reverend H. H. Brookins was pastor, a preacher who embraced the changing times for the church. Brookins was, with Vivian Parks, a part of Wichita's civil rights leadership. This was the same Brookins who went on to be "Hollywood's Preacher" at First A.M.E. in Los Angeles in the 1960s.

Another point of Fisk pride for Ron was his experience in being able to participate in one of the school's most treasured traditions, the Jubilee Singers. In this capacity, he joined that ensemble in being an ambassador for the school. This was Ron's return to an all-black experience. He loved the environment at Fisk. A few years earlier, he had attended a conference at the Charles S. Johnson's Race Relations Institute on the Fisk campus. Consequently, by choosing Fisk, he was returning to an institution he highly valued for its legacy.

From the Study of Africa to Black Studies

Nineteen sixty-three was the year of the marches. That year Ron graduated from Fisk. In the summer he moved to Michigan to live with me and work at Crittenden Hospital to save some money in anticipation of an August wedding. On June 6th, Detroit had its own Freedom March; among the headliners were Dr. Martin Luther King Jr., Walter Reuther of the U.A.W., and others. Because it was Sunday, Governor George Romney's Mormon religion meant he could not participate in the public activities, but the governor did declare the day "Freedom March Day in Michigan." There were 150,000 people attending the march and rally. Moving to Washington to attend American University, on August 28th Ron was able to attend the historic march on Washington at which he was among 250,000 participants.

After having his interest in Africa piqued at Fisk, Ron went to American University to pursue a PhD in the study of Africa, with a goal to the join the State Department as a part of the foreign service. One of the things Ron learned early on was that being black was a major barrier to entering the diplomatic corps. Not to be dissuaded, Ron played a leadership role in his graduate studies at American University. He served as president of the Graduate Student Association for the School of International Service and he was a member the Pi Sigma Alpha political science honorary society. Continuing with his interest in Africa, the title of his dissertation was "The Formulation of United States Foreign Policy Toward East Africa, 1958–1963." He did some of his coursework at Howard. After five years as a graduate student, Ron's first professorship was at Syracuse University in the fall of 1968. His major appointment was in the Political Science Department. While there, he was also associated with the East Africa Studies Center.

Nineteen sixty-eight was a tumultuous year and one that changed America. One could argue that it changed the life course of many, including Ron. In the summer of 1967 both Newark and Detroit erupted in flames, as did nearly two hundred other cities. President Lyndon Johnson appointed a commission to seek the causes of those rebellions. That next spring, on March 1, 1968, the National Advisory Commission issued its report on what caused the rebellions. According to the findings of the commission, "white racism" was determined to be the root of the problems. But before the problems could be addressed, on April 4th, 1968, Dr. King was assassinated. A few weeks after King's assassination, June 5th, a friend of civil rights, Bobby Kennedy, was assassinated.

In reaction to these events, like the student protests against the Vietnam War and civil rights, more generally, black athletes began to question their role in society and the Olympic movement. This questioning took the form of a threatened protest of the 1968 games that were to be held in Mexico City. There was no general boycott by the black athletes, but the black-gloved black power salute by

Tommie Smith and John Carlos as the U.S. National Anthem was played during the 200-meter medal ceremony at the 1968 Olympics to a worldwide audience was a powerful statement. On university campuses students began to take over buildings as a means to gain their demands for reform and student rights. All of a sudden the paradigm was being challenged with a call by black students for knowledge of the black experience to set the record straight and to understand the forces of subordination.

One such takeover was at Brandeis University. The purpose of this takeover was a demand that the school provide a Black Studies Department. As it happened, a black graduate student at Brandeis was a fellow Kansan whom Ron knew. During the Poor People's Campaign Ron received a call inviting him to interview for the director of a newly formed program in black studies. He was hired in May of 1969, making him the first, or one of the first, heads of the newly emerging black studies programs. In this regard, he was truly a pioneer. Two years later, it was in this same academic spirit that there were calls to make Howard University a "black university." Toward that end, Andrew Billingsley, the new vice president for academic affairs at Howard, recruited Ron to be chairperson of the Political Science Department. Others hired at the time were young forward-looking progressive black scholars who became Howard's class of 1971. It was from this platform that Ron was able to impact black scholarship in so many different ways.

A key factor to Ron's development and commitment to the struggle of black liberation was his soul mate and companion, Patricia Walters. Though not at an NAACP meeting per se, it was at a civil rights workshop at the University of Illinois-Urbana in 1957 that Ron met his companion for life, Patricia Turner of Columbus, Ohio. When he came back to Wichita, he proclaimed to all that he had met his love. A student at Philander-Smith, she was intellectually strong with a commitment to civil rights. In fact, as he described it, the two of them had stayed up all night talking civil rights. This meeting took place before the Dockum Drugstore sit-in.

From that night on, their life's work was fused. Whatever Ron's accomplishments, he did not do them alone. Pat was his constant support and critic. That night in Urbana led to a marriage just short of fifty years and a commitment to the black community and black politics that has been unparalleled and has taken us to a different place. Ron will be missed, but we can rest assured that in Pat his legacy will be preserved.

From Kansas to National Prominence: Ron Walters as the "Tallest Tree"

In reporting the passing of Dr. Walters, Talibah Chikwendu of the *Baltimore Afro-American*, attributed to Reverend Jesse Jackson that Ronald Walters was the "tallest tree" in our forest. Various scholars, politicians, and activists have placed Ron in the Du Boisian tradition of scholar-activism. Ron was no less a "race man" than Du Bois, and it was W.E.B. Dubois who was his role model. That activism ranged from being a resource for little-known community groups to presidents.

Being recognized as the "tallest tree" in our forest has a long tradition in the African American community. For his unrelenting opposition to segregation, Paul Robeson, the singer and activist, was a giant historical figure and was recognized by *The People's World* as "the tallest tree in our forest." It is in this spirit of Robeson and Du Bois that Ron is being recognized for his contributions to the struggle of African Americans. Being the "tallest tree" in our forest, Ron was often consulted by the nation's presidents. President Bill Clinton (2010) said of him:

> Ron never gave up on his ideals, and he never stopped working to put them into action. Using his gifts of intellect, education, and conscience, he played a role in everything from the development of the Congressional Black Caucus to ending Apartheid in South Africa, and he inspired others through his writings and teachings.

Likewise, President Barack Obama recognized Ron as a leading voice for the African American community. Even President Ronald Reagan felt the impact of Ron's influence to the point that he placed a personal call to Ron at his home to express his concern about some of Ron's criticisms of his policies. In one of Ron's early trips to South Africa, President Nelson Mandela made it known that he was familiar with Ron's book on his nation. To say that he was the "tallest tree" in our forest is no exaggeration. Few African American scholars have had such an impact on our nation's policies when it comes to politics and public policy. Whether it was the Gary Convention or being an adviser to candidates for the nation's presidency, Ronald Walters stands out.

His academic and professional accomplishments are well known and better documented elsewhere in this volume. The purpose of this essay is to place in context how he got there from the wheatlands of Wichita, Kansas. There is an expectation that giants of the struggle will have their roots in New York's Harlem or other urban black meccas such as Chicago or Detroit. There is little expectation that from Kansas, with its small population of African Americans, a pioneer in the struggle for justice and equality would become the "tallest tree." It was that pioneering spirit and leadership that was demonstrated as he made history right there in Wichita, Kansas in 1958. Of course, the significance of the later North Carolina sit-in cannot be overstated since it sparked a series of such demonstrations throughout North Carolina and the South in 1960. Yet, the Dockum Drugstore sit-in that preceded Greensboro by two years was not isolated in that similar demonstrations took place in the central part of the nation in cities in Kansas, Oklahoma, and Missouri (Morris 1984, 188–89).

This story about the formative years of Dr. Ronald Walters began with CBS News wondering about a challenge to segregation that took place outside the South, or stated otherwise the up-South, as Malcolm X used to refer to the North. In fact, Malcolm would chastise us by saying, "You need to stop talking about the South because everything south of the Canadian border is South." Wichita is south of the Canadian border, thus it is not an oddity that it produced one of the "tallest trees" in the African American freedom struggle.

References

Bettis, W. A. 1921. "Tulsa Mail Carriers Thank Brave White Citizens for Lawlessness in Mob Murder, Arson and Robbery." *The Wichita Protest,* June 24.

Clinton, William Jefferson. 2010. Letter of condolence. Washington, DC, September 16.

Drake, St. Clair. 1962. *Black Metropolis: The Study of Negro Life in a Northern City*. New York: Harper & Row.

Du Bois, W. E. B. 1970a. "Segregation (1934)." In *W.E.B. Du Bois: A Reader*, edited by M. Weinberg, 276–77. New York: Harper & Row.

———. 1970b. "Does the Negro Need Separate Schools." In *W.E.B. Dubois: A Reader*, edited by M. Weinberg, 278–88. New York: Harper & Row.

Eick, Gretchen Crass. 2001. *Dissent in Wichita: The Civil Rights Movement in the Midwest, 1954–72*. Urbana and Chicago: University of Illinois.

Ellsworth, Scott. 1982. *Death in a Promised Land: The Tulsa Race Riot of 1921*. Baton Rouge, LA: Louisiana University Press.

The Freedmen's Bureau Online. Freedmen and Southern Society Project. http://freedmensbureau.com/texas/index.htm.

Haynes, George E., Secretary of the Commission on the Church and Race Relations. 1924. (March 1943) Report of the Committee on Findings, The Conference on Race Relations, Wichita Council of Churches, February, 17–18, 1924.

Http://www.jimcrowhistory.org/scripts/jimcrow/lawsoutside.cgi?state=Kansas.

Johnson, Charles S. 1943. *Backgrounds to Patterns of Negro Segregation*. New York: Thomas Y. Crowell.

Johnson, Daniel, and Rex Campbell. 1981. *Black Migration in America*. Durham, NC: Duke University Press.

Lane, Robert Leon. 1977. *A Historical Study of the Development of School Desegregation in the Wichita Public Schools, 1966–1975*. Ann Arbor, MI: Xerox University Microfilms.

Morris, Aldon. 1984. *The Origins of the Civil Rights Movement: Black Communities Organizing for Change*. New York: Free Press.

Myrdal, Gunnar. 1944 (1962). *An American Dilemma: The Negro Problem and Modern Democracy*. New York: Harper.

National Advisory Commission. 1968. *National Advisory Commission on Civil Disorder*. New York: Bantam.

Norwood, Gerald. 2007. *Dunbar Elementary School Reunion: 1927–1971*.

Obama, Barack. 2010. Letter of condolence. Washington, DC: The White House, September 16.

Painter, Nell Irvin. 1976. *Exodusters: Black Migration to Kansas after Reconstruction*. New York: Alfred A. Knopf.

Rawley, James A. 1969. *Race and Politics: "Bleeding Kansas" and the Coming of the Civil War.* Philadelphia: Lippincott.

Rice, Lawrence D. 1971. *The Negro in Texas: 1874–1900.* Baton Rouge: Louisiana University Press.

Smallwood, James M. 1981. *Time of Hope, Time of Despair.* Port Washington, NY: Kennikat Press Corp.

Van Meter, Sondra. 1977. *Our Common School Heritage: A History of the Wichita Public Schools.* Wichita, KS: Board of Education of Unified School District No. 259.

Walters, Ronald W. 1983. "Reagan's Strategy: The Howard Demonstration against Symbolism for the Black Needy." *Spectrum: A Review of Politics* (March).

———. 2007, June 8–10. Speech delivered to the Dunbar Elementary School Reunion, 1927–1971, Wichita, Kansas. DVD of the proceedings.

Wichita Daily Eagle. 1924. (Wichita, Kansas), February 5, p. 1.

2

The Groundbreaking
Wichita Sit-In Movement

An Essay in Appreciation of Ronald Walters'
Scholarly and Political Contributions

ALDON MORRIS

This chapter seeks to illuminate the importance that low-visibility protests can have in producing social change. Such protests are usually initiated by relatively unrecognized activists and overlooked to a significant degree by those beyond the settings in which they occurred. As a result, these protests usually do not spark significant media coverage and are often invisible to many activists who participate in the larger movement produced, in part, by low-visibility protest. The central concern here is to understand how low-visibility protests may contribute to major social change movements. I focus on the important, but obscure, lunch counter sit-ins that occurred in the late 1950s prior to the famous lunch counter sit-ins launched by black students in the early 1960s. For analytical and historical reasons, the 1958 Wichita sit-ins led by Ronald Walters and his colleagues will serve as the prototype for the sit-ins of that period. I argue that such protests organized and executed by low-profile participants can have catalytic effects on large visible social change movements especially in their early phases. In particular, I highlight the importance of the 1958 sit-ins initiated by the local Wichita, Kansas Youth Council of the National Association for the Advancement of Colored People (NAACP) and their impact on the modern civil rights movement.

The Famous Civil Rights Movement

The modern civil rights movement produced famous confrontations that are etched in the collective memory of Americans and many people across the globe. The civil rights movement was a twentieth-century social movement that has become famous worldwide. The influences of this movement continue to be evident in the twentieth-first century. Indeed, the movements that rocked the Middle East in the spring of 2011 have been deeply influenced by the American civil rights movement. Those movements utilized many of the tactics of the civil rights movement and their major campaigns have been modeled, to a significant degree, on those made famous by the civil rights movement. Moreover, modern social change movements in Africa, Asia, and South America have been similarly influenced (Morris 1999). Closer to home, the contemporary Occupy Wall Street movement has drawn inspiration and tactical lessons from the civil rights movement.

Leaders of the civil rights movement, including Martin Luther King Jr., Rosa Parks, Malcolm X, Stokely Carmichael, and Angela Davis, are familiar to activists around the world. W. E. B. Du Bois, a major twentieth-century architect of the civil rights movement, is recognized in many corners of the globe as a great scholar and activist. Famous civil rights campaigns including the Montgomery Bus Boycott, 1960 student sit-ins, 1963 Birmingham Confrontation, and the 1965 Selma to Montgomery March are familiar to many activists throughout the world. Tragic events of the movement including the lynching of Emmett Till, the bombing murders of the four girls in Birmingham, Alabama's Sixteenth Street Baptist Church, the 1964 murders of three civil rights workers in Philadelphia, Mississippi, and the 1963 assassination of Medgar Evers, as well as the earthshaking 1968 assassination of Martin Luther King Jr., are parts of the consciousness possessed by numerous activists worldwide.

This visibility pertains to civil rights organizations of the period including the National Association for the Advancement of Colored People (NAACP), Southern Christian Leadership Conference (SCLC), Student Nonviolent Coordinating Committee (SNCC), and the Congress of Racial Equality (CORE). Cultural innovations in art and music during the civil rights movement have been widely recognized and transplanted into numerous freedom movements. Thus, the civil rights movement's national anthem, "We Shall Overcome," is the battle cry of many movements throughout the world. Likewise, high levels of visibility hold true for the repertoire of collective action tactics generated by the civil rights movement. Indeed, boycotts, sit-ins, mass marches, mass arrests that fill jails, freedom rides, and other forms of direct action were made famous by the civil rights movement.

By any criteria, the twentieth-century civil rights movement was a major development that achieved stunning victories. It overthrew Jim Crow in the southern United States and challenged racial oppression throughout America. Because of this success, this movement inspired the rise of numerous American movements that have challenged various forms of oppression. The modern women's movement, the antiwar movement, farmworkers' movement, disability movement, and the gay rights movement all drew inspiration and strategic lessons from the civil rights movement. As noted, the same has been true for movements beyond America's shores including the South African antiapartheid movement, the Intifada movement on the West Bank, the Middle Eastern movements known as the "Arab Spring," as well as the contemporary Occupy Wall Street movement.

Civil Rights Movement and Scholarly Analyses

Given the domestic and worldwide impact of the American civil rights movement, it is inevitable that questions arise regarding its causes and outcomes. Indeed, scholars and the general public have sought to understand why the civil rights movement emerged at a particular time in history. They seek to understand the reasons for its victories and defeats. They explore whether the movement was propelled by charismatic leaders or the multitudinous but underrecognized efforts of ordinary people. Were the famous, large, and drama-filled campaigns the essence of the movement, or was its transformative power generated by the convergence of smaller tributaries of protests? What role did emotions and culturally charged symbols play in the formation and outcomes of the civil rights movements? Was the movement stratified by gender such that women made major contributions while men received the lion's share of the credit?

Beyond the civil rights movement these are general questions movement analysts have attempted to answer. Though these questions have not been fully resolved, real progress has been made recently to account for the dynamics and outcomes of social movements. Because it was the pivotal movement in twentieth-century America, the civil rights movement has been a central focus of scholars seeking to answer these questions and to understand movements generally (Carson 1981; McAdam 1982; Morris 1984; Bloom 1987; Payne 1995; Andrews 2004). To understand the progress made in answering these fundamental questions, I provide an overview detailing what current scholarship reveals about movements.

First, movements are organized by people deeply embedded in the institutions, organizations, and cultures of their communities (Tilly 1978; Gamson 1975; McAdam 1982; Morris 1984). In this sense, the idea that movements are fueled by alienated individuals adrift in a sea of troubles has no merit. Rather, individuals who initiate and sustain movements are usually deeply connected to other people through personal, kinship, and institutional networks. Such ties provide the organizational and mobilizing resources needed to recruit people into movements and sustain their participation. Second, movements are not primarily the result of spontaneity but deliberate thought, planning, and organization (Morris 1984). This does not mean that spontaneity is absent in movements, for it certainly does occur and can impact movement dynamics and trajectories (Killian 1984; Robnett 1997). Yet, it is the planning and organization of movements that create the space for spontaneity to occur in the first place. Because movements are sites of innovation and improvisation, spontaneous creativity can spur and energize these processes. But "spontaneity" in this sense may be deliberately triggered by strategists and leaders who realize the need to anticipate and direct such spontaneity toward achievement of movement goals (Morris 1984).

Leaders are important to movements but not for reasons generally associated with movement leadership (Morris and Staggenborg 2004). The idea that a movement only becomes possible when a great charismatic Moses emerges and leads his people to the Promised Land has little merit. For example, as Morris (1984) has shown, in terms of the civil rights movement, local people in Montgomery, Alabama in 1955 had already begun to organize the bus boycott movement when they chose Martin Luther King as their leader. The "great men" theories of movements are overly simplistic and cloud rather than illuminate movement dynamics. Rather, movements of any substance are characterized by multiple leaders who vary in skills, gifts, and charisma. Mature movements are generally directed by leadership teams (Ganz 2009) where individuals combine their personal talents and skills to achieve movement goals. Closely related to the leadership of movements is the importance of strategies and tactics. Movements must devise appropriate strategies and tactics if they are to achieve change (McAdam 1983; Morris 1993). Social change movements are in the unenviable position of confronting powerful opponents who are intent on maintaining privileges and advantages. Thus, the strategic issue faced by movement leaders and activists is how to generate a counterforce that can provide the leverage to force powerful adversaries to accede to movement demands. To generate such power, activists must devise appropriate strategies and tactics and employ them strategically.

Cultural symbols and emotions are central to movements because they confront challenges regarding creating and sustaining solidarity between participants. Movements require ordinary people to engage in extraordinary deeds to accomplish change. Activists are required to make major sacrifices including risking injuries, economic reprisals, and even their lives in pursuit of change. As scholars have pointed out (e.g., Olson 1965), movements have to overcome the "free rider problem" if they are to be effective. This problem arises because most individuals are not willing to make great sacrifices to achieve a collective good. That is, why should an individual participate in risky collective action to achieve a collective good if he can reap the benefits of a movement without lifting a hand? Therefore, how can movements instill the courage and the willingness to make sacrifices to achieve a collective good? Emotional attachments, passion, and unswerving commitment to a set of values and ideals can provide the glue fastening individuals to high-risk activism often required by social change movements (Goodwin, Jasper, and Polletta 2001).

Research has shown that movements tend to be stratified by gender. This has been documented for the new left (Evans, 1980) and the civil rights movement (Giddings 1984; Robnett 1997; Ransby 2005). Throughout history men usually have held the most prestigious and glorified positions in movements. Women often find that formal leadership positions in movements are largely filled by men. Indeed, in terms of the divisions of movement labor, women often perform "female work" that is mirrored in the patriarchal structures of the societies from which they sprang.

Finally, the treatment of social movements by scholars as if they are one homogeneous mass of protest has been fairly typical. Thus, the massive black protests of the 1950s,'60s, and '70s are viewed as the "civil rights movement" or disparate protests by women are viewed simply as the "women's movement." Yet, the massive protests viewed as one movement are actually comprised of a multitude of local movements characterized by a great deal of variation. To capture this foundational quality of social movements, I (Morris 1984) developed the concept "local movement centers," which refers to a "distinctive form of social organization specifically developed by members of a dominated group to produce, organize, coordinate, finance, and sustain social protest. The ability of a given community to engage in a sustained social protest movement depends on that community's development of a local movement center" (Morris 1984, 284). This local emphasis enables the analyst to delve into both macro and micro processes of social movements.

Blind Spots in the Southern Perspective on the Civil Rights Movement

It is commonplace for Americans to believe southern race relations have differed fundamentally from those of the North. Until recently, scholarship on the civil rights movement has reflected this view by concentrating almost exclusively on the South. This focus is understandable given the explosive confrontations of the southern movement. Indeed, the dramatic confrontations in the South—Montgomery Bus Boycott, lunch counter sit-ins, freedom rides, standoffs at the doors of schools, and the epic battles in Birmingham and Selma, Alabama—have dominated both popular and scholarly attention. This attention has galvanized our attraction on historic personalities typified by Martin Luther King Jr. and "Bull" Connor. The overthrow of formal Jim Crow by the southern movement within a decade has also riveted scholarly attention on the South.

Nevertheless, over the last decade a new literature has emerged showing that northern civil rights movements have been as prominent and enduring as those in the South (Sugrue 2008; Lang 2009; Countryman 2005; Theoharis and Woodward 2003; Biondi 2003; Ralph 1993). Many northern movements preceded those that occurred in the South in the 1950s and '60s, while others paralleled southern movements. Northern movements were organized to confront deeply entrenched structural and cultural patterns of racial inequality rooted in northern forms of racism. These movements occurred across large and small cities and in rural areas throughout the Northeast, Midwest, and West (Sugrue). The presence of northern movements raises fundamental questions about the dominant scholarly narrative developed to explain southern movements that were organized to confront legally sanctioned Jim Crow in the South.

The literature on northern movements documents two important realities. First, racial inequality has always been deeply embedded in northern communities and has been enforced either by formal or informal rules or a combination of the two. In border states, versions of Jim Crow, including strict racial segregation, have often been the norm. Thus, northern racism may have differed in nuance and texture from that of the Deep South but not significantly in terms of substance. White supremacy in both locales required that blacks occupy the bottom rungs of the social order while whites dominated the middle and upper rungs. Yet, northern blacks have seldom borne racist oppression that restricted their life chances and assaulted their dignity quietly. The literature on northern black protests (Biondi 2003; Sugrue 2008; Countryman 2005; Lang 2009; and Murch 2010) clearly demonstrates that blacks, outside the South, have organized protest movements to attack racism in all of its myriad manifestations. As we will see, this was true for segments of the black community in Wichita, Kansas in the late 1950s.

Racism in Wichita and Seeds of Rebellion

It is not widely known that black students conducted lunch counter sit-ins in Wichita, Kansas during the summer of 1958. In sharp contrast, anyone casually familiar with the civil rights movement knows that in the early 1960s southern black students opened the floodgates of lunch counter protests by conducting hundreds of lunch counter sit-ins. Those sit-ins launched an intensive active phase of protest by interjecting unparalleled levels of youthful energy into the civil rights movement. Yet, unlike the sit-ins that followed those in Greensboro, North Carolina in February of 1960, the Wichita sit-ins lacked a contemporary model from which to gather strength. To be sure, CORE and the Fellowship of Reconciliation had initiated sit-ins against racial segregation in the 1940s. The Reverend C. T. Vivian and a small group of protesters in Peoria, Illinois conducted sit-ins against segregation in the 1940s. However, while the young Wichita protesters were taught about CORE's sit-ins of the 1940s, there were no immediate examples of sit-in protests they could adopt to confront segregation in the 1950s. In this sense, the Wichita protests truly pioneered the use of lunch counter sit-ins in the modern period. Thus, they deserve to be analyzed as a groundbreaking model and their larger significance needs to be unraveled. It is rare that a major leader of a pioneering protest also becomes an accomplished social scientist who provides a scholarly account of the movement in which he participated. This is exactly what the political scientist Ronald Walters accomplished. He led the Wichita sit-ins in 1958, and in 1996 he provided a first-rate social scientific analysis of those lunch counter sit-ins. Thus, my analyses of those sit-ins are heavily based on Walters' article entitled "The Great Plains Sit-In Movement, 1958–60." Those analyses will be augmented by my own research on the topic as well as other scholarly accounts and relevant data, especially those provided by Gretchen Eick in her book *Dissent in Wichita*.

Scholars of the northern civil rights movement emphasize that the black streams of migration from the rural South to northern cities during and following the first two World Wars were critical to the rise of northern protests. Because of the migration of southern blacks who sought to escape Jim Crow and find economics opportunities beyond the Mason-Dixon Line, northern blacks communities grew exponentially. In the process, these migrants planted solid cultural and structural roots on which collective goals could be pursued. These communities emerged as amalgamations of both southern and northern black culture (Gregory 2005). Walters' (1996) analysis demonstrates that Wichita, Kansas during the second half of the twentieth century fit this pattern:

Census data show that between 1950 and 1960 the total population of Wichita, Kansas, grew very quickly, from 168,000 to 255,000, and by 1960 its black population was nearly 20,000. This was a significant pattern of postwar population growth made possible by a developing aircraft industry, which, although it was structured to serve wartime production, rapidly made the transition to commercial markets. Indeed, national publications could write of Wichita as a "boom city" when a house-building frenzy took the city to twice its 1945 [size]. (86–87)

Therefore, by the 1950s blacks had established a substantial presence in Wichita and developed a tightly knit community of workers and consumers.

Yet, racial segregation and a northern brand of racism, greeted blacks fleeing to Wichita from the rural cotton fields and tobacco plantations. Walters (1996) explained:

But although the rising economy incorporated a segment of the black community who worked in aircraft and related industries, the social fabric of the city was distinctly segregated. Although Kansas had "bled" to keep slavery from its territory, Wichita resembled a Southern city in the occurrence of murder and lynching of blacks. Blacks had suffered a long history of discrimination and segregation in Wichita and even by the 1950s, although public transportation was integrated, blacks were not welcome in white elementary schools, theaters, churches, restaurants, parks, or other places of public accommodation. (87)

The sociologist Robert Newby, who was a friend of Walters and who would become a coparticipant in the Wichita sit-ins, observed, "In the South, everything was marked 'white' or 'black.' Just over in Kansas City [Missouri] signs were everywhere. But in Wichita there were no signs. Everyone just knew the rules and that you didn't break them" (quoted in Walters 1996, 87). Thus, in Wichita of the 1950s, racial segregation in public accommodations, coupled with racial discrimination in the labor market, was rampant.

Wichita's racial scene confirms the accuracy in Malcolm X's claim that "If you are black, you were born in jail, in the North as well as the South. Stop talking about the South. As long as you are south of the Canadian border, you are south." Yet, segments of Wichita's black community did not quietly accept the discrimination and economic exploitation they encountered. In the 1950s, the NAACP was the major organizing force in the black community resisting white domination. SCLC was not founded until 1957 and its base was largely southern. CORE was small, largely white led, and operated almost exclusively in large northern cities such as Chicago, Boston, and Los Angeles prior to the 1960s (Morris 1984). In contrast, the NAACP was national and could be found in border states such as Kansas. Regarding Wichita, Walters (1996) explained:

> As they had in many such communities, Wichita blacks had established a small but active NAACP chapter in the 1920s. The several chapters located in cities throughout Kansas, headed by state conference president Dr. C. A. Rocquemore, defined both racism and its opposition. The Wichita NAACP was headed by a youthful and dynamic attorney, Chester I. Lewis, and the December 1958 issue of *The Crisis*, the magazine of the NAACP, carried pictures of the local and state officers. (87)

Additionally, a cadre of individuals in Wichita's black community participated in and supported their local NAACP. As was the case nationally, Wichita's NAACP advocated the legal method as the weapon best suited to overthrow racial inequality. Because of this legal approach, lawyers constituted the power center within the NAACP and the courtroom was the stage where its battles for equality were fought. Moreover, the NAACP was a hierarchical protest organization wherein decisions had to be cleared through a chain of command that rested ultimately with the power of its elite leaders located in the New York headquarters.

This lawyer-centered protest organization did not always reflect the desires and viewpoints of its constituency. Indeed, racial inequality and segregation were more devastating in southern and border states than that experienced by northern NAACP leaders. In a brilliant analysis, Tomiko Brown-Nagin (2011) has shown that legal strategies of the NAACP's northern-based lawyers often conflicted with those of local black communities. The legal approach was often costly, time consuming, and involved only a few members of the black community. Thus, those members of the black masses who desired direct involvement in the struggle to overthrow racism were largely excluded by the legal approach, and NAACP lawyers were not enthused about involving masses because they could prove detrimental to well-honed legal arguments and back-door compromises.

By the 1950s, segments of black youth were especially dissatisfied with the pace of racial change. They often participated in local NAACP chapters because it was the only organized force in their communities challenging racial oppression. Within the NAACP, young people clustered in their own organizational spaces designated as Youth Councils. Those councils operated at the local, state, and national levels thus providing like-minded young people opportunities to interact, learn from each other, and share experiences. As Walters (1996) explained, Wichita had its NAACP Youth Council: "The Wichita Youth Council of the NAACP was headed from 1958 to 1960 by Ronald Walters, then a local college student. . . . The Youth Council included high school and college-age youth, the Little Rock generation. The Council was a novelty, since youth had not featured prominently in social change movements until this time" (87). Walters' reference to members of the Youth Council as the "Little Rock generation" is significant. It signals these youth identified with the bold action of nine black high school students who, under the leadership of Daisy Bates, desegregated Central High School in Little Rock, Arkansas in 1957. Black youth across America witnessed how those students pursued their goal relentlessly despite the mob action of white segregationists bent on keeping their school racially segregated. The youth in Wichita, like growing numbers of young black people nationally, were impressed by the courage and high-risk activism pursued by the nine students to desegregate Central High. They marveled how those desegregation efforts forced President Eisenhower, who was not an advocate of "forced" racial integration, to order the United States Army to protect students their own age from white violence and entrenched resistance.

Black youth in the 1950s were beginning to awaken politically. Indeed, the winds of change were blowing among these youth in Wichita by 1958. As Walters (1996) revealed:

> The Council recognized that nowhere in the city could blacks sit down to eat in a dignified manner in white-owned restaurants. The many blacks who worked downtown suffered from this disadvantage as well as the slight to their humanity of being served while standing behind a board at the end of the lunch counters at F.W. Woolworth, Kress and Company, and other stores. (87)

The members of Wichita's Youth Council were not merely interested in themselves. They empathized with the plight of their elders who worked downtown but could not eat in dignity in a northern Jim Crow restaurant. They were appalled to see their parents' generation endure such oppression and decided they would change the situation. Yet, as will become clear, their decision was not spontaneous; their action unfolded within the context of organized activity within the NAACP Youth Council.

Certain aspects of racial segregation were particularly humiliating. Segregation on buses was an example because black people were embarrassed when they paid the same fair as whites but had to ride in the back seats or stand if whites occupied those seats. The inequality of second-class citizenship on buses was excruciating because it occurred in a public space, making it evident that whites were treated as the superior race. Thus, for example, an elderly, dignified, black woman who had worked throughout the day had to give her seat to a white child because that was the law. Small wonder, then, in 1955, that Montgomery's black community initiated a yearlong boycott of the buses after Mrs. Rosa Parks' arrest for defying bus segregation. That act of defiance, as well as the 1954 murder of fourteen-year-old Emmett Till, was not lost on Wichita's "Little Rock generation."

A similar situation existed at segregated lunch counters. The act of eating with others is an intimate activity. When people eat in the same space, everyone's humanity is taken for granted. When members of one group, because of a marker like skin color, are singled out and forced not to eat in a shared public space, they experience a direct assault on their humanity. To have food handed through a back door so others will not be offended is a deeply degrading and stigmatizing act. This discrimination constitutes a public rebuke suggesting that the stigmatized group is contaminated and not fully human. Lunch counter racial segregation was widely practiced in

America during the twentieth century and it was painful. This is what Walters had in mind when he described the humiliation experienced by blacks at Wichita's segregated lunch counter as a slight to their humanity as they were being served while standing behind a board at the end of the lunch counters. Anger over this humiliation led some of Wichita's young people of the NAACP Youth Council to target the segregated lunch counters for protest.

As I argued earlier, until recently scholarly literature on the civil rights movement had focused on the South. Yet, Ron Walters was one of the first social scientists to recognize the inherent flaws of this regional approach. He lamented that many of the southern accounts of the movement ignored the important role that Wichita played in the origins of the civil rights movement. Walters (1996) critiqued the exclusive focus on the southern movement arguing that

> These accounts are inaccurate and incomplete, but they also symbolize the extent to which the civil rights movement in general has been written about almost exclusively from the perspective of what occurred in the south. Considering that journalists wrote the first accounts, it may have been their initial perspective that was responsible for the subsequent lapse by serious scholars. (88)

Walters' critique went beyond how such accounts skewed understanding of the civil rights movement; it revealed how they ignored northern racism that triggered protests. In this regard Walters (1996) wrote:

> Racism, of course, was encountered by blacks in the urban environment as the effects of the slavocracy of the rural south extended to the northern cities, resulting in patterns of exclusion of blacks from both public accommodations and private social functions. In both rural and urban environments, the freedom movement has confronted racism's iniquities. (92)

Thus, as a scholar, Walters led the way in the development of an approach that underscored the similarity of northern and southern racism and how these shared injustices provided the cultural and structural foundations on which a modern black freedom struggle would flower. As an activist in Wichita, Ron Walters provided leadership for the first major lunch counter sit-in of the modern civil rights movement.

Protest in Wichita: Groundbreaking Lunch Counter Sit-Ins

In the summer of 1958, members of the Wichita NAACP Youth Council walked into the Dockum drugstore and sat on its lunch counter stools reserved for whites only. Following the custom of racial segregation, servers refused to comply with the black protesters' request that they be served. These lunch counter sit-ins opened a new chapter in the modern civil rights movement; they launched a new tactical onslaught against Jim Crow–restricted public accommodations. The sit-ins were conducted by approximately two dozen young people ranging in age from fifteen to twenty-two years of age. The leaders, and most of the participants of this sit-in movement, were high school and college students and members of the Wichita NAACP Council. For more than three weeks, beginning July 19 of 1958, these protesters staged sit-ins at Dockum each Thursday and Saturday (Eick 2001, 7). On August 11, the owner of Dockum entered his establishment where sit-ins were being conducted and ordered his workers to serve the protesters. He "agreed to abolish all discriminatory polices" (Eick 2001, 9). The young activists had pulled off a major victory given that the new policy applied not only to Wichita but other locales as well, given that Dockum was part of a much larger chain. Moreover, black leaders from other cities and states in close proximity gazed across the border to absorb the lessons of the Wichita movement. Hence, it is instructive to examine the factors that led to victory in Wichita. Earlier I elaborated on the crucial factors social movement scholars have uncovered that are essential for successful collective action. Let's apply them to the Wichita sit-in movement.

Participants in movements, especially successful ones, are embedded in personal relationships including kinship and friendship networks as well as organizational networks. When the young Wichita activists are placed in context, we see they were deeply embedded within their community. Most knew each other, having attended the same high schools and colleges. Some were personally close, such as Walters and Newby who were long-term "best friends" (see chapter 1 in this volume). The two coleaders of the movement, Walters and Carol Parks, were first cousins, while Gerald Walters was the brother of Ron and cousin to Parks. Moreover, most of the activists were members of the local NAACP Youth Council, which meant they had a history of working together organizationally and interrogating the grievances that racism produced. Because their shared kinship, friendship, and organizational networks generated trust and solidarity, the young Wichita activists were able to mobilize participants to engage in direct action against border state Jim Crow.

It is crucial to understand that the young activists were embedded in the adult activist community of Wichita. This fact has been largely overlooked because the sit-ins have been portrayed primarily as a student movement. Even Ronald Walters (1996) gives this impression by focusing on the young Turks while shining little light on the foundational roles played by adult activists. Eick's account (2001) corrects this one-sided view. From her study we learn that the majority of the young activists' parents, relatives, and associates were members of Wichita's historic activist community. Some had been leaders in the local and national NAACP, such as Carol's mother, Vivian Park, and attorney Chester Lewis. Both were active in the national NAACP and both served as presidents of Wichita's NAACP. Lewis, the militant and talented civil rights attorney, succeeded Parks as president of the local NAACP and held this position during the Wichita sit-ins. Some of these adult activists had engaged in decade-long activism against race discrimination and segregation.

Wichita's activist community socialized those who would become "young Turks" in the art of resistance and exposed them to the storehouse of knowledge containing protest wisdom lodged in the historic black protest tradition. In this regard, the idea for the sit-ins emanated from that storehouse. Thus, Eick (2001) wrote:

> The idea for the sit-ins at Dockum Drug Store had germinated for at least two years. It was spawned during a late-night conversation that Carol and Ron had with the NAACP's western region director, Franklin Williams, two years earlier. In 1956, Williams, a young lawyer who radiated competence, had come from his California office to speak

to a citywide NAACP conference that Vivian Parks had organized. He stayed in her home. . . .Williams told Carol Parks
and Ron Walters about the sit-ins that the Congress of Racial
Equality . . . had organized in the 1940s. . . . over the next
two years [he] talked more with the youths, helping them
think about what they wanted to do locally to fight racial
discrimination. (3)

Following these discussions, "the youth group discussed the situation, and Carol and Ron shared what they had learned from Franklin Williams about the "sit-downs that CORE had organized in the
1940s." Clearly, the Wichita sit-in movement fitted squarely within
the black protest tradition, and Wichita's activist adults served as the
conduit linking them with that tradition.

This adult community made direct contributions to the sit-in
movement as it unfolded. Attorney Lewis provided legal assistance
free of charge, and as president of the local NAACP, he navigated
relationships between the young protesters, the national NAACP, as
well as with the opposition and the black community; parents and
adult supporters provided transportation for the young protesters
and stood short distances from the action, monitoring signs of trouble; and adults worked within the black community mobilizing its
support, which inclined the opposition to capitulate. Walters and
others emphasized the lack of support for the sit-ins coming from
the national NAACP. But it is crucial to underscore that the local
Wichita NAACP went on record defying the decision of the national
organization not to back the students and publicly proclaimed its
unswerving support of the sit-ins. This was not a move of the faint-
hearted because the national NAACP wielded enormous power
over it local branches and was not reluctant to excoriate and punish
local branches for insubordination. As a result, the breach between
Wichita's local NAACP and the national NAACP remained palpa-
ble for years following the sit-ins. Without strong support from the
local NAACP, the road to victory by the youth would have been difficult to say the least. The Wichita sit-in movement was a joint affair
between youth and activist adults, though it was spearheaded by the
youth and it was they who placed their bodies and careers squarely
in harm's way.

As pointed out earlier, the foundational essence of social protest is planning and organization and not spontaneity. The Wichita sit-in movement epitomizes this principle. As we have seen, the sit-in idea percolated for several years before it was executed. During this period, extensive planning for the protest occurred. The youth met with adult advisors who had secured space for them to practice and rehearse the sit-ins. Similar to the meticulous planning that would occur in sit-ins of the 1960s movements such as those in Nashville, the students' planning included role-play generating proper responses to all possible scenarios. In these planning sessions it was decided that students would be deployed in shifts so as to keep the lunch counter seats occupied at all times. Strategies were developed to recruit additional protesters outside the original group if the need arose. Measures were devised to react effectively to violence that might occur, keeping the safety of the protesters as the highest priority.

And there was an ultimate strategy to achieve victory. The lesson of the Montgomery Bus Boycott was not lost on Wichita's young insurgents. Walters (quoted in Eick 2001, 6) explained the victory strategy thusly, "this what we were hoping for—a shut off of the flow of dollars into this operation. . . . By the second week of the protest, we felt that we were winning because we were being allowed to sit on the stools for long periods of time. Surely the store was losing money." Thus, the Wichita movement attempted to leave nothing to chance by carefully planning the protest and anticipating the moves of the opposition so they could be effectively countered. Planning and organization were the hallmark of the Wichita sit-in movement and essential to its ultimate triumph.

I argued earlier that no individual leader is capable of generating, sustaining, and determining the outcomes of social movement. While the mesmerizing image of a Moses singlehandedly leading his people to the Promised Land may make for scintillating cinema, it is a poor proxy for how social movement leadership actually works. Powerful and successful movements thrive because they are led by leadership teams (Ganz 2009) rather than an overpowering charismatic personality. Therefore, the view that Martin Luther King Jr. was the all-powerful engine of the civil rights movement while all other actors paled in comparison actually detracts from King's leadership genius. Accounting for King's success, Lerone Bennett (1970) wrote, "King had . . . an unexcelled ability to pull men and women of diverse viewpoints together and to keep their eyes focused on the goal. . . . King . . . demonstrated . . . a rare talent for attracting and using the skills and ideas of brilliant aides and administrators" (32–33). The same holds true for the Wichita sit-in movement. Ronald Walters, given his post as president of the NAACP Youth Council and his exemplary action during the sit-ins, has been viewed as the movement's leader. Yet, the historical record paints a different picture. That is, though Walters was an outstanding leader of the movement, he was a central player in the leadership team that guided the movement.

A multilayered leadership team guided the Wichita sit-in movement. Walters was a key leader of the team by virtue of his presidency of the Youth Council and the formal powers that position afforded him. Another key member of the team was Carol Parks. Moreover, Vivian Parks was a staunch member of Wichita's activist community. Indeed, from the very beginning of the movement, the younger Parks was a leader given that it was "Ron Walters and Carol Parks [who] proposed that the youth group conduct a sustained sit-in at Dockum's" (Eick 2001, 4). Moreover, "Nineteen-year-old Carol and three other young women were the first to enter the drugstore" as the sit-ins commenced (Eick 2001, 5). Carol Parks, and other participants, occupied the lunch counter seats when the manager acceded to the youths' demand. At that time Ron Walters was absent from the drugstore to attend Army Reserve training. As part of the leadership team, Carol's mother, Vivian, continued to work behind the scenes consulting with community and organizational leaders while advising the young protesters.

Another key member of the leadership team was attorney Chester I. Lewis, who was a community leader by virtue of his position as president of the local NAACP and his stellar skills as a lawyer. Eick (2001) reveals how central Lewis' leadership was as a key mobilizer at the zenith of the movement:

> Lewis felt it important to let the black community know more about the sit-in and the students' plans and also soothe concerned parents who feared their children would be arrested.

The church was packed. Some participants narrated the story of the sit-ins at Dockum's and asked for community support. They had decided to expand the sit-in to additional days of the week. There were many questions from the audience and many concerns, but by the end of the meeting there was a great unity and solidarity. The students left the meeting knowing that the community was behind them and proud of them. (8–9)

The following day the opposition yielded to the movement's demands, and it was Attorney Lewis who consulted with that opposition and confirmed that the policy of the drugstore chain had indeed been changed. Lewis, therefore, was a key link in the chain of the movement's leadership.

To acknowledge that Walters' leadership unfolded within a team framework does not detract from the quality of his individual leadership. To the contrary, when Walters' leadership is so situated, we come to understand his personal leadership gifts, the least of which was having the confidence to colead with other strong and competent personalities. An example suffices to reveal the value-added dimension of Walters' leadership. At a key junction in the sit-ins, white thugs threatening to violently attack the protesters and were given latitude to do so because the police refused to protect the insurgents. Here is what happened next:

Anxious about what would happen without police protection, Walters went to the pay phone, called a local youth hang-out on Ninth Street, and spoke loudly into the receiver. "This is Ron Walters. We're having some trouble down here at Dockum's. Could some of you come?" the level of tension was building inside the store, as was the amount of taunting. Then, three carloads of black teenagers drove up; the teenagers piled out of the cars and entered the drugstore. Apparently, words were not necessary. The white gang left by Dockum's back entrance. As relief filled those sitting in, Walters realized that the black teenagers who had come to their rescue were armed with clubs, knives, and a pistol. The "rescue mission" could have been disastrous. (Eick 2001, 8)

This response by Walters exemplifies superb leadership. It averted a crisis that could have derailed the movement. Walters knew he was venturing outside normal protocol. He and his colleagues had been taught the principles of nonviolence and how it was paramount to remain nonviolent despite great threats of violence. Indeed, in addition to role-playing how not to respond violently to violence in advance, the protesters had studied the nonviolent techniques of Dr. King and the Montgomery Bus Boycott, having consulted a non-violent manual provided by King's organization, the SCLC. Nonviolence notwithstanding, Walters improvised in the heat of battle to keep the movement on track. Thus Walters' leadership was greatly enhanced because it sparkled in the context of a leadership team. His lifelong friend and fellow sit-in protester Robert Newby (in this volume) revealed how Walters embraced collective leadership:

> The sit-in was a success because the membership of the NAACP Youth Group believed in Ron Walters. They believed in his integrity, his commitment, his leadership. Ron was well-liked and popular. Even though there were apprehensions, Ron convinced us that we were not only right but had an obligation when it came to carrying out the sit-in. Whenever he was honored for his leadership of the sit-in, he quickly made sure that the praise would go to all of the participants. It is this characteristic, sharing the credit, sharing the glory, that Ron routinely spread to all of the participants. His leadership was shared with both Vivian and Carol Parks. He also had the essential support of Attorney Chester Lewis.

In short, Ron Walters' leadership was effective because it was a crowning jewel within the context of the leadership team. It was that team that propelled the movement to victory, establishing its pioneering role in the modern civil rights movement.

Gender diversity was evident throughout the Wichita sit-ins. Men and women shared in the movement's leadership, and they jointly shouldered the sacrifices of participating in risky collective action. I have already shown the leadership activities of women such as Carol Parks and her mother Vivian. Yet they were not alone. Thus, Rosie Hughes served as the adult advisor of the training sessions preparing the youth to confront Jim Crow at the lunch counter. Other women, such as Maxine Walters, monitored the environs as the students attempted to order cokes and hamburgers inside the drugstore. In terms of rank-and-file participants, "sometimes the group at the counter was all female'" (Eick 2001, 7). The evidence shows that the women were no mere helpers of the men and they did not seek male protectors before they acted. Men and women bore the work and fear of being insurgents and both genders were responsible for the successful outcome of the movement.

As I will discuss shortly, the Wichita sit-ins inspired the rise of numerous sit-in lunch counter movements. The point I wish to make is that women, as in Wichita, often played pivotal leadership roles in those movements. Belinda Robnett has shown that most of the top formal positions in the civil rights movement were held by men. Yet, this was not the case in the early sit-in movements (see Morris 1981 and 1984). Widespread female leadership existed in these movements because men tended to pass over leadership in NAACP Youth Councils because they viewed them as the domain of youths and not serious grown-up activities they desired to lead. To be sure, there were a few local NAACP chapters headed by women, including the Little Rock, Arkansas branch led by Daisy Bates and the Wichita chapter that had been led by Vivian Parks. Yet, the typical pattern translated into men leading chapters and significant numbers of women leading Youth Councils as presidents and adult advisors. The most famous example was Mrs. Parks, who headed the Youth Division of the Montgomery NAACP. Through NAACP Youth Councils, adult black women were able to function extensively as leaders and young black women were able to gain political experience as members of the councils.

In terms of women leadership in the NAACP, Wichita was favorably situated. During Vivian Parks' terms as president of Wichita's NAACP from 1955 to 1956, followed by her role as secretary of the branch, she involved women extensively in the political work of the organization and the larger community. By the time of the 1958 sit-ins, women were accustomed to participating in the political life of the black community. Although Walters was president of the Youth Council at the start of the sit-ins, the movement reaped heavy female participation because leaders like Parks had fertilized the soil ensuring such participation. Therefore, gender diversity was an essential quality of the Wichita sit-in movement. By understanding this fact, and not elevating Walters as "the leader" of the movement, the window was opened on the widespread participation of both men and women in the sit-ins and the centrality of the movement's leadership team.

A sustained protest movement is possible once some members of a dominated group develop a local movement center. Recall that such centers constitute a distinctive form of social organization specifically developed by members of a dominated group to produce, organize, coordinate, finance, and sustain social protest. Moreover, a movement center exists in a subordinate community when that community has developed an interrelated set of protest leaders, organizations, and followers who collectively define the common ends of the group, devise necessary tactics and strategies along with training for their implementation, and engage in actions designed to attain the goals of the group (Morris 1984, 40). It is clear that a segment of Wichita's black community had established a local movement center capable of launching and sustaining a sit-in movement. Indeed, adult and student leaders were in place; organizationally the local NAACP and its Youth Council were prepared to initiate protest; nonviolent direct action had been designated as the strategy and the movement's participants had trained to execute it; and an infrastructure consisting of legal skills, modes of transportation, and a protest tradition was entrenched. It was this center that enabled the movement to take firm root and achieve victory, making it a model that other communities could follow.

Wichita's Sit-Ins as Innovative Model

The protest spark that brightly glowed in Wichita would spread to other nearby states and cites, especially those bordering the South. A week after the Wichita victory, a lunch counter sit-in movement was initiated in Oklahoma City by the NAACP Youth Council under the adult leadership of Clara Luper and a fifteen-year-old activist, Barbara Posey. Others followed in Tulsa, Enid, and Stillwater, Oklahoma as well as in other cities in Kansas. Additional sit-ins spread to Missouri, Illinois, Kentucky, and West Virginia. Morris (1981), Walters, (1996) and Eick (2001) have established that these late-1950s lunch counter sit-ins were linked through personal and organizational ties and exhibited similarly tactical and organizational expressions. Given these shared qualities, the evidence confirms that Wichita sit-ins, having occurred first and achieved some visibility to black populations in close proximity, served as the inspirational, organizational, and tactical model for those sit-ins that followed in the late 1950s.

On February 1, 1960, lunch counter sit-ins occurred in Greensboro, North Carolina. Hundreds followed in cities throughout the South. The Greensboro sit-ins rapidly became designated by journalists, scholars, and movement participants as the first of such protests. Consequently, the border state sit-ins of the late 1950s faded from collective memory, and thus their pioneering significance was erased. Memories of the pioneering Wichita sit-ins vanished beyond Wichita and those activists who either initiated or were affected by them. Yet, as discussed earlier, those sit-ins played a pioneering role in triggering the cluster of those that followed.

However, evidence suggests that the Wichita protests, as well as those they help trigger, influenced the initiation of the Greensboro sit-ins. Like Walters and other youth participants of the Wichita sit-ins, the four students who initiated the Greensboro sit-ins were also members of their local NAACP Youth Council and attended nationwide meetings of that organization. Thus, Morris (1984) concluded that the Greensboro protesters knew about many of the other sit-ins conducted before 1960. This led him to proclaim, "the myth that four college students got up one day and on impulse went to sit in at Woolworth's—and sparked a movement—is not supported by the evidence" (198).Walters reached a similar conclusion:

> if . . . actors know how someone else has resolved a similar problem in the past, they may adopt the same style to deal with their own problem. Thus young people in Greensboro may have reacted to lunch counter discrimination with a sit-in not because of the Wichita and Oklahoma City sit-ins but because of their own unwillingness to tolerate discrimination. At the same time the style and rhythm of the Greensboro protest seem to have been colored by the earlier sit-ins. (92)

This essay shows that that low-visibility protests can play important roles in producing social change. Such change can occur despite the fact that the obscure protest may have been initiated by relatively unrecognized activists and overlooked to a significant degree by those beyond the settings in which they occurred. A case has been made in this essay that just a such protest in Wichita in 1958, followed by similar protests that those insurgents helped to generate, are exemplary instances demonstrating the power of low-visibility protests. Ronald Walters (1996) summed up the case:

> The actions of northern NAACP youth chapters in 1958 and 1959 were not "isolated" from the southern chapters of the NAACP—nor other organizations—and the campaigns of the northern chapters against segregated eating establishments constituted a national model and network for change by the time Greensboro sit-ins began. (92)

One does not have to agree with Walters absolutely to appreciate the wisdom of his analysis and the undeniable power of the hypothesis his work suggests. Namely, that social change potential may be camouflaged underneath low-visibility activism. Indeed, Professor Ronald Walters possessed a rare gift: he combined scholarly profundity and sterling activism, creatively enabling him to leave behind a better world!

References

Andrews, Kenneth. 2004. *Freedom Is a Constant Struggle: The Mississippi Civil Rights Movement and Its Legacy.* Chicago: University of Chicago Press, 2004.

Bennett, Lerone, Jr. 1970. "When the Man and the Hour Are Met." In *Martin Luther King, Jr.*, ed. C. Eric Lincoln, 7–39. New York: Hill & Wang.

Biondi, Martha. 2003. *To Stand and Fight: The Struggle for Civil Rights in Postwar New York City.* Cambridge: Harvard University Press.

Bloom, Jack. 1987. *Class, Race and the Civil Rights Movement.* Bloomington: Indiana University Press.

Bonastia, Christopher. 2006. *Knocking on the Door: The Federal Government's Attempt to Desegregate the Suburbs.* Princeton: Princeton University Press.

Branch, Taylor. 1988. *Parting the Waters: America in the King Years, 1954–63.* New York: Simon & Schuster, 1988.

Brilliant, Mark. 2010. *The Color of America Has Changed: How Racial Diversity Shaped Civil Rights Reform in California, 1941–1978.* Oxford: Oxford University Press.

Brown-Nagin, Tomiko. 2011. *Courage to Dissent: Atlanta and the Long History of the Civil Rights Movement.* Oxford: Oxford University Press.

Carson, Clayborne. 1981. *In Struggle: SNCC and the Black Awakening of the 1960s.* Cambridge: Harvard University Press.

Chafe, Williams. 1981. *Civilities and Civil Rights in Greensboro, North Carolina.* Oxford: Oxford University Press.

Countryman, Matthew. 2005. *Up South: Civil Rights and Black Power in Philadelphia.* Philadelphia: University of Pennsylvania Press.

Delinder, Jean Van. 2008. *Struggles Before Brown: Early Civil Rights Protests and Their Significance Today.* Boulder, CO: Paradigm Publishers.

Dittmer, John. 1995. *Local People: The Struggle for Civil Rights in Mississippi.* Champaign: University of Illinois Press.

Eick, Gretchen Cassel. 2001. *Dissent in Wichita: The Civil Rights Movement in the Midwest, 1954–72.* Urbana: University of Illinois Press.

Evans, Sara. 1980. *Personal Politics: The Roots of Women's Liberation in the Civil Rights Movement and the New Left.* New York: Random House.

Gamson, William. 1975. *The Strategy of Social Protest.* Homewood, IL: Dorsey Press.

Ganz, Marshall. 2009. *Why David Sometimes Wins.* Oxford: Oxford University Press.

Garrow, David. 1986. *Bearing the Cross: Martin Luther King, Jr., and the Southern Christian Leadership Conference.* New York: William Morrow and Company.

Giddings, P. 1984. *When and Where I Enter: The Impact of Black Women on Race and Sex in America.* New York: W. Morrow.

Goodwin, Jeff, James M. Jasper, and Francesca Polletta. 2001. *Passionate Politics: Emotions and Social Movements.* Chicago: University of Chicago Press.

Gregory, James. 2005. *The Southern Diaspora: How the Great Migrations of Black and White Southerners Transformed America.* Chapel Hill: University of North Carolina Press.

Hine, Darlene Clark. 1979. *Black Victory: The Rise and Fall of the White Primary in Texas.* Columbia: University of Missouri Press.

Killian, Lewis M. 1984. "Organization, Rationality and Spontaneity in the Civil Rights Movement." *American Sociological Review* 49: 770–83.

Klinkner, Philip, and Rogers Smith. 1999. *The Unsteady March: The Rise and Decline of Racial Equality in America.* Chicago: University of Chicago Press.

Lang, Clarence. 2009. *Grassroots at the Gateway: Class Politics and Black Freedom Struggle in St. Louis, 1936–75.* Ann Arbor: The University of Michigan.

McAdam, Doug. 1982. *Political Process and the Development of Black Insurgency, 1930–1970.* Chicago: University of Chicago Press.

Morris, Aldon. 1981. "Black Southern Student Sit-In Movement: An Analysis of Internal Organization." *American Sociological Review* 46, 6: 744–67.

———. 1984. *The Origins of the Civil Rights Movement: Black Communities Organizing for Change.* New York: Free Press.

———. 1993. "Birmingham Confrontation Reconsidered: An Analysis of the Dynamics and Tactics of Mobilization." *American Sociological Review* 58, 5 (October): 621–36.

———. 1999. "A Retrospective on the Civil Rights Movement: Political and Intellectual Landmarks." *Annual Review of Sociology* 25 (August): 517–39.

Morris, Aldon, and Suzanne Staggenborg. 2004. "Leadership in Social Movements." In *The Blackwell Companion to Social Movements*, ed. David A. Snow, Sarah A. Soule, and Hanspeter Kriesi, 171–96. Malden, MA: Blackwell Publishing Ltd.

Murch, Donna Jean. 2010. *Living for the City: Migration, Education, and the Rise of the Black Panther Party in Oakland, California.* Chapel Hill: University of North Carolina Press.

Olson, Mancur. 1963. *The Logic of Collective Action: Public Goods and the Theory of Groups.* Cambridge: Harvard University Press.

Ransby, Barbara. 2005. *Ella Baker and the Black Freedom Movement: A Radical Democratic Vision.* University of North Carolina Press

Parker, Christopher. 2009. *Fighting for Democracy: Black Veterans and the Struggle against White Supremacy in the Postwar South.* Princeton: Princeton University Press.

Payne, Charles. 1995. *I've Got the Light of Freedom: The Organizing Tradition and the Mississippi Freedom Struggle.* Berkeley: University of California Press.

Ralph, J. R. 1993. *Northern Protest: Martin Luther King, Jr., Chicago, and the Civil Rights Movement.* Cambridge: Harvard University Press.

Robnett, Belinda. 1997. *How Long? How Long? African-American Women in the Struggle for Civil Rights.* Oxford: Oxford University Press.

Sugrue, Thomas. 2008. *Sweet Land of Liberty: The Forgotten Struggle for Civil Rights in the North.* New York: Random House.

Theoharis, Jeanne, and Komozi Woodard, eds. 2003. *Freedom North: Black Freedom Struggles Outside the South 1940–1980.* New York: Palgrave Macmillan.

Tilly, Charles. 1978. *From Mobilization to Revolution.* Reading, MA: Addison-Wesley.

Walters, Ronald. 1996. "The Great Plains Sit-In Movement, 1958–60." *Great Plains Quarterly.* Paper 1093: http://digitalcommons.un1.edu/greatplainsquarterly/1093.

3

Reflections

RONALD W. WALTERS

M y most recently completed project was a coedited work, with Dr. Toni-Michelle Travis, on the District of Columbia, *Democratic Destiny and the District of Columbia* (Rowman & Littlefield 2010). This was a unique project that was brought to me by a group of freshly minted African American PhDs who had worked with me on a leadership conference on the black economic condition. Eventually, I agreed to edit the project, if Dr. Travis would join, and it became a very productive enterprise that was focused on politics and public policy. That is, the work interrogated, from the perspective of all of the mayoral administrations except the current one, and five selected public policies, to what extent the constitutionally mandated but strange relationship between the District of Columbia and the Congress has distorted the quality of democracy experienced by the governance of the District and the outcomes for citizens. We conclude that for many reasons, this relationship has been damaging to the just aims of government and must be changed. The initiation of this project was unorthodox inasmuch as authors generally initiate a project, but it was delightful to work with motivated contributors, for whom, except in a couple of cases, this would have been their first publication. In that sense, it was also exceptionally rewarding to me, and I am sure that this project would help to launch the careers of several new professors in the discipline of political science.

For over forty years, my research has sought to address the political condition of African American peoples. I came of age during the civil rights era and, like many of my colleagues, inherited the progressive values of that age with respect to how I would utilize my profession. The pressures were also substantial because it was the dawn of black studies, and the thirst of those who had inherited new political rights in 1964 and 1965 pushed many of us to engage the aspirations of our communities for empowerment tactics and strategies. I remember that a friend of mine and I would talk on the phone and one question we would ask each other at odd intervals was, "What does that have to do with the liberation of black people?" This question has guided my selection of research topics since that time.

My work is and has been interdisciplinary, since as a young scholar attempting to break through the rejection slips of the major journals, I came to understand the standards by which I was being evaluated for publication and decided that many of them, while useful to the discipline, were not useful to the truth I was attempting to discover, consistent with my larger objectives.

So, I came to be somewhat suspicious of the disciplinary narrowness, not only with respect to subject matter but methodologies, and came to believe that what was needed more than anything then was the correct interpretation of the studies that were done on African American political life. The sum total of that concern was that I was not led to produce much original data from self-initiated studies but to test the studies that were being done against what I knew from my deep involvement in community politics to arrive at concepts that were consistent with the black truth as I understood it.

Perhaps I should say that my work has been even more eclectic than usual because my MA and PhD degrees were in International Affairs, but when I began my profession as head of the Department of Afro-American Studies at Brandeis University, the student demand for courses in African American politics led me to specialize in this field. Thus, for most of my career I have carried two specialties— African American politics and comparative politics—which at many times provided enlightening insights in my work, especially on the African diaspora.

The two people who influenced my development most were Professors Marion Irish and Thomas Schelling. Dr. Irish came to American University as I was selecting the topic of my doctoral dissertation on U.S. Foreign Policy toward Africa, and although she was not an internationalist, she became my chair. That was a very special relationship because as a southern political scientist, she knew a great deal about what was happening in civil rights, such as the Emmett Till killing, Dr. King's writings, and other things that were consistent with the movement. So, she guided me on the methods and structure of my dissertation and held seminars with me on southern politics. In my course on theories of international relations, I encountered a book by Thomas Schelling, *The Strategy of Conflict,* and I began to wonder then about the limits of the kind of conflict to which his theory was applicable and came to believe that some of them were useful in the study of social conflict. The strange thing is that he went on to win the Nobel Prize for his theories that were essentially devoted to the study of nuclear warfare, and we ended up on the same faculty at the University of Maryland where, as an economist, he admitted a few years ago that he wanted to work on the problem of the extent to which his ideas had relevance to social conflict theory. In any case, my use of the idea of leverage was taken from his work (although the way in which he elaborates the theory was not useful), and it became a primary theory of my book, *Black Presidential Politics in America.* Beyond that, I have enjoyed collaboration with and learned much from Dr. Robert Smith in the field of African American leadership. While his focus was on empirical studies, mine was concerned with case studies, believing that much of the data that might inform more sophisticated theories of African American leadership was missing. To be sure, political scientists study African American leadership as they evaluate other political leaders, but they rarely apply the work of leadership scholars such as James MacGregor Burns and others.

Otherwise, my work has been characterized by the use of historical and conceptual themes, seeking to discover new subjects for presentation to the public. An example of this is a manuscript I have just finished on slavery in the twentieth century.

The readership that I usually have in mind for my work is students in the field of political science, generally readers who want specialized works in this field. Again, I have had a strong community orientation and find that people want to read works of black political scientists, but most of these works are inaccessible because of the heavy statistical and disciplinary bounding in which they are written. I believe that we could do much better at interpreting our work to such an extent that we are able to engage lay audiences with our ideas and findings. But what I believe has happened is that publication has turned in another direction because of the disciplinary pressures of tenure evaluation and the like.

As indicated, I have not paid much attention to the strictures of the discipline as a guide to the placement of my work or the selection of subject matter. So, if my work falls on the borders of the discipline, as long as it is in the mainstream of the African American community, I have been satisfied because of the many errors in works on racial politics that we take as authoritative. For example, in the late 1980s the work of Carmines and Stimson (*Issue Evolution*) emerged as a definitive work on African American politics. However, reading the work, I ran across the sentence: "We have repeatedly observed that the racial issue evolution proceeded at an impressive pace during periods such as the decade of the 1970s when racial concerns were not central to American party politics" (110). Moreover they assert that racial concerns in party politics were eclipsed by the Vietnam War. These ideas suggest a profound lack of understanding of the dynamics of the African American engagement with the Democratic Party system in the late 1960s and 1970s. The challenge of the civil rights movement placed great pressures on the Democratic Party for racial fairness and accountability. Several commissions were created in 1968 and 1972 to ensure fairness, and in 1974, as an adviser to the Black Democratic Caucus, I saw the commissions demand to be included in the writing of the Democratic Party charter (it had had no such document before that), which evoked considerable chaos in the party leadership. Then, in 1972 as a participant in the Gary Convention, I saw the convention challenge the party for policy accountability, as the National Black Political Agenda was taken to the candidates for their evaluation. Black conventions were held in 1974 and 1976 that were directly concerned with issues that the Democratic Party would take into the presidential campaign. I could go on with such details, but if it does not inform the theory of issue evolution one can have only so much faith in the statistical renderings one finds to support the concept. Moreover, it should be said that after forty years, the discipline of political science is better at the inclusion of African American faculty in its publications, but many white authors still practice what might be called "footnote Apartheid." Works on "race" by non–African Americans routinely do not include, or minimally include, African American scholarly works, reference the aforementioned work, or virtually any other. It is as though the entire subject of African American politics exists at the margins of the discipline; a curious thought, since racial dynamics are central to so much of what America is as expressed in the fabric of its daily concerns.

Part II

4

The Black Science in Political Science

KATHERINE TATE

The study of blacks in American politics was once an invisible field of inquiry. Since the 1980s, the field has since taken off. More scholars produce work in this field. And while publication in the top-tier journals remains rare (e.g., Smith 1981), many more scholars are publishing book-length treatments of African American politics. Members of this field have participated in the movement to create new journals receptive to the studies of minority groups. In 1989, the National Conference of Black Political Scientists (NCOBPS) began publishing the *National Political Science Review*, featuring political science work with a special emphasis on disadvantaged groups. In 2004, the *Du Bois Review* focusing on social science research on race was founded. In 2007, Wilbur Rich published an edited volume entitled *African American Perspectives on Political Science*, which provides an analysis of the discipline from the vantage point of many scholars working in the field of African American politics.

A blistering, important critique of the existing body of work in race and American politics emerged with the 1985 publication of Hanes Walton Jr.'s *Invisible Politics*. While Walton's critique was largely aimed at the new behavioral studies in political science, it applied broadly to studies of American politics. From Walton's work, it was clear that a true understanding of the politics of black Americans could not emerge comparatively, specifically in contrasting black political behavior against white political behavior. The politics of African Americans requires an exclusive focus on black politics, and it should constitute a separate field of study. Black politics scholars have a special mission. On the website of the National Conference of Black Political Scientists, Mack H. Jones, an NCOBPS founding member, is quoted stating that while "American political scientists in general serve to camouflage the illegitimate exercise of power, we as black political scientists bear the responsibility of clearly and brutally unraveling the devious ways in which the American political system serves to exploit the many for the benefit of the few" (http://www.ncobps.org/?page=AboutUs).

And yet, while no longer invisible, studies of black politics remain segregated from mainstream work. New works in black politics are rarely discussed in mainstream political science publications. A report on the treatment of African Americans in introductory textbooks on American government, in fact, finds that most still limit their focus to a single chapter on civil rights and that many also exclude major historical events involving blacks, such as Reconstruction, when twenty blacks served in the U.S. House of Representatives and two in the U.S. Senate (Wallace and Allen 2008). The segregation is so profound that the scholarship produced by those working within the field of African American politics and law can be called the "black science" in political science. It is the "black science" not so much because many scholars of black politics are also of black descent but simply because of its segregation within the discipline.

Labeling the type of scholarship produced within black politics as the "black science" will likely offend those who reject views that the mainstream suffers from a white racial cultural bias. Some may also contend that the preference of those working in the black science tradition is to remain separate and segregated from the discipline. However, black science views need to be represented in the scientific production of knowledge. The segregation of black science work prevents the integration of key research findings from black politics and allows factional views within the discipline to dominate. Thus, the segregation of research findings violates an important tradition of science, namely, that research is verified, reproduced, and extended by others through review, replication, and teaching. The exclusion of black science work in the classroom also means that the normative biases that exist in political science work are never challenged.

Obviously in attaching a racial label to a subfield of work, I reject assumptions that the politics and personal attributes of researchers are irrelevant to the science they produce. Postmodernists also reject broad claims of neutrality in science. Scientists produce work profoundly influenced by cultural biases. The enterprise of science is shaped as well by institutional and personal incentive systems, social networks, and the exclusion of marginalized groups. Others have claimed that bias is one-sided, found only among minority scholars who have an "ax to grind" and who are not as "objective" as white scholars (see a clear statement of this "black bias" in sociology by Fontaine in 1944; see also the brief rejoinder by Reuter who writes [rather weakly] that Fontaine's claim is not well supported and that white scholars, too, can be biased). Calling this work "black science" is not implying that it alone is free from racial bias. On the contrary, black science work is often more sharply critical of American politics, American political institutions, and American society than mainstream work. As a type of subfield, it competes with values rooted in white nationalism that generally dominates mainstream work. Thus, labeling seminal work produced in black politics as "the black science," I hope to call attention to both problems of bias in the discipline and its marginalization through intentional segregation.

Black Science Political Science Frameworks

The "black science" in political science refers to the new knowledge advanced by black politics scholars who expose and explain the inherent inequality in the political status of African Americans but who also work in the tradition of advocating group empowerment. I intend to discuss the work of three black science scholars, Ronald W. Walters, Linda F. Williams, and Derrick Bell.

All three scholars passed away recently. Williams died unexpectedly in 2006 at the age of fifty-seven, Walters and Bell, after serious illnesses, in 2010 and 2011. Walters' work moved the field past a debate between those critical of American institutions and society and those who embraced a pluralist perspective. The early work on blacks following Gunnar Myrdal's *An American Dilemma* (1944) focused on conditions leading to the integration of blacks into politics. *An American Dilemma* was hopelessly flawed. Even as it focused on the political exclusion of southern blacks, it still posited that black political rights would be restored through a liberalization of white social attitudes. It failed to predict the fifteen-year-long, bloody black struggle for civil rights that emerged in the late 1950s. Later, James Q. Wilson published a book in 1960 called *Negro Politics*. Wilson's book like the others affirmed a pluralist perspective insofar as blacks were equal participants in American political life in areas where they had access to the ballot, and the failure of blacks to realize political benefits from their inclusion was attributed to poor black leadership. Pluralism did not expose or explain the racism in both government and in society that rendered black votes ineffectual in winning equal treatment. Dianne Pinderhughes' (1985) work on Chicago politics provides an important critique of pluralism, explaining why although blacks were participants in the Daley political machine they were not rewarded with much because of institutional racism.

Ronald W. Walters' work went beyond the pluralist and pluralist critique debate. First, those works critical of pluralist frameworks recognize white racism in varying degrees, where Walters characterizes it as an unevolving feature of American society. This is most clearly stated in *White Nationalism, Black Interests* (2003). White nationalism, he writes, is a sociopolitical phenomenon used to protect and advance the racial interests of whites. It precedes the formation of the state. In pluralist critiques, however, the Constitution is accepted as egalitarian, which blacks aggressively and courageously have defended through nonelectoral as well as basic ballot-box forms of political protest. The pluralist critiques provide more of a "happy ending" perspective on American politics. For Walters, however, there is no implied "happy ending" under the current system. Walters' brilliant contribution to black politics is his unyielding lack of optimism about the willingness of Americans to back the necessary reforms to ensure the rights and freedoms of black citizens. Instead, African Americans must exploit opportunities whenever possible.

Here, Walters' scholarship gets interesting because it is often subversive. While black power analysts, including Ture and Hamilton (1992), advocate reform, they are often not specific about which reforms are necessary to secure the political rights and freedoms of black Americans. Moreover, whereas pluralist critique analysts can more astutely point out the very flaws in the American political system that are worthy of political reform, Walters moves ahead to outline political strategies for black Americans to secure a fair share of American political goods, in spite of American racism and the country's racially biased political institutions that were constructed and that are unlikely to be reformed. Walters recognizes the false assertion that a black can become president of the United States running on the issues blacks care most about, but he argues that blacks should use the electoral process regardless to put black issues onto the national agenda. In *Black Presidential Politics in America* (1988), he outlines how blacks can aggregate their votes and wrest more political goods from the system when they back a black presidential contender rather than waiting on the sidelines for postracialism.

Furthermore, Walters' black science work is often prescriptive. In *The Price of Racial Reconciliation* (2008), Walters argues that blacks must continue to push for reparations for black slavery. Reparations, he contends, are more than just a payment for past injury. They settle a debate over history. Reparations to the descendants of black slaves would redefine America. It would tell southern states celebrating the old Confederacy that history validates the black side of the American Civil War.

There have been reparations. American Indians have been compensated for the destruction of their land. The Jewish Holocaust victims have been compensated; while the amounts were very small, they still were meaningful. Payments from the Japanese were made to Chinese comfort women. The Japanese Americans interned during WWII were compensated—again, by small amounts. Why the descendants of black slaves are denied reparations, he argues, is simply based on racial hostility to blacks. Black American victims are invisible. He points at the fact that none of the speakers at South Africa's Truth and Reconciliation Commission were African Americans, although speakers discussed the Jewish genocide under the Nazi regime. The United States, he writes, is widely conceived as a land of opportunity and has little in common with El Salvador, Argentina, Chile, or Bosnia where the state participated in the murder and torture of civilians.

Blacks will need to make the case for themselves. Hannah Arendt in the 1950s said she supported the civil rights movement but then criticized it for prioritizing social concerns such as integration over basic human rights, such as overturning antimiscegenation laws. Ralph Ellison said that she wrote from an "Olympian position." When victims make the case, Walters writes, they ask for basic equality goods—not symbols of equality. Moreover, blacks and whites often offer different explanations for racial inequality, but blacks are the weaker voices. Alienated whites demand a sanitized version of history rather than what really occurred. They do not want to be labeled oppressors. Thus, African Americans must come forward to initiate something that will be painful for white Americans to accept.

Walters claims that the pain of white people would be enormous if this country focused on the crimes of whites against blacks, and thus, they remain covered up. Blacks are spiritually damaged, he writes, by the withholding of a truthful account about American race relations. The pain of slavery to blacks must be acknowledged. Furthermore, lynchings of blacks were social events, and this phenomenon continued from the 1890s through the 1950s. Chicago resident Emmett Till was murdered at the age of fourteen in Mississippi in 1955 after he supposedly whistled after a white woman. The murderers were acquitted by an all-white jury; they later confessed to the crime. In Till's murder, some blacks were involved. These blacks thought whites were only going to "pistol whip" Till. The tragic life of many blacks in race relations history is hidden. But jealousy, envy, drug and alcohol abuse, macho acts, and other extreme psychological traits are associated with having experienced abuse. Furthermore, Walters writes there is post-traumatic slavery disorder among blacks, causing anger, distrust, low or nonexistent self-esteem, and chronic flashbacks of "petty" incidences of racism. The stress and perceptions of racism lead to racial disparities in health. Blacks will never truly heal until the pain of American race relations is exposed and acknowledged.

While conservatives argue that reparations will reinforce black dependency on government, Walters states that reparations as a demand for justice would yield a number of important objectives. Reparations represent a human rights demand that recognizes blacks as equal Americans. Reparations restore dignity, which should be given to everyone. They restore lost resources. Finally, reparations for the descendants of black slaves would renegotiate the contract between blacks and America and establish a new official historical record on race relations. However, whites benefit psychologically and socially from being white, and most do not want to see these benefits end.

Like Walters, Derrick Bell incorporates a black power perspective in much of his work. Derrick Bell (2004), for example, asks us to think now if *Brown* had been decided differently, perhaps blacks would be better off; blacks, he contends, certainly cannot be any worse off with public education remaining so savagely, racially unequal. Bell considers the legal system permanently stacked in favor of white interests. American law operates in a racist world and is influenced by racist ideals. The *Brown* ruling therefore "dismisses *Plessy* without dismantling it." Had the High Court sustained *Plessy* but forced schools in the South to equalize their spending, that ruling would probably have led more forcefully to the end of dual systems than overturning *Plessy*.

Thus, while *Brown* was considered radical, it was not. Radical rulings, in fact, failed to win acceptance from the population and remain contested, while *Brown* became a celebrated ruling. *Brown* ushered in the view that *de jure* segregation is wrong, while *de facto* segregation remains tolerated. Additionally, radical rulings do not protect property against the recognized wrongdoers. In other words, while busing was deemed constitutional in 1973 by the Supreme Court, it was not widely practiced. Thus, while recognizing injustice, *Brown* did not disrupt the reasonable expectations of those not directly responsible for wrongs. No one had to pay for the history of racism practiced by states in the provision of public education.

The ruling, therefore, served as a "silent covenant," one that would not radically transform society and society's expectations about the future. It served to legitimate existing race relations. *Brown II* issued in 1955, which is famous for its "all deliberate speed" passage, was tantamount to issuing a decree that integration in public schools was never coming. The phrase was symbolic. The Court needed to issue a consent decree where the parties would have clear orders and a timetable. Some states in black-dominated rural areas simply closed the white schools and diverted public money to private all-white academies that sprang up. There was massive, national resistance to integrated public education. In the 1955 *Brown II* decision, the Supreme Court ruled that the lower courts should work out the details, but this ruling delayed the enforcement of black civil rights in education. White flight emerged as blacks continued to go to court. Later, public schools were heavily checker-boarded racially, meaning nearly all black/Latino and nearly all white. In 1974, in the 5 to 4 *Milliken v. Bradley*, the Supreme Court ruled that to achieve racial integration, school districts could not transfer students across districts, that is, from suburban school districts to urban ones like Detroit and vice versa. Popular opinion favored *Brown*, but in reality, few whites did. Had the courts forced state officials to immediately desegregate then whites would have massively rioted just as they did over court-ordered busing in Boston in 1974. The rioting by whites would have ruined the "silent covenant" over *Brown*.

Furthermore, in *Silent Covenants* (2004), Bell writes about his experiences as an NAACP attorney traveling to Mississippi to force the courts to require communities to desegregate their public schools. The accommodations in rural Mississippi segregation laws did not permit him to use hotels, and so he slept on the sofa of one family's house with a man stationed by the door holding a shotgun every night. Parents participating in the lawsuit against a noncompliant school district were fired from their jobs. *Brown* makes the problem of standing up for racial equality more difficult. When Bell asked a black civil rights veteran how she can muster the courage to continue to challenge white authority in the face of such violence, she gave a confusing response, which he professed admiration for: "I love to just harass White folks!" Taken literally, the elderly black woman's fight for integration appears unjustified and even unfair to whites since the laws had changed. Continued civil rights activism from blacks like Bell and the old woman transformed them overnight into "radicals" and even "reverse racists." Traditional declarations of freedom and justice in American laws and court rulings continue to hide patterns of deep inequality across the races (Smith 1995).

Bell argues blacks win politically only when black interests converge with white interests in policymaking positions. Their rights are recognized formally as equal to whites even as equality is denied. Litigation frankly often puts blacks as third parties in a lawsuit. As third parties, blacks are "fortuitous beneficiaries"—they cannot sue effectively if they fail to benefit from the new racial policy. They are the third party in the contract between a husband and a florist—the wife who no longer receives the flowers as contracted by the husband. To win justice, the wife must still wait for her husband to sue.

The problem with Bell's perspective is that he ignores some major gains that blacks have achieved because of *Brown*. Blacks were poorly educated in the Jim Crow South. Understanding that the United States still spends less on average to educate a black student as opposed to a white student, the end of dual educational systems

Table 4.1. Percent of U.S. Population with a High School Diploma for Blacks and Whites, 1940–2000

	1940	1950	1960	1970	1980	1990	2000
White	26.1	36.4	43.2	54.5	68.8	77.9	83.6
Black	7.7	13.7	21.7	31.4	51.2	63.1	72.3
Gap	18.4	22.2	21.5	23.1	17.6	14.8	11.3

Source: U.S. Census website, http://www.census.gov/hhes/socdemo/education/ data/census/half-century/tables.html.

improved graduation rates for blacks. The trend is one where the racial gap in diplomas has diminished over the decades. Data in table 4.1 show that in 1940 only 7.7 percent of blacks had a high school diploma compared to 26.1 percent of whites. Even in 1970, only one-third of blacks had a high school diploma compared to 54.5 percent of whites. But by 1980 a majority of blacks had a high school diploma, and the education gap between whites and blacks, while over 20 percent until 1980, dropped to 11.3 by 2000.

The 1940 U.S. Census reports that 45.9 percent of black males had less than five years of education compared to 8.5 percent of white males. In 1960, the educational gap between blacks and whites had narrowed. Whites between twenty-five and twenty-nine years of age had an average of 12.4 years of education, while nonwhites in that age category had an average of 10.5. The end of dual systems improved access to public education for blacks. America would not build enough schools for blacks to attend under Jim Crow. Yet studies continue to show that a segregated education still has a negative impact on the education of blacks and Latinos. While Bell believes racism continues to exert a powerful force in American education in light of recent studies showing that black school children are significantly more likely to be expelled than student groups of other races, the legacy of a dual educational system on American racism would have likely been worse.

Furthermore, *Brown* undeniably served as a catalyst for the civil rights movement. The movement could not be sustained for many reasons apart from the achievement of important civil rights victories. Symbols are not the direct causes diminishing black political efforts, but rather, blacks' gains are cut when whites collectively revolt. Black civil rights activists attempted to steer the movement toward economic empowerment, but a white backlash led to Republican ascendancy in Washington. Blacks then later put their efforts into winning descriptive representation in government (Tate 1994). In many respects, Bell's critique of *Brown* resembles the new critiques of black elected officials—that through winning political office, blacks are losing important political ground. These critiques ignore the benefits of black descriptive representation and ignore critical political developments—notably the rise of white conservative leadership in Washington.

Furthermore, while Bell points to white racism as underestimated in the politics shaping the lives of African Americans, he fails to document the ebb and flow of white racism. At the end of Reconstruction, southern Democrats instituted changes in the House empowering the committee system that obstructed the ability of liberals and blacks to win passage of civil rights protection laws. One committee issued a report demanding that Congress erase all Reconstruction measures from its "books" (King and Smith 2011, 59). White vigilante violence against blacks emerged under the newly formed Ku Klux Klan. The backlash against the empowerment of blacks after the war was, in fact, enormous. Blacks won with *Brown*, and as losers, resentful whites sought ways to maintain white privilege in the restructuring of government policies and laws.

Thus, as Walters (2003) argues, the post–civil rights era represents an important era of white anger and resentment. We need more scholars to investigate and document how white resentment against blacks is manifested in public policies and institutional reform. Michelle Alexander's *The New Jim Crow* (2010) reflects the intellectual agenda of Walters (2003), who similarly argued that the war on drugs represented a war on blacks. Furthermore, white animus against blacks is reflected in the major contestation over new photo identification voter laws; new social policies, such as health care reform; as well as new social rights demands that include blacks, such as amnesty for undocumented citizens and equal social rights for gays and lesbians.

Clearly, white racism remains a virulent force in American politics. Still, is it hegemonic? Like Walters and Bell, Linda F. Williams' *The Constraint of Race* importantly points to the political power of white Americans in creating a government that catered to their group's interest in remaining at the top of a racial hierarchy. Like Walters, she argues that opposition to a black civil rights and policy agenda intensified in the aftermath of the civil rights movement. She writes, "there was real retrenchment with substantial negative impacts on the poor and people of color in the years from Nixon through Bush. The inevitable counterrevolution King prophesied had begun" (2003, 217). Even while increasing numbers of scholars contend that blacks should broaden their social policy agendas to include "universal" policies, she warns as long as white skin privilege in the long run is favored, whites will reject social policies that benefit blacks. Thus, even though a universal health care policy in theory benefits middle-class and low-income whites objectively, subjectively they will reject it, seeing its benefits going to minorities. There are also cultural and moral dimensions of white skin privilege that extend the politics of white racial conservatives and means declining racism will not reduce white opposition to black political interests. Following the work of Antonio Gramsci, Williams claims that white racism is not hegemonic insofar as hegemony is absolute. Economic and political crises can create conditions that challenge hegemonic beliefs.

In the end, Williams argues that white skin privilege must be publicly confronted. "In short," she writes, "there must be an open, frontal exposure of right-wing politicians who interpret civil rights, equal opportunity, and affirmative action as distinct and unfair to the interests of poor whites" (2003, 398). Desmond S. King and Rogers M. Smith (2011) argue that racial politics is best conceptualized as having competing camps. They reject a static view of American racial power. Models of black politics should consider periods where white racism is less and periods when it is strongly on display in the many layers of American government. As important as the black science framework is in understanding American politics, white racism should not be portrayed as static.

Furthermore, historical periods should not be confused with one another. Aggressive racial conservatism continues to dominate the campaigns of Republican candidates, but these candidates, increasingly, are less effective. When Richard Nixon condemned busing as "evil" and sought to delay as long as possible civil rights enforcement during his presidency, he was a dominant political actor. Changes favoring the proportional allocation of delegates in the Republican

Party's presidential nomination system as well as the practice of rewarding solidly Republican states (those in the South) with additional delegates serve to empower racial conservatives. And thus movement away from race-card cultural politics toward policy debate that does not stigmatize groups is delayed by these electoral changes. In the future, the Republican Party will likely have to recruit minority candidates and avoid race-card politics as a strategic response to the changing racial and ethnic demographics of this nation.

Still, America is not postracial, and the Obama presidency may have intensified feelings of racial resentment among whites. Tesler and Sears find that attitudes about health care became "considerably more racialized after Obama became the loudest spokesperson for health care reform" (2010, 156). Furthermore, through accusations asserting that Obama is a Muslim or that he was born outside of the country, Obama's political opponents have continuously tried to establish his "otherness." This, scholars have argued, has driven up fears and anxiety among white Americans who worry that their position in society may be vulnerable. Barreto et al. (2011) contend that the election of the first black president, "and the change it symbolizes, represents a clear threat to the economic, political and social hegemony to which supporters of the Tea Party had become accustomed" (9).

In these black science frameworks, the degree of white racism is a constant and black political unity is presumed. The unchanging nature of black unity is problematic. Yet a black power framework presumes the emergence of an organically grown set of unified black interests whose cohesion is based on blacks' historical experiences and existence in a racist society. As white racism is ever-present, black interests are knit into a cohesive whole. Walters argues that the universality of white European racism, in fact, extends to the formation of black diasporic interests. In his book on Pan Africanism and the African diaspora (1993), Walters argues, convincingly, that people of African descent share a common set of experiences in a racist world, and from that develop a common set of political interests and political strategies. In his 2003 book on white nationalism, Walters surgically removes the ideologies of black conservatives from the black body politic claiming that they are flatly unrepresentative of black interests.

Black conservatives, however, represent an important group in black politics, defying broad claims of black unity. Other scholars have characterized the political ideologies of blacks as diverse and have portrayed black conservatism as, in fact, organic (Dawson 2001). Walters (2003) defines black conservatism as having features of accommodationism, support for national norms and white power, and hostility to America's enemies. There is also support for racial symbiosis or faith in racial integration, a deprecation of black culture, black political leadership, and black political goals. Black conservatives are, in short, antiblack. Byron D'Andra Orey (2004) examines this contention that black conservatives are antiblack rather than simply self-help proponents. He, too, believes that they promote views that are aligned with white conservative views about race, specifically that blacks are lazy and responsible for their lower socioeconomic status in the United States.

There has been important drift away from strong liberalism by black Americans as measured by opinion polls (Tate 2010). Scholars need to investigate not only the decline in black political liberalism but potentially a rise in black conservatism in the form of racial resentment against blacks. Cathy J. Cohen's (2010) study contends that young blacks seek advancement in society but lack agency to change conditions that deny them equal opportunities to advance. Yet they remained condemned not only by those in a white-dominated society but by elements in the black community as well. Lester Spence (2011) provides a view of black culture pointing to rap music as a source for neoliberalism, or the belief in the failure of American social policy and American institutions. Melissa Harris-Lacewell (2004) finds conservatism is produced in black-dominated venues, although her portrayal of black church leadership finds it is more liberal than conservative.

The failure of a black power framework to advance the interests of truly marginalized groups in society is something Walters' scholarship does not really consider. A small but growing number of black political theorists are documenting what represents a serious analytic flaw in black power frameworks, namely, the presumption that the cohesive set of black interests that springs forth from the oppression of blacks is, in fact, egalitarian and progressive. Cathy Cohen's (1999) and Hawley Fogg-Davis' (2006) scholarship recognizes the oppression of black gays and lesbians in the black community. Other critics of black politics, notably Adolph Reed (1999), point to the failure of black politics to treat black policy interests as differentiated by income and social class. Black politics is skewed toward the interests of the black middle class. That black collective interests support intolerance toward marginalized groups needs to be addressed in a black science framework.

There is a sociopolitical and institutional basis to black political conservatism. Walters (2003) argues that black conservatives are beneficiaries of the post–civil rights expansion of white nationalism. Others contend that black elected officials are changing, becoming more diverse as well (Gillespie 2010; Canon 1999). In my study of the Congressional Black Caucus (Tate 2013), I argue black candidates tailor their policy agendas and rhetoric toward a new electorate that includes moderate white voters. In my analysis of members of the Congressional Black Caucus, black House Democrats who later ran for statewide offices were significantly less liberal than less ambitious black House members. An age difference in the ideological scores of black Democratic lawmakers also emerges in this study. Younger black lawmakers are less liberal than older blacks in the U.S. House. I theorize that this age difference among black lawmakers is not organically rooted in a generation gap in the black community (as there is no strong evidence of this generation gap yet in public opinion polls) but rather reflects the different perceptions of the electoral universe they operate in. Older blacks are less poised to tailor their policy rhetoric to court white votes, having been raised in a Jim Crow, racist America. Young black politicians experienced improved race relations and see the universe of voters as less racially segmented than older blacks.

All in all, while black Democratic lawmakers remain significantly more supportive of black interests than white Democratic lawmakers, they are less liberal than those serving in the House during the 1970s and 1980s. In terms of ideological scores, the Progressive Caucus is more liberal than black Democrats in the House on average (Tate 2013). Linda F. Williams contends that the CBC could not impose discipline on its members during the debate over Clinton's welfare reform initiative (2003, 260), writing, "In the vacuum created by the lack of leadership in the CBC, it fell to the Progressive Caucus to organize an opposition in Congress" (2003, 262). The welfare reform bill was conservative, not only limiting welfare benefits to five years and thus ending the federal mandate for states to provide financial support to families below the poverty line, it also included mandatory drug-testing of all recipients, denial of aid to those convicted of drug felonies, and additional financial support for children born while the mother is on welfare assistance (Williams 2003, 259). This reform cutting off lifetime entitlement to welfare had majority support in the black community (Tate 2010). Thus, the black community is more diverse and more conservative than Walters and other scholars working in a black power tradition have yet to fundamentally acknowledge.

The Costs of Engaging in Black Science Research

There are some final comments to make about the study of black politics in this review of work by Walters, Bell, and Williams. Publications of black science work can cause alienation and cost some scholars important career opportunities. However, the costs borne by scholars whose research is not embraced by the mainstream are not easily documented. Walters and Williams both ended their careers at a public university—the University of Maryland, College Park. Derrick Bell states on his website (http://professorderrickbell. com/) that when he applied to teach at law schools in the mid-1960s, he was rejected before being hired by the University of Southern California. Harvard then hired him in 1969, and Bell became the law school's first tenured black professor in 1971. A black science framework is generally opposed in the academy precisely because it calls attention to white racism *and* the liberation of black people. Scholars adopting a black science framework in political science may be shunned.

An open display of the professional costs to scholars employing a black science framework occurred in 1993 when President Clinton withdrew the nomination of law professor Lani Guinier to head the Civil Rights Division of the U.S. Justice Department. Critics of Guinier in Washington claimed that her publications, which advocated reform of the American electoral system to benefit minority groups, made her too radical for such an appointment. Guinier, later, was hired by Harvard Law School, becoming the first tenured black female law professor there. However, Derrick Bell had engaged in a personal campaign to make Guinier's appointment possible. In fact, Bell withdrew from Harvard to remain at New York University to illustrate his commitment to opening the door to senior minority female professors. Bell understood what still many miss: that the promotional system in the academy remains hostile to females and especially minority females, that the white power structure has a strong male bias to it. One 1992 study of minority female law professors found that they were more likely than minority men to be at less prestigious law schools and have lower academic ranks (*The Chronicle of Higher Education* 5/6/92). Bell's campaign illustrates that such barriers, as a function of time, do not usually erode. The door opened to black professors under a changing sociopolitical and institutional context (Winston 1971). Further change is still needed to equalize professional opportunities for minority scholars and especially those working in marginalized fields.

A new campaign against radical black scholars recently surfaced. A conservative website in March 2012 released a video of President Obama at Harvard Law School hugging Derrick Bell in 1991. The conservative complaint is that Bell held views about American race relations much like Obama's former black pastor, Jeremiah Wright. Thus, the president should distance himself. These attacks may also have a chilling effect on black political scholarship. There is also generational change occurring in the academy. Because of their experiences in the civil rights/black power movement, Walters, Bell, and Williams had a revolutionary lens to their work. Thus, there are pressures against this tradition of research even as scholars once tenured remain among the most independent. If black politics scholars expect to impact the field of American politics in a serious way, the frameworks established by Walters, Bell, and Williams must be retained and extended. To this list of black science scholars, one can also include Manning Marable, who passed away in 2011. Marable kept scholarship focused on the black community and made it appealing. The *New York Times* named Marable's *Malcolm X: A Life of Reinvention* one of the ten best books of 2011, and it was awarded the Pulitzer Prize.

In the end, black politics scholars and the field of political science are harmed by intellectual segregation. Black politics scholars need to fight their segregation in the academy. They must also move into areas of exclusion, including adjacent fields of study, such as Latino politics. Black politics scholars engage in comparative studies (e.g., Jennings 1994; McClain 2006) and yet more need to respond in black politics to the racial diversification of America. Black politics scholarship should address concerns that some have who feared that a multiracial approach might limit attention to black economic and social problems. Others point out that blacks no longer represent the largest minority group in the United States and must be more attentive to the politics of Latinos, who have a long history of discrimination as well. In addition, black politics researchers need to pay greater attention to the class divide and government policies that deepen economic inequality. While the Occupy Wall Street movement did not engage many blacks, nor did it fundamentally call attention to black and Latino economic problems, the widening class divide has serious ramifications for black Americans. Analysts working in Latino politics are addressing the problems of economic stratification as political scientists may not necessarily consider how blacks are implicated in these movements and trends. Black politics analysts will have to enter into new fields to help direct research in political science toward the issues that significantly affect black Americans without abandoning their special mission, which, as Mack H. Jones asserts, is to explain the true nature of the American political system.

References

Alexander, Michelle. 2010. *The New Jim Crow: Mass Incarceration in the Age of Colorblindness.* New York: New Press.

Barreto, Matt A., Betsy L. Cooper, Benjamin Gonzalez, Christopher S. Parker, Christopher Towler. 2011. "The Tea Party in the Age of Obama: Mainstream Conservatism or Out-Group Anxiety?" *Political Power and Social Theory* 22: 3–22.

Bell, Derrick. 2004. *Silent Covenants: Brown v. Board of Education and the Unfulfilled Hopes for Racial Reform.* New York: Oxford University Press.

Canon, David T. 1999. *Race, Redistricting, and Representation: The Unintended Consequences of Black Majority Districts.* Chicago: University of Chicago Press.

Cohen, Cathy J. 1999. *The Boundaries of Blackness: AIDS and the Breakdown of Black Politics.* Chicago: University of Chicago Press.

———. 2010. *Democracy Remixed.* New York: Oxford University Press.

Dawson, Michel C. 2001. *Black Visions: The Roots of Contemporary African-American Political Ideologies.* Chicago: University of Chicago Press.

Chronicle of Higher Education, "Task of Hiring 'Woman of Color' at Law Schools Examined," May 6, 1992. http://chronicle.com/article/Task-of-Hiring-Woman-of/80759/.

Fogg-Davis, Hawley G. 2006. "Theorizing Black Lesbians within Black Feminism: A Critique of Same-Race Street Harassment." *Politics & Gender* 2, 1: 57–76.

Fontaine, William T. 1944. "Social Determination in the Writings of Negro Scholars." *American Journal of Sociology* 49, 4 (January): 302–15.

Gillespie, Andra, ed. 2010. *Whose Black Politics? Cases in Postracial Black Leadership.* New York: Routledge.

Harris-Lacewell, Melissa. 2004. *Barbershops, Bibles, and BET: Everyday Talk and Black Political Thought.* Princeton, NJ: Princeton University Press.

Jennings, James. 1994. *Blacks, Latinos, and Asians in Urban America: Status and Prospects for Politics and Activism.* Westport, CT: Praeger.

King, Desmond S., and Rogers M. Smith. 2011. *Still a House Divided: Race and Politics in Obama's America.* Princeton, NJ: Princeton University Press.

Marable, Manning. 2011. *Malcolm X: A Life of Reinvention.* New York: Viking.

McClain, Paula D. 2006. "Presidential Address: Racial Intergroup Relations in a Set of Cities: A Twenty-Year Perspective." *Journal of Politics* 68, 4: 757–70.

Myrdal, Gunnar. 1944. *An American Dilemma: The Negro Problem and Modern Democracy.* New York: Harper & Brothers Publishers.

Orey, Byron D'Andra. 2004. "Explaining Black Conservatives: Racial Uplift or Racial Resentment?" *The Black Scholar* 34, 1 (Spring): 18–24.

Pinderhughes, Dianne M. 1987. *Race and Ethnicity in Chicago Politics: A Reexamination of Pluralist Theory.* Urbana: University of Illinois Press.

Reuter, E. B. 1944. "'Social Determination': Rejoinder." *American Journal of Sociology* 49, 4 (January): 315.

Reed, Adolph, Jr. 1999. *Stirrings in the Jug: Black Politics in the Post-Segregationist Era.* Minneapolis: University of Minnesota Press.

Smith, Robert C. 1981. "Black Power and the Transformation from Protest to Politics." *Political Science Quarterly* 96, 3: 431–43.

———. 1995. *Racism in the Post-Civil Rights Era: Now You See It, Now You Don't.* Albany: State University of New York Press.

Spence, Lester K. 2011. *Stare in the Darkness: The Limits of Hip-Hop and Black Politics.* Minneapolis: University of Minnesota Press.

Tesler, Michael, and David O. Sears. 2010. *Obama's Race: The 2008 Election and the Dream of a Post-Racial America.* Chicago: University of Chicago Press.

Tate, Katherine. 1994. *From Protest to Politics: The New Black Voters in American Elections.* Cambridge, MA: Harvard University Press and the Russell Sage Foundation.

———. 2010. *What's Going On? Political Incorporation and the Transformation of Black Public Opinion.* Washington, DC: Georgetown University Press.

———. 2013. *Concordance: Black Lawmaking in the U.S. Congress from Carter to Obama.* Ann Arbor, MI: University of Michigan Press.

Ture, Kwame [Stokely Carmichael], and Charles V. Hamilton. 1992 [1967]. *Black Power: The Politics of Liberation in America.* New York: Vintage Books.

Walters, Ronald W. 1988. *Black Presidential Politics in America: A Strategic Approach.* Albany: State University of New York Press.

———. 1993. *Pan Africanism in the African Diaspora: An Analysis of Modern Afrocentric Political Movements.* Detroit: Wayne State University Press.

———. 2003. *White Nationalism, Black Interests: Conservative Public Policy and the Black Community.* Detroit: Wayne State University Press.

———. 2008. *The Price of Racial Reconciliation.* Ann Arbor: University of Michigan Press.

Wallace, Sherri L., and Marcus D. Allen. 2008. "Survey of African American Portrayal in Introductory Textbooks in American Government/Politics: A Report of the APSA Standing Committee on the Status of Blacks in the Profession." *PS: Political Science & Politics* 48: 153–60.

Walton, Hanes, Jr. 1985. *Invisible Politics: Black Political Behavior.* Albany: State University of New York Press.

Williams, Linda F. 2003. *The Constraint of Race: Legacies of White Skin Privilege in America.* University Park: Pennsylvania State University Press.

Winston, Michael R. 1971. "Through the Back Door: Academic Racism and the Negro Scholar in Historical Perspective." *Daedalus* 100, 3, The Future of the Black Colleges (Summer): 678–719.

Wilson, James Q. 1960. *Negro Politics: The Search for Leadership.* Glencoe, IL: Free Press.

5

Black Intellectuals in the Age of New Democratic Politics

Reflections on Ronald Walters, the Maryland Years

CEDRIC JOHNSON

In the fall of 2011, I was called upon to offer some words of reflection on the life and work of Ronald W. Walters as he was posthumously awarded the Frederick Douglass Award by the University of Maryland at College Park. Walters was my dissertation advisor, my boss at the African American Leadership Institute, my fraternity brother, my coauthor and my friend. As I prepared my remarks, I recalled how fortunate I was to work with Walters when I did, savoring how special the University of Maryland was during the 1990s as a place to study African American politics. When Walters succumbed after a lengthy battle with cancer, I felt as if lightning had struck the same place twice. In the same decade, we bid farewell to Linda Faye Williams. For members of my graduate studies cohort at the University of Maryland she was a guiding light, a tough-as-nails critic and cherished mentor. When I left College Park in 2001, I never would have imagined that I would lose both of my graduate school mentors so close together and so soon. As I paced the halls of the newly opened Samuel Riggs Alumni Center in anticipation of the Douglass awards ceremony, my mind drifted back to those years with a mix of nostalgia, sadness, and gratitude. So much of the personal and institutional substance that made our experiences so rewarding and intellectually rich had disappeared, leaving only traces. The physical

landscape of the campus was still familiar, but the energy and con-
junctural elements that made College Park such a fascinating and
stimulating place to study African American politics have moved on,
vanished in the crisp, Chesapeake air. Even the weathered inner-
ring suburbs of Prince Georges County with their ubiquitous strip
malls and thousands of red-brick postwar ranch homes, the places
where we worked and played, were at various turns unrecognizable.
The wheels of progress had continued to turn as new construction
replaced our old haunts and personal landmarks. The spirit was
gone, but the memories lingered.

In this essay, I want to situate Ronald Walters' work during the
late 1990s within the wider New Democratic political milieu and con-
vey the personal and institutional impact he had on those of us who
were studying African American politics at College Park before moving on to what I see as one of his signal political contributions during that period, namely, his public opposition to the African Growth
and Opportunity Act. I see these personal, institutional, and political developments as closely interrelated. Walters brought to College
Park a commitment to engaged-scholarship and actively mentored a
generation of black and left-progressive graduate and undergraduate students, encouraging us to make our intellectual work relevant
and useful to ongoing struggles. In turn, his own opposition to one
manifestation of neoliberal globalism took shape within the context
of the vibrant intellectual climate he helped to cultivate at Maryland,
and his courageous public stand served as an inspiration to many of
us as students who were already engaged in protests against corporate globalization following the 1994 North American Free Trade
Agreement (NAFTA) and thinking through the broader political
dynamics and implications of privatization that was taking shape all
around us.

On the University of Maryland's College Park campus, Walters, in a few short years, created an institutional space and secured
resources that enabled students to develop and flourish academi-
cally and politically. In his public life, he modeled a style of engagement that sought to defend earlier gains of sixties social struggles
and develop tactical and policy responses to the shifting contexts
of workfare and corporate globalization. In an effort to capture the
different facets of his intellectual work during the period, this essay
combines two different modes of writing—shared autobiography

and historical interpretation. The first part of this essay explores the context of Clinton's New Democratic reforms, provides some background on Walters' arrival at the University of Maryland in 1996, and reflects on what Walters' tenure meant for students with social justice commitments, particularly black doctoral students in government and politics. A central part of Walters' work during that time was his creation of the African American Leadership Institute, so in the second section of this essay, I describe some of the institute's activities and discuss their significance. I conclude this essay, by examining the reasons for his opposition to the African Growth and Opportunity Act, or "NAFTA for Africa," and the troubling new political alignments that made its passage possible.

Howard University at College Park

The wider social and political context of the Clinton years is pivotal for understanding the kinds of work that Walters produced and encouraged at Maryland and his impact on students there. Between the formation of the Democratic Leadership Council in 1985 to the election of Bill Clinton in 1992, the party leadership retooled its image and approach to governing by abandoning the left interventionism of the New Deal and Great Society periods in favor of its own brand of neoliberalism, which combined a socially liberal public relations style with forms of statist intervention and regulation that enhanced the movement and profitability of capital.[1] Clinton's affable character and political savvy helped to obscure the extent to which the "Third Way" centrism of his administration was, in effect, the more successful path of delivering pro-market reforms and served to deflect criticisms from those core, traditional constituencies of the New Deal coalition, organized labor, urbanists, African Americans, and social progressives who opposed the destruction of the social safety net and rollback of civil rights, labor, and environmental regulation. The African Growth and Opportunity Act was a neglected bookend to the Clinton administration's project of fiscal austerity and privatization at home and abroad.

Although the final years of his administration would be mired in the Monica Lewinsky sex scandal and congressional impeachment, the Clinton administration succeeded in transforming the Democrat

Party's mid-twentieth-century approach to state-market relations. On the domestic front, the administration fueled the prison buildup and hyper-incarceration of the urban poor with the passage of a draconian Omnibus Crime Bill in 1994, which expanded the types of crimes punishable by the death penalty and enforced the sentencing disparity between crack and powder cocaine. The Clinton Democrats claimed credit for welfare reform with the passage of the 1996 Personal Responsibility and Work Opportunity Act, which established time limits and work requirements for aid recipients, and the 1998 HOPE VI legislation, which federally funded the revanchist process of razing public housing complexes across the nation in favor of mixed-income developments (subsidized and market-rate housing units) under the pretext of deconcentrating zones of poverty and achieving greater social integration of the poor.[2] In the global sphere, the administration oversaw the passage of NAFTA, which eliminated barriers to trade and investment within the region, facilitating both the opening up of Mexican markets to competition and "dumping" from U.S. firms and the more extensive use of low-wage labor through increased maquiladorization along the U.S.-Mexico border and the Caribbean. The New Democrats succeeded in policymaking terms where their Republican predecessors had not and helped to advance market reforms that were difficult to contest even among those constituencies that were in the crosshairs of reform.

The Clinton years constituted an important political crossroads for black politics as it had evolved out of the civil rights and black power movements. Black political organizations emerged from the eighties, battered and demoralized by Reagan–Bush era assaults on social democracy, and yet after the 1992 election of Bill Clinton, the effectiveness of established modes of black political engagement and address were confronted with an era of renewed inclusion and nominal power with Clinton appointing a record number of black cabinet members and federal departmental staff; growing consensus around neoliberalization; and the social and economic shockwaves of post–Cold War globalization. Walters had witnessed the birth of the New Democratic movement within the party. In fact, in his role as a campaign manager and advisor during Jesse Jackson's two unsuccessful bids for the Democratic Party's presidential nomination, Walters and others within the campaign who sought a renaissance of the party's social democratic commitments helped to precipitate the formation of the Democratic Leadership Council that oversaw the party's rightward drift. Equally important, in his public arguments against the African Growth and Opportunity Act, or "NAFTA for Africa," Walters offered a withering critique of a nascent, black New Democratic politics, the collusion of a new class of black technocratic leaders and politicians around the agenda of neoliberal privatization. In this context and with these experiences, Walters came to Maryland, where graduate students already interested in questions arising from these historical circumstances were given intellectual and physical space to think through them with his help.

In the spring of 1995, I did an independent study with Linda Faye Williams on the black power movement and African American political activity since the end of the Jim Crow era. I was already interested in doing a dissertation on some of the neglected but clearly influential organizations and events from the black power era, namely, the 1972 National Black Political Convention in Gary, Indiana. At one point during one of our weekly sessions, Williams encouraged me to meet with Walters because of his role in the 1972 convention and involvement in the National Black Political Assembly and other organizations I wished to study. Within the next month, I drove from my apartment in Hyattsville down Riggs Road and over to Howard's campus. Although I showed up unannounced and he was obviously very busy, Walters obliged and met with me for over an hour on that first encounter. He welcomed me many times after that and seemed both amused and flattered by my passion for the subject matter.

My immediate connection with Walters was rooted in my interests in postsegregation black politics, but the bond grew deeper. From his earliest political stand during the 1958 Dockum Drugstore sit-ins in his hometown of Wichita, Kansas, to his last days, Walters was essentially an unapologetic race-man and in that regard, his manner, comportment, and worldview reminded me of the many mentors I had in south Louisiana, all doggedly antiracist and committed to the broader struggle for black people's advancement. Although I was honing my own criticisms of black nationalist and liberal integrationist politics at the time, I appreciated his public intellectual sensibility and progressive left commitments in a context where too many faculty seemed unwilling to support graduate students who wanted to pursue politically engaged scholarship. Politically, I was enamored by Walters because unlike some of the other Afrocentric and black nationalists intellectuals I had encountered from my teen years through my matriculation as a master's student in black studies, he offered a more politically engaged Pan Africanism that was not predicated exclusively on notions of racial kinship and a project of cultural recuperation but focused on building political solidarity and actively combating the forces that produced misery and structural underdevelopment on the continent.

Even before I met Walters, I had momentarily contemplated transferring to Howard because I initially did not think that I could do the kind of scholarship I wanted to pursue at Maryland. By the end of my first year, I found my niche, but I was certainly pleased to hear that Walters would be joining the faculty at Maryland. His presence made the beltway feel much smaller, as many of us were now drawn into the social orbit of black politicos in a way only he could facilitate. The world of black politicos was his world, and the sundry black organizations and personalities who populated the beltway were his "base." Walters commanded unparalleled respect and adoration within the national black leadership circles that clustered within the Washington beltway. He was a living bridge to the history of the civil rights and black power movements. This was incredibly helpful to my work on the black power era in that his name alone provided me with access to all manner of leaders and activists from the period. During one such interview, a veteran of the Carolina lunch counter sit-ins and classmate of Martin Luther King Jr. told me outright that he would never have talked to me if I had not been Ron Walters' student. Just the mention of Walters' name commanded immediate respect and access in some beltway circles.

The timing of Walters' decision to return to Washington, D.C. in 1971 and put down roots in the area is significant. Although he had lived in the area during his time as a graduate student at American University, Walters' decision to return to the area after living in Boston and upstate New York was especially serendipitous. He returned to Washington at the very moment when the region was experiencing profound political, demographic, and urban transformation. Walter Washington was finishing his term as mayor commissioner of Washington, D.C., and although he was appointed to that position in 1967, he was among the first blacks to hold chief executive power in a major American city. The ranks of the black middle class expanded rapidly during that period as well, largely due to integration in public-sector employment throughout the capital region. Authorities broke ground on the area's Metro rapid transit system in 1969 and its construction was at full tilt when Walters arrived at Howard. This massive public works project helped to radically transform Washington into a more cosmopolitan city. Walters once told me that he favored the D.C. Metro area because it possessed a unique, urbane character but was not as overpowering as New York City. Of course, Howard University was a principal node of the black power political activity during the late sixties and early seventies, serving as the site of powerful student protests for curriculum change that prefigured the black/Africana studies movement and as a locus of organizing for the African Liberation Day mobilizations, which sought to build solidarity for armed struggles against Portuguese colonialism and white settler rule in Southern Africa. His move from Howard to College Park was equally fortunate.

When Walters' arrival was announced, many hoped that the presence of several, influential black policy-oriented scholars at College Park might create synergy and resources for a formal institute. A 1996 article in *Black Issues in Higher Education*, titled "Creating a Powerhouse," focused on Maryland's hiring of Walters and Walter Broadnax, who had served as deputy assistant secretary of the U.S. Department of Health and Human Services as evidence of a growing trend—more robust recruitment of senior black scholars at large, majority-white universities. Much of the article lamented the implications for Howard University and other historically black colleges who might not be able to compete with well-funded research universities in luring and retaining senior black scholars.[3] Speaking to the motives for Maryland's recruitment of Walters and Broadnax, Williams said at the time, "We're trying to build a superior group to do work on race, policy and politics. . . . We're seeking the best scholars in these areas and plan not only to be a scholarly unit but also to add to the public debate in a real public way."[4] Williams alluded to the formation of a formal committee on race, policy, and politics, but the kind of academic unit she and others had hoped for did not materialize. Walters' African American Leadership Institute (originally the African American Leadership Program) at the James MacGregor Burns Academy of Leadership, however, was created shortly after his arrival and quickly became an important node of campus activity, a vital link to the wider policy debates of the capital beltway and a source of support for student and faculty research and activism.

In the 1990s, the University of Maryland's Government and Politics Department actively recruited African American students into its doctoral program. From the time I entered the graduate program in Government and Politics in 1994 to my graduation in 2001, there were twenty-five African American students admitted to the program, and in any given year during that same period there were at least twelve who were actively taking courses, working as teaching and research assistants, or completing dissertations. We formed a close-knit support group and struggled together through the day-to-day travails of becoming professional academics. Walters brought to College Park an ethic of service and mentorship that we cherished since many of us were alums of historically black colleges—Xavier University, Virginia State, Hampton, Southern University-Baton Rouge, Lincoln, and Howard. Many faculty members at College Park wanted us to succeed, but some construed that academic success as incompatible with the kind of broader social justice commitments that Walters and others actively nurtured. For some, race, class, and gender and other forms of social identity and stratification should be primarily examined as spigot variables within some ostensibly complex regression model rather than through the methods of historiography, ethnographic research, or textual/rhetorical analyses. After a formal job offer was extended to Walters and we all waited and wondered whether he would join the faculty, I can recall hearing that one senior faculty member in the Government and Politics Department had opposed Walters' candidacy for the senior appointment, claiming that he did not have enough peer-reviewed journal articles. Many of us were outraged and insulted by the accusation that Walters was not "good enough" for the department, because unlike the short-stack of esoteric journal articles authored by this naysayer, Walters' quarter-century of intellectual work spoke directly to our passions and was relevant to the very questions of racial inequality, power, and social change that had propelled many of us to graduate school in the first place.

Walters was a seasoned and effective mentor. When we arrived at College Park, he was a veteran who was already skilled in tending to the insecurities, bouts of overconfidence, and equivocations that too often hobble graduate students' progress. He offered helpful, patient, gentle—at some moments, not so gentle—feedback on our work. In a few terse words, he helped cure my perfectionist streak, a tendency that may have ruined my hopes of ever completing my doctoral dissertation. He modeled a work ethic and professionalism that had a big impact on me. Every weekday morning, he could be reached at his home office, writing, reading, and interviewing for various news programs and publications. He helped me to grow as a writer during those years by emphasizing the process rather than the end result and instilling a reverence for the daily regimen and work habits that boost creativity.

Although his public and intellectual contributions were well known and praised in many corners, Walters often demonstrated compassion for our well-being as students and as people in a manner that is not so common within some academic settings. One such instance of his willingness to step outside the role of director or dissertation advisor came in the summer of 1997. My partner and I were expecting our first child and during a routine prenatal visit, our doctor failed to get an accurate fetal stethoscope reading. As delicately as he could, he handed us some paperwork on miscarriages and explained that since it was a Friday and the ultrasound practice they used was already closed for the weekend, they could not tell us anything definitive until Monday. Needless to say, we were devastated, paralyzed with fear, and now faced a long weekend of uncertainty, alone with our emotions. The next morning, the first phone call I received was from Ron Walters. The sound of his voice was warm, reassuring, and I must admit, unexpected. Many of our own family members were still in the dark about our plight and few had called just yet. Luckily for us, the ultrasound results were positive that Monday morning and in January 1998, our first son was born. I've known many people throughout my life who are passionate and articulate about social justice and concern for humankind, but for too many, such sentiments are often largely an abstraction. In academe, many of the same self-styled radicals and progressives have difficulty holding a decent, civil conversation at a dinner party without engaging in "shop talk" and self-gratifying, intellectual acrobatics. And they are totally inept when it comes to talking in an honest, self-effacing manner about the personal challenges and frailties that make us human. Walters was not afraid of such ventures and I think this made his arguments for social justice all the more convincing.

The African American Leadership Institute

The African American Leadership Institute began as the African American Leadership Program shortly after Walters arrived in College Park, and it grew rapidly over the next few years, expanding from a staff of three to as many as ten. Such expansion was initially due to pluck and innovation but ultimately achieved through a generous grant from the W. K. Kellogg Foundation's Devolution initiative. The African American Leadership Institute was one component of the powerful but, unfortunately, short-lived James MacGregor Burns Academy of Leadership, a non–degree granting unit that began as a women's leadership program and grew into a multifaceted, dynamic center of academic courses, conferences, and training initiatives targeted at leadership development. Taliaferro Hall surged with activity during those days.

Georgia Sorenson was the founder and leader throughout the 1990s and the academy served as a haven for all types of idealists. The academy was socially progressive but not monolithic. A range of ideological positions and perspectives animated its programs— Alinskyite community organizing, GLBTQ activism, conventional notions of leadership as management, feminist politics, socialism, black nationalism, and liberal democratic politics. Some of the senior fellows at the academy during that period included former Houston mayor Kathy Whitmire and David Harrington, one of Walters' former students at Howard, then mayor of Bladensburg, Maryland and future Prince Georges County councilman and Maryland state senator. Grassroots activist Shelly Wilsey headed the Community Action Program, which trained hundreds of organizers from unions, antiviolence organizations, and tenants rights associations. Students had access to a wide range of politicos and professionals, including visiting faculty and Democratic Party strategist Donna Brazile; former deputy director of Lyndon B. Johnson's War on Poverty, Adam Yarmolinsky; and the academy's namesake, the Pulitzer Prize–winning biographer, James MacGregor Burns; Yarmolinsky and Burns served in advisory capacities.

Walters relished the ecumenical environment of the academy, but he did not value facile diversity over his commitments to social justice. Conflict unfolded when a young libertarian undergraduate student who was organizing his own leadership initiative suggested that the academy diversify its board to include more conservatives. Because of the argument that the liberal-leaning board was less likely to compete effectively for grants in a world of foundations and philanthropists that included many political conservatives, others took up the suggestion as a sensible proposition. The undergraduate student who initially made the suggestion forwarded House Speaker Newt Gingrich, whose coauthored *Contract with America* agenda guided the 1994 Republican Revolution, as a possible board appointee. When the nomination came up in a staff meeting, Walters offered a blistering critique of Gingrich as an archenemy of the very traditions of civil rights and social justice that the African American Leadership Institute was established to continue. In all likelihood, his powerful arguments against Gingrich only confirmed this student's impressions of the academy as a haven for liberal do-gooders, but Walters' words punctured the emergent climate of liberal tolerance that tended to suspend open, honest political debate even when such tolerance contradicted widely expressed commitments to social justice. His words also clarified the institute's political direction and focus.

If Walters was the architect of the African American Leadership Institute, Phyllis Jeffers was its construction manager. Jeffers was the assistant director of the institute when I joined as a researcher in 1996, and she helped to build and grow the programming even as she balanced her own coursework as a graduate student in English. During the early days, Phyllis was the leader of day-to-day operations, and Michele Miller served as undergraduate assistant. We all took part in the visioning and programmatic planning to various degrees. During these formative years, we developed practical administrative and leadership skills beyond our formal academic training and learned to work miracles with very little resources. Due to the growing success of our programming, the African American Leadership Program expanded into the African American Leadership Institute by around 1998.

One of the joys of the working with the institute and the academy was the sheer number of talented people who frequented the space. Some of the many graduate students who worked for the institute included Adolphus Belk, Guy DeWeever, Tamelyn Tucker-Worgs, Christopher Whitt, Nicole Mason, Ester Carr, Atiya Kai Stokes, and Tamara Masters, as well as others. Walters provided us with much-needed financial support through assistantships and work-studies. The lively intellectual culture of the Academy of Leadership breathed new life into my own work. Many of us who migrated to Taliaferro Hall for research assistantships found a resource-rich environment—new computers, office supplies, and other creature comforts that were the province of tenured faculty not graduate students. I think it was at the academy that I first encountered screensavers with streaming news and weather updates—a far cry from the sluggish, virus-prone terminals that were standard in our graduate computer lab. It was a place where our intellectual interests and work were appreciated and nourished. Under Walters' leadership at AALI, many of us were able to take our first steps as intellectuals, preparing white papers and reports; conceiving and organizing public events; achieving some of our first modest publications; and developing our presentation, writing, and analytical skills in ways that would prepare us for our lives as academics, policy researchers, and activists.

The political crises facing black leadership and the rethinking of African American politics they precipitated were reflected in several key books and articles during that period—Clarence Lusane's *African Americans at the Crossroads: The Restructuring of Black Leadership and the 1992 Elections* (1994); Adolph Reed Jr.'s 1995 *Village Voice* essay, "What Are the Drums Saying Booker?"; Joy James' *Transcending the Talented Tenth* (1996); Robert C. Smith's *We Have No Leaders* (1996); Kevin Gaines' *Uplifting the Race* (1996); Lea Williams' *Servants of the People* (1997); Manning Marable's *Black Leadership* (1998); Johnetta Rose Barras' sharp and spirited writings on local black leadership in the *Washington City Paper*, and Smith and Walters' compendium of their individual and coauthored writings, *African American Leadership* (1999). Such works were required reading at the time, and these and others shaped the questions and issues we addressed at the institute: Was the nature of "black leadership" determined by racial identity, institutional authority, or political commitments? In what ways had the very notion of African American leadership evolved in a manner that privileged black men, clergy, and elite brokerage at the exclusion of women, workers, and revolutionary politics? What particular styles and forms of political engagement were more efficacious and appropriate for achieving social justice in contemporary times? How had the expansion of the black middle class and their political integration rendered older norms and expectations of leadership authenticity and legitimacy of the Jim Crow era quaint and obsolete? These were just some of the many questions we posed, considered, and debated in Taliaferro Hall and the many public events organized by AALI during the late 1990s.

A principal focus of our work during the 1990s was assessing the role and relevance of civil rights organizations in contemporary struggles. On the one hand, the need for assertive civil rights organizations was greater than ever amid efforts to roll back civil rights era reforms, such as affirmative action and voting rights. On the other hand, the very organizations that had produced grand historical change, toppling Jim Crow segregation and initiating an unprecedented expansion of the black middle class, were now in turmoil with some facing fiscal insolvency, well-publicized leadership scandals, and the struggle to remain relevant to new crises and worsening social conditions faced by black urban poor and a new generation of youth who had come of age amid crack cocaine and the War on Drugs. To foster public debate around these matters, we hosted a series of annual panel discussions on the major civil rights organizations beginning with the NAACP and holding subsequent sessions on the Urban League and SCLC. Our session on the Urban League was held at the National Press Club and featured an uninvited, impromptu speech by then–league director Hugh Price, who was obviously concerned about how well his organization might be represented during the panel that mainly consisted of academics such as Linda Faye Williams and Jesse Moore. Unwittingly, Price's remarks merely confirmed the more barbed appraisals of the panelists who questioned the organization's continued emphasis on entrepreneurial activity amid the decimation of the social safety net. Waving off any insistence on the pursuit of left interventionist politics, Price was steadfast and asserted that there was only one stream to swim in the United States, the mainstream. One of our most well-attended and impactful events featured a transatlantic dialogue between Martin Luther King confidante and founding member of the Congressional Black Caucus the Reverend Walter Fauntroy and Guyana-born, British Labor MP Lord Bernard Grant. Developed as part of "Global Leadership Week" programming at Maryland, their conversation was especially powerful as it revealed common misgivings and struggles regarding the New Labour politics of British Prime Minister Tony Blair and the New Democratic thrust of Bill Clinton.

Rather than simply historical or nostalgic, our work also found ways to speak to contemporary struggles. AALI organized leadership training for an organization of young black professionals that featured a session by the late Lisa Y. Sullivan, veteran of the Black Student Leadership Network and founder of LISTEN (Local Initiatives, Support, Training, and Education Network). At times, the generational dynamics of these events and intellectual preoccupations of the moment produced interesting debates about black leadership and the place of ideology, gender, and class. Given the growing attention to the work of black women in the civil rights movement at the time and the actual division of labor within the AALI office, we also explored the questions of gender and black leadership at various turns. Even during those moments when he and his work were the target of such criticisms, Walters was gracious, welcoming our criticisms with generosity and good humor, often conceding that he was not too old to grow. Thankfully, Walters often offered perceptive firsthand accounts of the various historical personalities we debated and he had known and struggled alongside during the civil rights and black power movements.

The institute reached its apex of activity as the decade came to a close, after receiving a $2.5 million grant through the W. K. Kellogg Foundation's Devolution initiative.[5] Under this grant, the AALI served as the principal administrative host of the Scholar-Practitioner program that developed and circulated research on the social and policy impacts of workfare reform in five states (New York, Mississippi, Washington, Florida, and Wisconsin) and helped to build the capacities of local, state-level organizations and advocates to shape the new policy context. At the start of 1999, my own involvement with the AALI began to taper off. I remained on staff as a researcher, but I rededicated my energies to parenting my young son (and eventually to the birth of my second) and toward the completion of my doctoral dissertation. Reginald Tynes, a seasoned organizer and trainer, was hired as the assistant director and charged with administering the Scholar-Practitioner program. With the hiring of new staff, the AALI had outgrown its office in Taliaferro and was relocated to a floor of Holzapfel Hall for the duration of the grant period.

A number of well-known scholars and activists were recruited to serve as advisors or participants in the initiatives of the Scholar-Practitioner program. These included president of the Chicago-based

Center for New Horizons, Sokoni Karanja; political scientist Rodney Hero; CUNY anthropologist Leith Mullings; and Kensington Welfare Rights Union activist Cheri Honkala; among many others. At its best moments, the Scholar-Practitioner program created a vibrant network where liberal and left-progressive scholars and activists could assess the real sociological impacts of workfare rollout on communities. Reports and presentations developed by the various state teams recorded an array of new problems created by the devolutionary process, such as the unique transportation challenges faced by residents in isolated, rural areas and small towns; inadequate and/or underfunded childcare provisions for those now compelled to work; the patent limitations of creating a sub–minimum wage workforce as an antipoverty strategy and its implications for wage floors in various industries; as well as the ways that localized service delivery exacerbated existing patterns of discrimination against blacks, immigrants, and other aid recipients.[6] The various reports and papers created through the Scholar-Practitioner program provided useful information to those activists and politicos at the state level who were attempting to shape the new policy context in favorable terms—to make the most out of a bad situation.

Opposing NAFTA for Africa and the New Democrats

Walters was a pioneer of black public intellectual life as we have come to know it. Given his leadership of Howard University's Political Science Department and influential roles within Jesse Jackson's two presidential campaigns, Walters was increasingly called upon from the late 1980s onward by national television and radio news programs to provide commentary on current political affairs. His ascendancy predated the consolidation of major cable news networks and the concomitant transformation of norms and modes of public discussion such changes necessitated. Unlike latter-day public intellectuals whose legitimacy and styles of engagement are predicated on notions of charisma and telegeneity narrowly defined by corporate news, Walters derived his legitimacy and notoriety from his scholarship and extensive, long-standing engagement in real social struggles and organizations. The unfolding efforts to pass the African Growth and Opportunity Act, however, placed Walters in conflict with some of his former allies. His commitment to a left progressive vision of development in Africa, which placed labor rights, public investment, Western aid, and African sovereignty as essential elements, ran counter to the promarket reforms increasingly touted by the New Democrats and their allies.

Africa loomed large in Walters' politics since his youth. One of his first national publications was a fictional work titled "The Blacks," which was the winner of a national essay contest held by *Reader's Digest*. As the contest winner, Walters, then a senior at Fisk University, traveled to New York City and met John Williams, author of the novel *The Angry Ones*; South African writer Bloke Modisane; and William Melvin Kelly, author of *A Different Drummer*. Walters later said that this experience "only deepened my thirst fully to understand what I had written."[7] The essay reverses the middle passage of the Transatlantic slave trade—it reconstructs a dialogue between an African and an African American as they travel from America back to Africa. Walters would later recall, "That dialogue between 'The Blacks,' reflecting more than a century of unresolved tensions of what came before and after the Middle Passage of slavery, is still a subject deep in the recesses of my mind and, I think, of the Black mind in general, shaping such fundamental concepts as that of total allegiance to and identity with America."[8] As a graduate student, Walters specialized in international relations, and during the sixties, like many other young black intellectuals, he became a devotee of Martinican psychiatrist and anticolonial revolutionary Frantz Fanon. Walters was active in the African Liberation Support Committee and antiapartheid mobilizations and was a founder of key pro-Africa lobby organizations like TransAfrica and Constituency for Africa.

Unlike the domestic struggles over neoliberalization that were essentially a rearguard fight for the Left —a seemingly impossible attempt to stall reforms that had been gaining political momentum and cultural hegemony for two decades through an alliance of powerful, entrenched interests—the battle over "NAFTA for Africa" was characterized by a set of historical, political interests and different alliances. Also, labor unions, human rights organizations, and progressive lobbyist organizations working on poverty, health care, and development issues in Africa benefited from the prevailing criticisms of NAFTA and the visible impacts that trade legislation had on the workers and communities in the region. The Chiapas uprising, which began in January of 1994, and the struggles of the Ogoni peoples in Nigeria against Royal Dutch Shell, which drew international outrage after the 1995 execution of writer and environmentalist Ken Saro Wiwa, vividly illustrated the pernicious, violent effects of neoliberal globalization and served to fortify and expand opposition forces. The "NAFTA for Africa" legislation was a tsunami that emanated from the same seismic political shifts as domestic restructuring, but there was still time to sound a warning, to possibly stem its advance and diffuse its negative consequences. Walters used his pen and public stature to challenge this trade liberalization maneuver, and his opposition in writings and speeches on this subject is significant in three ways.

First, Walters offers a pointed analysis of the limitations and potential impacts of the legislation and as such, sketches a formative critique of neoliberal globalism as it pertains to the African continent, a critique that builds on Pan-Africanist, developmentalist, and anti-colonial traditions. Walters locates the origins of the African Growth and Opportunity Act in the Reagan era, noting that it was the Reagan administration that introduced a new approach to trade and investment that curbed aid and discouraged state-led economic growth in favor of creating the conditions for market competition. The Clinton administration followed with further encouragement of private sector–led development strategies spurred in part by significant rates of economic growth registered in some African nations after 1993. Democratic congressman Jim McDermott rolled out the idea that would become the African Growth and Opportunity Act in the spring of 1996. His proposal rested on three essential pillars— the accomplishment of a U.S.-Africa Free Trade area by 2020, the creation of U.S.-Africa Economic Cooperation Forum, and the establishment of a U.S.-Africa Trade and Investment Partnership modeled after APEC (the Asia Pacific Economic Cooperation Association). A year after McDermott's initial rollout, H.R. 1432 was introduced by Charles Rangel (D-NY) and Phillip Crane (R-IL) and, in addition to McDermott's original provisions, it included the following provisions: a $150 million equity fund and an $500 million infrastructure fund; an export-import bank initiative to expand loans for private projects, the elimination of trade quotas on textiles and the renewal and expansion of General System of Preferences for trade to Africa to allow an additional 1,800 products that were previously excluded

to now be traded with Africa for a ten-year period.[9] Supporters of
H.R. 1432 (henceforth, the Crane Bill) included former New York
City Mayor David Dinkins, Speaker of the House Newt Gingrich, and
former HUD Secretary under George Bush Sr. Jack Kemp. Various
corporations such as American International Group (AIG), Mobil
Oil, Chevron, Texaco, Exxon, Caterpillar, Occidental Petroleum,
General Electric, Enron, and Kmart, among others, lobbied for the
bill's passage.[10] Although the Reverend Jesse Jackson and Democratic Congresswoman Maxine Waters initially opposed the bill, they
later relented in favor of passage.

Walters' objections to the Crane bill focused on two aspects of
society that were most threatened by this trade liberalization package— state sovereignty and social democracy. He argued that the bill
would undermine the sovereignty of African nations through a continued emphasis on conditions, such as prohibitions against trade
with Libya, Cuba, or Iraq (nations that had supported postcolonial
development in numerous countries during the Cold War through
financial assistance and medical aid); the elimination of protection-
ist measures for national industries; and the reduction of business
taxes and regulations. Further, the bill lacked any assurances that
African leadership might maintain some control over direction and
implementation of new development initiatives or any measures that
might insure that the poorest citizens actually benefited from infrastructure improvements. Walters concluded, "if African leadership
does not have the human, financial and technological capacity to
lead in this area, they would be subject to the much larger and much
more sophisticated planning and financial capability and thus the
leadership of large corporations."[11] The Crane bill also promised to
decimate what little social democracy remained on the continent by
requiring cuts in government spending and the privatization of public services. Reflecting on the negative impacts of the shrinkage of
the public sector, Walters argued that "unregulated markets and private sector activity as a the primary engine of economic growth has
traditionally been unsuccessful at reducing widespread poverty," and
such market activity "throughout the Third World often sets prices
for goods at such a level that lower-income classes participate and are
often relegated to inferior goods."[12] Echoing the arguments made
by the AFL-CIO and COSATU (Congress of South African Trade
Unions) at the time, Walters argued that the bill did not mandate

any labor or human rights standards. "Without strong labor rights," Walters concluded, "the bill would have the same effect as the largely failed Caribbean Basin Initiative, which gave American firms access to the cheap labor of the Caribbean but stimulated little economic development in the region."[13]

Second, Walters exposes the new political alliances that congealed around the legislation and confronts the conundrum of black political acquiescence to New Democratic politics. In an earlier essay that first appeared in *The Black Scholar*, "Popular Black Struggle: Mass Mobilization in the 1990s," Walters addressed the widely held perspective that popular pressure tactics were passé and no longer relevant to contemporary struggles against inequality. In response to those who embraced "system-oriented leadership tactics" Walters argued, "the extent to which it is possible to 'routinize' leadership strategies through institutional means is largely fallacious, because it does not comport with the necessity to mount the requisite pressure on the political system that would produce 'large changes' sufficient to address the problems of most Black communities."[14] The argument, now familiar within studies of African American politics, holds that the black population has become more internally diverse and, by some accounts, more politically disunified as the adversarial certainty of the Jim Crow era has been abated, as an uneven social progress has transformed the material realties, and as experiences of African Americans have become more varied.[15] An immediate critique of this interpretative trope is that it presents the Jim Crow period and black political life as possessing more unanimity and simplicity that are not borne out by the historical record.[16] Walters' arguments, however, identified the political drift of some black political elites away from the strategies of mass protest and extensive commitments to the expansion of social democracy toward a politics of insider-negotiation and patronage. This conservative drift, however, was intensified by the ascendancy of the New Democrats and the corresponding emergence of a new generation of black public functionaries, politicians, and organizational leaders who were not socialized through the post–World War II civil rights movement and did not share the same commitments to left interventionist politics.

Walters took aim at the emergence of a comprador organization, the "National Summit for Africa," which he described as "the mechanism to achieve the movement of the African continent in the direction of 'pure' capitalism."[17] His analysis of this emergent political bloc and its implications for Africa policy and the fate of progressive alternatives is pure brimstone. He lays bare the ideological motives and power relations beneath the expensive conferences and suited environs of the "summit strategy":

> These Blacks are backed up by a new phalanx of young, hungry, business oriented professionals who see the world through the eyes of their corporate employers, who have unleashed them as the advanced guard of their presence on the African continent, and they pursue these interests at the tables of policy discussion and debate as ruthlessly as anyone. Then there are the new Black mayors who have been starved by the resource flight of the Federal Government, major businesses, and the middle class, who see in Africa, a potential new bonanza of economic salvation to their towns and cities, and who provide legitimacy for Federal government interests vis-à-vis grassroots blacks.[18]

This cohort was joined by the members of Congress and Africa-focused organizations who have embraced the neoliberal approach as the only alternative for changing the fate of the continent. "These would appear to be the elements of the new pro-business Black coalition on Africa," he writes, "which is backed up by its counterpart on the African continent: desperate heads of state, their ambassadors and an emerging business class, all of whom are running from the reduction of their fortunes in Europe to the new capitalist patronage in America."[19] The opposition to NAFTA for Africa was unable to stem the tide of support for the legislation. Clinton signed the bill into law in May 2000. In the years since its passage, we have witnessed a second "scramble for Africa," one led by multinational firms, with U.S. and Chinese firms serving as the principal beneficiaries within this new imperial milieu.[20]

Third, he outlines a more progressive route to economic development that respects labor rights, state sovereignty, and democratic processes and national development models over market-oriented poverty reduction measures. His voice was a part of a growing chorus of opposition to neoliberal globalism that attained popular media attention through the 1999 Seattle protest against the World Trade

Organization and subsequent April 26 demonstrations against the World Bank in Washington, D.C. Many of us participated in the latter demonstrations since it was in our own backyard. I can recall having a conversation with Walters as these events unfolded. Although he obviously shared the criticism of the new imperial relations that were taking shape and their pernicious impact on communities and the environment across the globe, he was less confident about the strategies that were being initiated by the anti-globalization forces. He argued that these forces had neglected any attempt to engage domestic black political organizations and to undertake the kind of coalition building that he knew was necessary for any sustained political movement to develop. He was leery of the theatrical aspects of the April 26 demonstrations and similar protests that were staged at the Democratic and Republican Party conventions later that summer of 2000. His criticisms stemmed from the sense that black people as a political force were being bypassed and excluded by the neo-anarchistic modes of politics responsible for Seattle and similar protests. His arguments, however, capture a core problem with their style of politics, which amounts to a rejection of politics as purposive activity and the limits of protests in an age where social conflict is so heavily integral to the central dynamics of news making and popular entertainment and where spectacle does not carry the same power to disrupt the normal ordering of business as it once did. The problems he identified then continue to plague left political forces that reemerged during the 2011 Occupy Wall Street demonstrations where media spectacle and fetishization of performative democracy have eclipsed the more difficult process of movement building and directly confronting institutional power.

Conclusion

In this essay, I have tried to pay homage to the late Ronald Walters by discussing three of his contributions during his time as a professor at the University of Maryland–College Park. First, he offered black and progressive graduate students mentorship that was wholeheartedly supportive and encouraging of an engaged scholarship. Walters impressed on us the need to serve. Dispassionate scholarship was someone else's luxury, not ours. He encouraged us to work toward our professional goals, but more importantly, he insisted that we pursue social justice and work tirelessly to leave the world more just and humane than the one we had inherited. Second, he created an institutional context that enabled us to flourish and develop professional and research skills that we may not have obtained otherwise. And finally, he modeled a quality of public engagement that was courageous and politically progressive at the historical moment when black politicos were converging in their support for neoliberal restructuring as the default form of statecraft and economic development in domestic and international contexts. Walters critique of both the dynamics of privatization and the place of new black political leadership in its advance is especially prescient now, when read against the backdrop of deepening global economic crises and the further consolidation of black politicos around neoliberal politics during the Obama administration. In his writings and speeches, Walters warned against the disastrous social impacts of neoliberal globalism and demanded an alternative that placed human needs, labor rights, and democratic power for the greatest number over the wealth and interests of the few.

Notes

1. See David Harvey, *A Brief History of Neoliberalism* (Oxford: Oxford University Press, 2005); Jaime Peck, *Constructions of Neoliberal Reason* (Oxford: Oxford University Press, 2010).
2. Sanford F. Schram, *After Welfare: The Culture of Postindustrial Social Policy* (New York: New York University Press, 2000); Jaime Peck, *Workfare States* (New York: Guilford Press, 2001); John Arena, *Driven from New Orleans: How Nonprofits Betray Public Housing and Promote Privatization* (Minneapolis: University of Minnesota Press, 2012).
3. The *Black Issues in Higher Education* article also focused primarily on black academic star power at the expense of acknowledging the broad, diverse group of faculty and staff that are needed to facilitate the successful matriculation of black graduate students. During the 1990s, we were fortunate at the University of Maryland–College Park to have a hosts of selfless, dedicated, and unsung faculty such as Ollie Johnson, Clarence Stone, Don

Piper, Dorith Grant Wisdom, Melissa Matthes, Ronald Tercheck, Joe Oppenheimer, Sharon Harley, Carla Peterson, Mindy Chateauvert, the late Rhonda Williams, and Gar Alperovitz, among many others, who provided constant advice, mentoring, and encouragement as we struggled with graduate student life.

4. Ibid.

5. For some background and analysis of the Kellogg Foundation's Devolution initiative, see Kay E. Sherwood, "The W. K. Kellogg Foundation's Devolution Initiative: An Experiment in Evaluating Strategy," *New Directions for Evaluation* 128 (Winter 2010): 69–86.

6. See "Racial and Ethnic Disparities in the Era of Devolution: A Persistent Challenge to Welfare Reform," A Report of Research Findings from the Scholar-Practitioner Program of the Devolution Initiative, the W. K. Kellogg Foundation, December 2001.

7. See Ronald W. Walters, *Pan Africanism in the African Diaspora* (Detroit: Wayne State University Press, 1993), 9.

8. Ibid.

9. Ronald W. Walters, "The African Growth and Opportunity Act: Changing Foreign Policy Priorities Toward Africa in a Conservative Political Culture," in *Foreign Policy and the Black (Inter)National Interest*, ed. Charles P. Henry (Albany: State University of New York Press, 2000), 20–21.

10. See "Lurking Below an Appealing Name, 'Africa Growth and Opportunity Act' Is Controversial Legislation with a Diverse Group of Opponents," *Public Citizen*, March 4, 1998, www.citizen.org/page.aspx?pid=3691.

11. Walters, "African Growth and Opportunity Act," 25.

12. Ibid., 25.

13. Ibid., 24.

14. Ronald W. Walters, "Popular Black Struggle: Mass Mobilization in the 1990s," in Ronald W. Walters and Robert C. Smith, *African American Leadership* (Albany: State University of New York Press, 1999), 173. See also in the same volume, his essay "Black Leadership and the Problem of Strategy Shift," and his formative appraisal of the 1972 Gary Convention, Ronald W. Walters, "The New Black Political Culture," *Black World* 21, 12 (1972): 4–17.

15. Michael Dawson, *Behind the Mule: Race and Class in African American Politics* (Princeton: Princeton University Press, 1995); Andra Gillespie, *The New Black Politician: Cory Booker, Newark and*

Postracial America (New York: New York University Press, 2012); Fredrick C. Harris, *The Price of the Ticket: Barack Obama and the Rise and Decline of Black Politics* (Oxford: Oxford University Press, 2012).

16. For analyses that either explore the ideological and class conflicts among African Americans during the Jim Crow era or that attempt to debunk the myth of a unified black political past, see Michelle Boyd, *Jim Crow Nostalgia: Reconstructing Race in Bronzeville* (Minneapolis: University of Minnesota Press, 2008); Cedric Johnson, *Revolutionaries to Race Leaders: Black Power and the Making of African American Politics* (Minneapolis: University of Minnesota Press, 2007); Preston Smith, *Racial Democracy and the Black Metropolis: Housing Policy in Postwar Chicago* (Minneapolis: University of Minnesota Press, 2012); Adolph Reed, Jr., and Kenneth W. Warren, eds., *Renewing Black Intellectual History: The Ideological and Material Foundations of African American Thought* (Boulder and London: Paradigm Publishers, 2010); Kevin K. Gaines, *Uplifting the Race: Black Leadership, Politics and Culture in the Twentieth Century* (Chapel Hill and London: University of North Carolina Press, 1996).

17. Ronald W. Walters, "The African Growth and Opportunity Act: A Renaissance for Whom?" *Black Renaissance* 2 (July 1999): 160.

18. Ibid., 160.

19. Ibid.

20. Chris Alden, *China in Africa* (London: Zed Books, 2007).

Part III

6

A Modest Proposal

A Call for Leadership Specialization and the
Recognition of Multiple Black Constituencies

ANDRA GILLESPIE

Introduction

In the conclusion of *African American Leadership*, Robert Smith and Ronald Walters made no apologies for their embrace of an "essentialist" view of black politics (Smith and Walters 1999, 249). While they were quick to acknowledge the constant political heterogeneity of the African American community and presciently identified the increasing integration of blacks into mainstream political, social, and cultural institutions as a disuniting force within the African American community (see Smith and Walters 1999, 250–58), they also argued that "Black leadership emanates from the Black community in the sense that the individuals who present themselves for leadership have their origin in that community and its culture and that they should reflect the needs and aspirations of that community" (249).

Ronald Walters' passing coincided with the publication of a number of popular books by cultural critics in which the authors grappled with the idea of essential blackness and heterogeneity within the African American community (e.g., Eugene Robinson's *Disintegration*, Ellis Cose's *The End of Anger*, and Touré's *Who's Afraid of Post-Blackness?*). While these authors chose to tackle this question from a broad, almost sociological perspective, it is clear that politics is the subtext of their examinations. For political scientists who assume the mantle left by Ronald Walters, it is imperative that we examine anew how growing intraracial diversity is reshaping black politics and how we think about it.

In the pages that follow, I begin to define the state of black political leadership in a "postracial," post-Obama," "postblack" era. After briefly outlining Walters' observations and conclusions in the second half of *African American Leadership*, I consider Walters' work in light of more recent developments. Two themes guide my discussion. First, I consider the possibility that black politics is too fragmented in the twenty-first century to consider it one unified body politic. I end by focusing my attention on modern racial social movements and consider the place of Walters' insider-outsider strategy in this new, racially transcendent era.

Black Political Leadership: A View from the 1990s

In the second half of *African American Leadership*, Ronald Walters anticipated the sweeping changes we see today in the African American community. In chapter 7 of the book, he noted that as blacks acquired more rights and more collective resources in the post–civil rights era, groups committed to the liberation of blacks altered their strategies. In particular, he notes the strategy shift from the non-violent protests to black nationalism to electoral politics. The mainstreaming or institutionalization of black politics coincided with the rise of the black middle class and the expansion of the pipeline professions for black leadership. Thus, as blacks became fixtures in elite business, cultural, and educational institutions and started moving into more prestigious elective offices at higher numbers, Walters noticed that blacks started to abandon protest strategies in favor of a more incremental approach that embraced lobbying and using elective office to seek change from within American political institutions (Smith and Walters 1999, 126–37).

Walters believed that incremental approaches were insufficient to fully achieving the large-scale redress that blacks sought. He argued that "the political history of Blacks suggests that *political strategies designed to produce large changes should be system-challenging*" (Smith and Walters 1999, 135, original emphasis). As such, Walters reiterates his support for the "insider-outsider" strategy. While Walters endorsed blacks holding elective office and moving, in the words of Bayard Rustin, "from protest to politics," he firmly believed that the U.S. government—even a descriptively representative U.S. government—would not fully address racial inequality and discrimination unless civil rights organizations used direct action techniques to maintain the salience of issues related to inequality (Smith and Walters 1999, chapter 9).

To illustrate his point, Walters cited a number of 1990s era protests, in which direct action—not behind-the-scenes legislative maneuvering—achieved material benefits for blacks. The most notable of these efforts included the boycott of Texaco. In 1994, after an Equal Employment Opportunity Commission (EEOC) investigation into promotion discrimination revealed audio tapes in which company executives made a series of offensive comments about blacks, local and national civil rights organizations joined forces to organize a boycott of the company in major cities across the United States. This put extra pressure on Texaco to settle the case out of court, and the black employees whose careers had been stalled as a result of the discrimination received compensation, retroactive pay raises, and guaranteed pay raises for the next five years (Smith and Walters 1999, 182–84).

Similarly, Walters noted the positive externalities of the Million Man March in 1995. Though not explicitly political, Walters argued that the march's controversial call for black men to resume their responsibilities as leaders within their families and communities had a positive effect on formal political participation. Walters contended that as a result of the march, black male voter turnout in the 1996 presidential election increased, a remarkable fact when one considers that black women turned out in lower rates that year. This increase is even more astonishing given the fact that 1996 witnessed the second lowest overall voter turnout in the United States from 1924 to 2008 (Smith and Walters 1999, 184–90; AU News 2008).

While Walters noted the continued efficacy of protest tactics, he also recognized the limitations of these strategies in the 1990s. For instance, while Walters attributed the turnout bump in 1996 to the Million Man March, he also recognized that the march's local organizing committees had trouble transitioning into sustained advocacy groups after the march. As a result, the groups lost momentum and were unable to translate the zeitgeist of the march into any appreciable movement for improving black communities (Smith and Walters 1999, 188–90).

Furthermore, Walters realized that by the 1990s, civil rights organizations faced numerous structural constraints that impeded their ability to act and to join in coalitions. In his case study of the National Black Leadership Roundtable (NBLR), which was supposed to create a national network by which to organize blacks at the congressional district level to put pressure on members of Congress to support issues that would benefit black communities (and to oppose efforts that were inimical to black interests, like budget cuts to job training programs or aid to cities). The roundtable explored ventures to create their own lending program for black-owned businesses and supported Jesse Jackson's 1988 campaign. However, the organization was defunct by 1991. Walters attributes the failure of the NBLR to a number of factors. First, the roundtable failed to secure nonprofit status, which made operations difficult. Most important, though, member organizations failed to pay their dues, making it difficult for the NBLR to meet its own budget (Smith and Walters 1999, chapter 8).

In a broader context, the demise of the NBLR is symptomatic of larger structural constraints within the universe of black civil rights organizations. Walters conceded that even by the 1990s, many forces conspired to prevent blacks from uniting around issues of common concern. That many black organizations relied on outside funding to survive suggested a lack of autonomy over their own agendas and would likely circumscribe direct action or even rhetorical critiques of certain institutions. Black communities were beset by cultural pathologies that would make it difficult to create a unifying political agenda. Most notably, Walters predicted that increasing class stratification within the black community would diversify "black interests" to such an extent that it would be difficult to unify blacks around a common agenda (Smith and Walters 1999, 146).

Has Anything Changed?

The problems that Ronald Walters observed in the late 1990s have only grown more acute in the past dozen years. The problems that plagued the NBLR and the local organizing committees of the Million

Man March were part of a larger trend of declining social capital and decreased human organization in traditional protest groups. Robert Putnam documented the precipitous decline of membership (as a percentage of the relevant constituency) in most of the prominent social, political, and volunteer organizations over the second half of the twentieth century. The NAACP, for example, saw black membership in its organization decline from about 3 percent of all blacks in 1950 to approximately 1 percent of all blacks by 1997. By 2006, even then-NAACP President Bruce Gordon admitted that his group had exaggerated its membership numbers for decades (Putnam 2000, 438, 442; Curry 2006).

In his analysis of the aftermath of the Million Man March, Walters recognized that modern social movement activity appeared to be episodic and short-lived. This observation mirrored his conclusions about the National Black Leadership Roundtable, which he argued was part of a national trend of "summitry" (Smith and Walters 1999, 170). Walters contended that the structural factors that guaranteed the survival of civil rights organizations served to mitigate their ability to engage in long-term protest activity. Walters identified broad-based funding and the need to limit political activity to qualify for nonprofit tax exempt status. Others have noted additional factors that may also contribute to civil rights organizations' limited capacity to organize. James Q. Wilson, for example, noted that the civil rights organizations that shifted away from protest and toward advocacy survived the heyday of the civil rights movement. Protest-based organizations, which require that their members sacrifice time and sometimes their safety and personal freedom, fared less well because most members will only commit to such costly activities for short periods of time. Moreover, Putnam also noted that advocacy groups lowered the bar for membership in an attempt to increase their numbers. Instead of requiring members to attend meetings and participate in activities, interest groups ask for donations. This kind of "checkbook" advocacy (Putnam 2000, 158) allows groups to claim large memberships, but those members are largely disengaged from the hard work the organization does. When these organizations need real-time commitments from their members, checkbook membership will not have inured the kind of accountability relationship that could realistically engage inactive members (Smith and Walters 1999, 195, 170–71; Wilson 1995, 50, 181).

The structural changes affecting civil rights organizations complement changes among black elites and black citizens. Katherine Tate observed that increased black political incorporation within mainstream political institutions has reshaped black public opinion. Whereas early public opinion studies found that most blacks espoused radical politics and left-of-center policy preferences, she found evidence to support the notion that blacks have moderated their policy preferences to reflect both their descriptive representation in mainstream institutions and the triangulation of conservative issues into the Democratic Party platform (Tate 2010, chapter 1).

While Tate implies that black voters are responding to descriptive and tactical changes within the black elite, it is important for us to consider that this relationship may be recursive. In short, both black elite behavior and black mass opinion may be responding to changes in the other group. For instance, there is evidence to suggest that there is a generational divide on some issues of particular interest to blacks. For instance, younger blacks, whether or not they hold elective office, are more likely to support school vouchers than their older counterparts.[1] Younger blacks are also less likely to list racism as the most salient issue affecting them (Bositis 2001). These differences do not reflect changes at the elite level so much as they reflect differences in socialization that would affect elite and non-elite members of the cohort alike.

In previous work, I have observed that black elites born after the civil rights movement approach politics differently. In general, they tend to embrace deracialized campaign tactics more than their older counterparts and are more ambitious. While strategy plays a key element in their tactical decisions, for parts of this new cohort of black leadership, deracialization is a core political value. Some of this cohort were not mentored by older black leaders and were socialized outside of traditional black political communities. We should not expect that they would frame issues or present themselves as candidates in the same way as previous cohorts of black political leadership (Gillespie 2009; Gillespie 2010).

In addition, while race is still clearly salient to most blacks, there is evidence that blacks are cognizant of class differences within the racial community. In 2007, the Pew Center released a poll in which 61 percent of blacks agreed with the idea that middle- and lower-class blacks had dissimilar values. In 2009, while America was in the throes of a Great Recession that disproportionately affected blacks, there was noticeably less agreement with that question, but a majority of blacks (53%) still agreed with the notion that middle- and lower-class blacks were different. These findings would not come as a surprise to Adolph Reed, who for years has argued that black politics has consistently marginalized the interests of poor blacks in favor of more bourgeois advocacy (Pew Center 2007, 1; Pew Center 2010, 14; Reed 2000, chapter 1).

Where Do We Go from Here? A Call for Specialization

The previous overview highlights the dynamic, complex nature of black politics at the dawn of the twenty-first century. Blacks are unified, yet diverse. They still grasp for equality, yet they are more pragmatic in their approach. They seek self-determination, yet they are not completely autonomous. Given these conditions, it would seem that now, more than ever, it would be more challenging to realize the goal of black liberation.

Paradoxically, though, recognizing the diversity of black interest creates new opportunities for the creation of a more robust black leadership cadre that more accurately reflects the diversity of the African American community. At the end of *Behind the Mule*, Michael Dawson predicts that the linked fate that he observed among blacks in the 1980s could give way to "two black movements" in the face of increased racism and widening intraracial class stratification (Dawson 1994, 210). To some, the notion of two black Americas connotes a division of strength and the potential weakening of black interests. However, if blacks were to actively organize around race and their other salient identities, I believe that there is the potential to create more targeted, effective advocacy.

While Walters acknowledged the diversity within the African American community, he viewed black liberation as a public good, to be shared equally by all blacks. As such, he prioritized intraracial political cohesion: "Cultural diversity is a fact of existence for any large group; however, when that group engages in competition within the political system as a group to attain its basic objectives, the *utmost political unity* is required" (Smith and Walters 1999, 215, original emphasis). If we choose to define discrimination and the fight against it in the broadest terms, then Walters' normative strategy of attack makes perfect sense. However, if we acknowledge, as critical race theorists have proffered for two decades now, that discrimination cuts differently depending on a person's additional marginal identities (see Crenshaw 1991), then we have to acknowledge that competing interests within the African American community may require a certain level of factionalism and specialization in order to properly represent the interests of a wider swath of the community.

Outlining Specialization

What type of factionalism do I propose? Simply put, while there are issues of common concern for nearly all blacks, there is enough heterogeneity within the African American community to warrant the creation of specialized lobbies with their own indigenous leadership. Discrimination looks different depending on the circumstances of the victim. We must acknowledge the qualitative differences in how discrimination manifests itself within the black middle class and the black poor, among black men and black women, between blacks in rural areas and blacks in inner cities, and across countless other identity cleavages. These subgroups perceive different strains of racism, have different needs and goals, and will likely need to employ different strategies in order to seek relief from their suffering.

A call for factionalism will undoubtedly be accompanied by concerns. Are there not issues that cut across class, gender, or orientation cleavages? Should civil rights organizations and black leaders model empathy within the black community and embrace the concerns of the doubly marginalized within their ranks, even if they believe that their issues do not affect them or most blacks directly? The answer to both of these questions is yes. However, the reality is that they do not. Cathy Cohen has ably documented how religious constraints, outright homophobia, and fear of retribution from the Reagan administration silenced the civil rights establishment on issues related to HIV/AIDS for the first decade of the AIDS crisis. Implicit in Walters' discussion of the failure of the National

Black Leadership Roundtable is the idea that the organization was so broad that it became unwieldy. It was difficult to create a cohesive agenda, and subsidiary organizations had a difficult time buying into the mission of the roundtable. This discussion echoes Robert Smith's analysis of the 1972 Gary Convention, which broke down in part because the interests of black radicals could not be reconciled with the interests of black officeholders and the leaders of mainstream civil rights organizations (Cohen 1999; Smith and Walters 1999, 217; Smith 1996, chapter 2).

Given the failure of black activists and elected officials to cohere beyond a targeted campaign to end broad-based, codified discrimination historically, it is highly unlikely that this type of factionalism will abate. It would make more sense to acknowledge the impasses and devise a new tactical framework that would help to maximize the representation of as many subgroups within the African American community as possible.

This new tactical framework involves rethinking the internal structure of civil rights efforts as well as external alliance strategies. As much as possible, these organizations should recruit from the grassroots and cultivate indigenous leadership with firsthand knowledge of the issues. For instance, people who have been poor are more effective representatives of poverty interests than affluent suburbanites who have never missed a meal. Someone who grew up on a farm is probably less familiar with the challenges facing inner-city dwellers and vice versa. Indigenous experts should be allowed to bring their experiences to bear to help identify problems and craft solutions.

Moreover, a factionalized interest structure should not preclude alliances within and outside of the black community. In fact, this type of structure more clearly embodies the original goal of the Congressional Black Caucus to have "no permanent friends, no permanent enemies—only permanent interests" (Singh 1998, xvi). Different subgroups will often find common ground to work on consensus issues that affect blacks across cleavage lines. Additionally, subgroup interests may find it normatively appropriate to show solidarity with other subgroups and embrace issues that on the surface appear to be tangential to their interests. They should feel free to join advocacy forces with other subgroups to achieve goals of mutual interest.

Addressing Concerns

On the surface, there are three concerns with this proposal. Critics will likely counter that the faction proposal creates a new form of essentialism by suggesting that only certain types of black people can represent certain types of black interests. Let me be clear: just as there is ample evidence that white legislators can represent black interests (see Swain 1993), there is nothing theoretically stopping a black person from one segment of the black community learning about and embracing the interests of blacks with an entirely different lived experience. Those who reach across cleavages and learn about the issues can be effective advocates. However, this does not always happen. The more common practice is for black leaders to either claim to represent all of the interests of the black community when they really represent only a portion of the community or to mask their parochial interests under the guise of catch-all racial populism (see Reed 2000, chapter 1).

In addition, there is a risk that some interests will still remain underrepresented or not represented at all. It would be unrealistic to assume that in a much more transparent environment where subgroups seek to organize around particular interests that some subgroups would have more access to resources and decision makers and thus be in a better position to have their demands met than other subgroups (see Cohen 1999). This is a valid concern. However, the proposed solution is still better than the status quo. As Walters showed in his case study of the National Black Leadership Roundtable, the attempt at broadening the agenda stymied the organization's effort and accomplished little. Allowing groups to specialize on achieving their own interests might actually allow something to happen, and it does not preclude creating subgroup alliances based on solidarity.

The biggest concern with implementing this proposal will be assessing the risk that fragmentation or specialization will leave blacks as a whole more vulnerable to the types of exploitation that will undermine all of the civil rights gains of the past fifty years. Walters was particularly concerned about such a possibility when he voiced his misgivings about younger, deracialized blacks being groomed for elected leadership so that mainstream legislators would no longer feel compelled to take the demands of more activist-oriented black leadership seriously (Martin 2003, 56). This is a legitimate concern, but as Walters' comments in 2003 indicate, the current consensus model of black politics has been unable to prevent the potential for this type of exploitation.

Would more transparent political factions within the African American community make politicians more susceptible to cooptation and exploitation? This is a testable question that should be explored. For now, though, we must consider the irony that factionalism might actually create greater accountability for black activists and elected leaders.

In any politically relevant minority constituency, there will always be instrumental individuals who seek political leadership for their own self-aggrandizement. The African American community is not immune from such grandstanders. While there is a legitimate concern that a more diffuse black body politic would amplify and support the self-serving efforts of self-appointed leaders, in reality, the process of recognizing disparate black factions and giving legitimate voice to their concerns through grassroots cultivation might actually help to distinguish the posers from the true leaders. In Adolph Reed's critique of Jesse Jackson Sr.'s 1984 presidential campaign, he indicted Jackson as being a leader without a constituency. Reed was clearly biased toward elected leadership being the only legitimate type of leadership, but he had a larger point. He argued that Jackson was an ordained minister without a congregation and the leader of a nonprofit advocacy group with no real membership base. In Reed's view, Jackson chose to run as a long shot for a national office instead of running for a local office he could win so he could present himself to the mainstream media as a spokesman for blacks (Reed 1986).

Moving toward a model of organized black political factions—if done correctly—could alleviate Reed's general concerns about self-aggrandizing leadership. If constituencies organize their own interest groups and select their own leaders through a democratic process, it may be harder for self-promoters to claim the spotlight. Yes, in an era of checkbook advocacy, it is easy for people to create nonprofits and thus claim a constituency. But the ease of doing so only underscores the importance of verifying claims. Anytime a leader claims a constituency, scholars and journalists have the responsibility to corroborate those claims. Does this "leader" have a following? How many members are in his or her organization? Does the organization have a real infrastructure, or are the members completely passive actors? Are there metrics by which to judge an organization's effectiveness or its leader's effectiveness or level of engagement with the community he or she claims to lead, and what does the data show?

The near unanimous support for Democratic candidates in the African American community obscures the sophistication that black voters employ when selecting candidates. As primary and general election results in 2010 demonstrated, black voters do make distinctions between black candidates, and their vote choices reveal discernible preferences about how they want to see black elected officials behave. Black voters in Washington, D.C. repudiated Mayor Adrian Fenty's perceived neglect of Southeast Washington and his allowing (in their view) D.C. public schools chancellor Michelle Rhee to run roughshod over the interests of teachers and parents in her restructuring of the public school system. And in Alabama, black voters held Congressman Artur Davis' opposition to the Obama health care initiative against him when he sought the Democratic Party's nomination for governor (Craig and Stewart 2010; Dean 2010). Regardless of whether one agrees with the logic employed by these voters, it is clear that black voters do not accept any and all forms of leadership. And at least in the electoral realm, there are imperfect mechanisms in place to hold officials accountable when they act against voters' salient interests.

In reality, both Fenty and Davis might have found greater success in other communities (though I should note that they are both native sons of the jurisdictions they represented). Their failure underscores the reality that not all black leaders are suited to serve all types of black communities. Sometimes a person's disposition and policy interests are incongruent with the political culture of the community they aspire to lead. Attempting to enforce a unified black body politic may obscure this harsh reality and place undue pressure on black candidates to conform to unnatural political postures that do not accentuate their best gifts. The reality is, some black leaders should not represent black communities, though they can support the interests of racial uplift through their support of legislation and initiatives that would improve the lives of blacks.

Specialization and Descriptive Representation

Embracing the idea of multiple black constituencies actually creates a place for exotic black leaders within the larger black polity and may serve to increase black descriptive representation. Jones and Clemons noted in 1993 that, at least a far as congressional redistricting went, it would be very difficult to increase black descriptive representation by drawing new majority-minority districts. At that time, they recognized that fielding deracialized black candidates in majority-minority districts was key to increasing black representation in Congress. Considering that Jones and Clemons wrote this before the passage of Supreme Court cases like *Shaw v. Reno* (1993), which deemed explicitly race conscious districting unconstitutional, their analysis is even more relevant (Jones and Clemons 1993).

Here is how this would work. Having descriptive representatives who do not represent the substantive interests of any segment of the black community is an undesirable prospect. Currently, though, there is little evidence to suggest that even the most deracialized black Democrats (i.e., the young politicians with the most tenuous ties to the black political establishment) support policies that are intrinsically opposed to the preferences of most black citizens (Congressman Davis' vote against health care notwithstanding). In their analysis of Jesse Jackson Jr.'s tenure in office, Randolph Burnside and Antonio Rodriguez found that the youngest black members of the 108th Congress (i.e., those born after 1960) were on the whole more conservative than their oldest, most deracialized colleagues. However, if we compare the voting records of black members of Congress across generational lines in the 110th Congress, we find nearly uniform voting for civil rights issues (as defined by the Leadership Conference on Civil Rights) among black members of Congress, regardless of their age or political demeanor (Burnside and Rodriguez 2010, 97; Leadership Conference on Civil Rights 2008, 18–35).[2] When the issue of whether Barack Obama's exotic upbringing disqualified him as a true race leader, Ron Walters defended the future president's civil rights bona fides by citing his progressive legislative record in the Illinois Senate (Walters 2007).

At least for the current cohort of deracialized politicians, this suggests that there is little reason to not encourage some politicians to specialize in winning elections in nonblack jurisdictions. They can be educated about black interests and policy preferences and held accountable by their peers through existing social networks such as the Congressional Black Caucus or the National Conference of Black Mayors.[3] While there is always the possibility that blacks who have no sense of how the history of discrimination affects contemporary politics will win office, in the short term at least, the voting records of the deracialized, Democratic set indicate that this is not an immediate concern.

Moreover, there may be evidence that black voters are strategic in their support of different types of black candidates at different levels of government. In her analysis of black support for Barack Obama in Illinois in his failed 2000 congressional race and in his successful 2004 senate race, Lorrie Frasure found evidence of what she termed "Jekyll and Hyde politics" (Frasure 2010, 136). Black voters had different levels of tolerance for Barack Obama's deracialized affect depending on the office for which he ran. When Obama ran against a more racialized candidate at the congressional level, voters expressed their preference for racialized leadership. However, many of these same voters recognized that Obama's deracialized persona was an asset to him as a statewide candidate. Thus, the professorial airs that were a disadvantage to Obama at the congressional district level were a huge help to him on a statewide ballot (Frasure 2010).

Specialization and the Insider-Outsider Strategy

Specialization also takes advantage of existing biases about black leaders both inside and outside the black community. Walters got at this idea in his discussion of legitimacy in chapter 10 of *African American Leadership*. In his construct, some potential leaders derived their authority from their support within black communities but had little credibility outside of their communities. For others, the exact opposite was true: they were warmly embraced outside of the black community but treated as suspect within it. There were some black leaders who enjoyed the respect of both black and nonblack citizens. Finally, there were those self-appointed leaders who are only legitimate to themselves (Smith and Walters 1999, 217).

Walters recognized that consensus leaders, or those who had earned the respect of both blacks and nonblacks, were in the ideal position to lead (Smith and Walters 1999, 217–18). His conclusion makes sense. However, with cunning and coordination, internal and consensus leaders can work together to play a vital role in helping to advance the interests of diverse numbers of blacks. Internal leaders can leverage their legitimacy within black communities to hold office within majority-minority jurisdictions. Most important, though, they can lead advocacy groups and stage protests that prime national attention to issues and place pressure on other consensus and external officials (especially those representing nonblack constituencies) to address the concerns of black communities.

Critics of deracialization have long raised the concern that deemphasizing race hamstrings candidates from effectively addressing racial concerns once in office. They note that deracialized politicians walk a delicate tightrope trying to keep their diverse constituency happy; they risk alienating vital parts of their constituency if they neglect one subgroup's issues of concern or appear to show policy favoritism toward another subgroup (see McCormick and Jones 1993, 77–78). That balancing act, though, could be made easier by the protest activities of other black activists representing other sectors of the community. As Walters articulated in his insider-outsider strategy (see Smith and Walters 1999, 135), protest activity can raise the profile of issues of importance to blacks such that elected officials have to address them. The media focus on the civil rights movement in the 1960s helped to engender sympathy among whites and Northerners for the plight of black Southerners. Though the media environment has changed and is more polarized, we need to give serious exploration to using protests to raising the profile of black issues among multiracial, liberal constituencies and the people who represent them.

Conclusion

Ron Walters was arguably the most astute strategist studying African American politics. More than a decade before his death, he predicted that the increased diversity within the black community would strain efforts for black activists and politicians to coordinate their efforts for the sake of black improvement. Professor Walters' instincts led him to push readers and practitioners to remember the unity imperative. Now that his predictions have come true though, I wonder if it might be best to navigate the waters of diversity in order to craft a strategy that seeks redress but honors the myriad, diverse interests within the African American community.

To that end, I have proposed formally acknowledging differences within black communities and organizing around those differences. In a perfect world, people respect others' different perspectives and seek common ground, but even in black communities, some interests still win out over others. It is impractical at this point to deny the misrepresentation of interests and the unequal allocation of resources within black communities. Formally acknowledging differences and encouraging organization along those cleavage lines frees black leaders from having to feign interest in issues they are ill equipped to represent. And hopefully, it will allow for the rise of indigenous advocacy that serves to advance the cause of self-determination.

I am under no illusions that my proposal will completely solve the problem of the underrepresentation of certain black interests. And I am forever mindful that if Professor Walters were alive, he would probably passionately argue against my proposal. However, I think black politics has matured to the point that we can at least acknowledge the shortcomings of the big tent model. Nothing in this proposal proscribes the creation of cross-subgroup alliances to create solidarity across cleavage lines. At best, my proposal should at least compel subgroups to compete openly instead of subversively undermining the interests of certain groups under the guise of unity.

Moreover, the electoral component of the plan should reap positive externalities for black elected leadership. The current model privileges blacks running in black districts even if the political culture and values of the district and candidate are not congruent. My proposal encourages aspiring black leaders to try to lead communities that actually value their leadership. The upside of this should increase black descriptive representation, and as long as most blacks (including these leaders) profess a belief in linked fate, then it is possible to use informal social networks and protest strategies to elicit the support of these important actors.

Notes

1. It should be noted that blacks in general are more supportive of vouchers than black elected officials (Bositis 2001, 29).

2. Keep in mind that there were no black Republicans in the 110th Congress.
3. While we must envision a day when black Democrats opt to not join these organizations, this time has not yet come. Moreover, a majority of blacks still report feelings of linked fate. There is little evidence to suggest that even prominent deracialized black politicians, despite their flaws, would not respond to appeals to racial solidarity (see Mack 2011).

References

AU News. 2008. "Much-hyped Turnout Record Fails to Materialize; Convenience Voting Fails to Boost Balloting." Press Release. American University. Washington, DC. November 6.

Bositis, David. 2001. *Changing the Guard: Generational Differences among Black Elected Officials.* Washington, DC: Joint Center for Political and Economic Studies.

Burnside, Randolph, and Antonio Rodriguez. 2010. "Like Father, Like Son? Jesse Jackson Jr.'s Tenure as a US Congressman." In *Whose Black Politics? Cases in Postracial Black Leadership,* ed. Andra Gillespie, 87–104. New York: Routledge.

Cohen, Cathy. 1999. *The Boundaries of Blackness: AIDS and the Breakdown of Black Politics.* Chicago: University of Chicago Press.

Cose, Ellis. 2011. *The End of Anger: A New Generation's Take on Race and Rage.* New York: Ecco.

Craig, Tim, and Nikita Stewart. 2010. "Gray Defeats Fenty as Voters Choose Conciliatory Approach Over Brash Tactics." *Washington Post.* September 15.

Crenshaw, Kimberlé Williams. 1991. "Mapping the Margins: Intersectionality, Identity and Violence against Women of Color." *Stanford Law Review* 43, 6: 1241–99.

Curry, George. 2006. "Bruce Gordon Hits It on the Numbers." *Chicago Defender.* July 12.

Dawson, Michael. 1994. *Behind the Mule.* Princeton: Princeton University Press.

Dean, Chuck. 2010. "Artur Davis' Loss in Alabama's Black Precincts 'Stunning.'" *The Birmingham News.* June 3. Retrieved from http://blog.al.com/spotnews/2010/06/davis_loss_in_black_precincts.html, accessed November 4, 2010.

Frasure, Lorrie. 2010. "The Burden of Jekyll and Hyde: Barack Obama, Racial Identity and Black Political Behavior." In *Whose Black Politics? Cases in Postracial Black Leadership*, ed. Andra Gillespie, 133–54. New York: Routledge.

Gillespie, Andra. 2009. "The Third Wave: A Theoretical Introduction to the Post–Civil Rights Generation of African American Leadership. *National Political Science Review*. 12(1): 139–161.

Gillespie, Andra. 2010. "Meet the New Class: Theorizing Young Black Leadership in a 'Postracial' Era." In *Whose Black Politics? Cases in Postracial Black Leadership*, ed. Andra Gillespie, 9–42.. New York: Routledge.

Jones, Charles E., and Michael Clemons. 1993. "A Model of Racial Crossover Voting: An Assessment of the Wilder Victory." In *Dilemmas of Black Politics*, ed. Georgia Persons, 128–46. New York: Harper Collins.

Leadership Conference on Civil Rights. 2008. *LCCR Voting Record: 110th United States Congress*. Washington: Leadership Conference on Civil Rights.

Mack, Brianna. 2011. "Where Did the Mule Go? Analyzing Linked Fate Trends Within the 40 and Under Black Population." Unpublished Manuscript Submitted to the Ralph Bunche Summer Institute (Duke University). July 2.

Martin, Roland. 2003. "Ready or Not . . ." *Savoy* (March): 52–56.

McCormick, Joseph, II, and Charles E. Jones. 1993. "The Conceptualization of Deracialization: Thinking Through the Dilemma." In *Dilemmas of Black Politics*, ed. Georgia Persons, 66–84. New York: Harper Collins.

Pew Research Center. 2007. *Optimism about Black Progress Declines*. Monograph. Washington: Pew Research Center.

Pew Center. 2010. "A Year after Obama's Election: Blacks Upbeat about Black Progress, Prospects." Monograph. Washington: Pew Research Center.

Putnam, Robert D. 2000. *Bowling Alone: The Collapse and Revival of American Community*. New York: Touchstone Books.

Reed, Adolph. 1986. *The Jesse Jackson Phenomenon*. New Haven: Yale University Press.

Reed, Adolph. 2000. *Class Notes*. New York: The New Press.

Robinson, Eugene. 2010. *Disintegration: The Splintering of Black America*. New York: Doubleday.

Singh, Robert. 1998. *The Congressional Black Caucus: Racial Politics in the US Congress.* Thousand Oaks: Sage Publications.

Smith, Robert C. 1996. *We Have No Leaders.* Albany: State University of New York Press.

Smith, Robert C., and Ronald Walters. 1999. *African American Leadership.* Albany: State University of New York Press.

Swain, Carol M. 1993. *Black Faces, Black Interests: The Representation of African Americans in Congress.* Cambridge: Harvard University Press.

Tate, Katherine. 2010. *What's Going On? Political Incorporation and the Transformation of Black Public Opinion.* Washington: Georgetown University Press.

Touré. *Who's Afraid of Post-Blackness? What It Means to Be Black Now.* New York: Free Press.

Walters, Ron. 2007. "Barack Obama and the Politics of Blackness." *Journal of Black Studies* 38: 7–29.

Wilson, James Q. 1995. *Political Organizations.* Princeton: Princeton University Press.

7

Still Walters Runs Deep

Synthesizing Ronald Walters' Theses on
Black Leadership and Black Nationalism

ERROL HENDERSON

Introduction

The work of very few scholars occupies pride of place in both academic and applied settings; that is, in the domain of both theory and practice. It is even less likely when the area of academic interest is African American/black politics, given that scholarship on black politics for most political scientists is on electoral politics, while scholarship on grassroots activist politics typically has been the domain of historians and sociologists (Wilson 1985). Professor Ronald Walters' scholarship comprises a body of work that consists of the informed analyses of a highly skilled and seasoned scholar as well as the passionate and committed concerns of a political activist. Dr. Walters' work represents a deep current in black politics and American politics, more generally. While his research spans issues from black electoral politics in the United States, to Pan-African thought in the African diaspora, to U.S. foreign policy and Africa, he has been particularly incisive in describing, explaining, and predicting the challenges and opportunities, successes and failures, occasioned by the struggles involving adherents and detractors of diverse ideological, theoretical, strategic, organizational, and institutional thrusts within the civil rights movement, the black power movement, and the subsequent era of "new politics" and "crossover politics."

While the current of Professor Walters' work runs deep in political science, in this essay, I focus on the confluence of two particular research streams: black leadership and black nationalism. Walters' analysis of black leadership is aimed at integrating a range of theses on the goals, methods, and rhetoric of black political leaders, and his major contribution (coauthored with Robert Smith in 1983 and revised in 1999) is an excellent engagement of this research (Walters and Smith 1999).[1] This work, while proffering an analytical framework for evaluating black leadership is descriptive, analytical, and prescriptive, and represents part of an ongoing and evolving attempt to provide a relevant framework for understanding both black leadership and black politics within the intellectual hegemony of mainstream, predominantly white, academia. His earlier analysis of black nationalism is much more oriented toward theoretical synthesis (Walters 1973). Interestingly, this drive toward theoretical synthesis with respect to black nationalism emerged largely from the exigencies of his work with the National Black Political Assembly (NBPA), one of the most important political formations emerging from the black power movement, and his attempt to moderate the conflicting tendencies within the NBPA in the early seventies. Both areas of research speak to and reinforce each other and the broader scholarly and activist communities in interesting ways that I will outline in this essay.

The remainder of this essay proceeds in five sections. First, I delineate several prominent contours in Walters' framework of black leadership, which rests on his conception of black politics. Second, I discuss how Walters' approach to black leadership in the context of his political activism led him to proffer a "modernized" version of black nationalism, which was intended to be more inclusive and to serve as a template for black political organizing in the NBPA. Third, I assess Walters' attempt to synthesize several prominent tendencies within the activist community, namely, nationalist and integrationist orientations under a single rubric. While this early attempt was problematic, it pointed the direction for a richer examination of the prominent black political ideologies and it was suggestive of the need for theoretical synthesis of the dynamics of ideological differences and shifts among the national black leadership. Fourth, I wed Walters' attempt at theoretical and pragmatic synthesis with Cruse's "pendulum thesis" to show the usefulness of Walters' explication of black leadership and black nationalism for further study of both phenomena. Fifth, and finally, I conclude with a summary of the main points of this essay.

Black Leadership

For Walters (1992), black leadership is grounded in black politics, which is characterized by the African American's struggle for power and racial uplift in a context of white supremacist institutions of power and privilege. Although white supremacy may take different forms, its consistency is rooted in its privileging of white power and its exercise of that power throughout the various communities within the United States. Black politics focuses on the competition for resources and adherents among black leaders and their organizations within black communities and in their interaction with other communities in the United States. Walters observes that black leadership does not simply emerge from or respond to a commonality of struggle against white supremacy, but more fundamentally it represents and reflects a commonality of culture of black people within the United States. He states that "the coherence of the Black community in particular is held together both by the forces of racial oppression as well as a history of common experiences and the evolution of a distinct shared culture" (145). It is further assumed that similar conditions and common culture breed similar orientations, which is a view that Walters would utilize in his analysis of the similarities in Pan-Africanist orientations throughout the diaspora, as well (Walters 1993). The objective of black politics is "to challenge institutionalized practices of racism and to foment the necessary changes in behavior that would result in the fair dispensation of goods, services, and principles" in the United States (Walters and Smith 1999, 202). Further, "a major goal of black politics" is to "develop institutionalized political power," as well as to establish "strong, progressive, and change-oriented" national political institutions. Black politics, for Walters, does not eschew coalitions, nor does it necessitate or favor an exclusive focus on blacks, but it suggests that "interracial political alliances and coalitions should be made with a bias toward progressive, reform-oriented whites, in keeping with the needs of the black community" while "black leaders should attempt to see that all who were under their perview (*sic*) benefited," even as "black needs were to be attended to as a priority" (202).

Walters notes that black leadership has "proceeded from the collective interests and concerns of people of African descent—including involvement in historical events defined by a 'racial uplift' tradition, and leadership to overcome the impediments to the full enjoyment of every aspect of American life (such as slavery, prejudice and discrimination, institutional racism, and any pattern of exclusion or racial inferiorization of Black humanity)" (Walters and Smith 1999, 122). Black leadership, in Walters' view, has "relied on social rather than economic resources because of the transfer of Black capital to Whites in the process of slavery." This leadership has "diversified into many different professions, political institutions, and arenas" (122). Following Holden (1973), Walters insists that black leadership has presided over a "black quasi-government" that is comprised of various enduring as well as more short-lived but prominent organizations and institutions having a national following characterized primarily by their service to the affairs of the black community, broadly defined (105). This leadership has been and continues to be both individual and collective. The primary objective of this leadership has been to facilitate "uplift" for black peoples, which over the history of black America has focused on issues of freedom, justice, and equality in a context of white supremacism.

Walters observes two prominent black leadership strategies. First, to utilize black politics

> to obtain the right to participate, which called for the use of a *tactic* of integration at one level, but which also was a *strategy* to define or redefine the character of American society altogether. This often called for such tactics as individual or collective protest, legal representation in the courts, or legislative strategies in order to acquire the necessary public policies that were important to empowerment. (117).

Second, black leadership sought to expand on the success of previous struggle such that once participation was secured, they attempted to "utilize it for the benefit of the Black community primarily. Exercising societal leadership in either the private sphere, for example, as head of major foundations, or in the public sphere as a publicly elected representative carr[ying] the responsibility to manage the interests of both the African American community and other groups as well" (117). Importantly, Walters insists that "as the end of the twentieth-century approaches, it is still the case, as determined by a wide variety of measures, that racism constitutes the major impediment to the forward progress of African Americans in the United States" (97). He adds that "although other powerful factors impinge on Black life-chances—such as the changes in the nature of the American economy with the rapid impact of technology on the process of production and thus, on fitness for the labor force and the globalization of the availability of productive work—the most damaging factor that compounds the effect of these is racism" (97).

While racism may be viewed as the greatest external challenge to black leadership, Walters does not ignore potential internal challenges to black leadership. For example, he along with Smith agree that although "Black leadership behavior is a function of factors external to the community," nevertheless, "two endogenous factors—class and culture—are also theoretically suggestive" (66). But Walters and Smith challenge the claim that an "unprecedented class conflict" is evident between the black middle class and the black underclass, an argument which they assert is "without scientific foundation." They note that while "there is some evidence of a leadership-mass cleavage on political methods, with the masses favoring more militant actions," nevertheless, "in terms of basic beliefs and policy preferences, one finds fundamental unity in the Black community at all class levels, and between the leadership and the masses in support of the ideology and policies of *liberal integration*" (66–67, emphasis added). These views seem quite inconsistent with more recent works that suggest that class differences are evident among blacks with respect to a variety of factors including issues such as ideological orientation (e.g., see Dawson 1994; Hochschild 1996; Brown and Shaw 2002). What is key is that the authors' contention about the relative insignificance of class is limited to the support of liberal integrationism, which continues to find widespread support across economic class within black communities. Appreciating the specific focus of the authors, they contend that

the theoretical insignificance of class in black politics is limited. This is not to deny that there are differences of sentiment, ethos, and opinion in Black America between the leadership and the masses. Rather, it is to suggest that these differences do not constitute class "antagonisms." Indeed, the class factor in studies of Black leadership may be best construed as an aspect of culture. While specialists disagree as to whether the Black community constitutes a separate and distinct political subculture . . . the data are unmistakable that there are significant differences between Black and White Americans in terms of their level of support for the system, their level of trust in the system, and political knowledge and efficacy. (Walters and Smith 1999, 67)

Notwithstanding the debate about the salience of class or political culture in the internal dynamics of black politics, it is clear that the prominent frame of reference that Walters relies on in explicating black politics is the race dominance/power approach. Through this analytical lens, Walters traces the various strategies that have been employed by black leadership to address the challenges faced by African Americans. Appreciating the dynamic nature of black politics, he also traces shifts in strategy prevalent among black political leadership. He notes, for example, that "recently, there have been three distinct periods of such shifts; the first of these occurred in the 1957–60 period with the civil rights movement, the second in 1966–67 with the Black Liberation/Pan African Movement and the third, in 1970–72, with the move toward Black electoral politics," which would reach its climax in the presidential runs of Jesse Jackson in 1984 and 1988 in which Walters played a prominent role (126). He notes that "in each of these periods the seeds of various movements existed simultaneously, although one would emerge as the dominant force in Black political strategy and ultimately gain prominence over that which preceded it" (126).

One of the major conclusions of Walters' research is that the incorporation of blacks in U.S. society has not been complete and, in fact, has stalled. He argues that

one of the salient issues is the continuing evidence of the practice of Black exclusion from many arenas of American life and active marginalization in most of those areas where they have been incorporated. This is reflected in the persistence of many Black organizations of an amazing variety; in the extent to which local and national Black leaders continue to sponsor "summits" and attempt to develop and implement "Black agendas" in their field of expertise; and in the empirical evidence . . . that there is a necessity for leaders to overcome negative conditions by the use of power. (p. 241)

But Walters is not simply concerned with incorporation; he is concerned to a much greater extent with the development of black political autonomy. For him, "an autonomous status of Black people in the United States would warrant an autonomous leadership class and structure similar to that enjoyed by White Americans." However, he contends that historically

this posture for the group was clearly impossible and thus, the Black leadership in the nineteenth century was caught on the horns of a dilemma as the most effective strategy for the expression of Black autonomy was remission back to Africa, and yet the consensus was to remain in the United States. This contradiction and the consensus that emerged led to the establishment of a highly integrative posture as the dominant political objective of the Black community, which the leadership tend[ed] to reflect in their practice, seeking "upward elevation" and successful entry into the mainstream of American society. As such, the continuing acceptance of the integrative ideology—even in the face of its substantial rejection by the majority in practice—defines the Black leadership crucible and its class.

It follows for Walters that "the nature of [black leadership's] political strategies must constantly take into consideration the etiquette of incorporation, a large element of which is the sensibilities and positions of the majority since it's their control over institutions and the political decisions within them that must be influenced to effectuate change" (243). These relationships are even evident in present discussions of the sine qua non of black politics: racism.

That is, there is an immediate challenge when one attempts to define racism in U.S. society, because a system of white racism persists in the United States that acts to prevent those within it from recognizing it, confronting it, indicting it, and therefore, changing it. Scholars analyzing racism in the United States are often confronted with the task of defining the concept in ways that do not offend extant racist sensibilities and institutions. In this context racists, themselves, have defined their racism out of existence through the creation of a "nonracist" discourse that obscures racist practices that persist in the society and instead targets relatively powerless expressions of bigotry among minority communities as more appropriate targets of state action. In such a context, mainstream scholars and policymakers willfully pervert definitions of terms such as racism in order to "deracialize," "naturalize," and "marginalize" white supremacism, which is at the core of U.S. society while often indicting as "racists" those who call this racist order into question (Henderson 2007).

Walters adds that

> thus, the radical solutions—and those who prefer them, because they have challenged both the notion and the etiquette of incorporation—have always been avoided, even deprecated by the mainstream leadership class. This is the source of their antipathy with Black nationalist, Marxist revolutionary, and other radical prescriptions for change. Nevertheless, with a substantially lessened concern for this etiquette, one might argue that strategies could be bolder and more flexible, but then, the leadership resource base would have to change to match the size and content of their ideas. (243)

Here Walters has struck at the heart of the issue: Black leadership as long as it seeks the acceptance of white racist mainstream political institutions and organizations while reducing black politics to interest group or "crossover" politics must be confronted and counterbalanced by reasoned, resolute, transformative, that is, "radical" alternatives deriving from the concrete challenges confronting the black masses. Therefore, integrationist strategies should be confronted with nationalist ones, patriarchal strategies with feminist ones, and elitist strategies with grassroots ones. It is important that these countervailing ideologies derive from the concrete reality facing the masses of black people and that the tendencies do not become ensconced in essentialist or vanguardist orientations. This view is consistent with Walters' admonition that it is "urgent that the focus of effective leadership continue to be addressed, not only to government but more emphatically directly to the local African American communities" such that "the critical issues that emerge necessitate the development of action strategies employing to a maximum degree the energy and skills of trained and dedicated leaders and followers" (244).

From his insightful analysis of black leadership and black politics, he states as his aim to determine and outline "those minimal issues that might facilitate the achievement of an effective unity among Black leaders both operationally and structurally" (p. 244). But here, Professor Walters succumbs to the siren call of the black unity thesis, which undermines many black nationalist endeavors. Black political unity is a chimera given that the competing ideological tendencies among blacks suggest not only very different objectives and strategies to attain them, but these differences are both historically grounded and evident today. They do not only represent abstract theoretical propositions on leadership, but in some cases they reflect the vested and entrenched interests of institutions and organizations articulating widely divergent ideologies from the NAACP, the Urban League, the mainstream black churches, on one hand to the Universal Negro Improvement Association (UNIA), Nation of Islam, the Pan African Organizing Committee (PAOC), or the Republic of New Africa (RNA) on the other. Robert Smith (1996) elaborated on the perilous pursuit of unity in his *We Have No Leaders*. The primacy of unity as a major objective of black leadership and the view that a common history of oppression should yield a common political ideology have rarely served as adequate foundations for comprehensive political praxis on a national scale. The problems inherent in such endeavors are evident in Walters' (1973) earlier attempt to reconcile the separate and conflicting ideological tendencies that were tearing at the fabric of unity in the NBPA. Key to this attempt at synthesis was his analysis of black nationalism.

Black Nationalism

In his "African-American Nationalism: Toward a Unifying Ideology," Walters attempted to demonstrate the underlying unity of several variants of racial uplift under the rubric of black nationalism, which although a major organizing force at the Assembly, was actually waning in power as a prominent ideology given the emergent power of black elected officials and their mainly integrationist orientation (Henderson 2000). Another tendency that was evident was a neo-Marxist perspective that was Pan-Africanist in orientation and actually integrationist with respect to its mobilizational focus but saw itself aligned with an international working class more than with a black nation in the United States (though these could be—and often were—reconciled under Maoism). Walters focused on developing a unifying ideology of black nationalism as a key to salvaging the NBPA's political identity and creating a "big tent" under which several tendencies toward racial uplift could find a home—primarily the various nationalist and integrationist factions struggling for dominance. In "The New Black Political Culture" published in *Black World* in 1972, he had observed "the growing tension between the politics of 'mass mobilization' and 'brokerage politics' in the black community (6) and in some ways the NBPA was an institutional representation of the attempt to reconcile these tendencies given that it housed both. His stated purpose in his 1973 article was to "provide an ideological framework for unity without uniformity," and at the center of this task was his attempt at broadening the definition of black nationalism, which, in his opinion had been "defined so narrowly as to make it a dysfunctional code for the masses of black people" (9).

His synthesis rested on his contention that "it has been demonstrated time and time again that those elements used to define a distinct cultural group apply to Black people in America" (Walters 1972, 11). He added that "one of the more important of these" is the "heightened sense of group awareness, based on an increased sense of identity formulated out of an expanding appreciation of our indigenous historical and cultural heritage" (11). In addition, group awareness, in his view, emerged out of "personal and collective white exploitation" (11). He observed that "there has developed a strong and vibrant sense of Black national consciousness; and . . . there have been liberation strategies which have proceeded from the previous basic assumption" (19). Commonality of culture as well as commonality of oppression seemed to suggest a commonality of political action in the form of racial uplift, which could be articulated through a black nationalist framework; however, the version of black nationalism as construed by most of the participants in the debate in the NBPA was limited in several ways, which Walters' would make clear in proffering his "modernized" and "mature" version of black nationalism.

Some of these limitations derived from misconceptualizations of black nationalism itself. Walters faulted white scholars with promoting much of this misconceptualization, given their tendency to dismiss black nationalism. Walters noted that even as black political awareness was expanding, "whites continue to assume that there is no such thing as Black Nationalism, that it is a mirage, and that it can be defined out of existence by the pen of an itinerant sojourner into the realm of the Black experience" (11). Nevertheless, Walters recognized that there were limitations in the current conceptualization of black nationalism held by its proponents, themselves, as well as their black ideological counterparts. He noted that "one is struck by the fact that the theory of nationalism has not changed to encompass new forces which have influenced the character of the nation-state, since such innovations in the use of economic, military, and technological power ultimately must influence any modern definition of nationalism" (16). Walters proposed that "if one conceives of himself, from the perspective of his Blackness, as being involved in nation building activity, then he is by definition a nationalist" (20). For him, black consciousness is key to black nationalism, but he was emphatic that "black consciousness is not a substitute for nationalism; it is a prerequisite." He then differentiated between "land oriented" and "social justice" perspectives within black nationalism. He largely dismissed the former as "substantially a fantasy," which had the potential to "distort and confuse the nationalist movement as long as it believes it is operating solely within the classical tradition of other nationalist movements" (9). For him, the social justice oriented version of nationalism was more appropriate in light of the condition blacks faced in the United States and given that it focused less on a "struggle over land" and more on "a struggle for resources and justice."

Walters did not downplay the difficulty of deriving a clear policy and strategy from his mature nationalism. For example, he pointed out that land is a specific commodity and, therefore, its relationship to nationalist objectives is much more concrete and the ideology which flows from that fact usually more capable of illustration. Justice on the other hand, is an ambiguous commodity and subject to misinterpretation, or over-interpretation, or no consensual interpretation at all. How, for instance, will the leaders of the nationalist movement based on "justice" know when the objective has been achieved? And how difficult it must be to develop a consistent and rational ideology based in such a fluid and dynamic idea. Such an attempt might seem to the casual, or to the serious but misguided, observer to amount to no nationalism at all; however, the expressions of this nationalism . . . are as certain as those which attend more classic nationalist's thrusts with more concrete base[s]. (14)

Walters argued that "all groups which can be said to have adopted a serious program devoted to bettering the spiritual and material contributions of black life are nationalists" (21). The rationale for such an expansive reconceptualization of nationalism was his view that "the façade of nationalist and anti-nationalist elitism and exclusion must be broken through to form a workable coalition with nationalists and potential nationalists of all types in order that the goals of the black nation are elevated above the squabble over means" (1973, 21). However, in redefining nationalism in this way, it seemed that "nationalism, like integration, was in essence a struggle for parity or equality of black access to the resources of American society" and little else (Smith 1996, 58).

Walters' attempt to reconceptualize black nationalism was commendable insofar as it aimed to situate nationalism as a fundamental ideological construct within black liberation struggles in the United States. Nevertheless, critics exposed the difficulty of Walters' reconceptualization of black nationalism in this way and the attempt to explain away ideological differences as simply "squabbles over means." For example, in a fraternal but, nonetheless, trenchant critique (which Walters seemed to agree with given its inclusion in his 1999 [46] coauthored text), Smith (1996) noted that although a valiant and understandable effort to try to reassert the principle of "operational unity" by focusing on ultimate goals rather than means, Walters' effort failed both as an intellectual and a political proposition. He noted that, first, the conflict cannot be so neatly compartmentalized into goals that all blacks agree on with only minor "squabbles" over means. The two are often, in any ideology, inextricably bound. Thus, the essay begged the question of just what is "a serious program devoted to bettering the spiritual and material conditions of blacks." The Pan Africanists say it is focusing on the liberation of Africa, and the land-based separatists say it is not; the liberal integrationists say liberal reform capitalism is such a program, while the Marxists say it is not—and the list of competing ideological claims goes on and on and on. (59)

Smith analogizes Walters' conceptualization with that of Malcolm X in the latter's formulation of his "ballot or the bullet" thesis, which posited, *inter alia,* that the objectives of nationalists and integrationists were similar, that is, freedom, but only the means were different. Smith notes that "if this formulation was viable then there would be no ideological conflict, since all ideologies at this level of abstraction or generality may claim to have the ultimate goal of freedom but differ only over means. Thus, Mao Tse-tung and Ronald Reagan both have the goal of freedom, only Mao thinks communism is the means while Reagan thinks it's capitalism. No mere squabble over means" (59).

Walters' attempt to expand black nationalism in such a way as to incorporate divergent and even competing ideologies under its rubric was as problematic as the attempt to prioritize unity as a key element of black leadership—and by implication as a basic ordering principle of black politics—insofar as it minimized substantial ideological and practical tendencies among black communities, organizations, and constituents. Smith, again, recognized this problem and associated it with the failure of the NBPA and the "unity without uniformity" notion undergirding it—especially as it attempted, in Congressman John Conyers' words at the Little Rock NBPA convention to "bring together the broad spectrum of black political views to organize grassroots politics" (Smith 1996, 64). For Smith, Conyers' remarks reflected a fundamental flaw in black political organizing insofar as it was this "broad spectrum of black political views" that "made it virtually impossible to reach any kind of consensus about the [black political] party or anything else" (64).

Greater gains may have been garnered by an examination of the valences of the competing ideologies that Walters was attempting to wrestle with and to link his project of "modernizing" nationalism, with the insights offered by Cruse (1967) in his study of the challenge to black intellectuals of the historical alternations between black nationalist and black integrationist leadership in black politics at the national level. To be sure, Walters appreciated these alternations and the significant role of black nationalism in them and he would later observe that "indeed, the fact that there are historically the inevitable explosions of Black militant nationalism may lie in the inadequacy of the accommodationist, incorporation[i]st, racial-uplift ideology that . . . left intact the racist logic of Black pathology . . . because it either left the racial integrity ideologies to the designs of the Black nationalists or . . . reaffirmed the integrity of Black nationhood from a weak or defensive posture" (Walters and Smith 1999, 243–44). Moreover, his drive to reconcile the divergent tendencies within the NBPA in order to salvage the assembly were understandable and in some ways even remarkable given the heady context of the times in which he made the attempt and the significance of the struggle in which he was engaged; nevertheless, it may have been just as—if not more—important to focus on the alternating ideologies in order to grasp which was ascendant and which was in decline so that advocates of one or the other approach could exercise a strategic retreat and provide at least a nominal endorsement of the leadership of the alternative viewpoint in order to take advantage of the transformation evident among black leadership and black communities. At the time of Walters' attempt at reconciliation, black nationalists were actually in decline nationally relative to black integrationists as represented by the emerging class of black elected officials (BEOs) concentrated in the Democratic Party. This almost assured that Walters' attempt to synthesize the valences in the divergent black ideologies—namely, nationalism and integrationism—using black nationalism as the linchpin was likely to fail in an era of rising black integrationist influence.

But these issues were not simply operative during the 1970s, they would arise again for Walters (and for blacks in general) following his work with the Jesse Jackson campaign in which he witnessed the movement of the most prominent black nationalist organization at the time, Louis Farrakhan's Nation of Islam (NOI), into a supportive role vis-à-vis Jesse Jackson in the latter's run for the presidential nomination of the Democratic Party. In this case, the previously "apolitical" NOI that eschewed electoral politics recognized the political salience of Jackson's presidential runs and sought to heighten the profile and accessibility of their leader using Jackson's coattails. Within less than a decade, the prominent national ideology among black leadership would shift again and it would be Jackson clamoring for "face time" on what was clearly Farrakhan's national stage at the Million Man March (MMM) in Washington, D.C. in 1995. An appreciation of the processes at work in these ideological shifts would have gone far to both explaining and predicting the transformation of black politics during the NBPA and the MMM, while also providing a blueprint for strategizing among competing interests within black leadership. Certainly, Walters appreciated the centrality of these developments in light of his assertion that "given the vital role of nationalism in the mobilization of Blacks for many types of causes, and as an internal antidote to White racism, Minister Farrakhan's role within the leadership structure would have to be created if it did not exist" (Walters and Smith 1999, 206). Nevertheless, an understanding of these relationships and their impact on black leadership and black nationalism are still underdeveloped today and would require the combination of scholarship and activism of a Ronald Walters in order to address this prominent lacuna in black politics.

Synthesizing Black Leadership and Black Nationalism

Walters' research on black leadership and black nationalism exposes a fundamental quandary in the study of black politics, which relates to the need to examine the dynamics of political phenomena that represent black political agency on its own terms. That is, for a black politics to be meaningful it should attend to the processes operative in black communities over long periods of time that maintain their salience in the present. Foremost among these are issues related to how blacks understand power and organize with respect to the collective expression of that power toward specific objectives that that power is assumed to allow blacks to attain. Simply put, we need to understand the means and ends served by leaders and followers in the black political arena. More directly, we need to understand the motive forces driving the adoption of diverse black political ideologies and the dynamic factors that lead to changes in the ideological outlook of black peoples with respect to which leaders they support and follow, utilizing whatever means and toward whatever ends.

In the United States, black nationalism was the first clearly articulated and institutionally supported black political ideology on a national scale. Even the most trenchant critics of black nationalism assert that it is not derivative of either American, French, or Jewish nationalism, but it represents an indigenous and independent strain of black political expression in the United States with a comparable historical pedigree (see Moses 1978, 1996). Its ideological counterpoise, black integrationism emerged sometime later as the option of mass black settlement in the northern United States became tenable. Although years ago W.E.B. Du Bois argued that black nationalism was a thought upsurging from the black masses, ironically, U.S. blacks continue to be dominated by liberal integrationist hegemony within mainstream electoral politics and quasi-radical or liberal integrationist dominance within the U.S. academy; and each of these tendencies denigrates black nationalism as a political ideology and even more so as a basis for political strategy or political organizing. One result is that scholars today usually reduce black nationalism to a "marginal" or "pathological" strain of black politics, while integrationist organization—either in its liberal or radical variant—is viewed as the "appropriate" framework through which black politics may be understood and collective strategies for racial uplift can be pursued. In such a context, scholars largely focus on some of the worst caricatures of black nationalism in order to condemn the black nationalist enterprise itself, while ignoring the progressive and more enduring core of black nationalism and its fundamental role in transforming U.S. society in the last three centuries. Ironically, since the mid-1800s black leadership has been dominated by integrationists. This may be owed partly to the fact that the leadership—often consisting of the more privileged classes—has pursued its class interests at the expense of mass interests; however, it is difficult to deny Du Bois' ([1940] 1991, 305) observation that "[t]he upper class Negro has almost never been nationalistic."[2]

One result of the ideological distance between black intellectuals and black nationalism is that black nationalism is among the most misunderstood concepts in American politics (Walton 1985). This misunderstanding is due, in part, to the failure of analysts to differentiate between statist and non-statist perspectives of nationalism (Henderson 2004). The former suggests that nations aspire to possess a state and advocates of this view tend to reject the nationalist claims of African Americans as both marginal and untenable. However, historically, in the United States, black nationalism has been rooted in a Pan-Africanist appreciation of the nationhood status of black Americans. In this context, historically polyglot cultural groups are amalgamated in a shared racial identity that forms the basis of their national identity. This black national identity is wedded to a common political purpose that suggests group autonomy though not necessarily statehood. In this conceptualization, nationalists may aspire to self-determination within a culturally plural state (see Cruse 1987) as opposed to territorial separation. Such a non-statist definition of nationalism is widely accepted among political scientists, in general (e.g., see Gellner 1983), but many black scholars—including scholars of black nationalism, as well—continue to assume that black nationalism is synonymous with "emigrationism" or racial separatism (e.g., see Dawson 2001).[3] This is "simplistic" and often self-serving, intended to show the lack of practicality of the black nationalist enterprise conceptualized as a black Zionist retreat from real political struggle rather than conceptualizing it as a political ideology rooted in the national self-determination claims of African Americans that may suggest a variety of possible outcomes with respect to the governance of the "black nation." In addition, black nationalists insist that African Americans as a distinct people should pursue collective political action rooted in their common history and their, ostensibly, common interests; but they don't necessarily assume that this convergence of history and interests results as a matter of course nor does it ignore fissures within the black community that problematize the prevailing views of identity within black communities (see Henderson 2004). Since the nation status of African Americans has been historically denied by European Americans, it stands to reason that the ideology of black nationalism would be denigrated, ignored, or treated as a pathology in mainstream, Eurocentric approaches. Nonetheless, the view that blacks comprise a nation persists throughout black communities in the United States. Where there is often disagreement among blacks is over what such an identification entails for their political, economic, and social interaction with European Americans and other citizens in the multicultural (or multinational) republic.

Appreciating black nationalism in its fullest sense is essential given Cruse's (1967) observation that "American Negro history is basically a history of the conflict between integrationist and nationalist forces in politics, economics, and culture, no matter what leaders are involved and what slogans are used." He concluded that "the pendulum swings back and forth, but the men who swing with it always fail to synthesize composite trends" (564). This suggests that understanding black nationalism is necessary in order to describe, explain, and predict black politics over the course of blacks' sojourn in the United States. Cruse's (1967) pendulum thesis acknowledges the ideological differences among black leadership and suggests the decreased likelihood of the development of a unified strategy for liberation and social justice. Instead of viewing this dichotomy as a breach in need of reconciliation, he noted it as a development rooted in the divergent class interests of black elites and black masses (7–8). Nevertheless, while Cruse is correct that black leadership has alternated between nationalism and integration, he does not provide a theoretical argument to account for the shifts. This absence reflects the dearth of systematic research on the correlates of black nationalism.

While several authors have examined the factors that give rise to black nationalism (Essien-Udom 1964; Walton 1985; Van Deburg 1992), these analyses are largely descriptive. In a previous study, Henderson (2000) essayed a tentative outline of the black leadership phases since the mid-1800s, and provided a theoretical rationale for the pendulum thesis and an empirical analysis of the factors that give rise to them. Building on Myrdal's (1944) argument that wars exposed the huge disjuncture between the American Creed of liberty, equality, and justice and the persistence of white racism, lynch-law, Jim Crow, and black privation, Henderson argues that in many of the country's wars blacks were faced with glaring contradictions between the ideals expressed to justify the war and the actual practices of domestic racism in the United States. This was apparent during WWI when black troops faced the hypocrisy of fighting a war abroad to "make the world safe for democracy" when they did not enjoy democratic rights at home. Similar sentiments were echoed during WWII in the popular "Double V" campaign initiated by blacks to signify the struggle for victory "over enemies from without [and] over enemies from within" (5). This incongruity was also apparent during the Vietnam War when the popular sports hero and draft recusant Muhammad Ali echoed a dominant theme among many blacks that "no Vietnamese ever called me nigger."

Henderson argues that during wartime, minorities may be viewed as a "fifth column," and blacks in the United States often faced internal repression especially by law enforcement agencies, which rationalized this persecution in the name of "national security" as was the case with Hoover's FBI, which branded King's nonviolent protesters as "communist agents" and threats to "national security," during the Vietnam War (Garrow 1981; Churchill and Vander Wall 1989; O'Reilly 1989), or his similar characterization of the fledgling Nation of Islam as a front for Japanese-sponsored subversion during WWII (Evanzz 1992, 24–26, 138–40). Such rationalizations serve to justify the repression of these groups, especially during wartime.[4] Facing wartime repression, blacks realize that they are viewed as a foreign caste or a sort of domestic alien population within the United States. In such a context, they are put upon by whites encouraged by the jingoism of war mobilization, who turn outwardly focused racist attitudes toward external enemies inwardly toward blacks and other domestic groups for which there is historic and ongoing racial antipathy (such as Japanese Americans during WWII, or Muslim Americans following the Al Qaeda attacks on the United States in 2001). This was evident during the Civil War, the expansionist wars at the turn of the century, following WWI, and during WWII (Hunt 1987). These periods witnessed some of the worst instances of white supremacist violence against blacks, such as the New York Draft riots of 1863, the Wilmington "coup d'état" of 1898 (Prather 1984), the Red Summer of 1919 (see Bennett 1965), the Tulsa Riot of 1921

(Ellsworth 1922), and the Detroit Riot of 1943. These relationships are consistent with Stohl's (1976) finding that in the United States from 1890 to 1970, there was a significant correlation between war and domestic violence. Such increasingly repressive environments bind and reaffirm African Americans in their common subjugation, common fate, and common identity. Increasingly faced with their caste condition, blacks reject integrationists' assimilationist arguments, and nationalist assertions become increasingly compelling. Therefore, shortly following U.S. war involvement nationalist leadership becomes ascendant.

In a multivariate logistic regression analysis of the fluctuation of black leadership between 1840 and 1996, Henderson (2000) found that U.S. involvement in war had the greatest relative impact on the rise of black nationalism, followed by a repressive political climate and phases of extroversion in U.S. foreign policy. Specifically, he found that, *ceteris paribus*, within three years of U.S. war involvement there is an increased likelihood of the ascendance of black nationalist leadership. Interestingly, his findings revealed that economic downturns were not significantly associated with pendulum shifts, which supports the view of scholars such as McAdam (1982) who argue that black political mobilization is rooted, mainly, in non-economic factors. On the other hand, it refutes Marable's (1985) view—and a persistent view of Marxists, socialists, and many integrationists—that economic factors are the most important correlates of black political change. Pendulum shifts, then, are, to a large extent, rooted in the interaction of macropolitical factors that affect the salience of group-based mobilization among blacks. Where group-based mobilization is mitigated by the absence of war and the presence of a period of introversion, integrationist arguments become increasingly salient and integrationist leadership becomes dominant. However, where group salience is heightened, such as in times of war, nationalism becomes ascendant. Under such circumstances the integrationist focus on assimilation appears quixotic. Simply put, when black oppression seems to be based on their caste (i.e., blacks are oppressed because they are black), nationalist leadership becomes ascendant; when black oppression seems to be based on their class (i.e., blacks are oppressed because they are poor), integrationist leadership becomes ascendant. War is a key factor that transforms the perception and practice of black oppression in the

United States, and in that role is a key element in the transformation of black politics in the United States. If one ignores or marginalizes black nationalism, one cannot explain this essential feature of black political development in the United States, and one is less likely to successfully implement black mobilizational and organizational strategies that can exploit the challenges and opportunities provided by the interplay of external and internal factors in black politics.

Understanding how war can lead to nationalist ascendance, one should also appreciate the factors in its decline, since this was the process operative during Walters' attempt to reconcile nationalist and integrationist perspectives in the NBPA under a nationalist rubric. It appears that in a relatively short period of time following war, nationalists are stymied by their failure to build substantial coalitions prior to the relaxation of more overt forms of repression as the jingoism of the war period wanes and the political cycle begins to shift toward introversion. This is evocative of the problems in the NBPA as the Vietnam War wound down and the country moved toward a more introverted foreign policy orientation and radical domestic politics (especially from the white Left) lost its salience and visibility. At the same time, the BEOs with their integrationist focus became ascendant in black communities, and they seemed to appreciate much better than the nationalists that the tide had turned toward electoral politics and the consolidation of gains wrought from the civil rights movement's successes. This allowed them to eschew black nationalist projects and reduce their espousal of black nationalist precepts to rhetoric as they sought solace, sanctuary, and personal success in the Democratic Party and largely abandoned the project of black independent politics. Drawing on their greater institutional support—especially through churches and mutual aid institutions—and the perquisites they derived from their interracial organizations, integrationists were able to offer tangible rewards to their black (and nonblack) constituents. At the same time, integrationists exploited black nationalists' myopia and the latter's apparent unwillingness to mobilize nonblack interests.

During peacetime, black nationalists cannot rely on the glaring contradictions between the American Creed and American racism to provide the impetus for black mobilization in the way that it does during wartime; instead, they must articulate meaningful programs that arise from blacks' legitimate claims of national self-determination.

Historically, black nationalist leadership has been largely ineffective
in providing such programs, and in the twentieth century, especially,
their attempts have too often been tied to ill-conceived "emigration-
ist" programs, nebulous community control initiatives, or abortive
insurgency strategies. These types of initiatives largely fail to address
the pluralistic politics to which blacks appear most responsive (see
Cruse 1987). One result is that black nationalists during peacetime,
like integrationists during wartime, are often unable to promote
policies and programs reflecting the overarching group interests
of blacks. Therefore, in the postwar era, integrationists reemerge
and largely pursue juridical concessions from the ruling white caste
elite. These concessions, while at times meaningful and lasting, are
limited in that they fail to ultimately address the caste basis of black
marginalization—a reality that is rejected by the white ruling caste,
itself. Nonetheless, by effectively eschewing group-based political
mobilization, integrationists reduce the amount of coercive pressure
that the black community can exert on an increasingly recalcitrant
white-dominated society. Concessions to black interests ultimately
engender white revanchism that serves to alter the dominant policy
mood of the country, helping to drive the next political cycle and
thus starting the pendulum process over again.

Conclusion

Walters' focus on black leadership and black nationalism allows us
to appreciate the importance of the nexus between academia and
activism. Walters is quick to remind us that "some of the strongest
critiques of Black leadership have been made by Black scholars, inevitably holding them up to high standards of performance." Importantly, he adds:

> This, however, is the origin of the political antipathy between
> many intellectuals and a Black leadership class that often
> views the perspective of scholars as "unrealistic" and divorced
> from the context of the daily realities they face. This is a
> reason why Black scholars may be invited to make presenta-
> tions at the various annual conferences of the major Black

organizations, but they do not generally function informally as a source of advice and information for the Black leadership, with, of course, a few historical exceptions. (244)

And Ronald Walters is one such exception. It is important, as Walters demonstrates, that black scholars involve themselves in the day-to-day politics of black communities at some level: international, national, state, or local.

It is also important to recognize that Walters' attempt to reconcile competing black political ideologies was hardly in vain given that integrationist and nationalist strategies both have strengths and weaknesses and can operate as complements even in their diversity. For example, the former appreciates the "American" nature of black oppression but too often rejects the significant culture group basis of black mobilization, while the latter appreciates the culture group basis of political mobilization but often fails to attend to the "American" nature of interest group and coalition politics. Although the perspectives are complementary, instead of a synthesis of the two, there is continued conflict among their adherents as each camp seeks to individually mobilize the black community. Interestingly, the ideological standoff does not preclude the usurpation of the successful programs of rivals. One result is that *nationalists* today "March on Washington" to "atone" in a manner that was nearly laughable for nationalists thirty years ago (the black nationalist, Malcolm X, labeled the 1963 march that was led by integrationists "The Farce on Washington"). By the same token, *integrationists* celebrate racial self-help initiatives, "buy-black" campaigns, and black studies programs that at least superficially reflect the black power perspective that integrationists eschewed in the 1960s.

Even as both camps borrow from the other, their ideological rift is maintained almost as a matter of identity. The consequence of this is that although both strategies have contributed to great improvements in the quality of life of African Americans—and Americans in general—a useful synthesis of the two approaches has not been forthcoming. One logical synthesis of the two strategies would wed the juridical focus of integrationist approaches to the community control initiatives of nationalists. One focal point of such a strategy could be a project to both defend and expand affirmative action initiatives through a focus on legal challenges drawing on arguments related to the eradication of "badges of slavery" implied by the Thirteenth Amendment as opposed to arguments relying on the Fourteenth Amendment's ambiguous "equal protection clause," which is, ironically, being used by opponents of affirmative action to dismantle such programs. This strategy may provide, *inter alia,* a legal foundation for black reparations and a more persuasive basis for black mobilization with regard to affirmative action than "diversity" arguments (see Henderson 1998). In addition, such a focus could provide a template for independent black political mobilization, which may take the form of an independent black political party, or a multicultural third party. Such a development would owe much to Ron Walters' insights and decades of hard work and struggle. Notwithstanding such developments, the suggestion of a synthesis of integrationist and nationalist approaches is not meant to imply that a diverse group of 40 million black people should be unified in a single political strategy. What is clear is that as black leadership wavers between nationalism and integrationism, black marginalization remains constant; a continuation of such a condition is unconscionable, and black intellectuals and political leaders, especially—though not exclusively—should do their best to both comprehend and provide remedies for this situation; and a fuller consideration of Ron Walters' research is a necessary starting point for such a project.

Notes

1. Smith wrote part 1, while Walters wrote part 2, and they collaborated on part 3.
2. For an alternative thesis, which posits that classical black nationalism was rooted in the separatist tendencies of eighteenth- and nineteenth-century black elites, see Moses (1978, 1996).
3. Walters and Smith (1999, 46) come close to equating black nationalism with separation at one point but only for purposes of systematic analysis, and they recognize that this is a "restrictive" definition of the concept.
4. The scapegoating of blacks during wartime is doubly ironic when we recognize that many blacks have long considered that greater

citizenship rights would reward their wartime sacrifice. In fact, military service was often viewed as a route for social uplift in the black community and even a stepping stone for the attainment of black leadership (Butler 1991). For example, according to Lewis (1993:,557–59), Du Bois sought an army commission in military intelligence during WWI.

References

Bennett, Lerone. 1965. *Confrontation: Black and White.* Chicago: Johnson Publishing.

Brown, Robert, and Todd Shaw. 2002. "Separate Nations: Two Attitudinal Dimensions of Black Nationalism," *Journal of Politics* 64,1: 22–44.

Butler, John. 1991. "The Military as a Vehicle for Social Integration: The Afro-American Experience as Data." In *Ethnicity, Integration, and the Military,* ed. Henry Dietz, Jerrold Elkin, and Maurice Roumani, 27–50. Boulder, CO: Westview.

Churchill, Ward, and Jim Vander Wall. 1989. *The COINTELPRO Papers: Documents from the FBI's Secret War on Domestic Dissent.* Boston: South End Press.

Cruse, Harold. 1967. *The Crisis of the Negro Intellectual.* New York: William Morrow & Co.

———. 1987. *Plural but Equal.* New York: William Morrow & Co.

Dawson, Michael. 1994. *Behind the Mule: Race and Class in African American Politics.* Princeton, NJ: Princeton University Press.

———. 2001. *Black Visions: The Roots of Contemporary African-American Political Ideologies.* Chicago: University of Chicago Press.

Du Bois, W.E.B. 1991 [1940]. *Dusk of Dawn: An Essay Toward an Autobiography of a Race Concept.* New Brunswick, NJ: Transaction.

Ellsworth, Scott. 1992. *Death in a Promised Land: The Tulsa Race Riot of 1912.* Baton Rouge: Louisiana State University Press.

Essien-Udom, Essien. 1964. *Black Nationalism: A Search for Identity in America.* New York: Dell.

Evanzz, Karl. 1992. *The Judas Factor: The Plot to Kill Malcolm X.* New York: Thunder's Mouth Press.

Garrow, David. 1981. *The FBI and Martin Luther King, Jr.* New York: Penguin.

Gellner, Ernest. 1983. *Nations and Nationalism*. Ithaca: Cornell University Press.

Henderson, Errol. 1998. "War, Political Cycles, and the Pendulum Thesis." Presented to the Conference in Tribute to Harold Cruse, University of Michigan, March.

———. 2000. "War, Political Cycles, and the Pendulum Thesis: Explaining the Rise of Black Nationalism, 1840–1996." In *Black Politics in Multiracial America*, ed. A. Alex-Assensoh and L. Hanks, 337–74. New York: New York University Press.

———. 2004. "Misunderstanding Black Nationalism: Failures, Fixations, Facades and Fabrications." American Political Science Association, Chicago, IL, September.

———. 2007. "Navigating the Muddy Waters of the Mainstream: Tracing the Mystification of Racism in International Relations." In *The State of the Political Science Discipline: An African-American Perspective*, ed. Wilbur Rich, 325–63. Philadelphia: Temple University Press.

Hochschild, Jennifer. 1996. *Facing Up to the American Dream*. Princeton, NJ: Princeton University Press.

Holden, Matthew. 1973. *The Politics of the "Black Nation."* New York: Chandler.

Hunt, Michael. 1987. *Ideology and U.S. Foreign Policy*. New Haven, CT: Yale University Press.

Lewis, David. 1993. *W.E.B. Du Bois: Biography of a Race*. New York: Henry Holt & Company.

Marable, Manning. 1985. *Black American Politics*. London: Thetford.

McAdam, Doug. 1982. *Political Process and the Development of Black Insurgency, 1930–1970*. Chicago, IL: University of Chicago Press.

Moses, Wilson. 1978. *The Golden Age of Black Nationalism, 1850–1925*. Oxford: Oxford University Press.

———. 1996. *Classical Black Nationalism: From the American Revolution to Marcus Garvey*. New York: New York University Press.

Myrdal, Gunnar. 1944. *An American Dilemma: The Negro Problem and Modern Democracy*. New York: Harper and Brothers.

O'Reilly, Kenneth. 1989. *Racial Matters: The FBI's Secret File on Black America, 1960–1972*. New York: Free Press.

Peeks, Edward. 1971. *The Long Struggle for Black Power*. New York: Charles Scribner's Sons.

Prather, H. Leon. 1984. *We Have Taken a City: Wilmington Racial Massacre and Coup of 1898*. Rutherford, NC: Fairleigh Dickinson University Press.

Quarles, Benjamin. 1968. *The Negro in the Making of America*. New York: Collier-MacMillan.

Smith, Robert. 1996. *We Have No Leaders: Africans in the Post–Civil Rights Era*. Albany: State University of New York Press.

Stohl, Michael. 1976. *War and Domestic Violence: The American Capacity for War and Reaction*. Beverly Hills, CA: Sage Publications.

Van Deburg, William. 1992. *New Day in Babylon: The Black Power Movement and American Culture, 1965–1975*. Chicago: University of Chicago Press.

Walters, Ronald. 1972. "The New Black Political Culture." *Black World* (October): 4–17.

———. 1973. "African-American Nationalism: Toward a Unifying Ideology." *Black World* (October): 9–27, 84.

———. 1992. "Two Political Traditions: Black Politics in the 1990s." *National Political Science Review* 3: 198–208.

———. 1993. *Pan Africanism in the African Diaspora*. Detroit: Wayne State University Press.

Walton, Hanes. 1985. *Invisible Politics*. Albany: State University of New York Press.

Wilson, Ernest. 1985. "Why Political Scientists Don't Study Black Politics, but Historians and Sociologists Do." *PS: Political Science* (Summer): 600–07.

Part IV

8

Usurper-in-Chief?

White Nationalism, the Tea Party Movement,
and President Barack Obama

ADOLPHUS G. BELK JR.

. . . white America is increasingly alienated and distrustful of all our
major economic and political power centers—the banks, big corporations, the government. And, for the first time in our lifetimes, outside the
South, white racial consciousness has visibly begun to rise.
  —Patrick J. Buchanan, MSNBC contributor and Tea Party sympathizer[1]

So you have this 21st Century plantation . . . where the Democrat party
has forever taken the Black vote for granted, and you have established
certain Black leaders who are nothing more than the overseers of that
plantation. And now the people on that plantation are upset because
they've been disregarded, disrespected and their concerns are not cared
about. So I'm here as the modern day Harriet Tubman to kind of lead
people on the Underground Railroad away from that plantation into a
sense of sensibility.
  —U.S. Representative Allen West (R-FL)[2]

Indeed, it would be illogical to assume that a powerful phenomenon
such as White racism has only a social or cultural impact and does not
have political manifestations.
  —Ronald W. Walters[3]

Introduction

For many Americans their introduction to Barack Obama came
with his appearance before the 2004 Democratic National Convention in Boston. Then a candidate for the U.S. Senate in Illinois,
Obama delivered a rousing address that included many well-tested

"New Democrat" ideas such as personal responsibility and opportunity, concepts that signaled the party was attuned to the concerns of the white middle class.[4] The speech also vaulted Obama into the national spotlight and had a number of observers thinking that he could be a serious presidential contender in the years to come. Few, however, thought that his opportunity would come so soon. On November 4, 2008, the junior senator from Illinois completed a stunning run to the White House. In the race for the Democratic nomination, he bested more seasoned candidates such as U.S. senators Joseph Biden (D-DE), Hillary Clinton (D-NY), and Christopher Dodd (D-CT) and Governor Bill Richardson of New Mexico. He then defeated the Republican nominee, Arizona senator John McCain, by winning 53 percent of the popular vote and taking the electoral vote by a margin of 365 to 173.

The American people were hungry for change in the wake of the election. Many believed that Obama, a man of mixed racial ancestry, would usher in a new era in race relations.[5] Just days after the balloting, Gallup found that 67 percent of Americans thought that relations between blacks and whites would eventually be worked out—the highest value that the polling organization had ever measured on the question.[6] Seven out of ten of those surveyed said that race relations would at least get "a little better." Lastly, over two-thirds of Americans thought that Obama's victory either was the most important advance for blacks in the past one hundred years or was among the two or three most important such developments.

A closer look at the 2008 exit polls reveals that these high expectations were somewhat unfounded. Although Obama won a majority of the popular vote, his support among whites was consistent with that of previous Democratic presidential candidates. From 1972 to 2004, Democrats garnered an average of 39.3 percent of the white vote, with Jimmy Carter setting the high mark of 47 percent in 1976.[7] By comparison, Obama secured 43 percent of the white vote and performed best with young whites, earning 54 percent of the vote from those between eighteen and twenty-nine years of age. Part of Obama's appeal was rooted in his rhetoric and style. Several scholars noted that Obama ran a "deracialized" campaign that eschewed race-specific language and targeted policies in favor of universalism and broad programs.[8] In the process, he deemphasized black concerns such as economic inequality and antipoverty programs, while simultaneously projecting a nonthreatening image to whites. As a result, many Americans believed that Obama could change the tone of the nation's politics and heal old racial wounds. In addition, given the multiracial nature of Obama's electoral coalition, several commentators openly wondered about the future of a Republican Party that was seemingly too reliant on older whites—white males, in particular—and southerners.[9]

What many analysts failed to appreciate, however, was the way in which Obama's run deeply divided racial conservatives from racial liberals, "as race was chronically more accessible to voters in 2008 than it had been in any previous campaign."[10] Furthermore, there was an almost immediate counterreaction against Obama and his policies. In the same November 2008 Gallup poll in which two-thirds of Americans said that they were "proud" to have Obama as their president, 27 percent of all respondents—and 56 percent of McCain supporters—said that they were "afraid."[11] With the economy mired in a debilitating recession, a new conservative movement began to unfold. Arguing that they were "taxed enough already," and reaching back to the struggles of eighteenth-century Bostonians, Tea Party activists and organizations emerged as some Obama's fiercest detractors. Although much of their criticism has pertained to issues such as government spending and the national debt, it soon became clear that there were racial grievances as well. At protests in the District of Columbia and across the states, some demonstrators held signs that depicted the president as Adolf Hitler, a half-naked African witch doctor, a monkey, or suggested that his master plan was to enslave whites.[12] Others challenged the authenticity of Obama's birth certificate and his legitimacy to lead by alleging that he was born in Kenya, thus giving rise to the "birther" movement.[13]

In the time since the protest movement surfaced in early 2009, Tea Partiers have flexed their muscles during the 2010 midterm elections, ultimately leading to the formation of a Tea Party Caucus in the United States Congress. One national group, Tea Party Express, collaborated with CNN to host the first ever Tea Party presidential debate in September 2011.[14] The rapid materialization of the Tea Party and its growing influence in the American political system clearly demonstrates that the nation has not transitioned into an idyllic postracial epoch. Instead, the ascent of the Tea Party raises serious questions for scholars of American politics, policy, and race, the sort of questions centered in the works of the late Ronald Walters. Building on his analysis of racism in American politics, this chapter asks, how can Walters' theory of white nationalism help us make sense of the Tea Party, its grasp on the national political discourse, and the movement's opposition to President Obama? I will argue that the Tea Party, generally aligned with the GOP, emerged out of the very conditions that Walters predicted would produce radical conservative uprisings. With the election of the nation's first nonwhite president and the economic hardships spawned by the Great Recession, some whites have experienced a sense of power deflation that has made them more receptive to the appeals of staunch conservatives. Consequently, white nationalism has animated the Tea Party movement and some of its opposition to the president and his policies.

The Role of Racism in Politics and Policymaking:
Walters on White Nationalism

There are generally three schools of thought when it comes to understanding the impact of race and racism on American society in the decades since the civil rights movement. The first, which includes Dinesh D'Souza, John McWhorter, Thomas Sowell, Shelby Steele, Abigail and Stephan Thernstrom, and others, suggests that racism "no longer has the power to thwart blacks or any other group in achieving economic, political, and social aspirations."[15] With groundbreaking U.S. Supreme Court decisions and the passage of far-reaching federal laws, the civil rights movement succeeded in transforming the nation and its people. Even though there are sporadic episodes of bigotry, the playing field is level and equal opportunity exists for the talented and industrious. If there are to be policy solutions to deal with lingering elements of the race problem, then they must be "strictly indifferent to race."[16] Racial minority groups—particularly blacks—must solve their own problems and cannot invoke white racism as an impediment to their progress. As evidence of the demise of racism, they point to the ascendancy of persons like General Colin Powell and former secretary of state Condoleezza Rice, imploring people of color to follow their example.[17] If minorities fail to thrive, then their lack of achievement is the result of their own deficiencies, be they intellectual, cultural, or moral.[18]

Next, adherents to the second school of thought have argued that while America remains a "color-conscious society," race and racism have declined as predominant forces in the lives of minorities. For instance, scholars like Paul Sniderman and Thomas Piazza have found that prejudice "no longer organizes and dominates the reactions of whites" and does not lead great numbers of them to reject policies intended to aid blacks or other nonwhites.[19] It is "simply wrong," therefore, to maintain that racism is the principal factor driving present-day arguments over the politics of race. In addition, researchers such as William Julius Wilson—juxtaposing the experiences of the black middle class and underclass—have long argued that socioeconomic status has become a more significant factor than race in restricting opportunities for people of color. As the African American middle class has grown and migrated from predominately minority central city neighborhoods to the suburbs, the gap between affluent blacks and the black underclass widened. With shrinking tax bases and residents in dire need of social services, cities have become financially dependent on a federal government that is less inclined to offer aid. Consequently, the black poor "have been plagued by higher unemployment rates, lower labor-force participation rates, higher welfare rates, and more recently, a slower movement out of poverty."[20] Thus, the "truly disadvantaged" are the ghetto poor who find themselves dislocated from opportunity and the American Dream.[21]

The final school of thought on race in American politics argues that it remains a powerful force in shaping both political debates and policy outcomes. While the civil rights movement dealt a mighty blow to the elaborate mechanisms of white hegemony, race and racism have transformed as the society has evolved.[22] Academics have used numerous phrases to describe post–Jim Crow racism, including "laissez-faire racism," "new racism," and "color-blind racism."[23] Although the terminology varies, the central thesis is the same: race continues to influence arguments over what government should do, for whom government should do it, and what level of government should act. Members of this school add that American racism is systemic and subtly and not so subtly affects our everyday experiences.[24] It is even possible for Americans and their elected officials to voice bigoted attitudes in public by using rhetorical tools and tactics devoid of pejorative epithets, hence giving rise to "racism without racists."[25]

Historically, political scientists have not had the best record analyzing race and racism.[26] Even so, several researchers have elucidated the role of race in shaping American political institutions and parties.[27] They also have explored the influence of race in the formation of group identities and ideology, the development and measurement of public opinion, and political participation.[28] Walters staked out his position on the role of race in American politics in *White Nationalism, Black Interests: Conservative Public Policy and the Black Community.* He sought to develop a theory that could explain how racism continued to threaten the economic, political, and social advancement of blacks in the post–Civil Rights era. From his vantage point, race has been a driving force behind the reorganization of the Republican Party since the late 1970s. Championed most famously by President Ronald Reagan, this movement has had deleterious consequences for blacks and other negatively constructed racial minority groups, as they are frequent targets of punitive policies. "[I]f a race is dominant to the extent that it controls the government of the state . . . it is able to utilize those institutions and the policy outcomes they produce as instruments through which it also structures its racial interests. In short, it may reward, punish and so structure outcomes as to protect and enhance racial interests."[29] How has such a racial project taken hold of the nation's political agenda? How do scholars discern the racial interests of the white majority when—due to the adroit use of coded language—policy is hardly ever formulated in ways that directly indicate partiality toward the dominant group? Walters provided answers to these questions with the theory of white nationalism.

White nationalism draws attention to that radical portion of the conservative movement that seeks to use both unofficial power and the official power of government to preserve white privilege by subordinating people of color.[30] White nationalists are persons or groups that either knowingly or unknowingly advocate policies that have a damaging impact on minorities, in general, or blacks, in particular.[31] While it can infect any region, white nationalism is purveyed in overt forms by southern politicians such as "Pitchfork" Ben Tillman and David Duke. Likewise, prominent blacks such as Booker T. Washington and Ward Connerly have served as surrogates for reactionary interests, thereby shielding white nationalists against charges of racism. Walters also illustrated the dominant tendencies within the white majority that fit the criteria of nationalism. First, members of the majority, though certainly not all whites, have a racial consciousness that renders them "distinctive" within the society.[32] Second, whites practice separation from other races, as evidenced by their proclivity to reside in nearly homogenous neighborhoods. Third, they have a shared cultural notion of "whiteness" and harbor attitudes about nonwhites that endure as stereotypes. Finally, whites exercise control over the nation's major political and economic institutions through numerical dominance and the subordination of other racial groups. Thus, white nationalism is entrenched in notions of racial chauvinism and has been used to organize whites across class lines.

Next, alienation is essential to the theory of white nationalism. In this context, it suggests that one feels antipathy toward state actors and institutions. This is critical because when a significant portion of the population becomes—or thinks that it has become—disconnected from government, it also embraces conservatism.[33] Infuriated with government, the disaffected develop an interest in reclaiming their traditional role in the social order and express a strong desire to weaken the state itself if it is deemed responsible for delivering remedy to persons regarded as inferior or undeserving. Therefore, although radical conservatives have long manipulated white rage to advance their interests, the key to understanding their success in organizing political movements lies in identifying the sources of white resentment. What are the most important determinants of white alienation? Walters pointed to increased competition from African Americans and white economic stagnation.

Since the civil rights movement, whites have experienced increased competition from blacks in both the political and economic spheres. In the political arena, black voter participation rates have greatly increased since the adoption of the Voting Rights Act of 1965 and the eradication of poll taxes and other impediments. Since the 1970s, when controlling for social class, blacks vote at nearly the same rate as whites.[34] In addition, the number of black elected officials has increased from 1,469 in 1970, to more than 9,000 in 2001, with southerners accounting for 68.5 percent of all black public officials.[35] As blacks and other minorities have established a greater presence in politics, their involvement has been viewed by some as a threat to white dominance—even within the Democratic Party—thus eliciting hostility.[36] In the economic arena, the rise of the black middle class is of special concern. Although black educational attainment continues to lag behind that of whites, they have made strides. In 1959, only 19.6 percent of black males and 21.6 percent of black females above the age of twenty-five held a high school diploma.[37] By 2006, those figures had increased to 80.1 and 81.2 percent, respectively. Similarly, in 1959, just 3.8 percent of black men and 2.9 percent of black women above twenty-five held at least a bachelor's degree. In 2006, 17.2 percent of black men and 19.4 percent of black women held at least a four-year degree. With regard to earnings, in 2008 dollars, black median income grew from $26,779 in 1980 to $34,218 in 2008.[38] There are, however, significant differences between the black and white middle classes. First, black households rely more on two wage earners.[39] Second, blacks, having been systemically denied opportunities to accrue wealth, trail whites in net worth and net financial assets.[40] Lastly, the African American middle class is more "bottom heavy," with blacks more likely to be represented among the "lower middle class" in terms of annual income.[41]

Even if it is clear that blacks have not attained political and economic parity with whites, according to Walters, evidence of black achievement has fostered bitterness among some whites. "Whites resent the fact that blacks are accorded access to social resources or that they appear to have achieved equal status."[42] Not surprisingly, "Conservatives have labored mightily to emphasize the progress that blacks have made from 1960 to the 1990s, largely to support their position that blacks do not need further so-called 'preferential treatment' in public policy."[43] Furthermore, in defining black upward mobility as a threat to white interests, many whites have adopted a "zero-sum" perspective on black progress.[44] That is, if African Americans have made gains, then they have unjustly done so at the expense of whites, thereby rendering whites victims of racial discrimination or liberal social engineering.

Economic stagnation is the second major determinant of white alienation. Since the 1970s, the standing and security of the American worker has eroded due to forces such as increased international competition, deindustrialization, mergers, and downsizing in both the private and public sectors. From 1978 through 1987, the richest fifth of the American population became 13 percent wealthier, while the poorest quintile became 8 percent poorer. In 1994, then U.S. secretary of labor Robert B. Reich observed, "The old middle class has become an anxious class—worried not only about sustaining their incomes but also about keeping their jobs and their health insurance. Our large corporations continue to improve productivity by investing in technology and cutting payrolls. In a recent survey, three out of four employers say their own employees fear losing their jobs."[45] For Walters, these trends created a circumstance wherein economic insecurity combined with racism to foster resentment among disaffected whites who struggled to explain their misfortune.[46]

In summary, white nationalism refers to radical conservatives who seek to use both unofficial power and governmental power to preserve white supremacy by subordinating racial minority groups. Increased competition from people of color and white economic stagnation create environments that are hospitable for white nationalist movements. The core features of such undertakings include heightened white racial consciousness, alienation from government, and a sense of "power deflation" that renders whites "losers" and threatens their position in the society. Once fully formed, white nationalist movements direct their ire not only at government, "but also *against the presumed clients of the state who are perceived to constitute the 'offending culture.'*"[47] The movement thus becomes the means by which radicals "fight back" to reclaim power over the state and its policies. Today, conservatism has become the acceptable civic form of white nationalist ideology in American politics.[48] In the pages to follow, this chapter will employ the theory of white nationalism to analyze the Tea Party movement, focusing on its emergence, platform, organization and leadership, and overall impact on American politics.

Reading the Tea Leaves: White Nationalism and the Tea Party

The Rise of the Movement

The Tea Party surfaced in February 2009, rising out of anger over President George W. Bush's $700 billion bailout of the banking industry and the Obama administration's $787 billion economic stimulus package.[49] It is the latest in a long line of conservative uprisings that have placed pressure on whichever of the two major political parties that was previously most receptive to white nationalist interests. In 1948, the States' Rights Party and an unflinching commitment to white supremacy fueled South Carolina senator Strom Thurmond's rebel presidential run. Twenty years later, Alabama governor George Wallace and the American Independence Party also bolted the Democratic Party to offer a strong white nationalist alternative to voters. In both instances, ultraconservative whites gave their support to candidates who promised to "take back" America from those who threatened their racial interests or called for an increased role for the federal government in the pursuit of equality. Today, according to a recent study of political typology by the Pew Research Center, about 9 percent of all Americans (11 percent of registered voters) are best described as "staunch conservatives."[50] Such persons "take extremely conservative positions on nearly all issues—on the size and role of government, on economics, foreign policy, social issues and moral concerns." Staunch conservatives are mostly white (92 percent), Republican (84 percent), older (61 percent above age fifty), and male (56 percent). They also are the only one of the eight typology groups wherein a majority of adherents, 72 percent, agree with the Tea Party.

Although the fiscal conservatives among the Tea Party faithful are mainly concerned with economic matters and government spending, a significant portion of the movement is also roused by racial concerns. Increased minority electoral competition in 2008 (and the resultant sense of power deflation) and white economic stagnation brought on by the Great Recession provided the impetus for the formation of the Tea Party movement. The election of President Barack Obama was arguably the greatest symbolic display of minority advancement in American history. Knowing that whites would comprise roughly three-fourths of the electorate, the Obama campaign sought to compete in nearly every state by appealing to middle-class whites. This was achieved by skirting controversial racial issues and associations, while emphasizing universal policies. The campaign also assembled a "minority-majority coalition" by mobilizing people of color in unprecedented ways.[51] In 2008, blacks, Latinos, and Asians accounted for about 24 percent of all voters, up from 21 percent in 2004 and 18 percent in 2000.[52] On Election Day, Obama won black (95% to 4%), Latino/a (67% to 31%), and Asian voters (62% to 35%) by wide margins and claimed 43 percent of the white vote.

Most Americans viewed Obama's victory as a sign of racial progress, with 67 percent of those polled by Gallup reporting that they were "optimistic" about him being elected president.[53] Others, especially McCain supporters, said that they were "afraid" or "pessimistic" about what was to come under an Obama administration. Further detailing the voting preferences and reactions of whites, Hanes Walton Jr. and Robert Smith observed:

> One area of the country where Obama did not make significant inroads was the South. Although he carried three states of the "suburban south" (Virginia, North Carolina, and Florida), he lost by substantial margins in the eight other states of the region. In many of these states, McCain won the white voter by margins of 9 to 1, with neither age nor education altering support for Obama. Clearly, traditional southern racism played a role in these outcomes. In interviews by the *New York Times*, many white southerners made it clear they were apprehensive about an Obama presidency. One respondent said she was bothered by the idea of a black man "over me," while another said Obama's election would make blacks "more aggressive."[54]

Clearly, some whites—particularly southerners—were melancholy regarding the outcome of the 2008 election, and their despondency was about more than McCain's defeat. Instead, they were fearful that having a black man in the White House would result in some sort of racial comeuppance and the pursuit of a policy agenda that favored people of color over them.

The second source of white alienation that gave rise to the Tea Party movement was provided by the Great Recession, which officially lasted from December 2007 until June 2009 but has persisted for many Americans. Labor economists Christopher Goodman and Steven Mance declared that America's most recent slump was striking "for its prolonged length, for affecting an especially wide range of industries, and for being deeper than any other downturn since World War II."[55] Since the inception of the Current Employment Statistics Survey in 1939, the United States has experienced eleven

Figure 8.1. Current Population Survey, Unemployment Rate, Seasonally Adjusted, January 2001 to September 2011

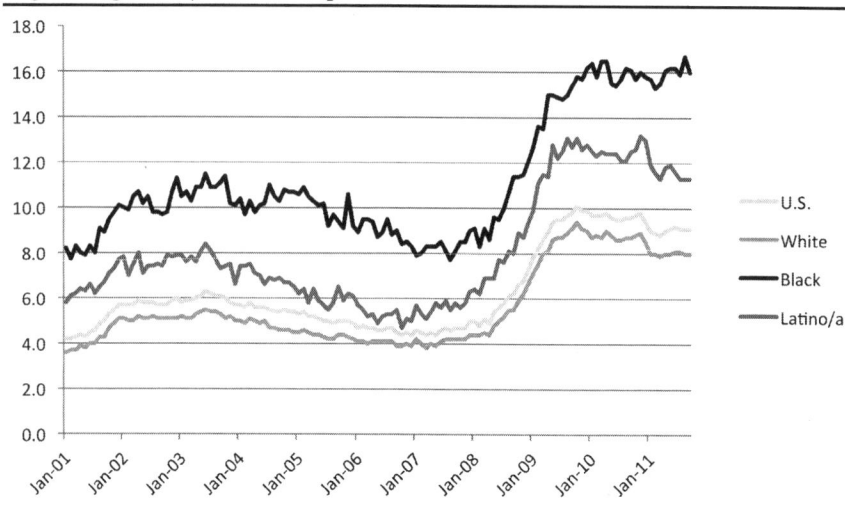

Source: Current Population Survey, U.S. Department of Labor, Bureau of Labor Statistics, October 2011.

periods of sustained employment declines. With the Great Recession, the nation writhed through its largest absolute decline in the history of the series, with 8.8 million net jobs lost from January 2008 through February 2010.[56] Amazingly, that level of job loss erased all of the jobs gained during the previous economic expansion from August 2003 to January 2008. The recession also affected a broad array of industries, from those that traditionally suffer during downturns like construction (2.2 million jobs lost) and manufacturing (2 million jobs lost) to more resilient industries such as retail trade (down 1 million) and leisure and hospitality (down 454,000). Consequently, as demonstrated in figure 8.1, the national unemployment rate swelled from 5.0 percent in December 2007 to 9.5 percent in June 2009. The white unemployment rate jumped from 4.4 percent to 8.7 percent over this same period.[57] Furthermore, with the shift from temporary layoffs to permanent sackings, as of September 2011, 44.6 percent of Americans (6.2 million people) found themselves out of work for more than twenty-seven weeks.[58]

As Americans scrambled to gain a foothold in a shaky economy, there was also a severe downturn in the housing market. From 1994

[[AU: s ply Jan figures galleys]

Table 8.1. Median Net Worth of U.S. Households by Race: 2005 and 2009

	2005	2009	Difference	Percent decline
All	$96,864	$70,000	-$26,894	-27.8
Whites	134,992	113,149	-21,843	-16.2
Blacks	12,124	5,677	-6,447	-53.2
Latinos/as	18,359	6,325	-12,034	-65.5
Asians	168,103	78,066	-90,037	-53.6

Source: Rakesh Kochar, Richard Fry, and Paul Taylor, "Wealth Gaps Rise to Record Highs Between Whites, Blacks and Hispanics," Pew Research Center, Social & Demographic Trends, July 26, 2011.

to 2004, the homeownership rate rose from 64.1 percent to an all-time high of 69.2 percent, a ten-year rate of increase not seen since the post–World War II boom.[59] As of early 2011, the homeownership rate dropped to 65.8 percent, its lowest level since 1998. Analysts estimate that nearly 3 million homes have gone into foreclosure since the earliest days of the recession. In addition, there has been a "five-fold increase in 'overcrowding' of remaining households—defined as more than one person per room."[60] With staggering job losses, foreclosures, and falling property values, many Americans suffered a severe blow to their overall worth. Table 8.1 shows that, from 2005 to 2009, the median wealth of U.S. households fell from $96,864 to $70,000, a reduction of nearly 28 percent.[61] Over this same period, the median wealth of white households declined by 16.2 percent, falling from $134,992 to $113,149.

While Americans of all races have struggled through the Great Recession, racial minority groups have suffered harm at a higher rate than their white counterparts. First, figure 8.1 indicates that jobless rates for blacks and Latinos/as—already greater than those of whites in the best of times—soared to even higher levels. Second, table 8.1 demonstrates that blacks and Latinos/as also saw their household net worth slashed by the recession, experiencing declines of 53.2 percent and 65.5 percent, respectively.[62] Nearly 25 percent of blacks and Latinos/as had no assets to report other than an automobile, compared to just 6 percent for whites. What is more, Asian Americans lost their position at the top of the U.S. wealth rankings, falling from \$168,103 in 2005, to \$78,066 in 2009. As a result, the wealth gap between racial minorities and whites reached its highest level since 1984. The purpose here, though, is to demonstrate the degree to which whites have experienced economic distress and how that privation has produced a new radical conservative movement that thrives off their sense of disaffection.

Anger in the Nation: Evidence of Alienation in the Tea Party

Since early 2009, a number of disgruntled Americans have thrown their support behind the Tea Party. Data from an April 2010 CBS News/*New York Times* poll indicate that 18 percent of Americans self-identified as members of the Tea Party.[63] Other polling groups, such as Gallup, estimate that 30 percent of Americans are Tea Partiers.[64] Next, as shown in table 8.2, the Tea Party is overwhelmingly white, with very few Latinos/as (3 percent), African Americans (1 percent), or Asians (1 percent) belonging to the movement. Seventy-five percent are above the age of forty-five, and 29 percent of all members report being older than sixty-four years of age. A majority of Tea Party backers are conservative (73 percent), male, and are more affluent and better educated than most Americans. Lastly, 54 percent consider themselves Republicans and 66 percent said that they always or usually vote for GOP candidates. Given the demographics of Tea Party supporters, it can be inferred that their reported perspectives on government, politics, and policy are a reasonable proxy for those of white nationalists.

Next, table 8.3 reveals the extent to which Tea Party members feel antipathy toward the state. When asked how much of the time they could trust the national government to do the right thing, 94 percent of Tea Party supporters said "sometimes" or "never," a mark 16 points higher than the general population. Likewise, when asked to describe their feelings about how things are going in the nation's capital, 94 percent reported that they were either "dissatisfied" or "angry," a figure 27 points greater than that of all respondents. Tea Partiers were especially infuriated by what they regard as an out-of-control central government that lacks fiscal discipline. In an interview with the *New York Times*, one respondent remarked, "The only way they will stop the spending is to have a revolt on their hands . . .

Table 8.2. Demographics of the Tea Party: 2010

		Tea Party	All Respondents	Difference
Race	White	89%	77%	+12
	Non-White	8	21	-13
Sex	Men	59%	49%	+10
	Women	41	51	-10
Age	18–29	7%	23%	-16
	30–44	16	27	-11
	45–64	46	34	+12
	Older than 64	29	16	+13
Party affiliation	Republican	54%	28%	+26
	Independent	36	33	+3
	Democrat	5	31	-26
How do you vote?	Always Republican	18%	9%	+9
	Usually Republican	48	19	+29
	Equally for both parties	25	31	-6
	Usually Democratic	3	16	-13
	Always Democratic	2	12	-10
How would you describe your political philosophy?	Very liberal	0%	4%	-4
	Somewhat liberal	4	16	-12
	Moderate	20	28	-18
	Somewhat conservative	34	22	+12
	Very conservative	39	12	+27
Total family income	Under $15,000	5%	10%	-5
	$15,000–$29,999	13	22	-9
	$30,000–$49,999	17	16	+1
	$50,000–$74,999	25	18	+7
	$75,000–$100,000	11	12	-1
	Over $100,000	20	14	+6

Source: "National Survey of Tea Party Supporters," CBS/*New York Times* Poll, April 5–12, 2010.
Total N = 1,580, Tea Party N = 881

Table 8.3. Distrust and Anger toward Government: 2010

		Tea Party	All Respondents	Difference
How much of the time do you think you can trust the government in Washington to do what is right?	Always	0%	4%	-4
	Most	6	16	-10
	Some	75	70	+5
	Never	19	8	+11
Which comes closest to your feelings about the way things are going in Washington?	Enthusiastic	1%	5%	-4
	Satisfied but not enthusiastic	4	26	-22
	Dissatisfied but not angry	41%	48%	-7
	Angry	53	19	+34

Source: "National Survey of Tea Party Supporters," CBS/*New York Times* Poll, April 5–12, 2010. Total N = 1,580, Tea Party N = 881

I'm sick and tired of them wasting money and doing what our founders never intended to be done with the federal government."[65] For most Tea Party backers, such un-American activities include reforming the nation's health care system, bailing out the banking industry, and using federal dollars to spur job creation in lieu of paying down the national debt.

When it comes to matters of race, Tea Party supporters believe that America is a meritorious nation and equality of opportunity exists for all. Seventy-three percent of those surveyed said that whites and blacks have the same chance to get ahead.[66] Even more telling, about half of all Tea Partiers, 52 percent, believe that "too much" has been made of the problems facing blacks compared to just 28 percent of all respondents. These observations make sense when one considers that, according to sociologists like Charles Gallagher, whites have embraced a "post-race, colorblind perspective" that allows them to believe that race no longer has an impact on one's ability to climb the social ladder. Today, most whites believe that the formula for success is simple: smarts, determination, and hard work. Gallagher writes: "This perspective insinuates that class and culture, and not institutional racism, are responsible for social inequality. Colorblindness allows many whites to define themselves as politically progressive and racially tolerant as they proclaim their adherence to a belief system that does not see or judge individuals by the 'color of their skin.'"[67] By rejecting the role that individual and institutional racism sometimes play in structuring or blocking opportunities, whites also negate the existence of white privilege and racial inequality. Moreover, scholars such as Michael Norton and Samuel Sommers have empirically shown that whites have adopted a "zero-sum" perspective on race. That is, "[b]oth within each decade and across time [1950s through the 2000s], white respondents were more likely to see decreases in bias against blacks as related to increases in bias against Whites—consistent with a zero-sum view of racism among Whites—whereas blacks were less likely to see the two as linked."[68] Whites have increasingly come to view advances by racial minorities as a threat to their own position in the society. Hence, "Whites now believe that anti-White bias is more prevalent than anti-black bias."[69] The Tea Party movement has provided a platform for such angst to be articulated in the public sphere and transformed into political action.

The Tea Party in State and Nation:
Organization, Structure, and Leadership

Stories about the Tea Party have dominated the news since it materialized in 2009. Thousands took to the streets during that spring and summer to rally against everything from corporate bailouts, to the stimulus package, to the Community Center at Park51 project, or as it was mislabeled, the "mosque at Ground Zero."[70] They also stormed the summer town hall meetings of several congressional representatives, challenging their positions on issues like health care reform.[71] At the voting booth, Tea Partiers assumed the role of spoiler during the 2010 midterm elections, either upsetting GOP-establishment candidates in ideologically charged primaries or helping Republicans pick up twenty-eight seats in the U.S. House of Representatives. Although many reporters touted the power of Tea Party voters, some analysts noted that the election returns were mixed, as several Tea Party–backed candidates struggled in metropolitan districts and more densely populated states.[72] After the elections, a group of veteran GOP lawmakers—including Representative Michele Bachmann (R-MN) and Senator Jim DeMint (R-SC)—collaborated with the Tea Party freshman of the 112th Congress to establish a Tea Party Caucus.[73] Republican presidential hopefuls in 2012 like Bachmann, former House Speaker Newt Gingrich, and Texas governor Rick Perry vied for the support of the movement. Another Tea Party darling, former Godfather's Pizza CEO Herman Cain, dropped out of the race following allegations of sexual misconduct.[74]

Even though the Tea Party brand quickly achieved notoriety, the movement itself is amorphous.[75] Nationally prominent figures such as former Alaska governor Sarah Palin, talk-show host Glenn Beck, or Senator DeMint are sometimes identified as Tea Party leaders, but the movement lacks a chief spokesperson. In addition, no single national association coordinates activities throughout the country. Nevertheless, the Tea Party exists both in the states and in the nation's capital. To understand the inner workings of the Tea Party at the local and state levels of analysis, investigators with the *Washington Post* conducted a months-long effort to contact every Tea Party group in America. The search unearthed more than 1,400 possible clubs, of which the *Post* made contact with 647, inquiring about details such as their membership and structure.[76] The survey revealed that most of the groups were small, with 51 percent reporting fewer than fifty

members. Forty-three percent claimed to have memberships ranging from fifty to one thousand persons, while 6 percent (39 groups)
declared memberships greater than one thousand. Of the nation's
647 active clubs, 325 were affiliated with major groups like Tea Party
Patriots (208), Americans for Prosperity (27), FreedomWorks (25), or
Tea Party Express (11). Reflecting on the connections between local
and national associations, Mark Meckler, a cofounder of perhaps the
most authentically grassroots group, Tea Party Patriots, said, "When
a group lists themselves on our Web site, that's a group. That group
could be one person, it could come in and out of existence—we
don't know."[77] Respondents from 272 local groups, though, said that
they did not work with any national organization. Finally, in terms
of structure, about three out of every four Tea Party clubs reported
their groups were informal and lacked a governance structure. They
also lacked capital, with most having raised less than $1,000 in 2010.
In a separate analysis, the Center for Responsive Politics found that
of the twenty federally registered political action committees with
"Tea Party" attached to their names, only seven donated to or spent
money on behalf of federal candidates.[78]

The people that populate the various Tea Party groups in American towns and cities are the same individuals that Robert Dahl once
labeled *homo civicus.*[79] Such persons are episodically involved in politics and their concern with governmental affairs is typically aroused
when their position is threatened. Only at that point does the average person deliberately set out to use his or her limited resources
to influence the actions of those in government. Many Tea Partiers
seem to fit that description, as 86 percent of the respondents to the
Washington Post canvass said that most of their members were new
to politics.[80] At the national level of analysis, in contrast, the dominant Tea Party organizations are the creations of *homo politicus.* Dahl
wrote, "Political man, unlike civic man, deliberately allocates a very
sizable share of his resources to the process of gaining and maintaining control over the policies of government."[81] In this instance, the
political animals and their well-moneyed allies have either formed
or worked through groups like Americans for Prosperity (AFP),
FreedomWorks, and Tea Party Express.[82]

First, although each of the aforementioned organizations is committed to neoliberal principles popular with Tea Partiers, such as
limited government, lowering personal and corporate income taxes,
and cutting the national debt, they have roots that are deeper than

the Tea Party movement itself. For instance, AFP and FreedomWorks, both of which were rebooted in 2004, are descendants of the now defunct Citizens for a Sound Economy, an organization created during the mid-1980s by billionaire brothers David and Charles Koch of Koch Industries.[83] Meanwhile, the Tea Party Express, which bills itself as "the most aggressive and influential national Tea Party group," is attached to the largest political action committee within the movement, Our Country Deserves Better.[84] Our Country Deserves Better was founded in 2008 to raise money for a conservative presidential candidate to oppose then senator Barack Obama.[85] It remained committed to his defeat in 2012.

Second, rather than being organized and led by the neophytes of the Tea Party movement, most of the major national associations are directed by experienced politicos and Washington insiders. AFP describes itself as "an organization of grassroots leaders," yet its headship includes people like the Koch brothers, Tim Phillips, James Miller, and Art Pope.[86] Tim Phillips, a GOP activist credited with organizing Tea Party demonstrations across the nation, serves as the president of AFP. Both Miller and Pope serve on the AFP board of directors. During the 1980s, Miller chaired the Federal Trade Commission under President Reagan. Pope is a past member of the North Carolina House of Representatives and major financial supporter of GOP office seekers. According to FactCheck, AFP spent more than $45 million during the 2010 election cycle, using radio and television advertisements to challenge the policy positions of particular candidates across the states.[87] Next, FreedomWorks is the brainchild of Dick Armey, a former member of the U.S. House of Representatives (one time majority leader) and a proponent of the "flat tax." Another veteran GOP strategist, Sal Russo, founded the Tea Party Express in 2009. Russo's career in politics started in California in 1966 with Ronald Reagan's gubernatorial campaign. Under Russo's direction, Tea Party Express has become the largest supporter of Tea Party candidates for federal office, having raised more than $7.6 million for the 2010 election cycle, or 96 percent of all money amassed by Tea Party–named PACs.[88] It has also organized several bus tours and demonstrations.

Third, since the early days of the movement, the national Tea Party groups have tried to tap into the energy of the movement and, as Brendan Steinhauser of FreedomWorks said, "institutionalize the revolution."[89] While rank-and-file Tea Partiers are sometimes ambivalent about their objectives, the power players have sought to use the crusade as a means of achieving more fundamental goals: reducing taxes, cutting federal regulations of big business, electing more Republicans to Congress, and running Obama out of office. To pursue these objectives, AFP operatives like Peggy Venable have said that they "help 'educate' Tea Party activists on policy details, and to give them 'next-step training' after their rallies, so that their political energy could be channeled 'more effectively.'"[90] The big Tea Party groups also claim to be grassroots. According to its president and CEO, Matt Kibbe, FreedomWorks has "hundreds of thousands of grassroots volunteers nationwide."[91] Furthermore, the group maintains that it is using the same organizing tools employed by liberal organizations like MoveOn, including "AstroTurf" lobbying, a practice derided as an artificial attempt to produce grassroots pressure. "If you look at MoveOn's model . . . if you consider that AstroTurfing, I'd probably have to say that we're AstroTurfing," said FreedomWorks spokesperson Adam Brandon.[92]

Finally, both state and national Tea Party organizations have had to defend themselves against charges of racism. At rallies across the United States, some Tea Partiers or their associates held signs that reeked of intolerance—some of which depicted President Obama as a Nazi. Others made appalling comments to the media, either in print or on television.[93] Soon thereafter, in a fashion similar to earlier radical conservative movements, Tea Partiers turned to a number of black representatives to shield their groups against allegations of bigotry. Some black members argued that the movement had been "infiltrated" by outsiders intent on discrediting their work.[94] The strongest black voices within the Tea Party include Republican congressmen Allen West of Florida and Tim Scott of South Carolina, both of whom rode the uprising all the way to the House of Representatives, and former business executive and presidential candidate Herman Cain.[95] While campaigning, West and Scott talked about how Tea Partiers had embraced them. Now in office, both men, as members of the Tea Party Caucus, have continued to speak favorably of the movement and challenge its detractors. For example, West has intimated that he frightens the "liberal establishment" because, as "a black man who was brought up in the inner cities, career military, a conservative, married going on 22 years, two beautiful daughters," his success could inspire other blacks to abandon the Democratic Party and follow his example. Lastly, Cain is arguably the most high profile of the Tea Party's black defenders. In speech after speech on the 2012 presidential campaign trail, he minimized the role of race and racism in American society, in general, and in the Tea Party movement, in particular. In explaining the troubles of some modern-day blacks, Cain said that they "weren't held back because of racism."[96] Instead, blacks "sometimes hold themselves back because they want to use racism as an excuse for them not being able to achieve." In responding to charges of racism within the insurgency that fueled his run for the White House, Cain said that he "would know racism if he saw it" and that racism "doesn't exist in the movement."[97] For people like West, Scott, and Cain, the real culprits are those in the "liberal media" who discourage people from participating in the Tea Party by denouncing it as racist. West and Cain have gone so far as to argue that African Americans have been "brainwashed" into not considering a conservative outlook.

In sum, the Tea Party movement functions very differently at the state and national levels of analysis. At the state level, it is decentralized and cash strapped, with most groups lacking a formal governance structure and large sums of capital. At the national level, the major associations—like Americans for Prosperity, FreedomWorks, and the Tea Party Express—were created by elite political and economic figures that have worked to "institutionalize" the Tea Party insurgency. Moreover, because they are connected to the wealthy and Washington power-players, the national Tea Party groups have greater financial and political resources. Next, in the final section of this chapter, we direct our attention to detailing the Tea Party movement's intense opposition to President Barack Obama and his policies.

"NOBAMA": The Tea Party and the President

The contempt that Tea Partiers have for the President Obama is both personal and political. Regarding the president's personality and values, Tea Party supporters are concerned about Obama's principles, citizenship, religion, and race, a matter that will be discussed in further detail shortly. When he was running for the Democratic nomination, some of Obama's critics—including his greatest rival,

Table 8.4. The Tea Party and President Barack Obama: Matters of Personality, 2010

		Tea Party	All Respondents	Difference
Do you think Barack Obama does or does not understand the needs and problems of people like yourself?	Yes	24%	58%	-34
	No	73	39	+34
Do you think Barack Obama shares the values most Americans try to live by?	Yes	20%	57%	-37
	No	75	37	+38
Do you think Barack Obama was born in the United States, or was he born in another country?	Born in U.S.	41%	58%	-17
	Born in another country	30	20	+10
What is your opinion of Barack Obama?	Approve	7%	43%	-36
	Disapprove	84	33	+51
	Undecided	7	17	-10
	Haven't heard enough	2	7	-5

Source: "National Survey of Tea Party Supporters," CBS/*New York Times* Poll, April 5–12, 2010.
Total N = 1,580, Tea Party N = 881

then senator Hillary Clinton—said that he was too professorial and aloof, even "elitist."[98] This was especially the case after an appearance in San Francisco when Obama said that small-town Americans "cling to guns or religion or antipathy to people who aren't like them" to cope with their own struggles. Three years later, Tea Partiers still think that the president is disconnected. Table 8.4 demonstrates that an overwhelming majority of Tea Party supporters, 73 percent, believe that Obama does not understand the problems or needs of people like them. Seventy-five percent do not think that he shares the values that most Americans try to live by.

Next, as noted earlier, unsubstantiated rumors regarding the president's citizenship and religion dogged him for months. Around conservative media outlets, numerous stories were floated that suggested that Obama was either born in Africa or was an undercover Muslim—a peculiar charge when considering that, for much the 2008 campaign, Obama's detractors argued that he was the wrong type of Christian due to his long association with a fiery black minister, Reverend Jeremiah Wright.[99] These perspectives were not just advanced by far-right fringe personalities, however. Rather, high-profile Republicans from Mike Huckabee, to Sarah Palin, to Newt Gingrich egged on the "birthers," who believed that Obama was not a natural-born citizen and was therefore ineligible to serve as president. Even after the president produced the long form of his Hawaiian birth certificate, critics still charged that it was a fake. The effect of this drawn-out controversy was reflected in data gathered by the CBS/*New York Times* Poll and other survey outfits. Table 8.4 shows that, when asked if Obama was born in America or in another country, 30 percent of Tea Partiers and 20 percent of all respondents said that they believed he was born elsewhere. Another 29 percent of Tea Party respondents said that they did not know where the president was born. Relatedly, the Pew Research Center found that 47 percent of all staunch conservatives—the political typology most supportive of the Tea Party—believed that Obama was born in another country.[100]

When Tea Partiers were asked to volunteer what they did not like about President Obama, the most frequent reply, which was offered by 19 percent of the Tea Party respondents, was that they "just don't like him."[101] Interestingly, the disdain that Tea Partiers have for the president is not limited to him alone. Rather, there is evidence that they also dislike the First Lady of the United States. According to the Pew Research Center's study on political typology, 69 percent of all respondents had a favorable view of Michelle Obama, with 56 percent of "main street Republicans" sharing that view. Sixty-eight percent of staunch conservatives, though, held an unfavorable view of the First Lady, "including 43% who say they have a very unfavorable opinion."[102] Such persons may have taken their cues from the likes of Sarah Palin, Rush Limbaugh, and others who have roundly mocked Obama's "Let's Move!" campaign, which is designed to fight childhood obesity.[103]

Regarding President Obama's politics and policies, supporters of the Tea Party movement are much more likely than people in the general population to disagree with his approach to a number of important issues. Ninety-two percent of the 647 Tea Party groups surveyed by the *Washington Post* opposed the policies of the Obama administration and the Democratic Party. Furthermore, table 8.5 reveals that 93 percent of Tea Party backers disapprove of the president's handling of the economy compared to 46 percent of all survey respondents, a difference of 45 points. Similarly, while most Americans, 53 percent, object to the president's handling of the national debt, Tea Partiers, at 91 percent, were much more likely to go against Obama on the issue. On the subject of health care reform, which featured a hot-tempered debate over the Affordable Healthcare Act of 2010, nine out of ten Tea Partiers object to the president's handling of the issue, compared to 51 percent of all respondents. All in all, Tea Party supporters (92 percent) are more likely than Americans in general (52 percent) to believe that the Obama administration's policies are pushing the nation toward socialism. To that end, roughly 56 percent believe that Obama has played the role of a modern-day Robin Hood by pursuing economic policies that favor the poor over the middle and upper classes. Thus, it is no surprise that almost nine out of ten Tea Party backers disapprove of the way that the president is handling his job.

Finally, the data also show that race drives some Tea Party backers to oppose President Obama. Even before Obama was inaugurated, and despite his efforts to avoid racial controversies, a sizeable segment of the white community feared that having a black president would yield a domestic policy program that favored people of color over whites. Table 8.5 shows that one out of four Tea Partiers believe that the president's policies have actually favored blacks over whites, compared with one out of ten Americans, in general. In a separate national survey conducted by the Blair Center of Southern Politics, when asked to think about the future, 46.1 percent of Tea Party members thought that things would be "worse" or "much worse" for whites, compared to 24.5 percent of non–Tea Party supporters.[104] What is more, the *Washington Post* canvass of Tea Party organizations found that about one in ten groups (11 percent) said that Obama's race, ethnic background, or religion was either a "somewhat important" or a "very important" factor in the support that their organization had received.

In summary, it is clear that supporters of the Tea Party movement strongly dislike President Obama and his policies. With regard

Table 8.5. The Tea Party and President Barack Obama: Matters of Policy, 2010

		Tea Party	All Respondents	Difference
Do you approve of the way that Barack Obama is handling his job?	Approve	7%	50%	-43
	Disapprove	88	40	+48
Do you approve of the way Barack Obama is handling the economy?	Approve	6%	43%	-37
	Disapprove	91	46	+45
Do you approve of the way Barack Obama is handling health care?	Approve	6%	41%	-35
	Disapprove	93	51	+42
Do you approve of the way Barack Obama is handling the federal budget deficit?	Approve	5%	29%	-24
	Disapprove	91	53	+38
In trying to solve the economic problems facing the country, do you think Barack Obama has expanded the role of government too much?	Too much	89%	37%	+52
	Not enough	3	18	-15
	About right	6	36	-30
Do you think Barack Obama's policies are moving the country more toward socialism?	Toward socialism	92%	52%	+40
	Not toward socialism	6	38	-32
Do you think the policies of the Obama Administration favor the rich, middle class, the poor, or do they treat all groups equally?	Favor rich	16%	17%	-1
	Favor middle-class	6	19	-13
	Favor poor	56%	27%	+29
	Treat all equally	9	27	-18
Do you think the policies of the Obama administration favor whites over blacks, favor blacks over whites, or do they treat both groups the same?	Favor whites	1%	2%	-1
	Favor blacks	25	11	+14
	Treat both groups the same	65	83	-18

Source: "National Survey of Tea Party Supporters," CBS/*New York Times* Poll, April 5–12, 2010.
Total N = 1,580, Tea Party N = 881

to the president's character, Tea Party members think that Obama does not care about people like them. They also believe that he does not live by the same values as most Americans, as they are apt to describe Obama as "un-American" or "socialist." Moreover, some continue to think of the president as a Muslim, despite the facts that have been presented to the public. Lastly, on matters of politics and policy, Tea Partiers strongly disapprove of the president's actions on nearly every major issue that the administration has faced, including the economy, budget deficits and the national debt, and health care reform. Some of them also feel threatened by Obama's racial identity and think that he has used the presidency to advance the interests of blacks over those of other Americans. Thus, Tea Party enmity for the president is both personal and political.

Conclusions and Outlook

Following Barack Obama's victory in the 2008 presidential election, a strong majority of Americans believed that he would help improve race relations, as it was thought that the nation's greatest glass ceiling had been shattered. What is more, many political observers wondered if the Republican Party was too reliant on older white voters and southerners to remain competitive in future contests. The immediate emergence and sheer force of the Tea Party movement, however, has proven that tales of the demise of radical conservatism were greatly exaggerated. To the contrary, some commentators, like Patrick Buchanan, have welcomed the increase in white racial consciousness, believing that it provides a basis for constructing an electoral coalition to defeat President Obama.

This chapter has employed Ronald Walters' theory of white nationalism to evaluate the Tea Party movement, assess its overall impact on the national political discourse, and to break down the movement's opposition to the president. White nationalism refers to radical conservatives who seek to use their own political and economic resources and the power of government to preserve white hegemony by subordinating people of color. The core features of a white nationalist political movement include heightened racial consciousness, alienation from government, and a sense of power deflation that renders whites victims of racism and threatens their position in the society. Once stirred, white nationalists focus their fury not only on state actors and institutions but also on the allegedly undeserving beneficiaries of government largess. The theory of white nationalism is useful because it helps researchers to explain how racism has evolved and continues to threaten the economic, political, and social advancement of people of color in the post–civil rights era.

Walters pointed to increased competition from racial minorities and white economic stagnation as the principal determinates of white nationalist uprisings. Such conditions were provided by the election of Barack Obama and the onset of the Great Recession, the nation's worst economic downturn since the 1930s. Alienated from government and suffering through a devastating recession, a segment of the white community grew increasingly angry about the state of affairs in America. In early 2009, the Tea Party movement provided a public space for white frustration to be articulated and transformed into political action.

Based on the analysis presented here, the following conclusions can be drawn about the Tea Party and its impact on American government and politics to date. First, it is the latest in a long line of radical conservative movements that has placed pressure on whichever of the two major parties was previously most receptive to white nationalist interests. The demographics of the Tea Party reveal that its supporters are overwhelmingly white, male, older, staunchly conservative, and Republican. They are also very angry and dissatisfied with government. Second, in terms of organization, structure, and leadership, the Tea Party movement is amorphous and lacks a central spokesperson. At the state level of analysis, groups are decentralized, lack formal governance structures, and are strapped for cash. At the national level, though, groups like Americans for Prosperity, FreedomWorks, and the Tea Party Express were creations of "political animals" that control greater financial and political resources. Such organizations have sought to use the power of the movement to pursue their own objectives. Finally, Tea Party supporters are fairly united in their disdain for President Obama and his policies. By and large, they believe that he is un-American and that his policies have placed the nation on the path toward socialism. Some Tea Partiers, about 25 percent, also feel threatened by Obama's race and think that he has advanced the interests of racial minorities over those of whites. Thus, Tea Party antipathy for the president is both personal and political.

The last few years have demonstrated that the Tea Party movement is a force with which to be reckoned. During the 2010 midterm election cycle, Tea Party supporters and organizations targeted congressional lawmakers that were deemed insufficiently conservative on issues such as the economy, government spending, and health care. Their efforts helped turn over the House of Representatives to the Republican Party and to cut into the Democratic Party's majority in the Senate. Looking to the 2012 election cycle, and considering the impact of the Supreme Court's decision in *Citizens United v. F.E.C.*, the national Tea Party groups were well positioned to raise tremendous sums of money to mobilize opposition against President Obama, the Democratic Party, and Republicans who stray too far from conservative dogma. Moreover, as staunch conservatives who harbor hostility toward government and believe that too much has been made of the problems facing people of color, Tea Partiers pose a serious challenge to the material- and rights-based interests of racial minority groups. Thus, it would be highly illogical to conclude that a powerful phenomenon such as white nationalism does not have political implications.

Notes

1. Patrick J. Buchanan, "Losing White America," *The American Conservative*, July 22, 2010. http://www.theamericanconservative.com/blog/2010/07/22/losing-white-america (September 15, 2010).
2. Jennifer Bendery, "Allen West: I Am the Modern Day Harriet Tubman [Update]," Huffington Post, August 18, 2011. http://www.huffingtonpost.com/2011/08/18/allen-west-harriet-tubman_n_930052.html (September 15, 2011).
3. Ronald W. Walters, *White Nationalism, Black Interests: Conservative Public Policy and the Black Community* (Detroit: Wayne State University Press, 2003), 22.
4. Jon F. Hale, "The Making of the New Democrats," *Political Science Quarterly* 110, 2 (1995): 207; "Illinois Senate Candidate Barack Obama," *Washington Post*, July 27, 2004. http://www.

washingtonpost.com/wp-dyn/articles/A19751-2004Jul27.html (August 15, 2011).

5. Adia Harvey Wingfield and Joe R. Feagin, *Yes We Can? White Racial Framing and the 2008 Presidential Campaign* (New York: Routledge, 2010).

6. Respondents were asked, "Do each of the following describe or not describe your reaction to Barack Obama being elected president?" They were then read the following words: proud, optimistic, excited, pessimistic, and afraid. Frank Newport, "Americans See Obama Election as Race Relations Milestone," Gallup, November 7, 2008. http://www.gallup.com/poll/111817/americans-see-obama-election-race-relations-milestone.aspx (June 24, 2011).

7. "National Exit Poll Table," *New York Times*, November 5, 2008. http://elections.nytimes.com/2008/results/president/national-exit-polls.html (August 15, 2011).

8. Christopher S. Parker, Mark Q. Sawyer, and Christopher Towler, "A Black Man in the White House? The Role of Racism and Patriotism in the 2008 Presidential Election," *Du Bois Review* 6, 1 (2009): 194; Hanes Walton, Jr., and Robert C. Smith, *American Politics and the African American Quest for Universal Freedom*, 5th Edition (Boston: Longman, 2010), 138; Andra Gillespie, "Judged by His Actions: How President Obama Addressed Race in the First Six Months of His Administration," *Journal of Race and Policy* 6, 1 (2010): 11. Also see Joseph McCormick and Charles Jones, "The Conceptualization of Deracialization in African American Urban Politics," in *Dilemmas of Black Politics*, ed. Georgia Persons, 66–84 (New York: HarperCollins, 1993).

9. Adam Nossiter, "For South, a Waning Hold on National Politics," *New York Times*, November 10, 2008. http://www.nytimes.com/2008/11/11/us/politics/11south.html (October 31, 2011).

10. Michael Tesler and David O. Sears, *Obama's Race: The 2008 Election and the Dream of a Post-Racial America* (Chicago: University of Chicago Press, 2010), 6.

11. Newport, "Americans See Obama."

12. "Signs of the Times: Tea Party Protests," Black Enterprise, July 15, 2010. http://www.blackenterprise.com/2010/07/15/signs-of-the-times-tea-party-protests (August 17, 2011).

13. Even former Arkansas governor Mike Huckabee, a serious

contender for the 2008 Republican presidential nomination, said, "One thing that I do know is his having grown up in Kenya, his view of the Brits, for example, (is) very different than the average American." The president eventually released the long form of his birth certificate. Philip Elliot, "Fact Check: Huckabee Claims Obama Grew Up in Kenya," Yahoo! News, March 1, 2011. http://news.yahoo.com/huckabee-wrongly-says-obama-grew-kenya-20110301-115817-303.html (March 2, 2011).

14. "CNN, Tea Party Express to Host First-Ever Tea Party Debate, Sept. 12," September 8, 2011. http://cnnpressroom.blogs.cnn.com/2011/09/08/cnn-tea-party-express-to-host-first-ever-tea-party-debate-sept-12 (October 28, 2011).

15. Dinesh D'Souza, *The End of Racism: Principles for a Multiracial Society* (New York: The Free Press, 1995), 525. Also see John H. McWhorter, *Losing the Race: Self-Sabotage in Black America* (New York: The Free Press, 2000); Abigail Thernstrom and Stephan Thernstrom, *No Excuses: Closing the Racial Gap in Learning* (New York: Simon & Schuster, 2003); Shelby Steele, *White Guilt: How Blacks and Whites Together Destroyed the Promise of the Civil Rights Era* (New York: HarperCollins Publishers, 2006).

16. D'Souza, *The End of Racism*, 551.

17. John Ridley, "The Manifesto of Ascendancy for the Modern American Nigger," *Esquire*, November 30, 2006. http://www.esquire.com/features/ESQ1206BLACKESSAY_108 (February 23, 2007).

18. Richard J. Herrnstein and Charles Murray, *The Bell Curve: Intelligence and Class Structure in American Life* (New York: The Free Press, 1994); William J. Bennett, John J. DiIulio, Jr., and John P. Walters, *Body Count: Moral Poverty . . . And How to Win America's War Against Crime and Drugs* (New York: Simon & Schuster, 2001).

19. Paul M. Sniderman and Thomas Piazza, *The Scar of Race* (Cambridge, MA: Harvard University Press, 1993), 5.

20. William Julius Wilson, *The Declining Significance of Race: Blacks and Changing American Institutions* (Chicago: University of Chicago Press, 1978), 134.

21. William Julius Wilson, *The Truly Disadvantaged: The Inner City, the Underclass, and Public Policy* (Chicago: University of Chicago Press, 1987).

22. Michael Omi and Howard Winant, *Racial Formation in the United*

States from the 1960s to the 1990s, 2nd ed. (New York: Routledge 1994).

23. Lawrence Bobo, James R. Kluegel, and Ryan A. Smith, "Laissez-Faire Racism: The Crystallization of a 'Kindler, Gentler' Anti-Black Ideology," in *Racial Attitudes in the 1990s: Continuity and Change*, ed. Steven A. Tuch and Jack K. Martin, 39–56 (Westport, CT: Praeger, 1997); Patricia Hill Collins, *Black Sexual Politics: African Americans, Gender, and the New Racism* (New York: Routledge, 2005); Eduardo Bonilla-Silva, *Racism without Racists: Color-Blind Racism and the Persistence of Racial Inequality in the United States*, 2nd ed. (Lanham, MD: Rowman & Littlefield, 2006).

24. Philomena Essed, *Understanding Everyday Racism: An Interdisciplinary Theory* (Newbury Park, CA: Sage Publications, 1991); Joe R. Feagin, *Systemic Racism: A Theory of Oppression* (New York: Routledge, 2006).

25. Bonilla-Silva, *Racism without Racists*.

26. Ernest J. Wilson III, "Why Political Scientists Don't Study Black Politics, but Historians and Sociologists Do," *PS* 18, 3 (1985): 600–07; Paula D. McClain and John A. Garcia, "Expanding Disciplinary Boundaries: Black, Latino, and Racial Minority Group Politics in Political Science," in *Political Science: The State of the Discipline II*, ed. Ada W. Finifter, 247–80 (Washington, DC: American Political Science Association, 1993); Wilber C. Rich, *African American Perspectives on Political Science* (Philadelphia: Temple University Press, 2007).

27. Ronald W. Walters, *Black Presidential Politics in America: A Strategic Approach* (Albany: State University of New York Press, 1988); Carol M. Swain, *Black Faces, Black Interests: The Representation of African Americans in Congress* (Cambridge, MA: Harvard University Press, 1995); Katherine Tate, *Black Faces in the Mirror: African Americans and Their Representatives in the U.S. Congress* (Princeton, NJ: Princeton University Press, 2003); Tasha S. Philpot, *Race, Republicans, and the Return of the Party of Lincoln* (Ann Arbor: University of Michigan Press, 2007).

28. Michael Dawson, *Behind the Mule: Race and Class in African-American Politics* (Princeton, NJ: Princeton University Press, 1994); Lucius J. Barker, Mack H. Jones, and Katherine Tate, *African Americans and the American Political System*, 4th ed. (Upper Saddle River, NJ: Prentice Hall, 1999); Fredrick C. Harris, *Something Within: Religion in African-American Political Activism* (New York:

Oxford University Press, 1999); Ollie A. Johnson III and Karin L. Stanford, *Black Political Organizations in the Post–Civil Rights Era* (New Brunswick, NJ: Rutgers University Press, 2002); John A. Garcia, *Latino Politics in America: Community, Culture, and Interests* (Lanham, MD: Rowman & Littlefield, 2003); Melissa Harris-Lacewell, *Barbershops, Bibles, and BET: Everyday Talk and Black Political Thought* (Princeton, NJ: Princeton University Press, 2004); Pei-Te Lien, M. Margaret Conway, and Janelle Wong, *The Politics of Asian Americans: Diversity and Community* (New York: Routledge, 2004); David E. Wilkins, *American Indian Politics and the American Political System* (Lanham, MD: Rowman & Littlefield, 2007).

29. Walters, *White Nationalism*, 2.
30. Ibid., 26.
31. First, Walters did not seek to calculate how many Americans are white nationalists, as it is difficult to quantify such a thing. Nor did he claim that white conservatives and white nationalists are always the same. Second, Walters never maintained that all whites were conservative or nationalists. "Just as every Jewish person is not a Zionist and every black person is not a Black Nationalist, every White person is not a White Nationalist." Finally, some whites have rejected the benefits of white privilege in order to advocate for social justice. Ibid., 21, 26.
32. Ibid., 21.
33. Ibid., 15.
34. Ibid., 178.
35. David A. Bositis, *Black Elected Officials: A Statistical Summary* (Washington, DC: Joint Center for Political and Economic Studies, 2003), 13.
36. Walters, *White Nationalism*, 29.
37. Bureau of the Census, "Current Population Reports, Educational Attainment in the United States: 2006." http://www.census.gov/hhes/socdemo/education (October 8, 2008).
38. Bureau of the Census, "Money Income of Households—Percent Distribution by Income Level, Race, and Hispanic Origin, in Constant (2008) Dollars: 1980 to 2008," in *Statistical Abstract of the United States: 2011*, 130th ed. (Washington, DC: US GPO, 2011, Table 689).
39. Bart Landry, *The New Black Middle Class* (Berkeley: University of California Press, 1987).
40. Melvin L. Oliver and Thomas M. Shapiro, *Black Wealth/White*

Wealth: A New Perspective on Racial Inequality (New York: Routledge, 2006), 88.

41. Karyn R. Lacy, *Blue-Chip Black: Race, Class, and Status in the New Black Middle Class* (Berkeley: University of California Press, 2007), 4.

42. Walters, *White Nationalism*, 29.

43. Ibid., 30.

44. Ibid., 3.

45. Quoted in Walters, *White Nationalism*, 32.

46. Ibid., 37.

47. Ibid., 21–22; emphasis added.

48. Ibid., 22.

49. Shannon Travis, "Tea Party at Second Anniversary: What Happens Next?," CNN, February 14, 2011. http://www.cnn.com/2011/POLITICS/02/25/tea.party.anniversary/index.html (June 21, 2011).

50. "Beyond Red vs. Blue: Political Typology," Pew Research Center for the People & the Press, May 4, 2011. http://www.people-press.org/files/legacy-pdf/Beyond-Red-vs-Blue-The-Political-Typology.pdf (July 19, 2011).

51. Walton and Smith, *American Politics*, 172.

52. "National Exit Poll Table."

53. Newport, "Americans See Obama."

54. Walton and Smith, *American Politics*, 173.

55. Christopher J. Goodman and Steven M. Mance, "Employment Loss and the 2007–09 Recession: An Overview," *Monthly Labor Review Online* 134, 4 (2011): 3.

56. The previous record was established in the period from November 1944 through September 1945, when the U.S. economy had a net loss of 4.3 million jobs.

57. "Current Population Survey, Unemployment Rate, Seasonally Adjusted" (Bureau of Labor Statistics). http://data.bls.gov (October 25, 2011).

58. Bureau of Labor Statistics, "The Employment Situation—September 2011." http://www.bls.gov/news.release/pdf/empsit.pdf (October 28, 2011).

59. Rakesh Kochar, Richard Fry, and Paul Taylor, "Wealth Gaps Rise to Record Highs Between Whites, Blacks and Hispanics," *Pew Research Center, Social & Demographic Trends*, July 26, 2011.

http://www.pewsocialtrends.org/files/2011/07/SDT-Wealth-Report_7-26-11_FINAL.pdf (July 26, 2011).

60. John W. Schoen, "Study: 1.2 million households lost to recession," MSNBC, April 8, 2010. http://www.msnbc.msn.com/id/36231884/ns/business-eye_on_the_economy/t/study-million-households-lost-recession (October 25, 2011).

61. Kochar, Fry, and Taylor, "Wealth Gaps," 13.

62. Ibid., 5.

63. Kate Zernike and Megan Thee-Brenan, "Poll Finds Tea Party Backers Wealthier and More Education," *New York Times*, April 14, 2010. http://www.nytimes.com/2010/04/15/us/politics/15poll.html (July 26, 2011).

64. Lydia Saad, "Americans Believe GOP Should Consider Tea Party Ideas," Gallup, January 31, 2011. http://www.gallup.com/poll/145838/americans-believe-gop-consider-tea-party-ideas.aspx (June 21, 2011).

65. Zernike and Thee-Brenan, "Poll Finds Tea Party Backers Wealthier."

66. "Polling the Tea Party," *New York Times*, April 14, 2010. http://www.nytimes.com/interactive/2010/04/14/us/politics/20100414-tea-party-poll-graphic.html (July 26, 2011).

67. Charles A. Gallagher, "Color-Blind Privilege: The Social and Political Functions of Erasing the Color Line in Post Race America," *Race, Gender, & Class* 10, 4 (2003): 22–37.

68. Michael I. Norton and Samuel R. Sommers, "Whites See Racism as a Zero-Sum Game That They Are Now Losing," *Perspectives on Psychological Science* 6, 3 (2011): 217.

69. Ibid.

70. Chris Good, "Signs of the Times: Slogans and Images from the Tea Party Rally," *The Atlantic*, September 13, 2010. http://www.theatlantic.com/politics/archive/2010/09/signs-of-the-times-slogans-and-images-from-the-tea-party-rally/62885 (November 1, 2011).

71. "The 2010 Republican Comeback: How It Developed," *New York Times*, November 4, 2010. http://www.nytimes.com/interactive/us/politics/20101104-CAMPAIGN.html (November 1, 2011).

72. Tom Moroney and Terrence Dopp, "Tea Party Election Results Diluted in Highly Populated States," Bloomberg, November 5, 2010. http://www.bloomberg.com/news/2010-11-05/

tea-party-results-diluted-in-high-density-states-as-christie-fades-at-home.html (November 1, 2011)

73. The House of Representatives has a Tea Party Caucus that is comprised of sixty members, including thirty-seven freshmen. Minnesota Representative and 2012 presidential candidate Michele Bachmann chairs the group. In the Senate, the Tea Party Caucus is comprised of just four members, three of whom are freshmen. South Carolina senator Jim DeMint leads the caucus.

74. Susan Saulny, "A Defiant Herman Cain Suspends His Bid for Presidency," *New York Times*, December 3, 2001. http://www.nytimes.com/2011/12/04/us/politics/herman-cain-suspends-his-presidential-campaign.html (December 29, 2011).

75. David Barstow, "Tea Party Lights Fuse for Rebellion on the Right," *New York Times*, February 16, 2010. http://www.nytimes.com/2010/02/16/us/politics/16teaparty.html (July 26, 2011).

76. Amy Gardner, "Gauging the Scope of the Tea Party Movement in America," *Washington Post*, October 24, 2010. http://www.washingtonpost.com/wp-dyn/content/article/2010/10/23/AR2010102304000.html (July 26, 2011); "An Up-Close Look at the Tea Party and Its Role in the Midterm Elections," *Washington Post*, October 24, 2010, http://www.washingtonpost.com/wp-srv/special/politics/tea-party-canvass (July 26, 2011).

77. Gardner, "Gauging the Scope of the Tea Party." Also see Alex Altman, "The 2010 TIME 100," *TIME*, April 29, 2010. http://www.time.com/time/specials/packages/article/0,28804,1984685_1984864_1985462,00.html (December 26, 2011).

78. Zack Newkirk, "Tea Party Activists Press Forward Despite Meager Finances, Varied Election Success," Center for Responsive Politics, February 23, 2011. http://www.opensecrets.org/news/2011/02/tea-party-activists-press-forward.html (November 2, 2011).

79. Robert A. Dahl, *Who Governs? Democracy and Power in an American City* (New Haven: Yale University Press, 1961), 19.

80. Gardner, "Gauging the Scope of the Tea Party."

81. Dahl, *Who Governs?*, 225.

82. Chris Good, "The Tea Party Movement: Who's in Charge?," *The Atlantic*, April 13, 2009. http://www.theatlantic.com/politics/archive/2009/04/the-tea-party-movement-whos-in-charge/13041 (June 21, 2011).

83. "About Americans for Prosperity," *Americans for Prosperity*, 2011. http://www.americansforprosperity.org/about (December 24, 2011); Jane Mayer, "Covert Operations: The Billionaire Brothers Who Are Waging a War against Obama," *New Yorker*, August 30, 2010. http://www.newyorker.com/reporting/2010/08/100830 fa_fact_mayer (August 17, 2011).

84. "Tea Party Express," *Tea Party Express*, 2011. http://www.teaparty-express.org (December 25, 2011); "Players Guide: The Tea Party Express," FactCheck, October 6, 2010. http://www.factcheck.org/2010/10/tea-party-express (November 2, 2011).

85. "Tea Party Express: What Is It?," CNN, July 19, 2010. http://articles.cnn.com/2010-07-19/politics/tea.party.express_1_tea-party-express-movement-fourth-term-primary-challenger (December 26, 2001).

86. Mayer, "Covert Operations."

87. "Players Guide: Americans for Prosperity," FactCheck, October 6, 2010. http://www.factcheck.org/2010/08/americans-for-prosperity (November 2, 2011).

88. Newkirk, "Tea Party Activists Press Forward."

89. Travis, "Tea Party at Second Anniversary."

90. Mayer, "Covert Operations."

91. "About FreedomWorks," *FreedomWorks*, 2011. http://www.freedomworks.org/about/about-freedomworks (December 25, 2011).

92. Good, "The Tea Party Movement."

93. Nossiter, "For South."

94. Philip Elliott, "Black Tea Party Members Dispute Racist Claims," MSNBC, August 4, 2010. http://www.msnbc.msn.com/id/38558455/ns/politics-more_politics/t/black-tea-party-members-dispute-racist-claims (December 30, 2011).

95. Jennifer Steinhauer, "Black and Republican and Back in Congress," *New York Times*, November 5, 2010. http://www.nytimes.com/2010/11/06/us/politics/06house.html (December 29, 2011).

96. Shannon Travis, "Cain's Race Not as Big an Issue with Conservatives as Obama's Was Three Years Ago," CNN, October 13, 2011. http://politicalticker.blogs.cnn.com/2011/10/13/cains-race-not-as-big-an-issue-with-conservatives-as-obamas-was-three-years-ago (December 29, 2011).

97. "Tea Party Favorite Herman Cain: Racism 'doesn't exist in the

movement,'" CNN, September 12, 2011. http://am.blogs. cnn.com/2011/09/12/tea-party-favorite-herman-cain-racism-doesnt-exist-in-the-movement (December 29, 2011).

98. Michael Finnegan, "Obama Expresses Regret for Remarks," *Los Angeles Times*, April 13, 2008. http://articles.latimes.com/2008/apr/13/nation/na-obama13 (December 30, 2011).

99. Jeff Zeleny and Adam Nagourney, "An Angry Obama Renounces Ties to His Ex-Pastor," *New York Times*, April 30, 2008. http:// www.nytimes.com/2008/04/30/us/politics/30obama.html (December 30, 2011).

100. "Beyond Red vs. Blue," 66.

101. Brian Montopoli, "Tea Party Supporters: Who They Are and What They Believe," CBS News, April 14, 2010. http:// www.cbsnews.com/8301-503544_162-20002529-503544.html (November 1, 2011).

102. "Beyond Red vs. Blue," 65.

103. Richard Pérez-Peña, "Skip the Sundae? Christie Is on the First Lady's Side," *New York Times*, February 27, 2011. http://www. nytimes.com/2011/02/28/region/28christie.html (December 30, 2011).

104. Angie Maxwell, "Tea Party Distinguished by Racial Views and Fears of the Future," Diane D. Blair Center of Southern Politics & Society, n.d. http://blairrockefellerpoll.uark.edu/5295.php (June 21, 2011).

9

White Nationalism, Black Interests, and Contemporary American Politics

COREY COOK

Professor Ronald Walters' varied contributions as a scholar, activist, and public intellectual are immeasurable. His work simultaneously informs the ongoing political and policy discourse and advances the academic literature. *White Nationalism, Black Interests: Conservative Public Policy and the Black Community* (2003) is perhaps his magnum opus. The book is a boldly conceived, meticulously researched, and compellingly argued analysis of the oft-cited but ill-explained conservative drift of American politics. Published at the height of the "conservative revolution," the first time in generations that the Republican Party controlled the House, Senate, presidency, and judiciary, the book was undoubtedly timely. It has turned out to be as prescient as it was provocative; nearly a decade later, its relevance has only increased. While Walters is correct that the 2000 election "completed the capture of the American political system by the radical Conservative wing of the Republican party" (Walters 2003, 1), the success of the Tea Party in capturing the entirety of the Republican Party and pursuing a more explicitly white nationalist agenda in the 2010 and 2012 elections only affirms his thesis.

On a personal level, *White Nationalism, Black Interests* came at a crucial time in my career and provided a desperately needed theoretical and conceptual underpinning for my dissertation research on the relationship between the descriptive and substantive representation of identity groups in Congress. My colleague Professor Robert Smith, who had listened to me struggle through an explanation of how I operationalized "white interests," suggested that Walters' book might help sharpen my thinking and refine my empirical measures. Though I had engaged many of the critical race theorists cited by Professor Walters, including Michael Omi and Howard Winant, I struggled to develop how to systematically discern and study the representation of white interests in Congress. Because proponents of these policies couch their agenda in race-neutral language, the intentions of these policies goes unstated and often undetected, rendering them opaque to many political scientists. As Dr. Walters explains, "given a condition where one race is dominant in all political institutions, most policy actions appear to take on an objective quality, where policy makers argue that they are acting on the basis of 'national interests' rather than racial ones" (Walters 2003, 2). But rather than shrink from the challenge of recognizing "the racial interests of the majority in policy making, since policy is rarely articulated in terms that directly imply favoring the dominant group" (Walters 2003, 2), he offers a compelling "inferential" approach for identifying these policies: that they seek to produce "racially disparate outcomes," challenge "the fundamental interests of Blacks," and maintain racial hierarchies of power and privilege (Walters 2003, 250 and 91). In this manner, Professor Walters has laid forth a new realm of research for scholars in American political science and history.

White Nationalism, Black Interests

In *White Nationalism, Black Interests*, Professor Walters challenges the conventional wisdom that the growing conservatism of American public policy is simply a pendulum shift away from the Great Society programs of the 1960s or a principled critique of big government. Rather, he asserts that this radical conservatism ought to be conceptualized as the culmination of a several-decades-long white nationalist movement committed to reinstituting and strengthening racialized hierarchies of power and privilege. He writes, "we appear to be living in an era when a dominant sector of the White majority seems to have lost confidence in the promise of a liberal democratic state . . . (and) is proceeding to concentrate economic and social power within its own group, using its control over political institutions of the state to punish presumptive enemies" (Walters 2003, 1). The ardent attack on the welfare state and the civil rights state is not so much a philosophical critique of government or the reformulation of the relationship between state and society, what others neatly call "neo-liberalism," but rather, as Professor Walters asserts, an effort by the white majority to seize political power and discipline the state appa-ratus to serve racial group interests: "to maintain White Supremacy by subordinating Blacks and other non-Whites" (Walters 2003, 26). Before discussing one empirical substantiation of Walters' work and a discussion of present-day conservative extremism and Tea Party Republicanism, I briefly highlight three themes of the book.

In the first part of the book, Walters offers a robust theoretical and historical discussion of white nationalism, documenting the rise of the contemporary movement in the United States, tracing its origins to at least the 1970s. He views this movement as analogous to the majority white backlash to the first reconstruction whereby white attitudes across the ideological spectrum converged in favor of racial group interests and a bipartisan consensus emerged to aban-don reconstruction, reconsolidate white political power, and disen-franchise African Americans. Walters shows that a similar process has emerged in the past several decades; he argues that a vocal and influential segment of the white community perceives the economic and political gains made by blacks and other minority groups during the past forty years as a threat to their economic and political privi-lege, experiences relative power deflation, and undergoes a growing racial consciousness. White nationalists "resent the fact that Blacks are accorded access to social resources or that they appear to have achieved equal status" (Walters 2003, 29). As such, these nationalists become "estranged and alienated from the state" and intend to dis-cipline the state "to once again serve the interests of the dominant cultural group" (Walters 2003, 16).

Next, Professor Walters explores the political and partisan dynam-ics of white nationalism and the formation of a policy rationale that embraces anti-statism and "the assertion of collective counter-rights" through a program of "racelessness" (Walters 2003, 21). Dr. Walters terms this policy framework "Gingrichism," after the architect of the Republican takeover of the House. He demonstrates how the nationalist political strategy initially sought to gain electoral victo-ries through the capture of the Republican Party but shows that the ultimate success of this movement depends also on two additional historical developments. First, after the 1994 election, the Democratic Party abandoned its black constituency and offered only symbolic gestures rather than substantive responsiveness, resulting in a convergence of white political interests "regardless of political ideology or policy" (Walters 2003, 6). And second, black conservatives committed to deconstructing the civil rights regime and opposing the use of the state apparatus to weaken racial hierarchies began to emerge to act as "proxy agents" of the white nationalist movement.

The bulk of *White Nationalism, Black Interests* supports Professor Walters' thesis that beneath the surface of radical conservative policymaking exists an unstated but unmistakably white nationalistic series of policy initiatives. Dr. Walters asserts that in endeavoring to deregulate the civil rights regime, radically modify and minimize the welfare state, wage a war on particular types of crime, and regulate access to educational institutions, white nationalist policymakers elevate white substantive interests and target nonwhites for punishment. He credits these policymakers with appropriating the language of civil rights while simultaneously enforcing Anglo cultural standards designed to underscore the legitimacy of white nationalists' right to govern and crafting racist public policies. In sum, "the White Nationalist movement created an ideology which has had a decisive impact on the political system, producing elected and appointed officials as policy makers who utilized this ideology to foment institutional racism with the courts, the Congress, and the executive branch" (Walters 2003, 250). Taken together, the book is an intellectual tour de force that challenges conventional understandings of the "Reagan revolution" and compellingly resituates race at the center of American politics. In and of itself, that is an enormous achievement. But the book also offers fertile ground for empirically oriented scholars to sow.

White Nationalism, Black Interests and
Research on Racial Representation

As noted earlier, something of a cottage industry has sprung up among students of racial, ethnic, and gender politics seeking to discern whether elected members of historically underrepresented groups are more likely to promote group interests while in office. These scholars assert, like Professor Walters does in his conclusion, that "Black interests are coherent . . . [because Blacks] operate out of an identity conceived from a relatively cohesive culture and a history in this country which has given them a roughly coherent outlook on American life" (Walters 2003, 252–53). After citing some combination of linked fates, group consciousness, common political socialization processes, and/or distinctive policy attitudes as evidence of a more or less tentative set of identifiable group interests these scholars utilize a wide array of measures and quantitatively rigorous methodologies to explore whether the election of blacks, Latinos, or women (most principally) "matters." Unfortunately, the literature fails to similarly examine the representation of dominant group interests: "White racial interests in objective majoritarian politics has drawn little attention" (Walters 2003, 253). While studies measuring representation of minority racial and ethnic group interests fill the scholarly journals, there are few scholarly explorations of the representation of white interests and none with the systematic rigor of the parallel literature on political minorities. *White Nationalism, Black Interests* recasts the literature on racial representation by displacing its conventional concern with the substantive representation of black or Latino interests to examine how white elected officials act to maintain racialized hierarchies of power and privilege. And it offers a viable design for approaching this research by providing a precise conceptualization of "white interests" that has deterred previous scholarship.

For instance, the leading study of racial representation in Congress, David Canon's *Race, Redistricting, and Representation: The Unintended Consequences of Black Majority Districts* (1999) explicitly dichotomizes legislation as either in promotion of "Black interests" or as "race-neutral." In contrast to this predominant literature that takes the claim of race-neutrality at its face value, Walters asserts that the "White Nationalist movement has helped racialize public policy" (Walters 2003, 92) by mobilizing political institutions to "reward, punish and so structure outcomes as to protect and enhance *racial interests*" (Walters 2003, 2; emphasis mine). And while "Whites are not homogenous with respect to their interests or racial and ethnic consciousness" (Walters 2003, 12), it remains possible to discern an objective "White interest" in maintaining "race privileges" (Walters 2003, 18). This notion became a principle concern of my research, and his operationalization of white interests provided the structural logic to how I coded the data in my empirical study. By effectively challenging the dominant paradigm, Professor Walters has blazed a trail for a generation of empirical work.

In my dissertation research, I study sponsorship, co-sponsorship, and roll call voting behavior from four Congresses from 1991 to 1999. In so doing, I coded over twenty thousand bills for their racial content, attempting to discern those that contain the intention of producing, whether explicitly or implicitly, "racially disparate outcomes." And while a complete retelling of the results is beyond the scope of this chapter (complete findings are available from the author), generally speaking, the empirical results overwhelmingly support Professor Walters' thesis. Just as he describes over a longer period, over the eight years of my study, white members increasingly sponsored and co-sponsored legislation implicitly or explicitly promoting white interests relative to legislation promoting black or Chicano interests. The ratio of bills coded as "white interest legislation" to bills coded as "black interest legislation" co-sponsored by white members rose from 3.2 to 1 in the 102nd Congress to 6.8 to 1 in the 104th Congress. Likely responding to the perceived growing racial hostility within the chamber, members of the Congressional Black Caucus increased their representation of black interests. The ratio of "black interest legislation" to "white interest legislation" co-sponsored by African American lawmakers increased rather steadily from 1.6 to 1 to 2.1 to 1.

The multivariate analysis of these sponsorship and co-sponsorship figures reveal that prior to the 1994 election, the most consistent predictors of a legislator's promotion of white interests is party affiliation. In every Congress, Republicans were more likely—controlling for region, district characteristics, and the race of the member—to support white interests. After 1994, race also becomes a significant predictor of these legislative priorities, with white members of Congress statistically more likely, regardless of the demographic characteristics of their districts, to sponsor and co-sponsor these bills. However, the impact of partisanship remained consistent before and after the Republican revolution.

My quantitative analysis of roll call votes during this period (using a negative binomial regression model) similarly confirms at the individual level what Dr. Walters observes at the institutional level. Roll call voting behavior is consistently explained by three variables in my

Table 9.1. All Co-Sponsorships in the U.S. House of Representatives, 1991–1998, Coded by "White Interest" and "Black Interest" Substantive Legislation

	102nd Congress	*103rd Congress*	*104th Congress*	*105th Congress*
Black Members (n)	26	38	41	39
Avg. black interest co-spons.	25.9	33.0	23.9	35.0
% of total	(6.0%)	(11.0%)	(14.5%)	(12.3%)
Avg. white interest co-spons.	16.3	17.0	10.9	16.6
% of total	(3.8%)	(5.7%)	(6.6%)	(5.8%)
Total Co-Sponsorships	428.3	300.1	164.4	284.9
White Members (n)	400	382	379	381
Avg. white interest co-spons.	20.4	23.0	23.7	23.6
% of total	(6.1%)	(9.0%)	(14.1%)	(11.0%)
Avg. black interest co-spons.	6.3	6.0	3.5	6.2
% of total	(1.9%)	(2.3%)	(2.1%)	(2.9%)

Table 9.2. Multivariate Analysis of White Interest Legislative Sponsorships in the House

	102nd	*103rd*	*104th*	*105th*
Intercept	-3.067	-2.259	-2.524	-2.123
South	**-0.386***	0.068	0.137	**-0.661****
% White VAP	**0.136***	**0.128***	0.091	-0.084
% Urban VAP	0.059	**0.071***	**0.082****	-0.015
Party	**0.476***	**0.479****	**0.763*****	**0.912*****
White	0.777	0.076	0.434	**2.158*****
Total Sponsorships	226	305	339	271

* = p < .05, ** = p < .01, *** = p < .001

model. In each Congress, southern, white, and Republican members were substantially more likely than their northern, nonwhite, and Democratic colleagues to vote consistently in accordance with white "racial interests" all else equal. The evidence of racial interest policymaking is overwhelming. But seemingly in contrast to his theory of political convergence, partisanship exerts a substantially stronger

Table 9.3. Multivariate Analysis of White Interest Legislative Co-Sponsorships in the House

	102nd	103rd	104th	105th
Intercept	2.176	2.249	2.066	2.367
South	-0.017	0.065	**0.239***	0.100
% White VAP	-0.018	-0.026	-0.011	-0.030
% Urban VAP	-0.025	-0.021	-0.023	-0.037
Party	**0.629***	**0.850***	**0.790***	**0.806***
White	0.073	0.316	**0.465***	0.307
Total Co-Sponsorships	3934	5865	6996	6149

*** = p < .001

Table 9.4. Multivariate Analysis of White Interest Roll Call Votes in the House

	102nd	103rd	104th	105th
Intercept	-1.812	-1.372	-1.771	-2.381
South	**0.746***	**0.872***	**1.332***	**0.874***
% White VAP	-0.047	0.034	0.075	0.001
% Urban VAP	-0.001	0.003	**-0.094***	-0.016
Party	**1.964***	**1.931***	**2.965***	**3.137***
White	**1.169***	**0.361***	**0.780***	**0.884***
Total Roll Call Votes	5	13	18	17

* = p < .05, ** = p < .01, *** = p < .001

effect on roll call voting behavior after Republicans seized control of the House than before. The coefficients in table 9.4 can be interpreted as log-likelihood odds ratios, meaning that all else constant, in the 102nd Congress, Republicans in the House were 3.2 times more likely than Democrats to support white interests. But in the 105th Congress, Republicans were twenty-three times more likely.

These data do not reveal individual-level partisan convergence. However, far from disputing Professor Walters' observations, these results add another layer to his narrative. My research confirms the argument that white nationalists were successful in seizing control of the Republican Party, attaining positions of power within the House of Representatives, and pursuing a vigorous agenda to promote white interests. As Dr. Walters convincingly demonstrates, after the so-called Republican revolution of 1994, President Bill Clinton adopted many of the central tenets of the Republican majority, including its insistence that "the era of big government is over," and the positions of the Democratic Leadership Council gained preeminence within the party. But while the Democratic establishment converged on Republican establishment positions to dismantle the remnants of the social welfare state and enact draconian crime bills, among similar acts, the fulcrum of partisan conflict shifted significantly to the right. It appears, particularly with the benefit of hindsight, quite predictably that as the Democrats converged on the Republican position, the leading edge of the white nationalist conservative movement pressed farther, thus maintaining a measurable distance between the parties. As Democrats agreed, for example, to support Republican positions on funding for affordable housing or so-called education reform, conservative Republicans proposed ever more reactionary and antistatist policies. And while the 2000 election in fact marked the capture of American political institutions by white nationalist forces, the rise of the Tea Party after the 2008 election marks another substantial surge in the mobilization of white nationalist sentiments and the takeover of the House of Representatives by extremist Republicans after the 2010 election assured further enactment of white nationalist public policies as once again Democrats sought out middle ground.

White Nationalism and Contemporary American Politics

Though *White Nationalism, Black Interests* was a compelling read in 2003, it is even more applicable to American politics a decade later. Though a complete update is well beyond the scope of this chapter, significant events, including the election of the first African American president, have not meaningfully changed the arc of history. Since the book was written, the nation has experienced both the lows of Hurricane Katrina, where the federal and state government both literally and figuratively abandoned African American residents in the Gulf Coast region, laying bare the systematic incapacity of a hollowed out state to maintain equal opportunity and equitable treatment under the law, and highs of a seemingly transformative 2008 election in which Senator Barack Obama outperformed the 2004 nominee John Kerry among white voters, notably excepting those from southern states.

During the 2008 election, Republican vice presidential nominee Sarah Palin traveled the South praising "the real America" and referred to various small towns as the "pro-America areas of this great nation," comments for which she later apologized. But the divisive tone of the waning days of the election, in which candidate Obama's patriotism, ethnicity, faith, and nationality were increasingly challenged, revealed a highly racialized campaign. Remarkably, at the same time, a new narrative emerged equating an Obama victory with a "postracial" America. In an editorial, in 2007, the *Washington Post* argued that Obama "promises to transcend the boundaries of what many voters see as the tired racial and party politics of the past. The excitement about Mr. Obama speaks in part to Americans' desire to believe, whether true or not, that this country has come to a point when it can rise above its ugly history of racism." This deeply flawed conception of "racial transcendence" leading to a "postracial America" was one Obama expressly contested. For instance, he told a *Newsweek* reporter that "I reject [postracialism] because it implies that somehow my campaign represents an easy shortcut to racial reconciliation. I just want to be very clear on this so there's no confusion. We're going to have a lot of work to do to overcome the long legacy of Jim Crow and slavery. It can't be purchased on the cheap." Nevertheless, voices on the right latched on to this conception and began spreading a triumphant "colorblind" narrative immediately after Obama's victory. As Dr. Walters presciently explains, "much of the emotional content underlying the ideology of white nationalism is predicated upon the view that the Black community has lost the moral capital to make further demands on the political system" (Walters 2003, 252). Obama's victory became fodder for this perspective as conservative thinkers, like syndicated columnist Jonah Goldberg of the *National Review Online*, asked:

> Is there racism in America? Of course. But if the race card was an ace last week, it seems to me it's a 6 of clubs now. If

not, the left needs to be forced to explain why it's not. They need to explain why we still need racial quotas in a country where a black president won in a near landslide. . . . con- servatives would be crazy to let their disappointment and frustration drive them to belittle the significance of having a black president. We should say it's a very big deal indeed, with great significance and symbolism. Not just because it's true, but because it makes it that much easier to argue that race-baiting hacks like Al Sharpton and Jesse Jackson are irrelevant fixtures of a bygone era and their political tactics have no place in a "post-racial" America. (Goldberg 2008)

The election of Obama might have been expected to derail the white nationalist agenda, coming as it did during a profound eco- nomic crisis resulting directly from the failure of the incapacitated American regulatory state to manage the growing financialization of the economy and revealing the frayed nature of the social safety net. And Obama was widely expected to repeal many of his predeces- sor's most egregious anti–civil rights actions including marginalizing the Civil Rights Division of the Justice Department, transforming the U.S. Civil Rights Commission into a body opposed to school desegre- gation and affirmative action and zealously concerned with "reverse racism," and politicizing the United States Attorney's office to focus on prosecuting bogus voter fraud cases. Indeed, several of the presi- dent's first-term legislative priorities were moderate expansions of national regulatory powers and increases in the provision of social welfare: an anti–wage discrimination law; legislation to end preda- tory lending by credit card and mortgage companies; new banking and consumer regulations; an increase in Pell grants; expansion of the S-CHIP program to provide health insurance to 4.1 million chil- dren, a $787 billion stimulus package; and health care reform. Yet it would be difficult to argue that white nationalist domination of American political institutions was in retreat.

Rather, As Walters would anticipate, the election of the first African American president, particularly at a time of profound eco- nomic upheaval, growing economic insecurity and wage stagnation seemingly incited increased racial resentment and consciousness resulting in overt appeals to "take America back." As in 1994, this expression of alienation from the state "reflects a latent desire for a clear and unambiguous regime for which people feel ownership and which nurtures their sense of personal and group integrity—in other words a sense of nationalism" (Walters 2003, 87). Within months of his election, radical conservative voices began baselessly blaming the financial crisis on the Community Reinvestment Act and the mandate to lend to black and brown homeowners and a new movement arose to contest the president's legitimacy, reaffirm white nationalist ideology, and enact legislation buttressing racialized hierarchies of power and privilege.

Though there are many distinct national and local Tea Party organizations, most trace their origin to the Obama inauguration and early months of the new administration. Many writers cite the February 19, 2009 rant by CNBC's Rick Santelli on the floor of the New York Stock Exchange as the seminal moment. Referencing Obama's proposed $75 billion loan modification plan to prevent foreclosures, Santelli bellowed, "This is America. . . . Let's reward people that can carry the water rather than drink the water. . . . It's time for another tea party." Fittingly, his critique was not about the size or role of government so much as a screed against those he deemed "undeserving" of assistance couched in explicitly nationalistic rhetoric.

That there are racist elements within the Tea Party movement is beyond dispute. As NAACP president Benjamin Jealous wrote in the preface to the NAACP's commissioned report on the Tea Party movement, "In March, members of the Congressional Black Caucus reported that racial epithets were hurled at them as they passed by a Washington, DC health care protest. Civil rights legend John Lewis was called the 'n-word' in the incident . . . local NAACP members reported similar racially charged incidents at local Tea Party rallies" (Burghart and Zeskind 2010, 5).

Still, the overt acts of racism and intolerance pale in significance to the Tea Party's rapid domination of the Republican mainstream and near instantaneous institutional power. David Campbell and Robert Putnam dispute the self-characterization of movement activists as "nonpartisan political neophytes." They interviewed over three thousand respondents in 2006 and returned to interview those respondents again in 2011. Their research offers insight into the characteristics of Tea Party supporters, before such a thing existed. Their research shows that "the Tea Party's supporters today were highly partisan Republicans long before the Tea Party was born" (Campbell and Putnam 2011). And that "concern over big government" is not the primary predictor of Tea Party support. Instead, they assert that Tea Partiers "are overwhelmingly white, but even compared to other white Republicans, they had a low regard for immigrants and blacks long before Barack Obama was president, and they still do" (Campbell and Putnam 2011).

This finding echoes survey research conducted by Gallup in 2010, which found that "there is significant overlap between Americans who identify as supporters of the Tea Party movement and those who identify as conservative Republicans. Their similar ideological makeup and views suggest that the Tea Party movement is more a rebranding of core Republicanism than a new or distinct entity on the American political scene" (Newport 2010). And that rebranding makes 1990s Gingrichism appear timid and moderate by comparison. As Devin Burghart and Leonard Zeskind write in their report on the Tea Party for the NAACP, "their storied opposition to political and social elites turns out to be predicated on an antagonism to federal assistance to those deemed the 'undeserving poor'" (Burghart and Zeskind 2010, 7–8).

Bursting on the national scene during the debate over health care reform, the white nationalist Tea Party movement gained steam during the 2010 midterm election, fueled by a seemingly inexplicable obsession over President Obama's birth certificate and an expressly nationalist appeal to "take back" the country from the "socialist" president and his liberal allies in Congress. Republican candidates in 2010 moved firmly to the right on immigration; many candidates employed identical footage of shadowy "illegals" sneaking into the country to take advantage of social welfare programs. They demonized unions, particularly public employee unions, and embraced radical fiscal plans coupling tax cuts for the rich with severe cuts to just about every nondefense government program. And in a low turnout election, they won.

"The Tea Party movement has unleashed a still inchoate political movement who are in their numerical majority, angry middle class white people who believe their country, their nation, has been taken from them" (Burghart and Zeskind 2010, 8). This white nationalist anger, couched in populist rhetoric, has systematically taken over the Republican Party and by extension the Congress of the United States. Beginning in 2010, Tea Party candidates defeated longtime

Republican incumbents and then-establishment favorites in House, Senate, and gubernatorial primaries. Previously "moderate" Republicans faced the choice of turning hard right themselves (such as John McCain) or finding themselves out of office (including Senators Bob Bennett [Utah], Lisa Murkowski [Alaska], and Richard Lugar [Indiana]). "Moderates" have been effectively purged from the party. The NAACP report card for the 112th Congress graded *every* Republican in the House and the Senate with an "F"; thirty-four of the forty-six Republican senators received a support score of 0. Reflecting a new politics of convergence, the NAACP found a much greater spread among the Democrats in Congress, with many "moderate" Democrats moving decisively, as before, to the right, to simultaneously discipline the state and challenge "the fundamental interests of Blacks" (Walters 2003, 91).

As in 1994, the House of Representatives has been the leading edge of this nationalist movement in government. Before even formally taking power, new chair of the House Committee on Homeland Security, Peter King of New York, announced plans for hearings on the "radicalization of the American Muslim Community." The House of Representatives passed legislation to repeal health care reform, to repeal funding for Obama's health care legislation as well as for school-based health centers—the majority of users of which are racial and ethnic minorities. And perhaps most significantly, the House passed the "Paul Ryan Budget" named for the House Budget Committee Chair and darling of conservative think tanks. That plan cuts spending to Medicaid, Medicare, Pell Grants, Head Start, Food Stamps, education, and job training programs while simultaneously enacting permanent tax cuts for the wealthiest Americans. Only four Republicans voted against the blueprint, one that was viewed as a politically toxic one a few short years earlier (Lizza 2012).

This capture of the American political system has extended as well to the Supreme Court, where Bush administration appointees have continued to deregulate civil rights while inventing civil and political rights for corporations. In his dissent in the case overturning Arizona's rigid anti-immigration legislation, Justice Antonin Scalia argues for a states' rights position, maintaining that states historically have had the right to keep out certain immigrants, specifically citing the ability of southern states to exclude freed slaves, a reference that caused minor shockwaves. Research using Martin-Quinn scores (named for legal scholars Andrew Martin and Kevin Quinn involved with the Supreme Court Database project) shows the Roberts Court to be the most conservative in generations. This research places justices along an ideological continuum and demonstrates both a demonstrable rightward tilt on the part of conservative justices and a convergence to a more conservative position from the courts more liberal members (see Gilson 2012). In its 2012–2013 term, the Court will consider several high-profile cases including challenges to affirmative action and the Voting Rights Act.

And heading into the 2012 presidential election, the radical conservative movement was after the biggest prize. The Republican primary election included the return of Gingrichism in body as well as spirit. Campaigning in the south, Gingrich began by labeling Obama the "food stamp president," an attack line that subsequently turned into a race-baiting fraudulent campaign advertisement by Republican nominee Mitt Romney about the president's alleged desire to remove work requirements from welfare. But beyond the tone of the campaign and its bear-hug embrace of the Ryan budget, made inevitable by the selection of Ryan as the Republican vice presidential nominee, perhaps the most significant role of conservative extremists has been the ability to push through state legislatures a host of laws designed to disenfranchise voters of color and suppress the vote on election day: the adoption of voter ID laws, purges of voter rolls, rolling back early voting, limiting poll worker assistance, intimidating nonpartisan voter registration groups (including the League of Women Voters), and the like. Surely the primary motive of this effort was to secure partisan advantage in Ohio, Pennsylvania, Florida, and other "swing states." But the entire discourse around so-called voter fraud is an expression of white nationalist ideology: a narrative of white racial victimization designed to foment institutional racism in the electoral system. Professor Walters' central thesis in *White Nationalism, Black Interests*, that this decades-long white nationalist movement remains committed to disciplining the national government and maintaining racialized hierarchies of power and privilege and threatens the legitimate and coherent interests of African Americans, remains a compelling and insightful framework for understanding contemporary politics. And it lays forth a robust research agenda for future research by both empirically and theoretically oriented scholars concerned about racial justice and the integrity of American democracy.

References

Burghart, Devin, and Leonard Zeskind. 2010. *Tea Party Nationalism: A Critical Examination of the Tea Party Movement and the Size, Scope, and Focus of Its National Factions.* Institute for Research & Education on Human Rights. http://www.naacp.org/pages/tea-party-report.

Campbell, David E., and Robert D. Putnam. 2011. "Crashing the Tea Party." *New York Times*, August 16, 2011. http://www.nytimes.com.

Canon, David T. 1999. Race, *Redistricting, and Representation: The Unintended Consequences of Black Majority Districts.* Chicago: University of Chicago Press.

Gilson, Dave. 2012. "The Supreme Court's Rightward Shift." *Mother Jones*, June 26, 2012. http://www.motherjones.com/politics/2012/06/supreme-court-roberts-obamacare-charts.

Goldberg, Jonah. 2008. "Obama and Transcending Race." *National Review Online*. November 5, 2008. http://www.nationalreview.com/corner/173462/obama-transcending-race/jonah-goldberg.

Lizza, Frank. 2012. "Fussbudget: How Paul Ryan Captured the GOP." *The New Yorker*. August 6, 2012. http://www.newyorker.com/reporting/2012/08/06/120806fa_fact_lizza.

Newport, Frank. 2010. "Tea Party Supporters Overlap Republican Base: Eight Out of 10 Tea Party Supporters Are Republicans." Gallup. July 2, 2010. http://www.gallup.com/poll/141098/Tea-Party-Supporters-Overlap-Republican-Base.aspx.

Omi, Michael, and Howard Winant. 1994. *Racial Formation in the United States: From the 1960s to the 1990s*, 2nd Edition. New York: Routledge.

Walters, Ronald W. 2003. *White Nationalism, Black Interests: Conservative Public Policy and the Black Community.* Detroit: Wayne State University Press.

Washington Post Editorial. 2007. "He's In." *Washington Post.* Thursday, January 18.

Wolffe, Richard, and Daren Briscoe. 2007. "Across the Divide." *Newsweek* 150, 3 (July 16): 22.

Part V

10

Ronald Walters and the District of Columbia

Action Research and the Odyssey of the Capital Colony

LENNEAL J. HENDERSON

Although born in Kansas, educated at Fisk and American Universities, and domiciled in Silver Spring, Maryland, Ronald Walters considered Washington, D.C. his headquarters as an action researcher. He successfully completed his doctoral work at American University; taught in and chaired the Department of Political Science at Howard University in Washington, D.C.; worked extensively with members of Congress and the District of Columbia government; and appeared at more than one hundred conferences, forums, and institutes in the nation's capital.

His last book, coedited with Toni-Michelle Travis, *Democratic Destiny and the District of Columbia,* published in 2010, was a comprehensive anthology on the history, evolution, and conflicts associated with home rule, advocacy for statehood, and the political economy of Washington, D.C. Under Walters' leadership, the volume conceptualized African American liberation as a major thrust for home rule in the nation's capital. However, the book was the culmination of nearly thirty years of work by Ron Walters on the political dynamics of Washington, D.C.

Six interrelated areas of research and action are critically examined as Walters' legacy in this essay: 1) His involvement of students, faculty, and researchers at Howard University in work on self-determination for Washington, D.C.; 2) his role as a journalist-activist-scholar writing hundreds of articles for the *Washington Informer,* the

Washington Post, and the *Washington-Baltimore-Richmond Afro-American* on almost every particular of black political life, including Washington, D.C.; 3) his work on the role of Advisory Neighborhood Commissions in Washington, D.C.; 4) his role as a *pro bono* consultant to the 1979 Constitutional Convention in Washington, D.C.; 5) his research on political leadership, black political leadership, and the leadership of the District of Columbia; and 6) his scholarship on the complex and convoluted issues of home rule and self-determination for Washington, D.C.

Action Research and the Role of a Public Intellectual

Before pursuing each of these six interrelated facets of Walters' impact on Washington, D.C., it is important to understand Walters as an exemplary action researcher and public intellectual. Action research (AR) is a research orientation focused on formulating, conducting, and utilizing research with and for the beneficiaries of the research and with the intent of improving life chances and economic, social, cultural, and political outcomes for them. The pioneer of action research is the late Kurt Lewin who, ironically, advanced his initial work on action research examining the role of "minorities" (Lewin 1948). He coined the term "action research" in 1944 and indicated that the practice was "work that did not separate the investigation from the action needed to solve the problem" (quoted in McFarland and Stansell 1993, 14). Since the 1940s, AR and its more dynamic partner, participatory action research (PAR) have been associated with four key themes, including: 1) empowerment of those individuals, groups, and institutions for whom the research is conducted; 2) collaboration through participation of those whose actions are informed by the research; 3) acquisition of knowledge by both the beneficiaries of research and those conducting it; and 4) social change (Stringer 2007; McIntyre, 2008).

Also, the growing participatory nature of "the People's Research" is a form of action research, particularly that which was designed to empower communities that tended to feel exploited by previous research efforts that entered communities through elitist and/ or privileged contexts, without concern for the conditions of the community once the research project was complete (see Park 1999;

Morris 2011). However, as Morris observes, these themes can also be found well before the 1940s, as they are a core component of the liberation scholarship and advocacy tradition in the African American community (Morris 2011).

Following the tradition of "activist" black scholars such as W.E.B. Du Bois, Carter Woodson, Charles Johnson, Kenneth Clark, and Derrick Bell, Walters always asked of his scholarship and his colleagues, "What does this have to do with the liberation of black people?" His scholarship and advocacy in the District of Columbia was driven by the same question. In his thirty-five years of work, action, and life in Washington, D.C., he witnessed and sought to intervene in the vicissitudes of life and liberation for black people in Washington, D.C. The subsequent sections of this chapter indicate what he witnessed in those thirty-five years and then what he sought to do in research and advocacy.

Ronald Walters, Howard University, and the Status of Washington, D.C.

Ron Walters was recruited to Howard University in 1971 as a result of a major Ford Foundation grant managed by former vice president for academic affairs Andrew Billingsley, himself a distinguished scholar. Washington, D.C. then was in the midst of significant but turbulent policy and administrative transition. In 1967, President Johnson had issued Reorganization Plan No. 3, replacing the old federally appointed three-commissioner governing board of the district with a presidentially appointed "mayor-commissioner" and nine-member council. Congress responded by approving the election of the School Board in 1968 and a nonvoting delegate to Congress in 1971 (Fauntroy 2003, 34–35).

As an astute student of African politics whose dissertation focused on U.S. foreign policy toward Africa, Walters understood the demographic, socioeconomic, racial, and political dynamics of the district's post–World War II history (Walters 1971). The conspicuous parallels between the district's status as a federal colony and the struggles of Africans against colonial control were compelling to him. Like the colonial centers of many African nations, Walters knew how vital government, as both policy and economic animator,

defines political power. As an architect of the 1972 Black Political
Convention in Gary, Indiana and the Pan-African Congress, Walters
knew that at the center of these colonial power struggles was the
cancer of racism. The District of Columbia and Africa were lurid
examples of racist politics separated only by land and water.

Walters was aware of the demographic and socioeconomic history
and foundations of this racism, particularly in Washington, D.C. The
behavior of the national government connects population, socioeconomic status, government employment, and race into a galactic web
of political intrigue. The population of Washington, D.C. remained
relatively stable until the Great Depression in the 1930s. To respond
to the profound economic desperation of the Depression, President Franklin D. Roosevelt's New Deal legislation expanded the
bureaucracy in Washington. Between 1933 and 1935, the United
States experienced the greatest proliferation of administrative agencies in its history. More than 90 percent of these agencies were physi-
cally located in Washington, D.C. World War II further increased
government activity, adding to the number of federal employees in
the capital. Because Washington, D.C. had truly become "a government town" and because African Americans depended more on government for employment, the federal government and black economic progress and employment were inseparable (Krislov 1967).
Like African economics and politics in the immediate post–World
War II period, the colony's nonwhite residents depended on government for both economic survival and political opportunity.

By 1950, when the district's population reached a peak of
802,178 residents, blacks had increased as a percentage of this population from 28.2 % in 1940 to 35 percent. However, shortly thereafter, the city began losing residents and increasing black population
due to suburbanization allegedly due to rising crime, traffic conges-
tion, rising cost of living and concerns about public schools as an
expanded highway network supported newer housing outside the
city (Gale 1990). The perception of many white and middle-class
black residents of the "disquieting" impact of social unrest, crime,
and the 1968 riots precipitated a dramatic exodus of population
from the District of Columbia to the suburbs. By 1980 Washington
had lost one-quarter of its total population while increasing the proportion of its black population from 35 percent in 1950 to 71.1 percent in 1970. Ironically, Walters argued, largely due to the modicum

of achievements of civil rights actions and policies, more of the city's middle-class black population also moved to the suburbs. Some lower-income African Americans relocated to impoverished areas of Prince George's County, Maryland (Johnson 2002), making it, according to Marion Barry, the unofficial ninth ward of Washington, D.C. The city's population continued to decline until the late 1990s, when gentrification efforts started to transform the demographics of distressed neighborhoods. The city's more business-oriented admin-istrations and accommodation to congressional directives may have helped that effort. However, as Walters indicated in his last book, a trend of commercial and economic growth since the 2000 Census provided the first rise in the District's population in fifty years but a major decline in black population as whites increased in number by forty-four thousand and blacks declined in number by twenty-seven thousand between 2000 and 2010 (Walters and Travis 2010).

These demographic and socioeconomic changes go back to the late 1960s. Resultant policy changes followed the horrific violence in Washington, D.C. in 1968 following the assassination of Martin Luther King Jr., destroying or damaging blocks of black neighbor-hoods in the 7th Street, 14th Street, U Street, Northwest, and H Street, Northeast, commercial corridors and homes. The life of the nation and the district was inextricably intertwined as "the riots," the assassination of Robert Kennedy, the Poor People's Campaign on "the mall" for forty-two fateful days, the violence at the Democratic National Convention, and the election of Richard Nixon would all resound in the streets and institutions of Washington, D.C.

In 1973, Congress enacted Public Law 93-198, the District of Columbia Home Rule Act. In addition to the tumults of the late and early 1970s, the influence of the then new Congressional Black Cau-cus, founded in 1971, and the Joint Center for Political Studies in 1970, is clearly evident in the lobbying for this legislation. Walters was close to both the Congressional Black Caucus and the Joint Cen-ter. (The Joint Center was initially a joint venture of Kenneth Clark's Metropolitan Applied Research Center and Howard University.) However, Walters was aware that this law, as momentous as it was, also affirmed the control by Congress of Washington, D.C., anchored in the United States Constitution. He once shared with me, as a scholar of "public administration," that the Home Rule statute "delegates" policy and administrative authority to the D.C. government almost as

a cabinet agency is delegated administrative authority from any statute to implement statutory policy mandates. He argued in a letter to
me that this continued the pre–Lyndon Johnson and Johnson tradition of the politics of administrative control over district affairs. Congress giveth, and Congress can taketh away, he argued. Subsequent
impositions of a control board, known as the District of Columbia
Financial Responsibility and Management Assistance Authority, in
1995 and the suspension of the federal payment to Washington,
D.C. in 1997 would more than fulfill his prophesy. Consequently,
throughout his career at Howard University, Walters consistently and
emphatically advocated for home rule for the District of Columbia.
In his research, work with students, and his work at Howard University's Institute for Urban Research, Walters closely followed the
tortured and complex struggle of Washington, D.C. to obtain home
rule, full congressional representation, and statehood. He super-
vised several doctoral dissertations at Howard University focused on
the District of Columbia and spoke to many audiences about the
travesty of congressional control, often in explicitly racial terms.

Walters as Activist-Journalist-Scholar in Washington, D.C.

In addition to his research, Ron Walters was a consistent, strategic,
and intense political activist. He was an academic, an organizer, a
strategist, and assessor of political trends. But he also wrote for the
masses. He was an effective but humble "public intellectual." Like
George Curry, Ron Daniels, Julianne Malveaux, and other effective
scholar-activist-journalists, Walters wrote some 450 articles in varied
newspapers and magazines ranging from the *Washington Informer*,
the *Washington Post*, and the *Washington-Richmond-Baltimore Afro-American* to activist, scholarly publications like *The Black Scholar*, *The Black
World* (formerly *Negro Digest*), and *The Focus*, the publication of the
Joint Center for Political and Economic Studies (formerly the Joint
Center for Political Studies). His syndicated column for the National
Newspaper Publishers Association, the African American newspaper
association, reached thousands of readers through more than 130
African American newspapers.

Consequently, his more than twenty newspaper and feature articles about the status of home rule in Washington, D.C. was a major

source of information and insight for readers *outside* of Washington, D.C. as well as those residing in the nation's capital. As good journalists do, he reported the facts confirmed from multiple and corroborating sources. But he was also an advocate in these articles for full voting representation for Washington, D.C. and against oppressive measures by Congress to control the budget, government, and politics of Washington, D.C. He was critical of "The Control Board," as a clear attempt by Congress to "make the District of Columbia financially accountable" to it rather than the district's people. To Walters, this was an attempt to circumscribe black politics in Washington, D.C., a politics often critical of federal and congressional policies. He argued that "the federal payment" (an annual allocation to the District of Columbia in lieu of a property tax on the federal government) was but a quarter of what it should have been. He brought to the attention of readers the status and strategies of those advocating statehood for Washington, D.C. but was realistic about the probabilities of any immediate constitutional action to make this possible.

However, his journalism was not just focused on Washington, D.C. in a national context; he wrote several articles on Washington, D.C. in a metropolitan context as well as the neighborhoods of Washington, D.C. He perceived the Maryland and Virginia suburbs as generally hostile to the economic and political interests of Washington, D.C. These suburban counties were often explicit in their opposition to any form of commuter tax for the Washington metro area, any attempt to share the severe burden of socioeconomic stress in many black neighborhoods in Washington, or even to full voting representation in Congress. He observed that "metropolitan planning" pursued by such institutions as the Metropolitan Washington Council of Governments, The Greater Washington Research Center, and several industry and business associations acknowledged the inequities suffered by Washington in the metropolis but rarely sponsored bold initiatives to address these inequities, particularly with financial resources from the suburbs. He instantly responded to former Maryland governor William Donald Schaefer's proposal to "retrocede" the District of Columbia back to the state of Maryland as a flawed proposal, likely to disempower rather than empower district residents.

His articles for the *Washington Informer,* a more local-oriented black newspaper owned and managed for many years by Dr. Calvin

Rolark, was a vehicle for Walters' view on neighborhood and internal political issues in Washington, D.C. Walters, like many others,
was horrified at the political descent of former mayor Marion Barry,
at the perception that Barry's successor, Anthony Williams, seemed
to have struck a deal with Congress and major business leaders in
the city to "stabilize" D.C. politics and fiscal decision-making, and he
questioned the wisdom of former mayor Adrian Fenty's decision to
make public school reform the centerpiece of his administration. He
wrote extensively about such issues as school vouchers, central business development, the racial divide among the city's wards, the city
council, and in citywide elections and the decision of city leaders to
"gentrify" several all African American neighborhoods in the name
of "economic development."

Walters and Advisory Neighborhood Commissions

A vital focus of Walters' research and advocacy in Washington, D.C.
was the controversial experiment with neighborhood participation in
public policymaking. Thirty-eight advisory commissions were established as part of the process of creating home rule in the District of
Columbia. In testimony before Congress on the enactment of the
District of Columbia Home Rule Act and subsequent amendments,
in papers given to the annual meetings of the Congressional Black
Caucus, and in work with the Senate and House District of Columbia Committees, Walters advocated the creation of formal neighborhood policy institutions in Washington, D.C. He was inspired by the
wave of scholarship and movement politics embodied in the Ocean-
Hill Brownville struggle for neighborhood control of schools in Bed-
ford-Stuyvesant, New York and works such as Milton Kotler's *Neighborhood Government*, Alan Altshuler's *Community Control*, and Stokely
Carmichael and Charles V. Hamilton's classic, *Black Power: The Politics
of Liberation in America*.

   With Diane R. Brown and Stephanie P. Honeywood, in 1980,
Walters published a seminal study of Advisory Neighborhood Commissions in Washington, D.C. entitled *Advisory Neighborhood Commissions: A Study of Citizen Participation in the District of Columbia* through
the Howard University Institute for Urban Affairs and Research.
These thirty-eight councils, with over three hundred Advisory

Neighborhood Commissions (ANC), were elected by designated neighborhoods in the District of Columbia. They were "advisory" to both the mayor and city council on matters ranging from public works to public parks, crime and public safety, health care, education, and economic development. Although significant as instruments of community voice, Walters saw these commissions as more symbolic than substantive sources of policy influence and impact. The ANCs could not veto any actions of the mayor or city council, even if they impacted the interests of their specific neighborhood jurisdiction. However, Walters and his colleagues believed that an empirical study of the ANCs could establish the foundation for more substantive policy roles for neighborhoods if and when the District of Columbia advanced to more substantive home rule. Walters and his colleagues established the framework for my own study of the ANCs some nine years later (Henderson 1989).

Statehood and the District of Columbia Constitutional Convention

Walters strongly believed in advisory neighborhood commissions, as the first vital step toward grassroots democracy in the capital, however, he believed that even this step would be meaningless if the District of Columbia was still subject to direct congressional control. Therefore, he was hopeful about the contributions of the statehood movement to some modicum of autonomy and democracy in Washington, D.C.

On November 4, 1980, 60 percent of the District of Columbia residents voted and approved the District of Columbia Statehood Constitutional Convention of 1979, which became DC Law 3-171. This law called for the creation of a state constitutional convention, which was a critical first step toward the establishment of a constitution for an eventual new state. In 1981, a DC Statehood Commission was established to advance the work of the constitutional convention and to critically examine the legal, fiscal, and administrative processes necessary to prepare for statehood. On November 4, 1981, forty-five delegates were elected to a constitutional convention to serve two- or three-year terms. Walters and I were among the *pro bono* consultants to the constitutional convention. The convention was charged with producing a working draft in ninety days. I focused on the fiscal and administrative issues in the constitution, having served as Mayor Barry's chair of the citywide Citizen's Budget Commission.

Walters advised the convention on the proposed electoral processes and the legislative institutions and authority to be reflected in the constitution. These electoral processes were a delicate and complex issue given their relationship to how elected officials and voters would interact and, most importantly, to how elected officials in the new state would interact with their former overseers such as Congress and the president and neighboring states of Virginia and Maryland. However, Walters also insisted that the ANCs be maintained and elevated to the status of formal policy resources to the governor, U.S. senators, and full House members anticipated in the new state. Grassroots needs and interests would be articulated in balance with statewide and intergovernmental interests through constitutional protections. He anticipated the need to reformulate federal powers in relation to the new state if this delicate balance between neighborhood and intergovernmental, including federal interests, was to function effectively (Harris 1995; Harris and Thornton 1981).

When the constitutional convention finally produced the draft of the constitution for the eventual state of New Columbia, Walters had succeeded in influencing the delegates to carefully design electoral institutions with his unusual sense of the realpolitik of neighborhood, district, federal, and neighboring state political power dynamics. He was realistic in understanding that the heart of this balance was ultimately racial politics both within the district and between the district and federal and state governments. He eventually wrote several op-ed articles for the *Washington Afro-American* and the *Washington Informer* about the process, prospects, and problems of the convention.

The elected delegates for the District of Columbia Constitutional Convention convened to write a constitution for the future state of New Columbia on January 31, 1982. On November 2, 1982, DC voters ratified the constitution for the state of New Columbia in a citywide referendum. The lasting legacy of the convention, and Walters' critical contribution to its work and product, is that should the District of Columbia ever become a state, its state constitution will have already been written and adopted.

In 1983, the bill introduced in Congress for the admission of the state of New Columbia into the Union was defeated, maintaining congressional control over the district with a municipal government in place and a nonvoting delegate to the House of Representatives. However, Walters' work remains, and he was essential to the eventual decision of Mayor Barry to support Jesse Jackson in his two attempts to win the Democratic nomination for the presidency as well as in Jackson's change of domicile to the District of Columbia to serve as one of two "shadow" United States senators from the district (Reed 1986; Henry 1990).

Walters therefore was again at the forefront of action and research and, as he demonstrated in his work at the national and global levels, clearly left a vital legacy in the struggles for racial liberation, the responsibility of those in struggle, and the reframing of a more authentic local democracy.

Walters and the Dilemmas of Leadership in the District of Columbia

Walters wrote constantly about leadership and the District of Columbia. He not only critiqued congressional leadership, both black and white, for its failure to effectively pursue home rule for the District of Columbia but did not hesitate to evaluate the behavior, ethics, and strategies of District of Columbia leaders. Although generally supportive of Washington, D.C.'s first elected mayor, Walter Washington (also its last appointed mayor), Walters openly criticized the mayor for failing to challenge Congress on such issues as the federal payment, local autonomy, police brutality, and education. Initially enthusiastic about the ascendancy of Mayor Marion Barry once he was elected to the school board, the city council and, eventually, as mayor, Walters both criticized the mayor for his moral and leadership shortcomings and Barry's detractors, such as U.S. Attorney Joseph DeGenova and the *Washington Post* for its use of those shortcomings to undermine a black political leader.

He was both supportive of African American leaders in the District of Columbia such as Mayor Barry, former council chairs Sterling Tucker, John Wilson, and Linda Cropp; former congressional delegate Walter Fauntroy; D.C. council members such as Hilda Mason, Wilhelmina Rolark, and Harry Thomas Sr.; and a variety of school superintendents, but he was also critical when they failed to exercise good judgment or pursue effective strategies supportive of African Americans in the district. He seemed less close to Mayors Sharon Pratt Kelly and Anthony Williams who represented more middle-class political perspectives and strategies. As Rachel Yon indicates, in less than twenty years, district residents had experienced extreme polarities in leadership with vast economic, political, and ideological consequences (Yon 2010). From Walter Washington as the last appointed and first elected mayor of Washington, D.C. to the populist Marion Barry to the more moderate and administrative and economically oriented Anthony Williams and Adrian Fenty, these leadership changes mirror key demographic, socioeconomic, financial, political, and intergovernmental relations in the drama of D.C. politics.

Georgia Persons has accurately captured the dilemma of black political leadership as both a matter of internal and personal discipline and external strategic acumen (Persons 1993). Walters applied these principles to his studies of African American leadership (Smith and Walters 1999) as well as to his observations about the discipline, skill, clarity, and consistency of district leadership in both its personal and strategic dimensions.

Democratic Destiny and Political Power in the District of Columbia

Given Walters' work on the ANCs, electoral processes, constitutional development, leadership, and political strategy in the District of Columbia and his skills as the ultimate example of an effective action researcher and journalist-activist, it is no surprise that his last book focuses on what he and coeditor Toni-Michelle Travis correctly label "the democratic destiny" of Washington, D.C. Published in 2010, this vital anthology includes essays by prominent scholars, activists, and district delegate Eleanor Holmes Norton. The book includes at least five interrelated critical dimensions: 1) It updates the diverse but scarce research on the electoral, institutional, and leadership issues characterizing district politics in the late twentieth and early twenty-first centuries; 2) it documents the continuing struggle with Congress over home rule, including the absence of any voting power for the delegate to Congress from the district, the erosion of the federal payment to the district, and the efforts of the Congressional Black Caucus to persuade oppositional House leadership to grant Washington full voting representation; 3) it includes both grassroots or neighborhood-level issues and politics as well as citywide political dynamics; 4) it locates district politics and struggles within the context of the African American political struggle, particularly at the leadership level (Walters 2007); and 5) it defines the district's political dynamics as part of national political dynamics and issues.

In her anthology *Whose Black Politics?*, Andra Gillespie and her colleagues underscore many of these dilemmas. For example, Rachel Yon's compelling essay on former D.C. mayor Adrian Fenty clearly indicates how the contrasting strategies of racial solidarity, reflected conspicuously by Marion Barry and "racial distancing," reflected in Fenty's campaign and governance style, is defining the destiny Walters and Travis examine in their book (Gillespie 2010). "Deracialization" in mayoral and national leadership is a controversy Walters critically examined nationally in his books as well as in the District of Columbia. Be they President Barack Obama or mayors like Adrian Fenty, these deracialized politicians and strategies are clearly connected to major public policy issues in the District of Columbia such as neighborhood power, fiscal issues, local autonomy, and relations with both Congress and the neighboring states of Maryland and Virginia.

True to his skills, training, and orientation as an action researcher, Walters pursued data and evidence to support his assertions. As a member of the executive council of the American Political Science Association and an active member of the National Conference of Black Political Scientists, he was well aware of the requirements of solid scholarship, expert testimony, and empirical evidence (Rich 2007). He recognized and deciphered the intimate interplay of analysis, action, assessment, reassessment, and strategy reformulation in politics and scholarship. Although he worked and acted on both a national and international stage, he was proximate to and fully aware of political and academic dynamics in his own backyard laboratory of Washington, D.C.

Walters urged national black political leaders to become outspoken in making full voting representation for the District of Columbia among their priorities. This was and is both a highly salient local

issue and a profoundly national issue in his view. Traveling throughout the world, including Africa, he often confessed to how embar-
rassing it was to concede that political liberation had not yet arrived
in the District of Columbia, his operating base. In addition, he
repeatedly urged President Barack Obama to exert more political
influence in advocating for full voting representation for the District
of Columbia. The United States Senate approved full voting rights
for Washington, D.C. in February 2009 by a vote of 61 to 37 but
could not secure support from the House of Representatives. On
April 16, 2010, President Obama urged Congress to enact full voting
representation for the district and to improve the D.C. Home Rule
Charter. Sadly, Ron Walters did not live to see full voting representation in the District of Columbia.

However, his academic, political, and ethical legacy will see the
District of Columbia achieve a more complete measure of legal and
political authority than it now experiences. Moreover, the emergence
of African American political leadership in the suburbs of Virginia
and Maryland will advance his theories and work to reflect a more
metropolitan black political dynamic than is evident today. African
American county executives have been elected in Montgomery and
Prince George's County, Maryland. African American members of
Congress, Albert Wynn and, subsequently, Donna Edwards, have
been elected from these two most populous counties of Maryland.

However, Walters' most lasting legacy likely will be his action
research impact on hundreds of younger scholar-activists who want
their research to contribute to social justice and their social justice
values to change the purpose and use of research. Much of that legacy resides in Washington, D.C. and its metropolis where Walters
lived, worked, taught, wrote, spoke, organized, strategized, and died.

References

Altshuler, Alan A. 1970. *Community Control: The Black Demand for Par-
ticipation in Large American Cities.* New York: Bobbs-Merrill.
Barker, Lucius J., Mack Jones, and Katherine Tate. 1998. *African
Americans and the American Political System.* 4th Edition. Engle-
wood Cliffs, NJ: Prentice-Hall.
Carmichael, Stokely, and Charles V. Hamilton. 1967. *Black Power: The
Politics of Liberation in America.* New York: Vintage Books.

Fauntroy, Michael. 2003. *Home Rule or House Rule? Congress and the Erosion of Local Governance in the District of Columbia.* Lanham, MD: University Press of America.

Gale, Dennis. 1990. *Washington, D.C.: Inner-City Revitalization and Minority Suburbanization.* Philadelphia, PA: Temple University Press.

George Washington University, Gelman Library System. 1982. *Guide to Washington, D.C.* Constitutional Convention Records, Collection Number MS2094. Washington, D.C.

Gillespie, Andra. 2010. *Whose Black Politics? Cases in Postracial Black Leadership.* New York: Routledge Press.

Harris, Charles W. 1995. *Congress and the Governance of the Nation's Capital: The Conflict of Federal and Local Interests.* Washington, DC: Georgetown University Press.

Harris, Charles W., and Alvin Thornton. 1981. *Perspectives of Political Power in the District of Columbia: The Views and Opinions of 110 Members of the Local Political Elite.* Washington, DC: National Institute for Public Management.

Henderson, Lenneal J. 1989. "Neighborhood Power in the Capitol: Advisory Neighborhood Commissions in Washington, D.C." *National Civic Review* 78: 209–15.

Henry, Charles. 1990. *Jesse Jackson: The Search for Common Ground.* Oakland, CA: The Black Scholar Press.

Johnson, Valerie C. 2002. *Black Power in the Suburbs: The Myth or Reality of African American Suburban Political Incorporation.* Albany: State University of New York Press.

Kotler, Milton. 1969. *Neighborhood Government: The Local Foundations of Political Life.* New York: Harper and Row.

Krislov, Samuel. 1967. *The Negro and Federal Employment.* Minneapolis, MN: University of Minnesota Press.

Lewin, Kurt. 1948. *Resolving Social Conflicts.* New York: Harper and Row.

McFarland, K. P., and J. C. Stansell. 1993. "Historical Perspectives." In *Teachers Are Researchers: Reflection and Action,* ed. L. Patterson, C. M. Santa, K. G. Short, and K. S. Smith. Newark, DE: International Research Association.

McIntyre, Alice. 2008. *Participatory Action Research.* Thousand Oaks, CA: Sage Publications.

Morris, Monique W. 2011. "Action Oriented Research as a Tool to Reduce Segregated Public Education." Unpublished paper submitted to the Fielding Graduate University, School of Educational Leadership and Change.

Park, Peter. 1999. "People, Knowledge and Change in Participatory Action Research." *Management Learning* 30: 141–57. Thousand Oaks, CA: Sage Publications.

Persons, Georgia A. 1993. "Black Mayoralties and the New Black Politics: From Insurgency to Racial Reconciliation." In *Dilemmas of Black Politics: Issues of Leadership and Strategy*, ed. Georgia A. Persons, 38–65. New York: Harper Collins.

Persons, Georgia A., and Lenneal J. Henderson. 1990. "Mayor of the Colony: Effective Mayoral Leadership as a Matter of Public Perception." *National Political Science Review* 2: 145–53.

Reed, Adolph. 1986. *The Jesse Jackson Phenomenon: The Crisis of Purpose in Afro-American Politics*. New Haven, CT: Yale University Press.

Rich, Wilbur, ed. 2007. *African American Perspectives on Political Science*. Philadelphia, PA: Temple University Press.

Smith, Robert C. 1996. *We Have No Leaders: African-Americans in the Post–Civil Rights Era*. Albany: State University of New York Press.

Stringer, Ernest. 2007. *Action Research*. Thousand Oaks, CA: Sage Publications.

Walters, Ronald W. 1971. "The Formulation of U.S. Foreign Policy Towards Africa, 1958–1963." Dissertation submitted to American University, Washington, DC.

———. 2005. *Freedom Is Not Enough: Black Voters, Black Candidates and American Presidential Politics*. Lanham, MD: Rowman & Littlefield.

Walters, Ronald W., Diane R. Brown, and Stephanie P. Honeywood. 1980. *Advisory Neighborhood Commissions: A Study of Citizen Participation in the District of Columbia*. Washington, DC: Howard University Institute for Urban Affairs and Research.

Walters, Ronald W., and Robert C. Smith. 1999. *African American Leadership*. Albany: State University of New York Press.

Walters, Ronald W., and Toni-Michelle Travis, eds. 2010. *Democratic Destiny and the District of Columbia: Federal Politics and Public Policy*. Lexington, MA: Lexington Books.

Yon, Rachel. 2010. "The Declining Significance of Race: Adrian Fenty and the Smooth Electoral Transition." In *Whose Black Politics? Cases in Postracial Black Leadership*, ed. Andra Gillespie, 195–213. New York: Routledge Press.

11

Ronald Walters as a
Political Empowerment Theorist

The Concept of Leverage Strategies

HANES WALTON JR.

Neither political theory nor major political theoreticians such as Ronald W. Walters are born in a political vacuum but instead in a crisis in the political environment. Otherwise they are dealing in fiction. Walters was born in 1938 in the age of African American political neophytes, which saw the political birth and rebirth of the African American electorate. This age demanded brilliant intellectuals, and Walters never failed to generate ideas and strategies that were indeed, then and now, outside the intellectual stream. When compared to earlier scholar activists such as W.E.B. Du Bois and Ralph Bunche, he excelled beyond their pioneering efforts.

Historian C. Vann Woodward pioneered the concept of African American political neophytes, writing that they were born in "a political revolution . . . under way in the Southern states, a revolution that is the first chapter in the history of the Negro voter in America."[1] This political revolution had been engineered by the four Military Reconstruction Acts of 1867–1868 passed by Congress and implemented by the U.S. military, which was stationed in ten of the eleven states of the old Confederacy. Beyond the matter of the origin of these neophytes, Woodward describes their initial moments at the ballot box in the South, observing that they were:

> unprecedented among American or any other known electorates. Their [freedmen's] very appearance at the polls in

261

mass, wearing the rags of slave days, and bearing the ancient
stigmata of oppression, conjured by every gloomy prognosti-
cation of the fate of democracies from Aristotle to the Federalists. Not Athens, nor Rome, nor Paris at greatest turbulence
had confronted their like. Here was the Federalist beast who
would turn every garden into a pigsty. . . . Here was the ultimate test to the democratic dogma in the most extreme form
ever attempted.[2]

According to Woodward, the Founding Fathers were completely
opposed to such political neophytes ever entering the American political process. They called upon their British heritage and
demanded that all political participants should have a "stake in society," that is, be property holders. On this fundamental value of the
Founding Fathers, voting expert Alexander Keyssar writes: "one such
consideration was the stake in society notion inherited from the
colonial period. Only men with property, preferably real property,
were deemed to be sufficiently attached to the community and sufficiently affected by its laws to have earned the privilege of voting."[3]
John Adams saw such political neophytes as the freedmen as "shift-
less and improvident Demos, pawn of demagogues and plutocrats
and menace to all order," while Alexander Hamilton claimed them
to be a "turbulent and changing" mass who "seldom judge or determine right" and whose participation would guarantee electoral instability in the political system.[4] Thus, it was inconceivable that former
slaves without property and a stake in society could be given the right
to vote. But this is exactly what the four Military Reconstruction Acts
did for the freedmen in 1867 and 1868.

Even though this electoral revolution occurred, it did not mean
that, given the values and ideals of the Founding Fathers that under-
girded the American political process, this democratic act would be
widely accepted at the elite or the mass levels, even after more than
a century of the democratic experiment in governance in America.
Woodward once again pioneered in responding to the negative reaction to the political neophytes' electoral revolution in the South:

The records left by that revolutionary experiment have been
widely used to discredit both the experiment itself and democratic faith in general. . . . No red glow of anarchy lit up

the southern horizon as a consequence of the revolution, and the enfranchised freedmen did not prove the unleashed beast of Federalist imagination. Moral pigsties undoubtedly developed, but they were oftener than not the creation of the other race, and more of them were to be found outside the South than within.[5]

Woodward seeks to tell us more about his group in a comparative manner. He begins by saying:

This new-born electorate of freedmen was plunged immediately into action by the election of delegates to [state] constitutional conventions. They followed by electing legislative bodies, state and local officials, and by full scale and continuous participation in all phases and aspects of political life in a period that was abnormally active in a political way . . . that the mass of these people had less education, less experience in public affairs, and less property of all sorts than the white voters is obvious.[6]

He adds:

The new electorate of freedmen proved on the whole remarkably modest in their demands, unaggressive in their conduct, and deferential in their attitude. In no state did they place power in anything approaching their actual numbers and voting strength. The possible exception was South Carolina, and there they held a majority of seats only in the lower house of the legislature. . . . In view of the subordinate role and few offices that the freedmen took, no state in the South could properly be said to have been under Negro rule or "domination" at any time.[7]

Woodward concludes by saying that it is neither accurate nor fair to heap all of the blame, insidious evaluations, nor negative assessments upon these political neophytes. In fact, "in retrospect," Woodward argues, one should be "more impressed with the success that a people of such meager resources and limited experience enjoyed in producing the number of sober, honest, and capable leaders and public servants they did. The appearance of some of this sort in every state is the main comfort the record provides to the democratic faith . . . and democratic theory."[8]

Overall, Woodward's reconceptualization of the African American electorate during the "Black Reconstruction" era (1867–1877) was not only smart intellectual thinking, it generated a wholly new political perspective as well as a new electoral portrait and laid the groundwork for our conceptualization of Ronald Walters as a political empowerment theoretician. Woodward demonstrates that the historians, political scientists, and sociologists of the Reconstruction era were comparing the African American neophytes with the southern white electorate, who were more educated, more experienced in public affairs, longtime voters and officeholders, and had nearly a century of political and electoral empowerment in Colonial Revolutionary and Antebellum America. Such comparisons biased their evaluations by making the white electorate the norm. Instead, the comparison should be made with other groups of political neophytes in American history.

Who were the other political neophytes in the American political process? They were the immigrants. Woodward explains that the "history of the Negro's political experience in Reconstruction has been studied too much in isolation and pictured as unique." African American uniqueness "does not constitute the only, nor the last, instance of sudden enfranchisement of large numbers of politically inexperienced people."[9] In point of fact, after the Black Reconstruction era, although "more than twelve million white immigrants . . . poured into the stream of American citizenship in the fifty years after 1880 from southern and eastern European counties, it is doubtful that more than a very small percentage had ever enjoyed any significant experience with American-style political and electoral democracy."[10]

With this group as the appropriate source for comparison and contrast, Woodward declared, "here were the real political neophytes of the American electorate." He adds:

> They greatly outnumber the Negro population. They too were dominated by bosses and influenced by handouts, and small favors. The record of the inexperience, naiveté, and ineptitude of these erstwhile peasants in the big city slums

is written in the history of corrupt city bosses, rings, and machines, a history that can match some of the darker chapters of Reconstruction government.[11]

The story of the immigrant political neophytes has been told and retold with mythic idealism when compared to the African American experience. If the African American neophytes had been compared with the immigrant political neophytes instead, the resultant portrait would not "support the stereotype of the Negro as the political tyro and neophyte of the western world, the laggard in the race for political maturity."[12] Therefore, when seen in this new perspective, which flows from Woodward's reconceptualization, one gets the "impression of [African American political neophytes] as people struggling conscientiously under desperate odds to live up to a test such as no other people had ever been subjected to in all the long testing of the democratic theory."[13]

Beyond the need for an appropriate standard by which to judge and evaluate the African American political neophyte, Woodward's reconceptualization firmly rooted his ideas into a now popular periodization: 1) First Reconstruction, 2) the most popular, Second Reconstruction,[14] and 3) the least well known, Third Reconstruction.[15] Embedded in this periodization is Woodward's theory about the political reform of the American democratic process and how the failure to fully implement all aspects of the reform led to the collapse of the First Reconstruction. This led to the Second Reconstruction, and when those reforms ended incomplete, that launched the Third Reconstruction. Central to each of these southern reconstructions as he saw it was the political agency of the African American voter rights activists and civil rights leaders.

Thus, with the coming of each different reconstruction is a new set of African American political neophytes.[16] Although neither Woodward nor his supporters or critics say it, each time that the failure of reforms gave birth to another reconstruction era, a new African American electorate entered the American political process. With each new group of political neophytes came a new struggle for African American political and electoral empowerment, accompanied by the need for a person such as Ronald Walters, a theoretician and voter rights activist. Otherwise, the reforms could not have attained their goals and objectives. In this matter Ronald Walters during the last reconstruction was the guiding star and intellectual trailblazer.

The Pioneering Theoreticians:
W.E.B. Du Bois and Ralph J. Bunche

When the major social science disciplines failed to select an appropriate case for comparisons with the African American political neophytes, which should have been European immigrants rather than the southern white electorate, this obfuscated the need of these neophytes for empowerment theorists like Walters. Public intellectuals such as Walters were needed to effectuate a strategy to ensure that the electoral reforms were successfully implemented as far as possible; otherwise they would be doomed before they started. Without such theorists there was no road map to show the way, and direction would come from their former masters and those few northerners who had come South in the Union League's Republican Party.

During the First Reconstruction era, the African American political neophytes had to rely upon the Republican Party for their theories and strategies of African American political and electoral empowerment. However, the party was not only not monolithic but also split into different factions over how to empower itself. The first scholar to analyze this phenomenon of Republican Party factionalism in the old Confederate South was historian Michael Perman. He studied the party in its formative years in the South, 1867 to 1870, and found that the "Republicans were potentially a minority party and so they needed to urgently increase their votes. Some of those votes could be obtained by better canvassing and organization of the party's major source of support, its black constituency, but a far more productive method was to broaden its appeal so that it could develop a reliable base among white voters."[17] Perman adds:

> To be viable outside of South Carolina, Louisiana, and possibly Mississippi where blacks on their own provided the party with a majority, the Republicans had to have a considerable white constituency. Secondly, it was not only the votes of whites which the party wanted; Republicans also needed their respect and acknowledgement that the Republican

Party was legitimate. . . . A final consideration that pushed the party toward a "competitive" strategy was the political risk involved in reliance on its black constituency. If an "expressive" approach were adopted, the Republicans would have to accentuate the prominence given to their cadres of black supporters. This would identify the party very closely with blacks and thus place obstacles in the way of whites recognizing or supporting it.[18]

These different strategies for building and institutionalizing the fledging Republican Party in the reconstructed South led eventually to a dual factionalism in each of the eleven state parties. Historians have given them different names: Radicals and Regulars, or Radicals and Centrists. Perman declares that the Radicals appeared first and quickly gave birth to the Centrists, then eventually morphed into the Regulars, so that it was initially the Centrists versus the Regulars that appeared in each of the eleven southern states. Here is his characterization of these two Republican factional groups in the South:[19]

The Centrists were invariably southerners with considerable political experience and they affiliated with the Republican Party in the hope that, and also on the condition that, they could reorganize and redirect it. Their intention was to fit the new party into a southern mold, incorporate it into the existing southern political system. Respectable and accepted, it would be led by traditional southern politicians like themselves and would rest on an electoral base consisting predominantly of native whites. Thus, constituted, it would naturally serve as the instrument for conservative economic development and social improvement rather than as an engine for racial justice and social change.[20]

The leadership of the Centrist factions, on the other hand, "was overwhelmingly native and local in origin," and as a consequence these "natives already possessed a record and a personal following and constituency, so that they would expect to build on that influence through the party's control of state government."[21] The mere existence of this local political and electoral base made them not only different from the northern whites in the Regular factions but also nearly completely reliant on the African American constituency base.

Describing the Regular factions, Perman writes that:

> With the exception of Texas, where the party's whites were overwhelmingly native, the Regular factions were headed by northerners. . . . A second characteristic of the Regulars was that they invariably derived their political viability from the control they possessed over federal patronage. Their northern origins and experience gave them preferment in obtaining nomination to Congress as well as in being selected as the federal government's agents and officeholders in its southern outposts. Consequently, with this as their base of influence, Regulars used their access to the northern wing of the party and their patronage power to restrain the drive of the Centrists toward a rather different orientation for southern Republicanism.[22]

In comparing these two factions, Perman found that the Regulars "unlike their rivals . . . did not want to change the existing composition of the Republican Party. . . . Rather the Regulars were the party loyalists and they strove to sustain and protect the institution as it was."[23] This meant that the African American political neophyte constituency was crucial to them. "They relied considerably on the party's blacks. Indeed, without them, the Regulars knew that their position in the party as well as the survival of the party itself were precarious. They therefore had to have the cooperation and backing of black Republicans."[24] Nevertheless, the electoral competition between these northerners and their African American political neophytes created great tension, conflict, and bitterness. Eventually, this would lead to another and different kind of Republican Party factionalism based solely on race, Black and Tan Republicans versus Lily-White Republicans.[25]

Before we get to the new Republican Party factionalism in the South, one must clearly understand that the factionalized Republican Party in the First Reconstruction period was unable to properly theorize and develop a strategy of African American political empowerment. Devoid of strategic scholars such as Ronald Walters, the empowerment of the African American political neophytes simply faltered and collapsed.

The first African American public intellectual to study this period was W.E.B. Du Bois in *Black Reconstruction*. Du Bois' theory arrived in 1935, far too late for the First Reconstruction (1868–1876) and too early for the Second Reconstruction (1965–). Moreover, this empowerment theory merely identified an electoral coalition partner (poor whites) for African American's but was incomplete in its discussion of how this coalition could be put together. Du Bois asserted that poor whites and African American political neophytes had a common interest, but that was not enough to effectuate an alliance. Overcoming the racism that persisted between these two groups was never carefully addressed in Du Bois' work. But it did leave a legacy for the future as well as demonstrate the need for African American public intellectuals to address this empowerment problem, which would certainly face the next wave of political neophytes. Walters would be influenced by Du Bois' scholarly effort.

Following Du Bois' incomplete theory of how to empower African American political neophytes was the theorizing of the first African American political scientist, Ralph Bunche. According to Du Bois' recent biographer, historian David Levering Lewis, key scholars from Howard University read Du Bois' *Black Reconstruction* manuscript and objected to its socialistic conceptions being applied to the African American working class.[26] These criticisms came from two African American professors in the Political Science Department—Emmett Dorsey and Ralph Bunche—and one in the Economics Department—Abram Harris. However, one year after the appearance of Du Bois' work, in 1936, Bunche wrote his first monograph, *A World View of Race*, which denounced racial analyses of the African American problem and declared the race problem to be everywhere a class problem with a Marxist solution.[27] From this moment in time both Du Bois and Bunche were proceeding along the same theory-building track.

In 1933 Du Bois attended an institute at Howard where Bunche delivered a paper that offered an economic analysis of the race problem in America that Du Bois found quite informative.[28] The growing admiration between the two men did not stop Bunche from offering a stinging critique of Du Bois' *Black Reconstruction*, as did Harris.

On this matter Professor Lewis writes: "Bunche and Harris were to be found among the severest critics of *Black Reconstruction.* That both men genuinely admired Du Bois is plainly evident from correspondence."[29] Nevertheless, "Harris and Bunche professed superior socialist understanding tinged with consideration for the author's advanced years." Bunche would remark that Du Bois "'racialism appears . . . a much too virulent breed to permit successful crossing with Marxism,' that the general strike proposition was 'untenable,' that Reconstruction state governments were petit-bourgeois creations, that southern white labor had been maligned, and . . . that the serious student of contemporary social forces and events must read [the book] with due caution."[30]

There was a white southern historian, C. Vann Woodward, who did like the work of Du Bois. Woodward had pursued an aspect of the Du Bois theory dealing with a coalition of poor whites and African American political neophytes, in conjunction with his work on Tom Watson, the white populist in Georgia, and the African American political neophytes' electoral coalition in the state.[31] Eventually, both Bunche and Woodward would move beyond Du Bois' work and address the problem of empowerment in their own ways.

Caught up in the ever-evolving New Deal programs and a World War that diminished in his eyes the problems with the Soviet Union and its leader Joseph Stalin, Bunche moderated his initial Marxist-based theory of political empowerment via a workers' revolution. He embraced an African American political dealignment from the Republican Party and realignment with the Democratic Party and its New Deal leadership of Franklin Delano Roosevelt.[32] Despite the problems that this alliance entailed, such as the white southern Democrats, at the moment it was the most viable solution to the numerous problems that African Americans faced. By then, Du Bois had moved into a series of third parties, particularly the Henry Wallace–led Progressive Party of 1948, and became a senatorial candidate in the New York–based American Labor Party (ALP) in 1950.[33] Neither of these new strategies answered the questions about African American empowerment of their political neophytes. There were only the legacies of those who had tried to find a theory of the rise of African American political neophytes made possible by the Supreme Court in *Smith v. Allwright* in 1944 and by the Voting Rights Act of 1965 and its subsequent renewals.

African American Political Neophytes and
Ronald Walters' Initial Leverage Theory

Contemporary with the *Smith v. Allwright* decision was the arrival of a new group of African American political neophytes and Ronald Walters into the political world of the African American community. This decision was followed by the 1957 and 1960 Civil Rights Acts, which were in reality new voting rights acts, and more African American political neophytes. In 1963 to 1964 there would be the formation of the Mississippi Freedom Democratic Party (MFDP) with its challenges at the 1964 Democratic National Convention in Atlantic City and its 1965 congressional seating challenges. Involved with both of these MFDP innovations was the rise of another kind of African American grassroots leader, Fannie Lou Hamer from rural America, who "spoke truth to power" in her famous speech at the 1964 Democratic National Convention. Walters was reaching political maturity amid these southern, rural neophytes, who were trying to further empower themselves, as were African American leaders from northern urban areas. Many of their efforts met setbacks due to the resurgence of institutional racism and political discrimination. Walters was involved in the birth and evolution of this confluence of rural and urban African American empowerment struggles. The Reverend Dr. Martin Luther King Jr. and his civil rights colleagues had center stage for the moment. Soon, however, the massive nationwide struggle would simply burn them out and collapse their organization's capacities. Walters would step into the vacuum.

Among the sundry forces unleashing African American political neophytes into the system during Walters' political maturity was the 1965 Voting Rights Act. This legislation introduced the largest number of African Americans into the American political process since the first Reconstruction in the 1860s. These individuals needed a new theory of political and electoral empowerment, because it was clear that the older theories had severe weaknesses. Truly, something had to be done following the electoral reform efforts in single southern states, such as the MFDP in Mississippi, or the National Democratic Party of Alabama (NDPA), and the 1972 seating challenges from Georgia led by Julian Bond and from Illinois by Jesse Jackson. A new National Black Convention movement followed in 1972. The 1972 election campaign saw African American congresswoman

Shirley Chisholm's pioneering campaign for the Democratic Party's nomination. Walters was involved with all these political and electoral empowerment formations, and soon after Jackson's presidential campaigns for the Democratic Party nomination in 1984 and 1988 he would, like all of the previous scholar-activists, commit his ideas to paper in the form of articles and books.

Walters' first book-length study of his empowerment theory for African American political neophytes was entitled *Black Presidential Politics in America: A Strategic Approach.*[34] Having advised the leaders' numerous innovative, challenging formations, as well as actually participating in these new formations and ad hoc organizations during the sixties, seventies, and the Jackson presidential campaigns of the eighties, Walters took the dominant "Balance of Power" theory to task and replaced it with a wholly new theory that he called an "Independent Leverage Strategy." It was the first breakthrough empowerment theory for African American political neophytes since the initial efforts of Du Bois and Bunche.

Walters began this book with an initial chapter that analyzed the "evolution of a Black electoral theory," which revolved around a dominant dualism: a moral suasion strategy and an electoral politics strategy with the presidency as its central focus. Eventually, out of this dualist strategy emerged a consensus theory that came to be known as the "Balance of Power." It evolved from the experiences of free women and men of color with the simultaneously evolving American political party system after the ratification of the U.S. Constitution. Initially there were Federalists vs. anti-Federalists, Jeffersonian Republicans vs. National-Republicans, Whigs vs. Jacksonian Democrats, Whigs vs. Democrats, and finally the Republicans vs. the Democrats from 1856 to the present.

In addition to these two major political parties, the American party system began in 1824 to evolve an array of minor political parties ranging from the anti-Masonic to the antislavery parties, such as the Liberty Party and the Free Soil Party, to the proslavery parties such as the American or "Know-Nothing" Party and the Southern Democratic Party.[35] Despite some spotty affiliation with several of the major parties such as the Federalist and the Whigs, in the decade of the 1840s free men of color became not only voters and activists in the antislavery parties but delegates and observers in the national presidential conventions of the Liberty and Free-Soil parties and eventually in the electoral coalition of the Republican Party just prior to the Civil War.[36] Walters covers all of these before he develops his theories of dependent and independent leverages in African American empowerment strategies. Dependent leverage as Walters defined it emerged from "the dependence of the Black community upon the Republican Party to continue its benevolent immediate post–Civil War policies that resulted in the emancipation of slaves and in the Reconstruction regime."[37] However, in his evaluation of their type of leverage, Walters declared: "this paternalism initially demanded loyalty to the Republican Party based on the sentiment of past favors, dictating the two-fold logic that by being part of a strong party institution Blacks were often able to protect their own interest" as well as to possibly advance it.[38] For Walters, this dependent leverage simply allowed the Republican Party to control the "Black vote for Republican candidates" through handpicked leaders via political appointments and economic grants to African American community institutions and their leaders. Such small political handouts did not significantly influence an impoverished community and left the African American political neophyte in a dependent status.

Soon this Republican Party–originated system reversed itself with a realignment to a similar Democratic dependent leverage, starting during the New Deal and ending with the presidencies of Kennedy and Johnson during the civil rights movement. Out of political efforts to reform the Democratic Party via political inventions such as the MFDP and the NDPA, and with charismatic grassroots leaders such as Martin Luther King, Ella Baker, and Fannie Lou Hamer, came the African American presidential campaigns of Chisholm in 1972, Jackson in 1984 and 1988, and former U.S. senator Carol Moseley Braun and Reverend Al Sharpton in 2004. While each had some varying degrees of influence and impact, Walters made it clear that this was still dependent leverage, inside one party, which he called an "intra-party presidential politics." Of the dependency of the Jackson campaigns he writes:

> Yet, despite its independent features, at every point in the major scenarios of the election process there is an interactive relationship. . . . For example, the primary process is governed by party rules and thus is an obvious extension of the party system . . .

In the convention process, the dependency factor was evident in the extent to which the process of participating in the development of the Democratic Party platform resulted in Jackson's Four Minority Reports. But the status of the campaign was nowhere more evident than in the post-convention period when its demobilization was required out of deference to both Federal Election Laws and the Mondale campaign, which at that point represented the Democratic Party.[39]

Walters saw that dependency on others was missing in the proud emotional portrait that emanated from the two Jackson presidential campaigns. He understood that in the primary electoral process, it is the party's rules that control things. In the convention process, the platform committee denied all four of Jackson's minority reports, and after the convention he had to turn over his campaign resources to the winning candidate and pledge to support him, without attaining any substantive public policies for the African American political neophytes and their communities. Power stayed within the Democratic Party national structure and with its presidential and vice presidential nominees. This indeed is dependent leverage. The only independence in the Jackson campaign effort was the autonomy embedded in it.

Walters defines the independent leverage strategy as follows:

The challenge of disciplining the Black vote through organization is therefore, the key to the exercise of independent-leverage, the meaning of which is that the Black vote will be controlled by the Black community rather than by the major (Republican or Democratic) party nominee. Shared control of the Black vote, or outright control of it by forces outside of the Black community, damages the credibility of policy bargaining. Autonomous control establishes a neutral fulcrum in the "balance of power" and provides the basis for making credible public policy claims based on the performance of the Black vote, because it is part of a "true leverage system." Control establishes leverage because it enhances the possibility of *direct*, rather than indirect or dependent, political influence.[40]

He concludes by saying that "we perceive that two positive outcomes are possible through the autonomous control of the Black vote by Blacks: first, the satisfaction of policy demands and second, the side-benefit of political resources."[41]

What are examples of independent leverage strategies? According to Walters they are "the Black Political convention, a form of episodic organization" and "the Black presidential or vice presidential candidacy." He adds that "these two political processes—conventions and parties—should logically function together but, except for a few brief attempts . . . they have often been separate activities rather than reflective of a genuine presidential candidate."[42] And how do these independent organizations link up with the leverage strategy? On this final point, Walters leaves no one in the dark.

> In this is an argument for the position that independent leverage is achieved through the establishment of autonomous organization which acquires political resources in the development of a disciplined Black vote which has the ability to become the "balance of power" through its flexible application to electoral coalitions as the strategic situation demands. Expectations that the winning party will satisfy the policy and political interests of Blacks are enhanced both by explicit bargaining and by the ability of their organization to levy sanctions as an accountability measure.[43]

Overall, Walters had developed out of the two Jackson presidential campaigns a theory of empowerment for African American political neophytes, as well as the "Jackson Model," a theory about "intra-party presidential politics" that could and would be played inside the Democratic Party, given the attachment of African American political neophytes and their elected officials to this currently accessible major political party.[44] It was these theoretical insights that were developed in *Black Presidential Politics in America.*

However, the major question about this highly insightful and keenly relevant theory was that it was built upon the Jackson model in two elections. Would it hold up and prove to be useful in future elections? How effective and predictive would it be? No one knew at the time Walters crafted this theory of leverages, but he had developed a point of departure that was original and innovative.

African American Political Neophytes and
Ronald Walters' Refined Leverage Theory

In the ever dynamic U.S. presidential election system, Walters saw the problems and limitations with his Jackson model in the seventeen years that covered the four presidential elections from 1992 to 2004. His second book on the topic, *Freedom Is Not Enough: Black Voters, Black Candidates, and American Presidential Politics*, updated and refined his leverage theory of African American electoral empowerment. He noted that the remarkable victories of Democrat William J. Clinton in 1992 and 1996 came at a price. The first Democrat since Franklin Delano Roosevelt to win two terms in the White House, Clinton had distanced himself and the Democratic Party from Jesse Jackson and his organization, the Rainbow Coalition, and the African American community. Republicans, beginning with President Nixon, refined the party's southern strategy by advancing the critique that the Democratic Party had prioritized African American interests over white Democratic middle- and working-class interests. With this political argument, Nixon swept the South twice in 1968 and 1972, and dealigned whites from the Democratic Party. Republicans Ronald Reagan and George H. Walker Bush won again in 1980, 1984, and 1988. After the Republican landslide victory in 1984, congressional and southern state Democratic leaders formed the Democratic Leadership Council (DLC) and moved the Democratic Party to the right of center. The DLC endorsed Clinton, and he led the organization as the party acquired a conservative demeanor and public policy stance. Jackson was out; Clinton rebuffed him as a possible vice presidential candidate. And Jackson's previous independent efforts were basically abandoned.

In the 2000 presidential election, Republican George W. Bush beat Clinton's incumbent vice president even in a booming economic environment favorable to the Democrats, by skillfully manipulating the election rules in one of the major battleground states, Florida. African American voters were rendered ineffective and without leverage.

Another civil rights leader, Reverend Al Sharpton, and former Illinois senator Carol Moseley Braun attempted to replicate the Jackson model in the 2004 Democratic presidential primaries. Both campaigns failed miserably and were unable to achieve any type of meaningful leverage with the Democratic nominee, Senator John Kerry. Senator Kerry designated Barack Obama as the convention's keynote speaker.

From these efforts, Walters discerns that Jackson was a unique candidate and that few African American politicians at the time could replicate his performance. Like the Democratic Party, the African American candidates in this presidential election had changed, as had the role and function of the African American electorate. Walters' initial leverage theory had to be modified and updated. Chapter 6 in his second book is devoted to the problems with the leverage theory, evaluated from the Sharpton and Moseley Braun campaigns, and contrasted with the Jackson model. He focused his discussion on: 1) candidate motivation, 2) the need for an African American community base, 3) social justice mobilizing and campaigning, 4) public policy acumen, 5) demonstrated electoral support in winning presidential primaries, especially in the South, and 6) bargaining and negotiation with the party nominee for policies relevant to the African American community, as well as making the party accountable on these matters. These six dominant characteristics of the Jackson model were refined in light of the failure of the two 2004 campaigns.

In an unusual reflective effort, Walters used the career of Barack Obama to talk about his independent leverage theory "in speculation that the 2004 Senate victory of State Senator Barack Obama from Illinois may eventually lead to a presidential candidacy."[45] Later in his book, he declared that:

> The fact that Barack Obama, a Black politician from Illinois, won election to the U.S. Senate has already stimulated many references to his potential role as a future candidate for either the presidency or the vice presidency. If either of these roles materializes, the question of whether he will choose to initiate leverage politics on behalf of the Black community will be a major consideration.[46]

Using Obama's election to the U.S. Senate in 2004 to refine his theory and criticize the dependent leverage of the Sharpton and Mosley Braun campaigns, Walters concluded with vision and empirical evidence on the ever-important role of the African American political neophyte in American presidential elections. Although 2004 saw the easy election of incumbent Republican president George W. Bush, which once again suggested the irrelevance of both the mature and the neophyte African American electorate, Walters argued that although the Black voter turnout did not break records, it had substantial and positive results:

> It reflected one of the highest increases in modern times, eradicated the voter turnout deficit with white voters, contributed to the expansion of the CBC (Congressional Black Caucus) from thirty-nine to forty-two members, and elected Barack Obama from Illinois to be another Black member of the U.S. Senate.[47]

Although it did not seem clear at the time, the African American electorate had just elected the next president of the United States of America. Walters was right: this electorate was still relevant. In this second book, Walters alluded to the importance of an African American presidential candidate garnering independent leverage in American politics.

Ronald Walters and an African American President: Another Modification of the Theory

Three years after Walters updated and refined his theory of African American political empowerment, the unexpected happened when Senator Obama from Illinois won the Democratic Party's nomination and went on to win the 2008 general election over Republican nominee U.S. senator John McCain.

After watching Jackson and Sharpton, Walters noted that "the future of Black presidential candidacies will undoubtedly resemble the future of candidacies in the larger society, in which individuals with experience in legislative bodies or high governmental administrative appointments stand for office."[48] He gave Moseley Braun and Obama as examples. Notwithstanding Walters' leverage theory and Jackson model, Obama won both the Democratic primaries and the general election without a black agenda or progressive public policies for the African American community but with unprecedented support and backing from the African American electoral neo-phytes. This occurred in a political and electoral context with the nation's economy and housing situation in shambles. Such a crisis forced the first African American president to prioritize the nation's weak economy and recovery above any help and assistance specifi-cally for the African American community. Walters criticized Obama for his lack of any response to the African American community, a black agenda, or targeted progressive public policies. Were these criticisms another modification of his independent leverage strat-egy based on the Obama presidential candidacy? No! Unfortunately, Walters' untimely death in 2010 cut short the full modification of his empowerment theory.

Ronald Walters' Leverage Theory: An Appraisal and Evaluation

More than anyone, Ralph Bunche specifically sought to develop an empirically based academic theory to explain the empowerment of African Americans in both segregated America and colonial Africa. Despite his best efforts, he was unable to do so. However, such a theory emerged from Henry Lee Moon, a publicist for the NAACP (National Association for the Advancement of Colored People) in 1948. Many African American leaders and academics had talked about the role and function of the African American voter; from both practical experiences and reading political science they advanced the idea that a strategy known as the "balance of power" could help a political and electoral minority such as African Americans. African Americans could use the institutions of political parties and the Constitution-based electoral system to establish public poli-cies that would eliminate their second-class citizenship, remove Jim Crow laws, undermine the illegal system of segregation, and reverse the power and influence of the South in national and state politics. The African American southern political context cried out for such a theory.

What made the theory of the balance of power so appealing and useful, especially in the 1940s, was that the great migration out of the rural South and into the major urban centers was already paying dividends. African Americans were beginning to appear as elected officials at the city council, county commission, and state legislative levels across the country. The future promised more, and with this tide of elected officials came a look toward influence at the presidential level. Moon's theory, which had been cobbled together from leading African American crusading journalists since Black Reconstruction and the Era of Disenfranchisement as a way to use the political and electoral system after the abandonment of the freedmen by the Republican Party was a vision offered to the African American political neophytes. Moon's book, *Balance of Power: The Negro Vote*, appeared in 1948, in the midst of the presidential election contest between incumbent Democratic president Harry Truman and Republican challenger Thomas Dewey.[49] Truman's advisor Clark Clifford not only accepted Moon's thesis but also based Truman's reelection strategy upon it. President Truman launched the process himself when, after the disastrous 1946 midterm elections when Democrats lost control of both houses of Congress, he created the President's Committee on Civil Rights. He was looking for new coalition partners for his reelection bid. African American political neophytes had just won the 1944 *Smith v. Allwright* decision and were winning other state cases that wiped out the white primaries. Voting in large numbers would help their case. Civil rights leaders and voting rights activists had their strategy. Truman did not stop with the establishment of the committee. In 1947, he became the first American president to address the NAACP, at the Lincoln Memorial, and released his Report on Civil Rights. He mentioned it in his 1948 State of the Union address, sent a Special Message to Congress on Civil Rights on February 2nd, and put a civil rights plank into the platform at the Democratic National Convention, which caused a walkout of southern delegates. Lastly, Truman made a speech in Harlem on October 29th, just prior to the presidential election.[50] Clearly he was actively courting the African American electorate that had been set free by the Supreme Court white primary decision. The 1948 election signaled a breakthrough when President Truman won the election against huge odds. The viability of the African American vote was without question and the balance of power strategy was now a fact in presidential elections.

Conversely, however, the African American vote was of no consequence in the 1968 election of Republican president Richard Nixon. This led African American journalist Chuck Stone to pen a book, *Black Political Power in America*, where he vigorously attacked the balance of power theory, declaring that it was inaccurate, had serious weaknesses, and was primarily unreliable. He called upon African Americans to discard it as an electoral strategy and to adopt his concept of a "third force."[51] By 1988 Walters joined Stone and declared that the balance of power theory was inadequate simply because there was no way to make party leaders and presidential candidates accountable. The only way to make the theory work was via independent instead of dependent leverage. Walters stood alone in crafting this theory of leverage.

Political science as a discipline, with its adoption of behavioralism, first refocused the analysis of political parties to a new concept known as political partisanship, an individual-based psychological concept, and made it relevant in terms of the search for variables that determined how individuals acquired it and/or how they shifted and remade their partisanship. Emphasis switched from older concepts such as empowerment to microanalytic questions such as individual partisanship and its different manifestations.

Second, the discipline in this era of behavioralism focused on the voting behavior of individuals and shifted the focus from actual voting behavior to the matter of predicting an individual's vote choice. Actual voting behavior was redefined as vote choice simply because prediction made this social science discipline more exact, like the natural and physical sciences. Hence, emphasis was put upon the variables that predicted and determined vote choice. The discussion of empowerment theory turned to political consultants, campaign managers, pollsters, and other key campaign people. Strategies were designed from individual candidates not groups. The emphasis here was upon how to win, how to help candidates to win, and not on the empowerment of specific groups of voters so that they could improve their communities.

As a consequence of these contextual changes in the discipline, Walters' brilliant theorizing on the limitations of long-deficient electoral strategies did not excite disciplinary scholars. His work has become undervalued except in the African American community, where every entering class of African American political neophytes needs a refined theory of political empowerment to deal with the backlog of unsolved problems that have staggered into the present with huge negative consequences and needs numerous public policies that offer solutions just to keep pace with conditions that continue to deteriorate. Problems here and in the African diasporas continue to mount, almost always without attention from the political system and the political leaders who ride in on the backs of the African American voters. Walters became a matchless theorist, and his ideas will continue to cast a positive intellectual shadow on the nation's democratic order and political system. His influence is formidable. It offers new dimensions to political party analysis, voting behavior, and racial politics in making a mature democratic system such as America truly democratic. It is a new look at democratic theory itself. Thus the discipline, in ignoring Walters' theorizing, delays its own growth and progress as a democracy.

Notes

1. C. Vann Woodward, "The Political Legacy of Reconstruction," in *The Burden of Southern History*, updated 3rd edition (Baton Rouge: Louisiana State University Press, 1993), 98.
2. Ibid., 99–100.
3. Alexander Keyssar, *The Right to Vote: The Contested History of Democracy in the United States* (New York: Basic Books, 2000), 9.
4. Woodward, "Political Legacy," 100.
5. Ibid.
6. Ibid., 99.
7. Ibid., 100–01.
8. Ibid., 102.
9. Ibid., 103.
10. Ibid.
11. Ibid., 104.
12. Ibid., 103.
13. Ibid.
14. Richard Valelly, *The Two Reconstructions: The Struggle for Black Enfranchisement* (Chicago: University of Chicago Press, 2004). See also his "Introduction: Of Reconstructions and the South," in C. Vann Woodward, *The Strange Career of Jim Crow* (New York: Oxford University Press, 1957), 3–12.
15. Hanes Walton, Jr., Josephine A. V. Allen, Sherman C. Puckett, and Donald R. Deskins, Jr., "Beyond the Second Reconstruction: C. Vann Woodward's Concept of the Third Reconstruction in the South," *American Review of Politics* 32 (Spring 2011): 105–30.

16. Ibid., 110–20.
17. Michael Perman, *The Road to Redemption: Southern Politics, 1869–1879* (Chapel Hill: University of North Carolina Press, 1985), 94.
18. Ibid.
19. Ibid., 22–56.
20. Ibid., 44.
21. Ibid., 42.
22. Ibid., 52.
23. Ibid.
24. Ibid., 53.
25. See Hanes Walton, Jr., *Black Republicans: The Politics of the Black and Tans* (New Jersey: Scarecrow Press, 1975) and Donald Lisio, *Hoover, Blacks and Lily-Whites: A Study of Southern Strategies* (Chapel Hill: University of North Carolina Press, 1985).
26. David Levering Lewis, *W.E.B. Du Bois: The Fight for Equality and the American Century, 1919–1963*, vol. 2 (New York: Henry Holt, 2000), 363.
27. Ralph Bunche, *A World View of Race* (Washington, DC: Associates in Negro Folk Education, 1936). See also Charles Henry, "A World View of Race Revisited," in *Ralph Johnson Bunche: Public Intellectual and Nobel Peace Laureate*, ed. Beverly Lindsay (Urbana: University of Illinois Press, 2007), 45–59.
28. Lewis, *W.E.B. Du Bois*, 318.
29. Ibid., 375.
30. Ibid., 376.
31. Ibid., 376–77.
32. Hanes Walton, Jr., "Political Science Educational Contributions: Integrating Theory and Practice," in *Ralph Johnson Bunche: Public Intellectual and Nobel Peace Laureate*, ed. Beverly Lindsay, 62–66 (Urbana: University of Illinois Press, 2007). See also Hanes Walton, Jr., and Maxie Foster, "Ralph Bunche as a Political Consultant: The 1939 Bunche Report to the Republican National Committee," *Government and Politics Journal* 3, 7th edition (Spring 2007): 15–21.
33. Lewis, *W.E.B. Du Bois*, 552.
34. Ronald W. Walters, *Black Presidential Politics in America: A Strategic Approach* (Albany: State University of New York Press, 1988).
35. Hanes Walton, Jr., *The Negro in Third Party Politics* (Philadelphia: Dorrance, 1969).

36. Ibid., 49.
37. Walters, *Black Presidential Politics in America*, 19.
38. Ibid.
39. Ibid., 179.
40. Ibid., 112.
41. Ibid.
42. Ibid., 114.
43. Ibid., 114–15.
44. Ronald Walters, *Freedom Is Not Enough: Black Voters, Black Candidates and American Presidential Politics* (Lanham, MD: Rowman & Littlefield, 2005).
45. Ibid., 47.
46. Ibid., 156.
47. Ibid., 181.
48. Ibid., 47.
49. Henry L. Moon, *Balance of Power* (Westwood, CT: Greenwood Press, 1977). See also Michael Gardner, *Harry Truman and Civil Rights: Moral Courage and Political Risks* (Carbondale: Southern Illinois University Press, 2002), 14–27.
50. Gardner, *Harry Truman and Civil Rights*, 28–146.
51. Chuck Stone, *Black Political Power in America* (Indianapolis: Bobbs-Merrill, 1968).

Part VI

12

Ronald Walters

Theory and Practice of Foreign Policy Justice

KARIN L. STANFORD

Introduction

It was during the height of the antiapartheid movement when I first learned that Ronald W. Walters, a scholar at Howard University, was a leader in advancing theoretical conceptualizations of African Americans in international affairs. At that time, I was a student at the University of Southern California and troubled by the outrageous racism practiced by the South African government. I was equally infuriated by the South African government's comfortable and profitable relationship with U.S. corporations and government. It was then that I joined the picket lines of the Free South Africa Movement (FSAM), an organization that drew attention to apartheid by protesting against artists and businesses who entertained and conducted business with South Africa. I was already familiar with the names of Congressman Walter Fauntroy (DC-D), TransAfrica president Randall Robinson, law professor Eleanor Holmes Norton, and Civil Rights Commission chair Mary Francis Berry. Their arrest in 1984 highlighted the atrocities of the South African government and elevated African American concerns about the repression and exploitation of that country's black citizens.[1] Although courageous, their bold actions were not surprising considering that they were already famed as politicians or political activists. However, it was rather unusual for me to witness scholars also function as activists in international affairs. Yet, Ronald W. Walters connected both platforms—as activist and scholar—to promote a theory and practice of foreign policy justice that was designed to liberate African descendants and other dominated people from domination.

My interest in international affairs preceded my introduction to the man who would become my academic advisor, dissertation chair, and mentor. Before becoming a doctoral student at Howard University, I had already received instruction on the most accepted academic debates on U.S. foreign policy toward Africa. The focus of the information and research was on the actions, successes, and failures of elite state actors, such as the secretary of state, ambassadors, and cabinet officials. The scholars studied were essentially framed as objective observers, theoreticians, and commentators on foreign policy ideas, tasks, and accomplishments. Activism by nonstate actors was usually separated from foreign policy theory, and the work of scholars was unconnected to activists. This approach to scholarship guided my studies, until I was introduced to Ronald Walters' practice of serving as scholar, theoretician, policy analyst, strategist, and activist for the global movement against colonialism. It was during the antiapartheid movement, which elevated attention on African American international activism and the work of individuals such as Ronald Walters, that I understood that one could be an activist and a respected scholar of international affairs. Acting within that capacity as scholar-activist, one could actually have an impact upon the international arena without being a foreign service officer or having matriculated at an Ivy League institution. I attended Howard University in hopes of receiving instruction from Ronald Walters and to benefit from his tutelage.

The preeminence of Dr. Walters' scholarship on domestic politics makes it quite easy for some to overlook the fact that his Doctorate of Philosophy was in International Affairs. This misconception is negligible, since Walters, as most African Americans, constructs "the same paradigm of justice seeking in foreign affairs as in the domestic arena."[2] Accordingly, Walters did not support the argument that in order to legitimate scholarship, one had to reject an active role in the African liberation movement. As stated by Ronald Daniels, president of the Institute of the Black World 21st Century, "in the tradition of W.E.B. Du Bois, Dr. Walters was an authentic intellectual, an action-oriented theorist who never wavered in his conviction that the lessons learned in the academy must be translated/applied in terms of activism in the community."[3] Walters was consistent in connecting domestic and international affairs in his efforts to explain the predicament of African-descended people.

In this chapter, I will examine Ronald Walters' contribution to our understanding of African Americans in the global context. I offer an assessment of how his scholarship and work on African Americans and African descendants in the global context inform his readers and the body politic. This chapter considers the work of Walters over his entire academic career. In particular, it traces the development and evolution of his international perspective, his early engagement with African and international studies, and his work as a scholar-activist in the international realm. This chapter will also present an analysis of selected writings by Walters on global issues. These works provide a survey of his academic work on African Americans and international affairs, U.S. foreign policy and race, and his conceptual framework of foreign policy justice.

Global Consciousness

By the time Ronald Walters retired as Professor of Government and Politics at the University of Maryland, College Park in 2009, he had received a multitude of awards for his prolific work on African American politics within the United States. Such awards include the Best Book Award from the National Conference of Black Political Scientists for *Black Presidential Politics in America* and the Award for Distinguished Service to the Devolution Initiative by the Kellogg Foundation.[4] The significant role he played as advisor to the Jesse Jackson campaigns for the presidency in 1984 and 1988 has also been well documented.[5] Attributions for Ronald Walters' work on domestic issues are important, considering the fact that discrimination and inequality inside the U.S. remain an ever-present reality. The focus on domestic subsistence invariably calls attention to Walters' work on internal racism and white supremacy, as exemplified in his book *White Nationalism, Black Interests: The Conservative Movement and the Black Community*, published in 2003.[6] For these reasons, it is unlikely that conventional dialogue about Walters' contribution to the fields of political science and black studies would recognize that global affairs was central to his academic work and political life.

Ronald Walters was an undergraduate student at Fisk University during the modern civil rights movement. He points to his senior year, in 1963, as the period when he became conscious of Pan Africanism.[7] His views on the subject were expressed in an essay, entitled "The Blacks," published in *Reader's Digest* as the winner of a national essay contest. In the essay, Walters underscored the importance of Africa to African Americans and indicated the need for dialogue among descendants of Africa. After writing that essay Walters began to associate with other internationally minded black activists in the United States and abroad. He worked with individuals who would become leading figures in liberatory politics, including Maulana (Ronald) Karenga, Amiri Baraka, Stokely Carmichael, Owusu Sadauki, and South African writer Bloke Modisane.

After graduating from Fisk University with a Bachelor of Arts Degree in History and Government, Walters attended American University as a graduate student of African Politics. Determined to impact global affairs, he joined the foreign service as a career diplomat and enrolled in the Junior Officers program at the Department of State. However, the contradictions between State Department policies and the needs of African people were too blatant for him to ignore. He noted that the State Department was not receptive to African Americans and that it operated as "an old boys' network."[8] Undeterred, Walters reshaped his career aspirations and academic studies. He became a doctoral student at American University in International Affairs but also enrolled in courses at Howard University in African studies and even studied the East African language of Swahili. After completing his doctoral studies in 1971, Walters accepted a position at Syracuse University in the Department of Political Science, as a specialist of East African History. The student movement then propelled him into the position of founding chair of the Afro-American Studies Department at Brandeis University, where he developed courses in Afro-American politics. Although the fervor of the modern civil rights movement required intense focus, Walters did not abandon his dedication to Africa and international affairs, but he carried both fields as essential components during his entire academic career.

The early scholarship of Ronald Walters emphasized international affairs and African politics. As a graduate student, Walters cofounded *The Africanist*, a journal of the African Studies Program at Howard University in 1968, and he cofounded the *Journal of International and Comparative Studies* at American University. In June 1971, he published "Pan Africanism: Africa and the Diaspora," in *Black Lines,* a periodical of the University of Pittsburgh, and "The Global Context of U.S. Foreign Policy toward Southern Africa," in *Africa Today,* October 1972.[9] His first book, *South Africa and the Bomb: Responsibility and Deterrence,* combined and expanded his earlier work and warned of the dangers of the South African's government's quest to obtain nuclear weapons and technology transfers to South Africa from the United States.[10] The impact of the 1986 book was so significant that Dr. Horace Campbell, the well-respected international peace and justice scholar, deemed it an important educational weapon for activists who fought against the white minority regimes in Rhodesia and South Africa.[11] Although Walters' early work centered on South Africa and other global issues affecting the black world, he did not ignore critical domestic issues. Signaling the era of heightened civil rights and black nationalist activism, Walters publicly commented on education, black political activism, and black power and acknowledged race as a significant factor in explaining the condition of black people in the United States.

Walters can be distinguished from other scholars of international affairs in several respects. First, his scholarship was dedicated to investigating how race permeates global affairs, even when avoiding the issue might have granted him higher esteem among his mainstream colleagues. Moreover, Walters advanced progressive ideas in his scholarship and political work that could enhance freedom and self-determination for African posterity.

Ronald Walters: International Activist and Scholar

In 1969, a group of African American scholars seceded from the African Studies Association (ASA), the primary academic organization on Africa. Charging the ASA with elitism, African American scholars including James Turner, Herschelle Challenor, and Willard Johnson established the African Heritage Studies Association to "engage directly with foreign policy instead of assuming the more traditional role of organizing conferences and scholarly debates."[12] Ronald Walters played a central role in the breakaway group. Already familiar with strategies of protest, Walters had engaged powerful systems of discrimination before. One of his most noted organizing efforts occurred in July 1958, as a youth leader of the NAACP when he led a successful sit-in protest against a segregated drugstore in Wichita, Kansas. Civil rights scholar Aldon Morris credits the Wichita sit-in with providing an example for similar sit-ins during the civil rights movement.[13]

The African Heritage Studies Association was founded to support liberation struggles in Africa and organize African Americans to promote social and racial justice in foreign policy. The organization formed alliances with the African Liberation Support Steering Committee, established the Black Forum on Foreign Policy, and aligned themselves with politicians and policymakers. Ronald Walters served as president of the organization from 1974 to 1979.

The basis for Walters' support of the African Liberation Support Committee (ALSC) was its call for liberation in Africa, Pan-Africanist orientation, and advocacy of confrontational strategies such as boycotts. As a member of the ALSC, Walters was able to extend his work in international politics by participating in meetings and learning from early African revolutionaries, such as Amilcar Cabral, the African revolutionary who led the war for independence of Guinea-Bissau from Portugal. The efforts of the committee members also contributed to the recognition of the African Liberation Day celebration on May 25th. Unfortunately, the ALSC dissolved in the mid-seventies, based on ideological conflicts.[14]

The demise of the ALSC created space for Walters to form a closer collaborative relationship with U.S. policymakers on Africa. An advocate of grassroots and systemic organizing, Walters promoted the view that the movement for liberation and justice would not triumph without intense communication and coordination among activists. Following that line of thinking, Walters accepted the position of senior foreign affairs consultant for Congressman Charles Diggs (D-MI) in 1976. Diggs was chairman of the Subcommittee on Africa of the Committee on Foreign Affairs. Walters' primary role was to assist Diggs in formulating and crafting an action plan for Africa and clarifying those ideas to activists and other policymakers. The productive working relationship Walters had previously established with the activist community allowed him to effectively communicate their ideas and concerns to Congressman Diggs.

During this period, Walters contributed to organizing the sixth Pan-African Congress, held at Dar es Salaam in Tanzania in 1974. Walters, however, did not attend the Congress. He explained his reasons for that decision during an interview in 2003. First, many diasporic activists and dissenters from established African and Caribbean governments were not allowed to attend, which meant that important voices would be excluded. Second, he questioned the potential productivity of the conference. Meetings held to organize the international conference had become engulfed in intense ideological debates and diatribes about the direction of the movement, which only allowed for a two-directional choice between Pan Africanism and Marxism. Walters feared that the debate would resurface at the conference, which he believed would not yield any benefit to the cause of liberation from colonialism and oppression. Ultimately, Walters elected to disengage from the international meeting he had helped to organize.[15] As predicted, the veracious atmosphere that occurred at the sixth Pan-African Congress on issues of race and class led some to discount the significance of the conference in the struggle for African liberation.[16]

As senior consultant, Walters worked alongside Congressman Diggs and his staff, including administrative assistant Randall Robinson, to implement Diggs' idea of establishing an African American Lobby for Africa and the Caribbean. The previous groups, including the Black Forum on Foreign Policy and African Heritage Studies Association, contributed to important discussions on African Americans and foreign policy but had not benefited from community resources to effectuate policy successes. Understanding those deficiencies was an important galvanizing idea for the formation of TransAfrica in 1977, as the African American Lobby for Africa and the Caribbean. Established to change the public debate on U.S. support for the South African apartheid government, its strategy combined direct action techniques, lobbying, and educational activities. Ronald Walters contributed to the germination and founding of TransAfrica in his role as senior consultant and as a member of its board of the directors. Walters also wrote the initial proposal for TransAfrica Forum, which was the educational arm of the lobby, and he organized its first board of directors. Randall Robinson served as the first director of TransAfrica until his resignation in 2001.

In addition to his focus on Africa, Ronald Walters engaged the international conversation about self-determination and liberation in the Middle East. Advancing a Third World perspective, Walters articulated the views of African Americans in that area of the world as expressed through its leadership.[17] Evidence of African American knowledge and perspective on the Middle East can be found as far back as 1866 when Edward Wilmot Blyden traveled to the area, visiting Lebanon, Syria, and Palestine. Believing that Jewish repatriation would not have a negative effect on Palestine, he referred to the Jewish quest for a homeland in his description of Zionism as "that marvelous movement."[18] African Americans also expressed outrage toward Adolf Hitler's atrocities committed toward Jewish people.[19] Although many African Americans supported the settlement of Israel in 1948, they also supported the rights of Palestinians. Signifying the importance of the Israeli-Palestinian quagmire to the African American community was the forced resignation of Andrew Young as U.S. Ambassador to the United Nations in 1979. Young was accused of holding an unauthorized conversation with Palestine Liberation Organization (PLO) representative Tariq Aziz. This "meeting" was viewed by U.S. officials as contrary to their support for Israel, however, and Young's forced resignation was denounced by African American leaders. To demonstrate their independence from U.S. government policy, members of the Southern Christian Leadership Conference and Operation Push embarked upon a fact-finding mission to the Middle East seeking to learn and then articulate their own perspectives on the conflict. Reporting on the ventures, Walters stated that both African American delegations advocated mutual respect and balance in their conversations with high-level officials. He also concluded that African Americans identified with the Palestinian cause because they were also "victims of white Western European oppression." Notwithstanding African American understanding of the Jewish quest for a homeland, supporting the Palestinian cause as well was "consistent with the Black Third World perspective on the question of national liberation movements."[20]

Walters' holistic approach to liberatory politics necessitated a discussion about securing resources for effective advocacy and nation building. He concluded that reparations for African descendants must be an essential component of his organizing work. Therefore, Walters became one of the initial founders of the National

Coalition of Blacks for Reparations in America (N'COBRA) in 1987, an organization that has become recognized as the leading voice for reparations in the United States. In addition to N'COBRA, Walters belonged to the Reparations Coordinating Committee (RCC), which was founded to win reparations for African Americans and determine various options in pursuit of that goal. The RCC used legal strategies to raise the issue of the "legal right of African descendants to reparations based on the continuing vestiges of slavery" (www.ncobra.org). Members of the RCC included Randall Robinson; professors Charles Ogletree, Cornel West, and Johnnetta Cole; and attorneys Johnnie Cochran and Willie Gary.

In his traditional methodology, Walters theorized the importance of reparations in his scholarship and became a local, national, and international spokesperson on the issue. There is ample information on Walters' activism on reparations, as he testified before members of the House of Representatives concerning the need for passage of H.R. 40, a reparations bill sponsored by Congressman John Conyers of Michigan; testified before the Maryland General Assembly for passage of the bill; served as a panelist at Reparations Town Hall meetings; lobbied members of the House and the Senate; and conducted lectures at the University of Maryland and the University of the District of Columbia to raise student awareness.[21] Perhaps, his most significant contribution to reparations was the writing and publication of his book *The Price of Racial Reconciliation*, which uses a comparative methodology to explain and support the idea of reparations for African descendants.[22]

Walters considered the work of reparations important not only to African Americans but also African descendants globally. He chaired the American delegation to the International Conference on Reparations held in Abuja, Nigeria, hosted by the Organization of African Unity. That meeting was held to situate the consequences of slavery into an international context and address the African side of reparations. Walters urged attendees to consider not only the resources taken from the continent as a result of slavery but also colonialism and imperialism. He also set forth his view that reparations were essential for rehabilitating the "African self and history."[23] One important outcome of the conference was that the Organization of African Unity (OAU) established an International Committee on Reparations to continue the struggle for reparations on a global level. Also connected to reparations and the fight against racism was Walters efforts in 2001 at the United Nations' World Conference against Racism, Discrimination, Xenophobia and Related Intolerance. At the conference, he served as a delegate from the Centre of Advanced Studies of Africa, located in Capetown, South Africa and as part of the leadership group of African Americans. Upon his return, Walters reported on the U.S. delegation's efforts to avoid criticism of Israel and discussions of reparations.[24]

A Black Internationalist Approach to Scholarship

As a young scholar, Walters conceptualized U.S. foreign policy differently from senior scholars, including Hans Morgenthau and Joseph Nye, who utilized the Cold War scenario to examine and explain U.S. policy in the international arena. Oppositional schemas that centered on the perceived polarity between realism and idealism formed the basis of their descriptions of the U.S. relationship with the Soviet Union. For U.S. scholars, the Soviet Union was a superpower that needed to be contained, despite negative consequences for other nation-states and domestic economic stability. The common language of "realpolitik" and the bipolarity of foreign policy "hawks vs. doves" dominated discourse, and Third World nations were viewed as pawns in a chess game as both superpowers armed oppositional forces in those countries. The devastating consequences to smaller nations included assassinations, starvation, economic instability, underdevelopment, and ecological disasters.

Building upon the literature of African American and Third World scholars who rejected the Cold War scenario as the essential analytical tool in the discourse on U.S. action in the world, Ronald Walters used African American history as the basis for his analysis of international affairs. According to Walters, "slavery shaped Black interest in domestic and foreign affairs, as rehabilitative projects to construct positive relations between Africans and peoples of African Descent, and between the nations and continents that contain such peoples." Moreover, the brutality and injustice of the slave trade and the institution of slavery caused "blacks to construct the same paradigm of justice seeking in foreign affairs as in the domestic

arena."[25] Thus, his analysis is rooted in African American existential-
ism, which critiques domination and emphasizes the power to define
one's experiences. Walters also viewed the black freedom struggle
post slavery as also important for shaping African American views on
U.S. policy.

The writings of Ronald Walters were published as books, scholarly articles, and opinion editorials and served opportunities to
educate activists, policymakers, and the general public. It was common for Walters to utilize radio, television, and internet resources to
report about essential areas of action. He often communicated critical information from sites of policy formation and places of debate,
as occurred from the African American fact-finding missions from
the Middle East and the Durban Conference against Racism. Walters also proposed and published action plans in hopes of moving
progressive policies forward. By this strategy, Walters challenged and
encouraged scholars in a variety of subfields to thoughtfully consider
African Americans' views on international relations.

Several themes dominated Ronald Walters' scholarship on U.S.
foreign policy and global issues affecting African Americans and
other descendants of Africa. First was the contradictory nature of
U.S. policy in relationship to African people. Walters' early work on
South Africa highlighted those contradictions, with the goal of prop-
agating doubt among the public about the actions of the United
States toward the apartheid government. One case in point was discussed in his article "The Global Context of United States Foreign
Policy toward Southern Africa," published in *Africa Today*. Walters
pointed out the inconsistency between President Richard Nixon's
public support for black Africans and his actual policies. At the time
of his writing, at least 350 U.S. companies were benefiting from a
financial relationship with South Africa. The U.S. and South Africa
were also working together on space tracking facilities and nuclear
weaponry and power, which indicated a collaborative military relationship. According to Walters, the goal of receiving financial benefits in the global economy dictated the relationship between the
United States and South Africa instead of altruism toward black
South Africans.[26]

Because Walters' activism was embedded in his scholarship, he
set forth an agenda for activists and policymakers that might force

administrative officials to craft and implement progressive policies. Walters also encouraged African Americans to establish linkages with black South Africa as part of a Pan-African strategy to support their struggle. Building coalitions with other Third World people around issues of exploitation and subjection was another important component to the idea of linkages. Also essential, according to Walters, was to gain access to power by using modern weaponry and geographic authority.[27]

The contentions of several scholars of the African Heritage Studies Association published in *Africa Today* in 1973 were similar to the suppositions Walters set forth in his "Global Context" article of 1971. Nine scholars, including Walters, jointly exposed the various ways the U.S. government had collaborated with the South African government and how the country's resources were being used to defend minority privilege and exploitation. Published during the Vietnam War, the scholars warned that this scenario could lead to a similar quandary for the United States in South Africa. The African Heritage Studies scholars eventually advocated for a foreign policy that reflects the basic values and moral concerns of the United States and is rooted in support for human rights.[28]

Walters prioritized apartheid and South Africa's potential global threat in his first book and several articles. In the book *South Africa and the Bomb: Responsibility and Deterrence* (1986) and two articles, "Apartheid and the Bomb: The U.S. and South Africa Military Potential" (1976) and "The United States and the South African–Namibian Uranium Option" (1983), Walters methodically outlined nuclear cooperation between the United States and South Africa and situated that collaboration as a violation of nuclear resolutions that the United States had previously supported. Walters also warned of the United States' growing reliance on the strategic minerals in Namibia (Southwest Africa), a border state illegally occupied by the apartheid regime of South Africa. Namibian uranium was being supplied to the United States at the behest of South Africa. Again, Walters highlighted the contradictions in U.S. foreign policy, as the United States publicly asserted support for black Africans, but its policies ignored the devastating plight of the indigenous population of Namibia. One example was U.S. National Security Memorandum No. 39, also known as the "tar baby" option, which argued that "constructive change in the region of southern Africa could only come about through relations with whites."[29] Essentially, the United States would continue its relationship with the apartheid government and benefit from its racist policies and illegal occupation. Walters introduced the concept "white settler nationalism" to describe the actions of the South African government and boldly proclaimed U.S. action as supportive of that ideology.

Walters believed that African Americans could support black Africans in their quest for self-determination. Members of the Congressional Black Caucus and the two African American Foreign Service officers stationed in South Africa at that time could create opportunities to positively affect U.S. policy. Second, he called upon African American interest groups, such as the National Urban League, to work to pursue justice for Africa. In the case of Namibia, Walters insisted that the United States should comply with decree number 1 of the UN Council of Namibia, which sought to protect Namibian resources. He also suggested strong coalitions be organized between antiapartheid groups, unions, the antinuclear war movement, and others who are opposed to the importation of foreign source uranium into the United States.[30]

The antiapartheid activism of African Americans received widespread attention during the 1980s, as they worked to defeat President Ronald Reagan's policy of Constructive Engagement with the South African government. Walters had charged Reagan with developing policies toward the region that combined conservative ideology and color consciousness in his article "Beyond Sanctions."[31] The article detailed the flaws of Reagan's policies and how African American activism and pressure provided enough leverage for Congress to pass a Comprehensive Sanctions Bill in 1986. After an analysis of the victory, Walters argued for enhanced sanctions to prohibit the South African government from formulating ways to overcome their effectiveness. Walters also highlighted the concerns of nine neighboring states of South Africa, who were organized under the umbrella of the South African Development Coordinating Conference (SADCC). The SADCC nations were suffering from South Africa's damaging military and economic actions by emphasizing regional security. In "Beyond Sanctions," Walters advocates economic development of the SADCC states by delinking their economies from South Africa's whenever and wherever possible, in order to promote economic autonomy. Walters ended his article advocating for Reverend Jesse Jackson's call for a Marshall Plan for Africa, which would increase financial support for struggling countries, as occurred in Europe after World War II.[32]

Economic development for Africa was the subject of another article written by Ronald Walters. In "The African Growth and Opportunity Act: A Renaissance for Whom?" in *Black Renaissance*, published in 1999, Walters criticized attempts to promote capitalism on the African continent.[33] He raised the concern about the economic direction of the continent in the wake of the Ford Foundation sponsored National Summit for Africa and after the introduction of the African Growth and Opportunity Act (AGOA), embedded in H.R.1432, legislation introduced by Congressman Charles Rangel in spring 1997. The National Summit for Africa was established to transform the national conversation on Africa by reducing African American concerns about European malfeasance, thus making it more mainstream. The African Growth and Opportunity Act promoted economic development by emphasizing free trade and partnerships. Walters recognized the importance of this legislation but was concerned that the mantra "trade not aid," advanced by Republican leaders, would lead to further exploitation of the continent.

In the article, Walters highlighted divisions within the African American community over the African Growth and Opportunity Act and reasoned that the conflict served as a window into future disagreements. The opposition to the bill was spearheaded by members of TransAfrica, who believed that the legislation placed conditions on African states that could violate their sovereignty and inferred that trade would be prohibited with countries unfriendly to Western nations. Opponents of the bill also argued that the bill did not protect basic labor rights and would not protect nor benefit the poor. Members of the Congressional Black Caucus (CBC) were split, with twelve of its members voting against it. Two of the most outspoken members of the CBC, Maxine Waters (D-CA) and Ronald Dellums (D-CA), argued for more progressive policies.

The divisions among African Americans on economic policy toward Africa also included employees of the State Department and White House, who Walters viewed as functionaries of the U.S. government. Other segments mentioned were business-oriented African

Americans who supported their corporate employers and black mayors who saw Africa as a possible source of economic support for their starving cities.[34] Walters' observations have become increasingly relevant considering the rise of black foreign policy actors within the U.S. State Department and globalization.

Unmistakable in Walters' writings is the idea that African descendants must work together to resolve common problems and build closer relationships, irrespective of geography. As a social scientist, however, Walters recognized the complexity of the African experience, which interfered with attempts to create such a functional international community. This recognition influenced his decision to write *Pan Africanism in the African Diaspora*, published in 1993.[35] In this book, Walters dissects how race has impacted Africa and its diaspora by utilizing a comparative method. He also demonstrates how African communities have endeavored to overcome race as a negative factor in their lives, but also how they have utilized race as a basis for progressive international relationships. Walters compares specific aspects of white dominance against Pan-African communities, African Americans, blacks in Britain, and blacks in the Caribbean and Latin America. He examines the environment in which they live and argues that the local context provides shape to Pan-African relationships. He also considers political movements in each country and the extent that Pan-African connections became important in political activism. Notwithstanding the importance of the scholarly achievement of *Pan Africanism in the African Diaspora*, Walters refuses to neglect advocating his personal and political perspective. In this case, the reader can appreciate why Ronald Walters appeals to African Americans and other African descendants pursuing Pan Africanism.

In reply to critics of *Pan Africanism*, who suggested that he needed to consider the issue of culture and Pan Africanism, Ronald Walters clarifies his view that black culture must be considered uniquely different in the world. His research findings indicate that people of African origin express certain similarities of culture, which include the broad experience of racial subordination, economic exploitation, political exclusion and marginalization, and one-way acculturation. Although those experiences might differ in the local context, Walters argues that the shared experience remains. The similarity in experiences leads Walters to argue that African Americans should use an Afrocentric perspective to define their world.

In addition to the Pan-African perspective advanced, Walters develops a research methodology rooted in social science that provides an important contribution to Pan Africanism. Historians, he asserts, should be commended for developing a body of important literature on the origins and cultural basis of Pan Africanism. Social scientists, however, needed a unique methodology for the study that would allow for various levels of interpretation and comparison. Walters created and utilized the two methodologies of comparative race analysis and the Pan-African method to examine Pan Africanism. In that regard, Walters analyzed five types of Pan-African relationships 1) among Africans states; 2) among African states and African origin states in the diaspora, as in Caribbean; 3) among African states and African origin people (communities) in the diaspora; 4) among African-origin states in the diaspora and African-origin communities in the diaspora; and 5) among African-origin communities in the diaspora.[36] Walters then compared the political dynamic that emerges from the vertical relations between the dominant white and subordinate black communities and used a Pan-African analytical approach to determine the degree of functional interaction between communities. Walters looks within the nation-states or within the horizontal relation of transnational African communities as a resource for each other. He concluded that the Pan-African analytical approach should be considered a black studies methodology, in that it recognizes the dominant influence of the racial variable within the context of domestic relations, while the Pan-African method recognizes the dominant influence of African identity, history, and culture in the transactional relations of African-origin peoples in the diaspora. He presents a typology of potential unifying relationships among African people, which reflects the continental and diasporic context for each relationship.[37] He concludes that the Pan-African movement persists because of continental necessity and the importance of extra-continental dimension in world affairs.

Theorizing Foreign Policy Justice

The fundamental idea in Walters' writings on international affairs is the concept of social justice, which he argues is rooted in the African American pursuit of freedom from oppression and the quest for self-determination and liberty. Although this approach is evident in all of his scholarship, its components are not fully articulated until later in Walters' life. The article "The U.S. War on Terrorism and Foreign Policy Justice" explicates a detailed presentation on Walters' view of social justice internationally.[38] Published in the book *The Paradox of Loyalty* edited by Julianne Malveaux, the exposition was written in the midst of the U.S. war on Iraq in 2004, to explain the problems and contradictions of U.S. foreign policy in the Middle East. Focused on the Israeli and Palestinian conflict, Walters takes issue with the U.S. posture as an "honest broker" in the dispute, especially since the United States is the largest sponsor of Israel and the Israeli government serves as an outpost of American interest. Walters also asserts that the U.S. government imagines that the Arab revolution is unconnected to the just struggle for self-determination among Third World people and that the political situation of Israel and Palestine are equal. In reality, according to Walters, Israel is much more powerful than Palestine because of U.S. support. Moreover, U.S. policy requires that the weaker of the two nations, who is often the disproportionate victim of violence, exercise more responsibility than the more powerful. This contradictory behavior of the United States Walters contends is "foreign policy injustice."

Foreign policy justice is defined by Walters as a "just" protocol that provides attention to the political demands of both sides and balances the interest of both Israelis and Palestinians. Walters defines the Palestinian opposition to occupation as a "just war" as it was for Americans who fought against the British, or South Africans who fought against apartheid, or Algerians fighting against the French. The term "foreign policy justice" affirms the importance of moral and racial content. Foreign policy justice must consider unequal power and unequal loss.

An even more in-depth explanation of foreign policy justice is set forth by Walters in his article "Racial Justice in Foreign Affairs," published in 2009.[39] In this essay, Walters brings together the most important concepts that he has advocated as important to African American internationalism, which are a progressive foreign policy, Afrocentrism, and finally foreign policy justice. He explains the reasons why black international interest is not rooted in American nationalism but instead lies in Afrocentrism, its Third World perspective, and human rights. This African-centered perspective of

African Americans is reflected in their overwhelming opposition to most wars involving the United States.

In his later years, Walters laments the decline of African American interest in foreign affairs since the 1980s as evidenced by their lack of activism around the atrocities that occurred in Rwanda and Darfur. Walters agrees with Charles Henry, a scholar of political science, who argues that the decline is parallel to the emergence of a conservative political culture, which continues to challenge the cultural integrity of the black community. However, Walters also suggests other factors to consider as significant, such as the end of the liberation period in the 1960s, which led to the decline of international liberation organizations in number and in strength. In addition, the popularity of Pan Africanism in theory and practice waned as the social movements that had sustained it declined.

A second reason for the decline in African American activism in international affairs is the rise of black state leadership. When Walters began academic writing during the late 1960s, few African Americans were considered influential in international affairs. However, as political and economic conditions shifted, opportunities for African Americans to become official actors in U.S. foreign policy apparatus increased. Many of these new African American middle-class professionals attended schools that provided little or limited information that would support African American internationalism and an Afrocentric perspective. Moreover, there is pressure for African Americans to conform to the mainstream direction of U.S. foreign policy as an expression of their loyalty.[40] For example, former secretaries of state Colin Powell and Condoleezza Rice were received positively for their loyalty to the administrations for which they were appointed. When Colin Powell questioned President George Bush's invasion of Iraq, he was ostracized and considered disloyal for his legitimate critique. Walters describes African Americans who ignore racial interests in foreign affairs as "African American in identity, but they represent interests that are antithetical to that community." This view supports Robert Smith's findings on the behavior of black appointed officials, which indicates that "they are not free agents" but "follow instead a silent theory that their presence and excellence in the performance of their duties advance the prospects of racial equality."[41]

According to Walters, another reason for the decline in black interest and activism in foreign affairs is the devaluation of the intellectual legacy of direct action and revolutionary change. In the current climate, revolutionary activists and activities, especially black revolutionaries and their white progressive allies, are not given legitimacy and voice in public debates. Likewise, African heads of states and other Third World leaders are not incentivized to support African descendants in the diaspora. Certainly, there are few negative consequence for African leaders who ignore the concerns of African people living in white-dominated societies. One example occurred in the case of South African president Nelson Mandela, who visited the United States after he was elected as president of South Africa. In Mandela's honor, the U.S. government held official proceedings involving U.S. government officials, while those African American leaders who had fought and led the movement to end apartheid in South Africa were excluded from the celebrations and ceremonies. Certainly, "the new posture of governance often broke the linkage among Africans fighting their own subjugation with their allies in the Diaspora."[42] Walters' commitment to Pan Africanism caused him to critique Mandela's posture as the first black South African president was being revered throughout the world.

Finally, Walters argues that globalization has had a negative effect on Pan Africanism. Globalization has increased economic stress for some countries, which in turn redirects the energies of people to their own survival. A weakening social structure leads to disinvestment, crime, gentrification, and mass incarceration, which displaces workers and others who could contribute to society. As a country suffering from economic devastation turns inward, it no longer has the resources to utilize the human and financial resources of its diaspora.[43]

Walters' death limited his full critique of President Barack Obama's foreign policy design. However, he offered guarded optimism on the young president's willingness to support racial justice toward Africa and its diaspora. The reasons for Walters' outlook were many. Certainly, he had hoped that Obama's Kenyan heritage might translate into sensitivity toward the African continent, which could possibly change the direction of U.S. policy, from exploitive to one that is compassionate and benevolent.[44] Second, Obama promised to end the Iraq War and made statements about strengthening ties to African and Caribbean states, which also led to Walters' idealism. The appointment of Susan Rice, an African American woman, as U.S. Ambassador to the United Nations was viewed by Walters as equally positive. Assuredly, Walters' astute observations in the past meant that he was not blindsided by Obama's race, so he remained aware that President Obama had not yet articulated policies in the interest of Africa and its diaspora. For that to occur President Obama would have needed to develop a new definition of U.S. strategic interest that included funding for HIV/AIDS; programs to alleviate hunger; and progressive policies toward the environment, climate change, energy and other issues that might help stabilize countries. Walters predicted that President Obama's support for a foreign policy based on justice would be dependent on several things, including the global economy. In the end, Walters believed President Obama's pursuit of justice in the world would be dependent first and foremost upon "the degree of commitment among African Americans to mobilize those interests."[45]

Conclusion

Becoming a pioneer of academic work on African Americans and international affairs could not satisfy Ronald Walters' desire to build a strong Pan-African movement, guided by the principle of social justice and rooted in an Afrocentric perspective. Certainly, Dr. Walters was a scholar in thought and academic performance; however, he was equally an advocate and practitioner who utilized his skills to establish structures that would carry his ideas forward. He also assiduously trained others to use his method.

As a student of Ronald Walters, I accomplished my objective of receiving his instruction through courses and his support of my research. As the chair of my dissertation committee, Dr. Walters advised me from the beginning through the defense process. He also opened his private files for my study and introduced me to individuals who might grant interviews and/or access to additional data. After I graduated from the Department of Political Science at Howard University, Walters remained involved with my scholarship. He guided me on publishing my first book and even wrote its foreword.

But, in addition to supporting my academic efforts, I was encouraged by Dr. Walters to adopt the Du Boisian tradition of the scholar-activist. For Walters that meant I had to understand and work with organizations focused on African Americans and internationalism. From the Washington Office on Africa, the Constituency for Africa, and the RainbowPush Coalition, I advocated, supported, and worked alongside activists involved in foreign policy justice. Under the direction of Ronald Walters, my scholarship became purposeful.

During the HistoryMakers interview in 2003, Dr. Walters was asked how he wanted to be remembered. His answer was, "I would like to be remembered as someone who gave his life and his resources to the idea of the dignity of the African person, the unity of people of African descent and the contribution that the idea could make to human civilization."[46] Ronald W. Walters continued the quest for justice well into his final years and made sure that others would stand in for him while he rests.

Notes

1. Francis Njubi Nesbitt, *Race for Sanctions* (Bloomington: Indiana University Press 2004), 123.
2. Michael L. Clemmons, *African Americans in Global Affairs* (Lebanon, NH: Northeastern University Press, 2010), 1.
3. Ronald Daniels, "The Life and Legacy of Dr. Ronald Walters," Free Speech Blog, September 15, 2010. www.freespeech.org/blog/life-and-legacy-dr-ronald-walters, accessed September 1, 2011.
4. Ronald W. Walters, *Black Presidential Politics in America* (Albany: State University of New York Press, 1988).
5. Ronald W. Walters, "The Issue Politics of the Jesse Jackson Campaign for President in 1984," in *The Social and Political Implications of the 1984 Jesse Jackson Presidential Campaign*, ed. Lorenzo Morris, 16–48 (New York: Praeger Publishing, 1990); "Ron Walters, Rev. Jesse Jackson Advisor and Long Serving Howard University Professor Dies," Newsone Staff, September 13, 2010, accessed October 15, 2011, newsone.com/nation/newsonestaff4.
6. Ronald W. Walters, *White Nationalism, Black Interests: The Conservative Movement and the Black Community* (Detroit: Wayne State University Press, 2003).

7. See Ronald W. Walters, *Pan Africanism in the African Diaspora* (Detroit: Wayne State University Press, 1997), 9, for additional discussion on the essay and Walters' burgeoning consciousness of Pan Africanism.

8. Ronald W. Walters (The HistoryMakers A2003, 121) Interview by Larry Crowe, July 15, 2003, The HistoryMakers Digital Archive. Session 1 tape 3, Story, Ronald Walters explains why he left the U.S. State Department to pursue a PhD in African Studies. http://www.idvl.org/the historymakers/icoreclient htm.

9. Ronald W. Walters, "Pan Africanism: Africa and the Diaspora," *Black Lines* (June 1971): 7–17; Ronald W. Walters, "The Global Context of U.S. Foreign Policy toward Southern Africa," *Africa Today* (October 1972): 12–21.

10. Ronald W. Walters, *South Africa and the Bomb: Responsibility and Deterrence* (Lexington, MA: Lexington Books), 1986.

11. Horace Campbell, "Africa: Ronald W. Walters—A Fighter against Global Apartheid," September /allafrica.com /stories/printable/201009230743, accessed September 1, 2011.

12. Nesbitt, *Race for Sanctions*, 99.

13. Aldon Morris, *The Origin of the Civil Rights Movement: Black Communities Organizing for Change* (New York: The Free Press, 1984).

14. Nesbitt, *Race for Sanctions*,108.

15. Walters, HistoryMakers Interview.

16. For commentary on the credibility of the sixth Pan-African Congress, see "No Easy Victories: African Liberation and American Activists over a Half a Century, 1950–2000," www.noeasyvictories.org/select/08_hill.php.

17. For examples of ideas and activism of African American leaders related to Africa and international affairs, see Hanes Walton, Jr., and Robert C. Smith, *American Politics and the African American Quest for Universal Freedom* (Glenville, IL: Longman, 2012), chapter 16.

18. Robert G. Weisbord and Richard Karzarian, Jr., *Israel in the Black American Perspective* (Westport, CT: Greenwood Press, 1984); Karin L. Stanford, "Race and the Persian Gulf War, 1990–1991: African American Perspectives," *International Journal of Africana Studies* 12, 2 (2006): 194–212.

19. African American concerns about Adolf Hitler are expressed in Clarence Lusane, *Hitler's Black Victims: The Historical Experiences of*

Afro-Germans, European Blacks, Africans and African Americans in the Nazi Era (New York: Routledge, 2003).

20. Ronald W. Walters, "The Black Initiatives in the Middle East," *Journal of Palestine Studies* (Winter 1981): 13.
21. Some of Ronald Walters' work related to reparations is listed on N'COBRA's website. See N'COBRA's tribute to Dr. Ronald Akili Walters. http://groups.yahoo.com/group/trueblackness/message/46910.
22. Ronald W. Walters, *The Price of Racial Reconciliation* (Ann Arbor: University of Michigan Press, 2009).
23. Walters, The HistoryMakers Interview. Ronald Walters discusses the reparations movement in Africa and the diaspora.
24. Ibid. Ronald Walters recalls the World Conference against Racism in Durban, South Africa.
25. Ronald W. Walters, "Racial Justice in Foreign Affairs," in *African Americans in Global Affairs: Contemporary Perspectives*, ed. Michael Clemmons, 1–30 (Lebanon, NH: University Press of New England, 2010).
26. Walters, "The Global Context of U.S. Foreign Policy toward Southern Africa."
27. Ibid., 28–29.
28. Willard R. Johnson, Goler Butcher, Herschelle Challenor, Karl Gregory, Elizabeth Landis, John Marcum, Ronald Walters, Peter Weiss, Carol A. Bloomberg, "United States Foreign Policy Toward Africa," *Africa Today* (Winter 1973): 15–44.
29. Ronald W. Walters, "Apartheid and the Bomb: The United States and South Africa's Military Potential," *Africa Today* (1976): 26; Ronald W. Walters, "The United States and the South African–Namibian Uranium Option," *Africa Today* (1983): 13–36.
30. Walters, "The United States and the South African–Namibian Uranium Option," 58–59.
31. Ronald W. Walters, "Beyond Sanctions: A Comprehensive United States Policy for Southern Africa," *World Policy Journal* (1986/1987): 109.
32. Ibid., 95.
33. Ronald W. Walters, "The African Growth and Opportunity Act: A Renaissance for Whom?" *Black Renaissance* (Summer 1999): 161–69.
34. Ibid., 6.

35. Walters, *Pan Africanism in the African Diaspora.*

36. Ibid., 4.

37. Ibid., 325.

38. Ronald W. Walters, "The U.S. War on Terrorism and Foreign Policy Justice," in *The Paradox of Loyalty: An African American Response to the War on Terrorism,* ed. Julianne Malveaux and Regina A. Green (Chicago: Third World Press, 2002).

39. Walters, "Racial Justice in Foreign Affairs," 3.

40. Ibid.

41. Ibid., 24 and 25; Robert Smith, *We Have No Leaders: African Americans in the Post–Civil Rights Era* (Albany: State University of New York Press, 1996), 139.

42. Walters, "Racial Justice and Foreign Affairs," 20.

43. Ibid., 22–23.

44. Ibid., 25.

45. Ibid., 27.

46. Walters, The HistoryMakers Interview, Ronald Walters discusses how he would like to be remembered.

13

Ronald Walters

Pan Africanism and International Struggles for Social Justice

HORACE CAMPBELL

Introduction

When progressive Pan Africanists met at the Henry Sylvestre Williams Conference in Trinidad in 2000 and were articulating the goals of political change of the twenty-first century, there was recognition that the reconceptualization of Pan Africanism had to elevate the questions of dignity and humanity away from the state centered preoccupations of the period up to the end of apartheid. Questions of health, life, peace, and the saving of planet earth had brought the questions of a new century in line with the social forces who were at the forefront of the struggles for social justice. It was basically agreed in meetings and discussions among progressive intellectuals that revolutionary changes had to take place in order to end the mode of economic organization that placed profits before humans. Throughout the Pan-African world from Brazil to Nova Scotia and from Cape Town to Cairo, youths were using new tools of the information revolution to accelerate the pace of communication and inspiration in the Pan-African world.

In January 2011 the bottled up aspirations exploded and echoed from the streets of Tunisia to Tahrir Square in Cairo, Egypt. Within days the unrelenting protests against dictatorship (economic and political) that began in Tunisia in January subsequently cascaded across Egypt leading to the downfall of President Ben Ali and Hosni

Mubarak. From Egypt, the bridge between Africa, Asia, and Europe, these protests spread into Yemen, Syria, Bahrain, and Libya to Wisconsin in the United States and then to Spain, Portugal, and Italy. In the midst of a chronic and deepening crisis, there was now a new global spirit of resistance to corporate plutocrats and the governments that defended them. This spirit was trampled upon by the massive NATO intervention in Libya. Using the United Nations as a tool, under the mantle of a United Nations Security Council Resolution of "responsibility to protect," the Western powers of France, Britain, Italy, and the United States launched a war of regime change in Libya. Sirte, which had been the seat of the declaration for the new face of the African Union in 1999, was bombed to smithereens as President Gaddafi was executed.

Despite the efforts of the corporate media to detach the uprisings and war in North Africa from the rest of Africa, African activists and thinkers grasped the continuities between these new struggles for social justice and peace. Firoze Manji of the Fahamu Network for Social Justice correctly summed up the interconnections between the revolutions in North Africa and the continued struggles in the rest of Africa. He argued,

> Indeed, I think it would be a mistake to consider the shifting political and social climate in Africa being based on the overt, large-scale uprisings alone. There is growing evidence in a number of countries of social movements re-emerging during the last 10 years, providing a framework through which the disenfranchised have begun to re-assert their own dignity, proclaiming—even if only implicitly—their aspiration to determine their own destiny, their own right to self-determination. The emergence and activities of movements such as Bunge La Mwananchi, Bunge Sisters and the Unga Revolution in Kenya, Abahlali base Mjondolo, the Anti Eviction Campaign, the Landless People's Movement in South Africa, the anti-water privatization movement, the growing militancy of the LBGTI movements, the formation of alliances of peasant and farmer organizations, the growing demands from organised labour, all these are manifestations of an underlying mood of discontent and disenchantment with the political order.[1]

The important point raised by Firoze Manji and other Pan Africanists was that while the Western media attempted to use the formulation "Arab Spring" to detach Egypt, Libya, and Tunisia from the rest of Africa, the uprisings were part of the international movement against neoliberal capitalism. In less than one year, this global movement exploded into the Occupy Wall Street movement, in which 99 percent of humanity were making their claim for changes in the international system. These global manifestations along with the NATO invasion of Libya demand engagement from progressive Pan Africanists with the kind of clarity that emanated from the movement at the time of the Italian invasion of Abyssinia in 1935.[2] This author agrees with the writer Esam Al-Amin, who characterized the Egyptian revolution as a perfect storm that has changed world history.

> Like perfect storms, several factors have to simultaneously and collectively come together for popular uprisings or protests, even massive ones, to turn into a revolution. That is why only a few of them have been successful in world history. A revolution is, by definition, a successful struggle embraced by the masses that radically alters the existing political, economic, and social order.[3]

This same author went on to argue that the revolutionary process never proceeds in a straight line, "Popular revolutions are rare in history because they face the daunting task of establishing a new political and socio-economic order in society based on the people's will."[4]

Al-Amin then outlined three major challenges facing the revolutionary process. These were: 1) that the revolutionaries are not in charge, 2) the role of Islam in society, and 3) the role of foreign powers. From this analysis I will argue that this revolution is only in its embryonic stage with the overthrow of the Mubarak regime dictator.

From the cascading processes in Africa and the Middle East it is imperative that within the Pan-African world there is clarity on the convergence between the African Awakenings and the popular uprisings in Yemen, Syria, Bahrain, and elsewhere in what is known today as the Arab World. The interconnections at the level of ideas, strategies, and goals of these revolutionary processes challenged old conceptualizations of Arab-African divisions and demanded a new and sharper philosophical basis for Pan Africanism, calling for those who know history to remember the era of Nasser when the Pan-Arab and Pan-African struggles were at the center of the nonaligned movement.[5]

Youth and women who were developing new forms of politics were also claiming new leadership roles in this phase of twenty-first-century Pan-African struggles. The energy and power of the grass-roots workers, women, and youths of Egypt, Tunisia, and Libya called for new forms of solidarity beyond the shallow anti-imperialism of many of the contemporary leaders of Africa who sought to place themselves at the front of the global Pan-African movement. Leaders such as Robert Mugabe of Zimbabwe, Meles Zanawi of Ethiopia, and Yoweri Museveni of Uganda are representative of leaders who came to power with promises for change, only to entrench themselves in office while the conditions of the majority of the citizens deteriorated.

Ronald Walters was a scholar in the United States who in his life dedicated himself to people-centered Pan Africanism, and in this essay that pays tribute to his life I will also take this opportunity to salute his internationalism. As a political scientist, Ronald Walters used his training to explore and elaborate on the meaning of Pan Africanism and this he did clearly in the book *Pan Africanism in the African Diaspora: An Analysis of Modern Afrocentric Political Movements.* This book appeared one year before the seventh Pan-African Congress in Kampala, but the twin challenges of reconstruction and destruction placed the issues of Pan-African revolution beyond the old ideas of congresses and meetings with Pan-African declarations.[6]

Progressive Women Intervene to Reshape
the Pan-African Discourse

In 1994, the formal end to apartheid and the coming to power of Nelson Mandela had brought to an end the euphoria of the liberation of states as opposed to the liberation of the people. The issues that have been raised since the end of apartheid relate to the ideas of emancipatory politics and how the Pan-African movement can move in a new direction where the emancipation of the people start from the fact that Africans think and are human beings with the right to live on the planet. For over sixty years decolonization and Pan-African liberation were formalized to mean that African males entered the corridors of the old oppressive regime and sought to use this apparatus as the vehicle for social development of the people. This has deepened the masculinization of political spaces by those who occupy positions of power in Africa. This lesson in South Africa reinforced the lessons from Algeria, Angola, Kenya, Mozambique, Zimbabwe, and Namibia and all of the societies where the working poor made major sacrifices for the liberation of Africa. It was a simple lesson that the colonial state could not be used as the basis for reconstruction and transformation.

In many parts of Africa, the fact that the same leaders who were at the forefront of the Pan-African movement are at the forefront of repression ensure that many African women do not want to associate themselves with Pan Africanism in the way it is presently formulated by the leaders of yesterday. The youths are even clearer, and they want to form a new basis for community solidarity and peoples' cooperation away from the politics of exclusion and the ideological illnesses of the past generation. This challenge of doing things differently and focusing on African knowledge and self- reliance principles has been a theme put forward at meetings in all corners of Africa, especially at meetings of women.[7] These meetings critique the negative direction of the present leadership that focuses on the further integration of Africa into an unjust social system that has been the source of insecurity since colonialism and the partitioning of Africa. The positions of African workers, scholars, grassroots organizations, and civil society organizations continue to be clearly different from the leaders of the Group of 8 and international organizations such as the World Bank and the IMF that believe in working for the United Nations Millennium Goals and "fighting poverty" without the end of the structural imbalances and inequalities of the global system of capitalism. The organized African women's movement had redefined the tasks of liberation to broaden the questions of freedom to include the freedom from all forms of oppression. Radical feminists from all four corners of Africa are raising the questions of sexuality, violation, reproductive health, and the dangers of deformed masculinity.[8]

As scholars evaluate Ronald Walters and his internationalism, the context of his life and work provide another opportunity to focus on the redefinition of Pan Africanism that had been sharpened by the political work of radical African women. Increasingly, African women such as Ifi Amadiume, Ama Atta Aidoo, Nawal El Saadawi, Micere Mugo, Barbara Ransby, Dorothy Roberts, and Ulla Taylor are charting new directions in the understanding of Pan-African politics. In the face of the masculinist leaders such as Robert Mugabe posturing as progressive, these networks of women are making a clear distinction between the Pan Africanism of leaders and the Pan Africanism of the ordinary people. At the same time Ifi Amadiume makes a distinction between daughters of the goddess and daughters of imperialism. Ifi Amadiume and Micere Mugo sought to, as it were, reenvision Pan Africanism. Micere Mugo in her essay "Re-Envisioning Pan Africanism: What Is the Role of Gender, Youth and the Masses?" noted that

> though not cited in intellectual discourses that have so far come to be the literary cannon on Pan-Africanism, in their activism, as well as participation, women were and have always been the heart of Pan-Africanism's essence, or if you like, substance. My point is that Pan-Africanism may be seen as manifesting itself in two major ways, which are equally important: through the movement itself and through its lived aspects. As a movement, Pan-Africanism has been characterized by fluctuation, registering bouts of life and dormant lulls. On the other hand, its lived aspects, actual substance, or essence, have always remained alive and persistent over historical time. Ordinary people, or the masses, including the majority of Africana women, have been the key keepers or carriers of this essence.[9]

Philosophically, a new cadre of intellectuals has been interrogating the essence of Pan Africanism and its importance to the working peoples in order to bring back the core of Pan Africanism away from leaders who have distorted the full meaning of Pan-African solidarity. By focusing his work on Pan Africanism in the diaspora, Walters had of necessity to deal with the articulation of Pan-African voices from below. Walters had been part of the faculty at Howard University where Joseph Harris had convened the major study on the African diaspora and gave serious weight to the impact of the trans-Atlantic slave trade in the formation of the political consciousness of Africans.[10] Michael West deepened the analysis of Walters and Harris by noting the emancipatory component of the idea of Global Africa. Michael West argued persuasively that

> The Global Africa idea holds that Africans and people of African descent worldwide share a common set of historical experiences, most notably, slavery, colonialism, racial oppression, and their many consequences. Politically, the global Africa idea assumes that these shared ordeals constitute a template on which Africans—at home and abroad, on the African continent and in the diaspora—should unite to effect their mutual liberation. In fine, the global Africa idea was founded on the premise that shared experiences of oppression constitute the basis for a common struggle for emancipation.[11]

West then went on to anchor the intellectual ferment in the African diaspora that arose from the revolutionary traditions in Haiti. This dialectic of revolutionary advances and setbacks, in short the zigs and zags of revolutionary struggles, have always dogged the Pan-African movement. The hopes and fears of the Pan-African movement came together at the same moment at the end of the last century when the very moment of the victory over apartheid was overshadowed by the fastest genocide in the history in Rwanda. This turning point brought to the forefront the idea that it was the people not governments that would be the guiding force behind Pan Africanism in the twenty-first century. Thus far, in the written versions of African liberation, the centrality of African women has been in the main unrecorded in the dominant discourses on Pan Africanism. In the words of one activist, "women did not write books, but wrote history." Radical African feminists are not only calling for liberation but a redefinition of the past in order to prepare for a different future.

One could see the ideas of radical women such as Nawal El Saadawi finding material form with the young women who emerged at the forefront of the Nile revolution (called the Arab Spring by the media) that is still underway. In particular, it is important to salute women such as Amal Sharaf and Asmaa Mahfouz of the April 6 Youth Movement of Egypt who showed exemplary leadership in challenging the much-dreaded Mubarak regime. These women are part of a new generation of revolutionaries who are fighting to shift the power in society from patriarchs and capitalists to the working men and women. In the Pan-African world, issues of rape in the Democratic Republic of the Congo and the killing of innocent women in Côte d'Ivoire have placed the questions of Pan Africanism in the forefront of discussions on Africa. These discussions hold leaders in Africa accountable and should be distinguished from the degeneration of the ideals of Pan Africanism where there are those who want to compare Laurent Gbagbo to Patrice Lumumba.[12]

Tunisia's Mohamed Bouazizi entered the annals of revolutionary martyrs when he sacrificed himself to rally the youths in Tunisia to stand up and fight. The Tunisian example gave confidence to youths all across Africa and the Middle East. But it is the outstanding leadership of Egypt's women, especially Asmaa Mahfouz, that must be studied by Pan Africanists, especially political scientists. Asmaa Mahfouz is a young revolutionary who was one of the founders of the April 6 Youth Movement.[13] This movement was formed by young Egyptian revolutionaries, including Ahmed Maher and Amal Sharaf, in 2008 to support the workers in the industrial city of El-Mahalla who were on strike for better working conditions, better wages, and protesting rising food prices. The April 6 Youth Movement used the tools of social media and brought new ideas about the politics of inclusion as well as new ideas about political organizing to the forefront of Egyptian politics. Though mainly from the educated classes of the Facebook generation, this group of men and women struggled to translate online activism into real mobilization of humans to stand up for their rights. Esam Al-Amin in his brilliant analysis of the implications of the Egyptian revolution wrote that

> As the demonstrations continued, every day broke new ground. It started with the educated youth, both middle class and affluent. They were soon joined by the oppressed and uneducated poor. Within a few days, the protests swelled to include all segments of society, including judges, lawyers, doctors, engineers, journalists, artists, civil servants, workers, farmers, day laborers, students, home makers, the underclass and the unemployed.[14]

Professor Ronald Walters joined the ancestors on September 10, 2010 before the revolutionary processes in Africa and Arabia had matured, but he was very aware of the reasons that Afrocentric political movements had to be internationalist. It is this internationalism that did not lead Walters to repeat the idea from some who define themselves as Pan Africanists yet seek to deepen the divisions between Arabs and Africans. John Garang, the former leader of the Sudan People's Liberation Movement, sought to cut through these divisions when he said, "Argentineans speak Spanish and are Christians, but they are Argentineans not Spaniards, and are proud of being Argentineans." His point was that there are Sudanese who speak Arabic but are not Arabs, they are Sudanese Africans who live in Africa. This vision stood in contrast to those Pan Africanists who would divide the continent between Africans north and south of the Sahara.

Walters was very aware of how scholarly divisions over the definition of who is an African played itself out at the level of politics, and he articulated a conception of unity that minimized the kind of feuds, splits, and vendettas that plagued the black liberation struggles in the United States. His grasp of the impact of the trans-Atlantic slave trade and slavery in Africa made him conscious of the legacies of antislavery ideas and anti-Arab sentiments in North Africa. Over the fifty years of his life as a scholar-activist within this Afrocentric movement, Walters strove to be an example to rise above all forms of chauvinism, whether racial or male-centered chauvinism. From his early years in Kansas, in the movement against Jim Crow he was involved in demonstrations and sit-ins to change society.

Walters emerged as a major international spokesperson for reparations, peace, and social justice. He was at the forefront of the campaigns of the African Liberation Support Committee in the early 1970s and was a participant in the World Conference against Racism in Durban thirty years later. He wrote passionately against apartheid and worked to build a grassroots movement across Africa to oppose global apartheid. In the process he has established a body of scholarship for younger scholars to build on.

As one of the activists behind the antiapartheid struggles, he saw firsthand how the system responded to the activities of Congressman Charles Diggs, who carried forth the antiapartheid work from the halls of Congress. Serving as Diggs' senior advisor, Walters sharpened the international understanding of the Rhodesian and South African apartheid regimes and gave intellectual power to the political organizing that was percolating in that era. He was at the base of the mobilization of blacks to exercise their right to participate in the political system in the United States and wrote extensively on its political processes. Other contributors in this book have elaborated on Walters' work with Charles Diggs, but for this commentary it is the interface between his work and his internationalism that set him apart from those who sought to use access to the corridors of power to domesticate black politics in the United States and cut it off from its anchor in the anti-imperialist traditions.

As one of the forces behind the Rainbow Coalition and the Jesse Jackson campaigns in 1984 and 1988, Walters wanted to carry forward the struggles for full democratic rights. He is better known for his scholarly writings on domestic U.S. politics, for example, *Black Presidential Politics in America: A Strategic Approach* and *White Nationalism, Black Interests: Conservative Public Policy and the Black Community*. This latter book can assist us in understanding the rabid racist movement that continues to try to dominate public spaces in the United States.

But Walters opposed global white supremacy and white nationalism and worked hard to alert students to the realities of the United States in the international state system. It was his objective to work for a new society where all humans could live in dignity. His support for the rights of oppressed peoples led him to articulate a brand of Pan Africanism that supported the rights of oppressed blacks and indigenous peoples in all parts of the world. For instance, he supported the rights of self-determination of Palestinians. His scholarship and activism is a beacon for those who want to understand the meaning of commitment. He struggled hard to break the conservative stranglehold on mainstream political scientists.

Walters' Brand of Pan Africanism

The biographical notes of Walters' work tell the story of a scholar who toiled for change even as a teenager.[15] Writing in the preface of his book *Pan Africanism in the African Diaspora: An Analysis of Modern*

Afrocentric Political Movements, Walters described his early days as a student and activist. His first awareness of Pan Africanism occurred in 1963 when, as a senior at Fisk University, he wrote an essay titled "The Blacks," which won a *Reader's Digest* national essay competition. Whether it was his activity as the president of the youth chapter of the National Association for the Advancement of Colored Peoples (NAACP) or as a budding scholar, Walters had marked a path for struggle since his undergraduate days at Fisk University. His fruitful years at Fisk led him to work closely with Diggs, another Fisk graduate.[16] Walters was fully aware that he was maturing in a context where both activists and scholars had made tremendous contributions to Pan-African thoughts and practice, and in the preface to the book on Pan Africanism he was explicit about his debt to these thinkers in the Pan-African movement. Long before the sit-ins by youths in Greensboro, North Carolina made national and international news, Walters was organizing against racism in the South.

His book details his association with the Pan-African movement and his work with Jimmy Garret, Stokely Carmichael (Kwame Ture), Amiri Baraka, Courtland Cox, Howard Fuller (Owusu Sadaukai), and William Strickland. Walters also wrote of his activities in the African Heritage Studies Association (AHSA). The AHSA was the effort of those who opposed the domination of the African Studies Association (ASA) by those who served the interests of empire. Walters worked with Pan Africanists such as James Turner, John Henrik Clarke, Ron Karenga, Leonard Jeffries, Molefi Asante, and countless others. It is in this collaboration with activists of differing intellectual and ideological persuasion where Walters distinguished himself in his commitment to Pan-African unity.

Struggles in the Academy

Dr. John Johnson, a colleague of Ron Walters' when he taught at Syracuse University in 1969, has spoken of his passion and work among youth on and off campus. Walters was very clear that black students on white campuses had a special responsibility to ensure that their scholarship did not alienate them from the day-to-day world of the black community. Johnson recalled Walters' electric presentation on the question of black awareness in higher education. This was the period of the black uprisings on the Cornell and Syracuse university campuses in upstate New York. His relationship with James Turner was special during this period of struggles, and as we remember Ron Walters, it is also germane to grasp the ways in which the academy is seeking to roll back the gains of the black studies movement. John Henrik Clarke bears special mention in this reference to Pan-African scholars who sought to maintain a tradition of linking the Black Revolution to Pan-African studies.[17] Like John Henrik Clarke, Ron Walters worked in a tradition that fused African knowledge systems with his formal training in the Western academy. As a communicator, Walters was continuously working, traveling, speaking, advocating, fighting, and proposing peace and reparations. (For those who did not know Walters, it is now possible to get his view of his growth as a scholar from the Oral History Interview with Ronald W. Walters at www.historymakers.com. Conscious of the role of oratory in preserving the history and culture of Africans, Walters produced an eight-part video of the history of his life.)

Although he was trained in the U.S. university system, he broke with the traditions that placed scholarship in the service of oppressors. Walters was acutely aware of the role of social science as imperialism, and he helped to transform the terms of scholarly debate within the field of political science.[18] In this work, he was a founding member of the National Conference of Black Political Scientists (NCOBPS) and was one of the few senior political scientists to challenge head-on the efforts to marginalize Pan Africanism by the foundations and the gatekeepers in the academy. This was a major battle at a moment when the State Department and the foundations had mobilized to distort the true meaning of Pan Africanism.

Mainstream Academia and the Study of Pan Africanism in the Era of the Cold War

We started out this commentary by drawing attention to the current revolutionary upheavals in North Africa. These movements will have to draw from the clarity and commitment that had been shown by scholars and activists such, C.L.R. James, George Padmore, Paul Robeson, W.E.B. Du Bois, and other antiracist activists who linked Pan Africanism to global struggles for peace and social justice in another period of capitalist depression. Hollis Lynch has brought out the contribution of these Pan Africanists during the period of the last major capitalist depression, and it is not by accident that C.L.R. James wrote the important book *The Black Jacobins* in order to inspire revolutionary action in the Pan-African world.[19] This brand of Pan Africanism was anti-imperialist and antifascist. As the frustration of workers in Europe was exploited by racists and fascists, the Italian dictator Mussolini invaded Abyssinia. From all corners of the globe Africans protested this invasion and warned that this was the start of an era of war all across the world. One of the manifestations of this worldwide opposition was manifest in the deification of the Emperor of Abyssinia and the deification of Haile Selassie.[20] Black intellectuals on both sides of the Atlantic mobilized and opposed this invasion, and one of the most well known groups of these intellectuals was the Council on African Affairs in New York.[21] The counterpart to this organ in Europe was the International African Service Bureau that worked with George Padmore and others to oppose fascism and war. At that historical moment when there were united fronts against fascism and war, the British government tolerated these Pan Africanists during the struggles against Hitler and Mussolini but worked to undermine and co-opt this Pan Africanism after the important convening of the fifth Pan-African Congress in Manchester in 1945. It was after the dynamism of this movement in giving intellectual coherence to the anticolonial struggles that mainstream British academics entered the discussion on Pan Africanism, seeking to determine the trajectory of research, scholarship, and activism on the subject. Scholars such as George Shepperson had made the distinction between Pan Africanism with a big P and Pan Africanism with a small p. [22] However, in his work, Ron Walters drew heavily from the work of St. Clair Drake who made a distinction between the cultural relations of people to Pan Africanism and the more formal rendition of international Pan-African conferences.[23]

Following the traditions of Garveyism and the activism of the Council on African Affairs, a brand of Pan-African scholarship developed that linked Pan Africanism in the United States directly to the lived experiences of peoples of African descent. Given the vibrancy and potency of the activist-scholarly tradition, the ruling forces in the United States worked hard to redefine the meaning of Pan Africanism and inscribe it in the ideological battles of the Cold War.[24] After the Second World War, leading scholars of political science such as Joseph Nye and David Apter were involved in research and writing on Pan Africanism in a period when the top Ivy League institutions received support from foundations for the study of Africa. Melville Herskovits of Northwestern University established a tradition among liberals where there were attempts to silence other narratives of Africa by generally omitting "any reference to the long-standing tradition of African Studies at historically black colleges and universities, only rarely giving a nod to African American professional and lay scholars of Africa, and seldom acknowledging the existence of epistemic communities based in Africa."[25]

It was in this intellectual environment where there emerged in the academy a "racial division of labor between African Studies and Afro-American Studies where white people did African Studies, while black people did Afro-American Studies."[26] It was the subtext of this discourse that Africans could not be serious scholars on Africa and Pan Africanism because of their emotional attachment to Africa. Herskovits dismissed Du Bois as a propagandist and political activist rather than a serious scholar. This ensured that liberal whites dominated the research and teaching spaces in the country's leading universities.[27] Scholars such as W.E.B. Du Bois, Franklin Frazier, Ralph Bunche, Alain Locke, and Carter Woodson were denigrated by the academic establishment in the United States. Blacks were important to the system only insofar as they could be co-opted to serve empire as Ralph Bunche did with his service in the Congo.

Walters was entering the field of political science a generation after W.E.B. Du Bois when the "philanthropists" and government institutions were bent on funding scholarship that would perpetuate white hegemony in the white academy. Ron Walters took a position at Syracuse University, but he learned early that the study of Africa within this institution did not take as its starting point the interests of the liberation of the peoples of Africa. Walters had to seek refuge in the historically black colleges and universities in order to survive the intellectual environment of Cold War scholarship on Africa.

Scholars from the dominant white universities sought to develop a monopoly over the reproduction of knowledge about Africa, and it was in this context where hundreds of thousands of young Africans were recruited as students of these experts. Pan Africanists such as Patrice Lumumba were assassinated, and this physical assassination was accompanied by an intellectual enterprise that justified the killing of serious African leaders. Eduardo Mondlane of Mozambique, who had worked within this African studies enterprise, was assassinated when he returned to Africa to support the decolonization process in Mozambique.

David Apter excelled in this environment and contributed to a body of scholarship on Ghana, Nkrumah, and Pan Africanism, while building an organization called the American Society of African Culture.[28] Research by thinkers for the empire was bent on distorting the history of Pan Africanism. Under the direction of political scientists such as Apter and John Marcum, a major study, *Pan Africanism Reconsidered*, was published.[29] Joseph Nye had written on Pan Africanism and integration in East Africa at a moment when the Nkrumah project of African unity was still on the international agenda. It later turned out that the American Society of African Culture, one of the principal platforms for intelligence gathering, and this organization were heavily funded by the intelligence agencies and the foundations. Walters belonged to that group of scholars, black and white, who were opposed to the mobilization of the social sciences for military purposes. These scholars understood that the intellectual battle had to be engaged in order to support the spontaneous and organized struggles that were going on in everyday life for Africans. Intellectual struggles against violence and exploitation had to unmask the pseudo discourse of poverty and the vicious cycle of violence.

Walters belonged to that group of African American scholars who formed a black caucus within the African Studies Association (ASA), the professional association in the United States for the study of Africa. Walters devoted considerable space to this caucus in his book on Pan Africanism.[30] The black power movement in the United States had inscribed a new momentum in relation to black thought and action, and the black scholars who supported black power opposed the links between the intelligence agencies and the professors of the African Studies Association. There was a major rupture within the African Studies Association at a meeting in Montreal in 1969. Black scholars objected to the integration between the intelligence services and the research priorities of the ASA. This integration ensured the domination of the field of African studies by the Ivy League institutions that excluded blacks from leadership positions. It was at this point that the African Heritage Studies Association

(AHSA) was formed to bring Pan Africanism back to its base—among those who opposed racism, colonialism, and apartheid. It was in this same period in 1969 when Walters joined those black political scientists who formed the NCOBPS.

After the rupture in 1969, the subject of Pan Africanism was dropped by mainstream political scientists (although Andrew Apter followed in the footsteps of his father David when he wrote the book *The Pan-African Nation: Oil and the Spectacle of Culture in Nigeria*). The study of Pan Africanism fell under the rubric of black studies, and mainstream political scientists relegated this subject to the back-burner. In this period it was unfashionable to write and speak about the global Pan-African struggles. But Walters refused to go along with this and carried his passion for justice to the centers of intellectual debate.

Research funds from the major foundations dried up. Funding from the Department of Education disappeared. There were few centers where graduate students could do doctoral research in this field. Walters directed one such center when he served as a professor of political science at Howard University in Washington, D.C. From this base he trained a new generation of thinkers and activists to link the local to the global.

Pan Africanism and the African Liberation Support Committee (ALSC)

As a committed intellectual, Walters did not confine his work to the Howard University campus. He was one of the key thinkers behind the formation of the Congressional Black Caucus. As mentioned earlier, he served as an advisor for Congressman Charles Diggs, who waged a relentless battle against American support for the illegal government of Ian Smith in Rhodesia. It was while working with Diggs, Shirley Chisholm, Charles Rangel, Louis Stokes, and others that the Pan-African struggles to boycott chrome from Rhodesia took the spotlight in the United States. Walters also wrote on the apartheid bomb. His book *South Africa and the Bomb: Responsibility and Deterrence* became a reference for the antiapartheid campaign, and he wrote scholarly articles and op-ed pieces about the U.S. government's support of the oppression of blacks in Africa. (Today, the U.S. government is working hard to sow confusion about humanitarianism and the so-called War on Terror in Africa to disguise new efforts to militarize the continent. It has established the U.S. Africa Command, with the supposed mandate of supporting peace and good governance.)

Of the more than one hundred scholarly articles Walters published, his most fruitful period of publication was those years when he was fighting apartheid in the United States and in Africa. At that moment, he was organically linked to the black liberation movement.

This academic work was done alongside Walters' activism in the African Liberation Support Committee (ALSC). The ALSC represented one of the highest points of the organizing for Pan-African liberation in the second part of the twentieth century. The energy and spirit of the people were manifest in demonstrations, protests, books, films, and other forms of political statements on the struggles in Africa and the struggles of Africans in the diaspora. Scholars such as Walter Rodney and Amiri Baraka have written on the importance of the ALSC for the building of political consciousness.[31]

Walters was one of those caught in this ferment with the ideological explosions from such a dynamic moment. Many "scholars" did not survive to continue in the movement for liberation. Divisions over ideological lines blurred deeper divisions among those who worked for the long-term needs of liberation. Walters used all the resources available to support the ALSC and was in the midst of these deliberations.

As outlined earlier, the turbulence and intellectual ferment of this movement has been captured by numerous scholars, but it was Geri Augusto who was able to bring the insights of an African American woman to the historical record. Walters himself provided his own insight into this period in his book *Pan Africanism in the African Diaspora*. This was a period when black political representatives, such as Charles Diggs, were challenged to link the opposition to apartheid in South Africa to apartheid conditions inside the United States. At this time, those from black political spaces dominated the news on the opposition to apartheid and colonialism. Diggs had used his position in Congress to work with the ALSC and the forces of freedom to expose U.S. corporations that were profiting from the exploitation of black labor. So incensed were the ruling forces in the United States that they worked hard to silence Diggs and removed him from Congress.

Removing Diggs was an effort to silence the antiapartheid forces from the center of national organizing. The system sought to humiliate not only Diggs but the entire black liberation force in order to prop up white supremacy at home and abroad.

Walters understood all of this and worked even harder to find spaces to oppose racism. In the 1980s he emerged in the forefront of electoral politics as a close advisor to the Jesse Jackson campaign.

Working Inside and Outside the Political System to Combat Racism

While immersed in electoral politics, Walters was writing about the limitations of the same electoral process, based on the experience of blacks. He spelled out the need for multiple forms of struggle in the book *Freedom Is Not Enough: Black Voters, Black Candidates and American Presidential Politics.* After his involvement in the established political system, Walters was writing for the younger generation to show them that the democratic façade of elections concealed greater challenges for society.[32]

This author was a beneficiary of the rich insights of Walters, and I remember that in 2007 when he came up to Syracuse to speak on the Obama phenomenon, we spent hours reflecting on the need for a movement that would be clear about the need to work inside and outside the system. Ron Walters wrote weekly columns on the need for multiple forms of struggle. He prepared us to develop the needed strategies to combat the neo-fascist forces that are now mobilizing under the banner of the Tea Party while building the new movement of the majority called the 99 percent. From his scholarship we understand that the Tea Party nation is only one manifestation of the deep racism of this society. His book *White Nationalism, Black Interests* outlined the institutionalized forms of racism and the dangers for black and brown peoples. It is now urgent for engaged scholar-activists to grasp the dangers of the Tea Party's form of populism in a period of extended capitalist depression. It was for this reason that while he was on his deathbed, Walters found his voice to speak out forcefully against conservative commentator Glenn Beck's work to manipulate the memory and meaning of Dr. Martin Luther King Jr.

I alerted him when I started writing my book *Barack Obama and Twenty-First-Century Politics: A Revolutionary Moment in the USA*. He supported and encouraged me and was always full of optimism borne out of concrete experience in the struggle. I asked him to write a blurb for the book, and he readily accepted, sending back the words of solidarity that now grace the book. I did not to know then that he was terminally ill because he did not share his pain with us. He worked up to the last moments of his life.

It is in the context of Walters' life and work that we can grasp the impact of the Arab Spring for Africa because this revolution is helping Africa to break the shackles of dependence and domination. The Mubarak regime was one example of a government that spent billions to oppress the people, and the new confidence of the Egyptian and Tunisian peoples has pointed the way for millions as Algerians, Djiboutians, Guineans, Senegalese, Libyans, and others catch the spirit of the Nile revolution to confront exploitation, police violence, manipulation, unemployment, and the oppression of women.

Revolutionary energies are now being unleashed, and the question of Pan Africanism and the unification of peoples beyond ethnic, religious, regional, and racial lines are now center stage in Africa. This was clear from the theories and philosophies that emerged in the Egyptian and Tunisian revolutions and was integral to Walters' diasporic internationalism.

Notes

1. Firoze Manji, "On the African Awakenings," *Pambazuka News*, July 13, 2011, http://www.pambazuka.org/en/category/features/74882. See also *African Awakening: The Emerging Revolutions*, ed. Sokari Ekine and Firoze Manji (Cape Town, Dakar, Nairobi, Oxford: Pambazuka Press, 2011).

2. S.K.B. Asante, *Pan-African Protest: West Africa and the Italo-Ethiopian Crisis, 1934–1941* (London: Longman, 1977).

3. Esam Al-Amin, "Anatomy of Egypt's Revolution," Counterpunch,

February 17, 2001, http://www.counterpunch.org/2011/02/17/
anatomy-of-egypt-s-revolution/, accessed, November 6, 2011.

4. Esam Al-Amin, "Three Big Challenges Threatening the Arab
Uprisings," Counterpunch, September 16–19, 2011, http://
www.counterpunch.org/2011/09/16/three-big-challenges-
threatening-the-arab-uprisings/.

5. Samir Amin, *The Arab Nation* (London: Zed Press, 1978).

6. Tajudeen Abdul-Raheem, *Pan Africanism: Politics, Economy and
Social Change in the Twenty-First Century* (London: Pluto Press,
1996).

7. Zanzibar Declaration of the Pan-African Women Working for a
Culture of Peace, May 1999. http://www.unesco.org/cpp/uk/
declarations/zanzibar.htm.

8. Ifi Amadiume, *Daughters of the Goddess: Daughters of Imperialism*
(London: Zed Books, 2000) and Patricia McFadden, "Impunity,
Masculinity and Heterosexism in the Discourse of Male Endan-
germent: An African Feminist Perspective," Working Paper
Series, Center for Gender and Development Studies, University
of the West Indies, No.7, March 2002.

9. Micere Mugo, "Re-envisioning Pan Africanism: What Is the Role of
Gender, Youth and the Masses?" in *Pan Africanism and Integration
in Africa*, ed. Ibbo Mandaza and Dan Nabudere, 52–69 (Harare:
SAPES Books, 2002).

10. Joseph Harris, ed., *Global Dimensions of the African Diaspora* (Washington, DC: Howard University Press, 1982).

11. Michael O. West, "Global Africa: The Emergence and Evolution of an Idea," *Review* (Fernand Braudel Center) 28, 1 (2005):
17–35.

12. This comparison was made at the Forum of the World Africa
Diaspora Union in April 2011, http://www.wadupam.org/
wadu-africa-burning-forum-urged-diaspora-action.

13. For an analysis of the role of the youth in the uprisings in Egypt,
see Samir Amin, "Egypt: How to Overthrow a Dictator," *Pambazuka News*, February 24, 2011, 518, http://pambazuka.org/en/
category/features/71173.

14. Esam Al-Amin, "When Egypt's Revolution Was at the Crossroads:
Twelve Moments That Shook the World," Counterpunch, http://
www.counterpunch.org/amin03092011.html.

15. For biographical details, see http://www.nytimes.com/2010/

09/15/us/15walters.html and http://www.thehistorymakers. com/biography/biography.asp?bioindex=627&category=educat ionMakers.

16. For an analysis of the nature of this collaboration, see Ronald Walters, "Apartheid and the Bomb: The United States and South Africa's Military Potential," *Africa Today* 23, 3, "Southern Africa and U.S. Foreign Policy," *Black Renaissance* (July–September 1976): 25–35. See also Ronald Walters, "The Global Context of United States Foreign Policy toward Southern Africa," *Africa Today* 19, 3, Black Perspectives on Africa (Summer 1972): 13–30.

17. See special issue of *Africa Today* on "The Black Revolution and African Studies," 16, 2, African Studies and the Black Protest (April–May 1969): 26–38.

18. Claude Ake, *Social Science as Imperialism: The Theory of Political Development* (Idaban, Nigeria: Ibadan University Press, 1979).

19. C.L.R. James, *A History of Pan-African Revolt* (Chicago: Charles Kerr, 1995). See also *The Black Jacobins: Toussaint L'Ouverture and the San Domingo Revolution* (New York: Vintage Books, 1989).

20. Horace Campbell, *Rasta and Resistance: From Marcus Garvey to Walter Rodney* (Trenton, NJ: Africa World Press, 1987).

21. Hollis Lynch, *Black American Radicals and the Liberation of Africa: The Council of African Affairs, 1937–1955* (Ithaca: Africana Studies and Research Center, Cornell University, 1978).

22. George Shepperson, "Pan Africanism and 'Pan Africanism': Some Historical Notes," *Phylon* 23, 4 (1962): 20–32. See also St. Clair Drake, "Diaspora Studies and Pan Africanism," in *Global Dimensions of the African Diaspora*, ed. Joseph Harris, 185–203 (Washington, DC: Howard University Press, 1982).

23. Drake, "Diaspora Studies and Pan Africanism," 193.

24. Penny M. Von Eschen, *Race against Empire: Black Americans and Anti-colonialism, 1937–1957* (Ithaca: Cornell University Press, 1997).

25. Pearl T. Robinson, "Area Studies in Search of Africa," UCIAS Edited Volume 3, Article 6, 2003: 17.

26. Ibid., 26.

27. Jerry Gershenhorn, *Melville J. Herskovits and the Racial Politics of Knowledge* (Lincoln: University of Nebraska Press, 2004).

28. Frances Stonor Saunders, *Who Paid the Piper: The CIA and the Cultural Cold War* (London: Granta Books, 1999).

29. See David E. Apter, *Pan-Africanism Reconsidered* (Berkeley: University of California Press, 1962).

30. See Ron Walters, *Pan Africanism in the African Diaspora* (Detroit: Wayne State University Press, 1997), 364–67. See also John Henrik Clarke, "African Studies in the United States: An African American View," *Africa Report* 6, 2 (April 1969): 3–13.

31. Walter Rodney, "Southern Africa and Liberation Support in Afro-America and the West Indies," United Nations, African Institute for Economic Development and Planning, www.rodney25.org/biblioWRworks.htm; Amiri Baraka, *The Autobiography of LeRoi Jones/Amiri Baraka* (Chicago: Lawrence Hill, 1984). See also the doctoral dissertation of Fanon Che Wilkins, *In The Belly of the Beast: Black Power, Anti-Imperialism, and the African Liberation Solidarity Movement, 1968–75*, PhD dissertation, New York University 2001. For a penetrating analysis of the layered struggles in this period, see "No Easy Victories Interview: Geri Augusto," in *No Easy Victories: African Liberation and American Activists over a Half Century, 1950–2000*, ed. William Minter, Gail Hovey, and Charles Cobb Jr. (Trenton, NJ: Africa World Press, 2007).

32. Samir Amin, "Elections versus Democracy," *Monthly Review* (July 2011), http://mrzine.monthlyreview.org/2011/amin170711.html. See also Issa Shivji, "Democracy and Democratisation in Africa: Interrogating Paradigms and Practices," *Pambazuka News*, November 30, 2011, http://www.pambazuka.org/en/category/features/78361.

14

Reparations, Citizenship, and the Politics of Identity

CHARLES P. HENRY

The black revolution is much more than a struggle for the rights of
Negroes. It is forcing America to face all its interrelated flaws—racism,
poverty, militarism, and materialism. It is exposing evils that are rooted
deeply in the whole structure of our society . . . and suggests that radical
reconstruction of society is the real issue to be faced.
                                        —Martin Luther King Jr.

The week after the election of Barack Obama as the forty-fourth
president of the United States I spoke at Purdue University.[1] Following my talk, which focused on the status of African Americans in
general and the issue of reparations in particular, I agreed to answer
questions. Immediately a middle-aged white man in the rear raised
his hand and then stated he did not ever want to hear about the
plight of African Americans again. After all, he said, a majority of
the citizens in Indiana had just voted for a black man for president.

For this man and undoubtedly many others, the election of
Barack Obama was viewed as a form of reparations. I want to argue
here that Obama's election was not a form of reparations. In fact, to
the extent to which he is either unable or unwilling to address the
specific conditions of African American disadvantage, his administration approaches a type of anti-reparations. That is, to the extent
that African American issues are considered a type of interest group
politics and to the extent that the peculiar history of the black presence in the United States is ignored or rewritten, there will be an
increased need to address reparations. Reparations is not an issue

333

subject to interest group bargaining (economic issue). It is an issue central to the politics of recognition (social and moral issue).

Today's post–civil rights/postmodern society has left us with two primary political options. Color-blindness has been the path of those who argue the civil rights movement was successful in creating a level playing field for individuals representing any racial or ethnic group. Its adherents claim any difference in socioeconomic status between such groups is the product of cultural differences (pathologies) not structural inequality. Eduardo Bonilla-Silva calls this approach "colorblind racism." A second approach has focused on the privatization of what had been public goods. Just as blacks and others were making increased material claims on the welfare state, the obligations and responsibilities of those government institutions were curtailed and in many instances—from schools to prisons—privatized. Some have characterized this process as the abandonment of nonwhites to a state of war and a violation of the social contract.[2]

The reparations movement has challenged both approaches arguing that formal equality has not eliminated white normativity, and therefore color-blindness is a false notion meant to hide continuing white privilege. It also confronts abandonment by the state by insisting that the state be held responsible for the historic and continuing subordination of its black citizens. The unwillingness of the general public to seriously address the issue of reparations and the relative absence of intellectual interest in the subject are reflective of a historical resistance to centering issues of social justice related to blacks in the interest of societal (i.e., white) stability. In short, the almost universal condemnation of reparations discourse reflects an unwillingness to see its positive contribution to democratic political participation.

The contribution of reparations to the post–civil rights public arena is best seen in conversation with the reasons the civil rights movement ended. Unlike some who take a long view of civil rights, I argue that movements by definition are short-term, widespread disruptions of routine or incremental politics. People have limited time and resources, and movements seek to maximize the opportunity to bring about change through intense involvement.[3] Therefore the civil rights movement, although preceded by a long series of events that created the conditions for takeoff and followed by another long series of aftershocks, roughly encompassed a five-year period beginning with the lunch counter sit-ins in Greensboro, North Carolina on February 1, 1960 and ending with the outbreak of violence in Watts, California in August 11, 1965. Three primary reasons may be cited for ending the movement on that date. First, white backlash prevented any additional civil rights legislation from passing Congress, such as King's proposed fair housing bill. Second, both the location and objectives of the movement shifted from the South to the North and from political and civil rights to economic rights. King called this the second stage of the movement. Finally, the movement had generated a new black pride and self-confidence that also led to increasing impatience with the lack of progress in the North and with mainstream leadership of blacks and whites.

When John Lewis contends that Barack Obama's election marks the fulfillment of the civil rights movement, he is correct in the sense that blacks have achieved a kind of political or civic citizenship that enables them to participate in and win elections at the highest possible level.[4] But the political organization that enabled Obama's victory was not a civil rights movement organization grounded in a moral principle. Furthermore, the election of Obama has failed—to this point—to bring about King's ultimate objective of "the beloved community."

The 1965 Voting Rights Act signed just days before the violence in Watts would be the last major piece of civil rights legislation to pass Congress as insurrection swept the nation's urban centers in the late sixties. The passage of four pieces of civil rights/political rights legislation from 1957 to 1965 on the one hand, and the widespread urban violence on the other, created a general attitude summed up by a 1966 *Newsweek* cover asking "What does the Negro want?" Taking down the legal barriers of Jim Crow and establishing formal (procedural) equality was viewed by many white Americans as leveling the playing field. Of course this leveling of the playing field would be adopted by the newly emerging neoconservative movement as a mantra. Any lack of black success would now be characterized by it as the result of pathological behavior, not structural or legal disadvantage.

To his credit, in a remarkable June 1965 speech at Howard University, Lyndon Johnson stated that equal opportunity was not enough and that special action must be undertaken to level the playing field for those who had been disadvantaged for so long. He foresaw a new "more profound stage" of battle ahead—to seek "not just freedom but opportunity . . . not just equality as a right and a theory, but equality as a fact and as a result."[5] Yet Johnson would become alienated from the black political community as the war in Vietnam increasingly took his attention and American tax dollars.

While it is fashionable to blame the rise of black power for white backlash, polling data reveals eroding white support for civil rights as early as 1964. Moreover, Goldwater's success in capturing the Republican presidential nomination and his subsequent attacks on the 1964 Civil Rights Act during the campaign are just the beginning of a long-term decline in public support for civil rights. The 1964 presidential election was the decisive turning point in the political evolution of racial issues not the rise of black power.[6] Although Johnson and Kennedy were right in predicting that their support of civil rights would cost the Democrats the South in future presidential elections, they probably would not have believed that no Democratic presidential candidate has won the majority of white votes since 1964. And while the legislative success of the civil rights movement opened up the political arena for black politicians, it could not and did not attain substantive equality. Thus this failure of the civil rights movement raises a crucial question about the rights of minority citizens in conflict with the majority population. Reparations not only addresses the question of the right to redress but also suggests that the position of the white majority on reparations is reflective of white identity politics or white nationalism.[7]

Reparations in this instance is a call for full inclusion in the public arena of demands that are group based and essentially moral rather than political. They raise questions about citizenship that are not adequately addressed by earlier theories of citizenship.[8] And as previously subordinated citizens have called for greater rights globally, they have faced backlash from those in superordinate positions. Yet while the demand for political participation is a rights-based demand, the actual objective of reparations advocates rests on obligations rather than rights.

One way of viewing the relationship between reparations and citizenship is to distinguish between political (state) citizenship and ethnic (nation) citizenship. The first type of citizenship is inclusive, universal, and limited. Citizens are equal in their rights, voting for example, and their obligations such as taxes. In short, political citizenship is largely procedural. It gives you access to the political arena and obligates you to accept the rules of participation.

Ethnic citizenship, on the other hand, is informal, voluntary, and often exclusive. Unlike political citizenship, not all ethnic participants are equal. Citizenship must be more than a set of formal rules if a nation-state is to function. Citizenship is cultural and the extent to which individuals are human, or Christian, or white, or speak English has a profound effect on their status as ethnic citizens. Historically, those who were cultural "others" found it difficult if not impossible to claim political citizenship. The dominant view was if one wanted to be a citizen, one needed to assimilate the dominant culture. Thus for some minorities this meant being more "American."[9]

What changed with the development of "black power" was a rejection of ethnic sameness and a demand for cultural plurality. It was a demand for the democratization of ethnic citizenship. The development of "identity politics" has been critiqued as the disuniting of America or the balkanization of politics. This criticism, however, presumes a unity of purpose that never existed and a cultural conformity that was forced not voluntary.[10]

Like the black power advocates, who represent the core of reparations activists, the call for reparations goes beyond a demand for formal or procedural equality. It wants recognition that rights were denied and acknowledgment that group harm flowed from the denial of rights. Political or legal rights alone assume a level playing field without taking responsibility for past substantive harms caused by the denial of rights. Thus there is a disconnect between the law on one hand and moral values on the other.

According to Howard McGary, "for John Locke and other liberal political theorists to deny a person's right to reparation amounts to a refusal to recognize the full moral status of the person. In fact, acknowledging a duty of reparation is good evidence that one views the wronged party as a bona fide member of the moral and political communities."[11] I understand this to mean that a person's right to reparation is a right to demand redress, not a right to a particular outcome. On the other hand, it is the obligation of the state, as representative of its citizens, to seek social justice and to insure that in the future similar violations of rights be prohibited. What constitutes social justice is a political and moral issue, while prohibiting future violations is a legal issue.

The reliance on legal suits by reparations activists has been criticized for its dependence on rights claims and state power for redress. In attacking Patricia Williams' reliance on rights discourse, political theorist Wendy Brown states, "if the provision of boundary and protection from 'bodily and spiritual intrusion' offered by rights are what historically subjugated peoples most need, rights may also be one of the cruelest social objects of desire dangled above those who lack them."[12] Brown continues, "in the very same act with which they [rights] grant her selfhood, they turn back upon the individual all responsibility for her failures, her condition, her poverty, her madness—they privatize her situation and mystify the powers that construct, position, and buffet her."[13] This leads Brown to condemn the moral absolutism of rights discourse and the reliance on the state for the enforcement of rights.

Williams, in responding to the criticism of the civil rights movement leveled by critical legal studies (which are in some ways similar to Brown's), contends that the focus should not be on deconstructing rights in a world of no rights but rather "the goal is to find a political mechanism that can confront the denial of need" (reparations is precisely a mechanism to confront this denial of need). She adds, "the argument that rights are disutile, even harmful, trivializes this aspect of black experience specifically, as well as that of any person or group whose vulnerability has been truly protected by rights."[14] For Williams the danger is not from the state's excessive enforcement of rights but rather its failure to commit to defending the rights of all its citizens.

At another level, Brown worries that the pursuit of legal redress in the form of reparations marks a departure from the pursuit of freedom. This sounds very much like the debate between negative rights and positive rights; however, it has a racial dimension. Brown is not making the conservative argument that minorities are claiming victimhood as an excuse for the lack of individual and group initiative. Rather she is concerned about the traps that identity politics can place on minorities limiting their vision to notions of revenge and moral absolutes. Lawrie Balfour suggests this position is "symptomatic of a more general tendency among political theorists to reproduce a white perspective in the course of analysis."[15] I believe Williams would agree with Balfour and add that the differing experiences of blacks and whites are not attributable to such divisions as negative/positive or bourgeois/proletariat but fundamentally rooted in race consciousness: "It is only in acknowledging this difference, however, that one can fully appreciate the underlying common ground of the radical left and the historically oppressed: the desire to heal a profound existential disillusionment. Wholesale rejection of rights does not allow for the expression of such difference."[16] Thus for Balfour, and by extension Williams, the rejection of reparations discourse is a failure to acknowledge the different histories of blacks and whites and furthermore is a failure to see the positive aspects of the black perspective for the whole society.

An important contribution of reparations discourse to the public arena is its concern with economic rights and group rights. It is a mischaracterization of the reparations movement to say it is primarily concerned with legal redress. Given the many legal obstacles reparations cases face in the U.S. legal system, some of the most successful efforts have been the result of legislative activity at the state and local level.[17] It is equally disingenuous to contend that revenge is the major motive of reparations activists. In fact, reparative justice, not retributive justice, has been the primary goal of such activists.

Martha Minow's aptly titled *Between Vengeance and Forgiveness* correctly locates the demands of most reparations advocates. Indeed, the global popularity of truth and reconciliation commissions points to an alternative between retribution of the one hand and erasing the historical record on the other. The goals of the seventeen truth and reconciliation commissions formed since 1974 include discovering and acknowledging past systemic abuse, responding to the needs of victims, contributing to justice and accountability, recommending reforms, and promoting reconciliation. Such commissions make a distinction between individual reconciliation and actions that lead to political or national reconciliation.[18]

In a major contribution to the literature on reparations, Ronald Walters compared the cases for reparations in the United States and South Africa. His book, *The Price of Racial Reconciliation*, highlights the importance of material or economic reparations in the healing process. Led by Archbishop Desmond Tutu, the South African Truth and Reconciliation Commission (TRC) was active over a period of seven years, heard the testimony of twenty-two thousand people, reviewed six thousand applications for amnesty, and issued a five-volume report. Yet although nineteen thousand victims had been declared entitled to reparations, the government decided no payments would be made until a final report was issued in 2003. Moreover, a poll on the work of the TRC found that a substantial majority of all racial groups in the country believed the process had made matters worse.[19]

Tutu contends that the idea of retributive justice is largely a Western concept and African understanding of justice is far more restorative.[20] Minow believes "the process of seeking reparations, and of building communities of support while spreading knowledge of the violation and their meaning in people's lives, may be more valuable, ultimately than any specific victory or offer of a remedy."[21]

According to Walters, "the forgiveness sought by Tutu has not worked on a mass basis in South Africa because of the connection of memory to the present condition of black people in that country."[22] That is, the material gap between the races remains too large to "cultivate the generosity of the spirit," to absolve the white minority regime of its past crimes. And the current black majority government apparently lacks the will to pay the TRC-recommended $400 million over six years to the certified victims.[23] Even if it did pay, however, reparations are not about achieving equality in wages, says Walters, but equality in wealth. It is this wealth-based equality that is the "key to achieving individual, family, and group self-determination on a par with whites."[24]

In his analysis of the TRC, Mahmood Mamdani suggests that justice is more important than the truth. In the case of the TRC, the truth was provided by both victims and perpetrators. Each believed what they said was the truth, but it often led away from reconciliation. For Mamdani, the TRC failed because it was more concerned about delivering truth than justice. It forgave perpetrators for their crimes *and* allowed them to keep the status and economic resources accrued during apartheid.[25]

In his *The Burden of Memory, The Muse of Forgiveness*, Wole Soyinka also suggests the primacy of justice in South Africa while acknowledging the role of political expediency. He states, "the problem with the South African choice is therefore its implicit, *a priori* exclusion of criminality and, thus, responsibility. Justice assigns responsibility, and few will deny that justice is an essential ingredient of social cohesion."[26] Soyinka sees social strategies such as the TRC and the reparations movement in general as having an ultimate goal of a sort of historic closure. Yet such a closure could not happen in South Africa because remorse leading to repentance and some measure of restitution were missing from the TRC process.[27]

Walters, Mamdani, and Soyinka all see justice as an overriding goal of any reparations model or process. Storytelling or giving voice to those historically silenced is not enough. Justice must be a part of the truth-telling process, and economic redistribution is central to achieving justice.

Obviously there are important historical and demographic differences in drawing lessons for the United States from South Africa. Blacks in South Africa now represent a political majority, yet the preponderance of economic wealth rests with the white minority. Although blacks are the demographic majority, only a tiny fraction participated in the TRC process itself. Land redistribution was a form of economic equality discussed in South Africa that is absent from contemporary U.S. discourse. Finally, South Africa has undertaken a major reconfiguration of its national identity. The multiracial character of the country is firmly enshrined in its new Constitution.[28]

Despite these significant differences, two questions emerge from the reparations movements in both countries that are vital to their success. First, what does economic equality mean? We know that roughly political equality means one person, one vote, but where do we draw the line on economic redistribution? In short, economic equality raises the issue of group rights in a much more complicated way than political or civil rights. Second, is the call for reparations constructive or destructive? Most racial groups in South Africa saw the TRC process as harmful. Yet reparations for Japanese American internment camp survivors have generally been viewed as positive, and the U.S. government has taken a leading role in pushing for various forms of restitution for Jewish survivors/families of the Holocaust. Does the attempt to protect minority white privilege in South Africa help us understand majority white attempts in the United States?

As mentioned earlier, as the civil rights movement shifted from the South to the North, it also focused more on economic inequality. And while King was careful to talk about widespread poverty among all racial groups, there was little general consensus on what economic equality meant. Moreover, as James Forman and other black power advocates demanded reparations in the late sixties, the group boundaries of reparations became apparent.

Opposition to group rights generally takes two forms. One argues that equality must be measured solely on the basis of individual comparison. The other argument against group rights asserts that it essentializes group characteristics while ignoring the variability and flexibility of individual attachments.

Political theorist Iris Young states that comparing the situation of individuals makes no sense when making claims about social justice. Justice is a relational concept, and only by evaluating inequality in terms of social groups can we claim some inequalities are unjust, says Young, "because such group-based comparison helps reveal important aspects of institutional relations and processes."[29] That is, by identifying inequalities according to group categories we can reveal structural inequalities.

The emphasis on structural inequality returns us to Walters' concern that we measure black and white inequalities of wealth rather than income. Judgments of equality or inequality are simply factual comparisons of amounts or degrees of some variables between or among entities. A wage differential between a black worker and a white worker, for example, tells us nothing about the skill level or productivity of the individual. Thus, we can only make a weak moral claim at best for wage equality. By looking at intergenerational wealth between the two racial groups, however, we can discover systemic inequality by showing a pattern of average difference in status or well-being along several parameters including wealth, making our moral claim for redress much stronger.[30]

The argument that identity politics expressed through the call for reparations reifies an essentialist perspective on race is certainly a danger. Yet it ignores two significant contributions reparations discourse makes at both a micro and macro level. According to Eric Yamamoto, reparations can raise the issue of differential racialization and disempowerment. Differential racialization encompasses racialized differences between groups but also within groups. It creates differing racial meaning for racial groups and subgroups that relate to political agency as well as individual identity and collective consciousness. Differential disempowerment acknowledges the differences in power and resources between groups and recognizes some degree of group agency and responsibility. Rather than reinforcing essentialism, Yamamoto's approach is more complex and more likely to produce the empathy necessary for building alliances than either an anticolonial or nationalist approach.[31]

Insisting that equality and liberation entail ignoring difference has oppressive consequences in three respects according to Young. First, blindness to difference disadvantages groups whose experience, culture, and socialized capacities differ from those of privileged groups. Second, the ideal of a universal humanity without social group differences allows privileged groups to ignore their own group specificity (i.e., white nationalism). Third, denigration of groups that deviate from an allegedly neutral standard often produces an internalized devaluation by members of those groups themselves (i.e., resisted by black power).[32]

The rise of identity politics has frequently been accused of fragmenting or undermining a sense of national community and purpose. Arthur Schlesinger Jr., the well-known liberal historian, called it the "disuniting of America" in his book of the same title. Yet what black power and black pride did was not disunite America but reveal a dominant white norm that masked white privilege.

Reparations as an issue further uncovers the historic advantage accrued by whites and challenges the notion of American exceptionalism. How else could a term that means "to repair" be seen by so many as a threat or divisive. It implies that there is nothing to repair or that any efforts to repair past injustices will be more harmful than the status quo. Perhaps James Baldwin said it best:

> People who imagine that history flatters them (as it does indeed since they wrote it) are impaled on their history like a butterfly on a pin and become incapable of seeing or changing themselves or the world. . . . This is the place in which it seems to me most white Americans find themselves. Impaled. They are dimly, or vividly, aware that the history that they have fed themselves is mainly a lie, but they do not know how to release themselves from it, and they suffer enormously from the resulting personal incoherence.[33]

We are regularly treated to both popular and scholarly efforts at rewriting history. In March 2010, the Texas Board of Education passed more than one hundred amendments to the 120-page curriculum standard for the state, revising history, sociology, and economics guidelines from elementary to high school. Under the revised guidelines evolution and the separation of church and state will be deemphasized. The conservative resurgence of the 1980s and 1990s including leaders like Phyllis Schlafly and the Moral Majority will receive increased attention. Students will be required to study the unintended (read negative) consequences of the Great Society legislation, affirmative action, and Title IX. Textbooks will now stress that Germans and Italians as well as Japanese were interned in the United States during World War II, to counter the idea that the internment of Japanese was motivated by racism. Efforts by Hispanic board members to include more Latino figures as role models for the state's large Hispanic population were repeatedly defeated. Given the size of Texas, the board's action is likely to have an impact on textbook publishers across the nation.[34] Two months later the state legislature in Arizona went further than Texas in banning outright the teaching of ethnic studies, specifically Chicano or Mexican American studies, in Arizona schools. Supporters of the legislation called such classes divisive.[35]

Chicanos were also the primary target of another action taken by Republican senators Lindsey Graham of South Carolina and Mitch McConnell of Kentucky. They have suggested a reassessment of the Fourteenth Amendment's guarantee of citizenship to anyone born in the United States that was passed in 1866 to prevent Southern states from denying citizenship to freed slaves. Fellow Kentucky senator Rand Paul contends that the public accommodations section of the 1964 Civil Rights Act interferes with private businesses' First Amendment right to discriminate. He provided no explanation for his novel reading of the First Amendment.[36]

In April 2010 the governor of Virginia, Robert McDonnell, proclaimed April "Confederate History month" in a proclamation emphasizing the bravery of those who fought to preserve the Confederacy but neglecting to mention the role of slavery in the Civil War. The governor's action revealed that while contemporary scholars agree on the centrality of slavery in the conflict, how the reasons for the war are translated to students in southern classrooms varies greatly. [37] The 2012 presidential aspirant Michele Bachmann also drew fire for her signature on "The Marriage Vow" pledge promoted by a conservative Christian values group that was aimed at opposing gay marriage. However, the document also included the following passage: "Slavery had a disastrous impact on African-American families, yet sadly a child born into slavery in 1860 was more likely to be raised by his mother and father in a two-parent household than was an African-American baby born after the election of the USA's first African-American President."[38]

In response to criticism of her action Bachmann said she believed that "slavery was horrible and economic enslavement [i.e. the current U.S. debt] is also horrible."[39] In fact Bachmann hates slavery so much she has revised the history of America's "founding fathers" to indicate they "worked tirelessly" to eliminate it. When pressed to name one, she selected John Quincy Adams who was a child at the founding and died seventeen years before the Civil War.[40]

Efforts to rewrite history to support one's political goals are an unceasing aspect of politics. By viewing the primary goal of reparations as revenge and primarily legal, the educational and democratizing aspects of the movement are overlooked. Yet how else can one explain the rise of what some have called an "age of apology." From the Catholic Church's apology to Galileo to the U.S. Senate's apology for not enacting anti-lynching legislation, reparations discourse is more prominent than at any time in the past. Elazar Barkan states, "Contemporary international discourse underscores the growing role of guilt, mourning and atonement as part of a reconfiguration of national identity, including the national revival of indigenous groups on the verge of extinction or other historically victimized groups who do not enjoy full sovereignty."[41] By giving voice to those groups that have historically been silent, one can argue that the first benefit of reparations discourse is a "democratizing" of the past.[42]

According to John Torpey this "rise of regret in all its forms is a sign of the failure of the state to generate adequate psychological defense mechanisms, not the state's success in doing so."[43] Rather than operating at an absolutist level above politics, apology has entered the political realm where it was previously absent. The battle over the remembrance of events that have to do with our nation's obligations and entitlements is both political and moral. Minow believes that social and religious meanings rather than economic values lie at the heart of reparations.[44]

The struggle for reparations represents at its most fundamental level an attempt to reshape the moral identity of the nation. As such it is what Young would call a radically democratic pluralist project that "acknowledges and affirms the public and political significance of social group differences as a means of ensuring the participation and inclusion of everyone in social and political institutions."[45]

To return to our earlier discussion, citizenship must involve a sense of solidarity and common purpose in a multination state. Only by recognizing and accommodating rather than subordinating national identities will unity emerge. It is not enough for subordinated minorities to share the same procedural values and principles of the dominant group. They also require a shared *identity*. That identity cannot exclude the history of nonwhites. People from different national groups will only share an allegiance to the larger polity, says Will Kymlicka, if they see it as the context within which their national identity is nurtured rather than subordinated.[46] This is echoed by Young who argued groups cannot be socially equal unless their specific experience, culture, and social contributions are publicly affirmed and recognized.[47] Reparations should be seen as an effort to rework our national identity to be more inclusive and more just. As stated by Walters:

> The demand for reparations, then, is not simply a request for payment for slavery; it is a demand for something greater, something more difficult to achieve: a major step toward racial reconciliation through the power of Black self-determination. The monetary award of reparations may assist in that endeavor, but it cannot achieve it. That reconciliation is absolutely vital if Blacks are finally to claim their rightful place in America, and feel that it is their rightful place because it is *right*.[48]

Notes

1. Ronald Walters, as chair of the Political Science Department at Howard University in the fall of 1973, gave me my first job as a political scientist.
2. See, for example, Patricia J. Williams, *The Alchemy of Race and Rights* (Cambridge: Harvard University Press, 1991) and Charles W. Mills, *The Racial Contract* (Ithaca, NY: Cornell University Press, 1997). On color-blind racism, see Eduardo Bonilla-Silva, *Racism Without Racists* (Lanham, MD: Rowman & Littlefield, 2010).

3. See, for example, Sidney Tarrow, *Power in Movement* (Cambridge: Cambridge University Press, 1998).

4. John Lewis, Remarks as Prepared for Delivery, Democratic National Convention, August 28, 2008.

5. Johnson is quoted in Taylor Branch, *At Canaan's Edge* (New York: Simon & Schuster, 2006), 232.

6. Edward G. Carmines and James A. Stimson, *Issue Evolution* (Princeton: Princeton University Press, 1989), 47; Donald R. Kinder and Lynn M. Sanders, *Divided by Color* (Chicago: University of Chicago Press, 1996), 100–01. See also Thomas B. Edsall and Mary D. Edsall, *Chain Reaction* (New York: Norton, 1992) on the impact of black power on public opinion.

7. Carol M. Swain, *The New White Nationalism in America* (New York: Cambridge University Press, 2004) and Ronald W. Walters, *White Nationalism, Black Interests* (Detroit: Wayne State University Press, 2003).

8. Thomas Janoski groups citizenship theories into three categories. One school of thought centers around T. H. Marshall's typology of citizenship rights—legal, political, and social —that develop in a particular order and must be balanced with citizenship obligations such as taxes and military service. For Marshall, citizenship rights grew out of the conflict between capitalism and equality. Following this perspective, Nikhil Pal Singh argues that the principles that underlie the market and those that apply to the nation-state are often in direct conflict. The market presumes atomistic freedom and opens the way for the play of differences while the state presumes equality and is organized around sameness.

   A second group of theories revolve around the Tocquevillian/Durkheimian approach to civil culture. This perspective goes beyond formal citizenship rights to focus on the participation of volunteers and private groups in the public sphere. Thus it is civil society rather than formal rights that provide the context for citizen participation. More recently this approach has formed the basis of communitarianism.

   Finally, a third approach adopts the Gramscian/Marxist theory of civil society that attempts to guard against both state abuses and market greed. The efforts of Jürgen Habermas and others to improve democratic communication are an example of its emphasis on complex democracy and social movements.

According to Janoski, although citizenship is a frequently used concept across the political and academic worlds, it has not been a central idea in the social sciences. He defines citizenship as "passive and active membership of individuals in a nation-state with certain universalistic rights and obligations at a specified level of equality." Thomas Janoski, *Citizenship and Civil Society* (Cambridge, UK: Cambridge University Press, 1998), 9. See also Nikhil Pal Singh, *Black Is a Country* (Cambridge: Harvard University Press, 2004), 25 and Herman R. van Gunsteren, *A Theory of Citizenship* (Boulder, CO: Westview, 1998), chapter 3.

9. In his 1944 classic *An American Dilemma* (New York: Harper & Row, 1964), Gunnar Myrdal states that the best thing "Negroes" can do to advance their status is to be more like whites.

10. Renato Rosaldo, *Culture and Truth* (Boston: Beacon, 1993) and Thomas R. Rochon, *Culture Moves* (Princeton: Princeton University Press, 1998). See E. D. Hirsch, Jr., *Cultural Literacy* (New York: Vintage, 1988) for a counterargument.

11. Howard McGary, "Achieving Democratic Equality," *Journal of Ethics* 7, 1 (2003): 99.

12. Wendy Brown, *States of Injury* (Princeton: Princeton University Press, 1995), 128.

13. Ibid.

14. Ibid., 152.

15. Lawrie Balfour, "Reparations *After* Identity Politics," *Political Theory* 33, 6 (December 2005): 789.

16. Williams, *The Alchemy of Race and Rights*, 152.

17. Charles P. Henry, *Long Overdue* (New York: New York University Press, 2007), chapters 3 and 4.

18. Priscilla B. Hayner, *Unspeakable Truths* (New York: Routledge, 2001), 24.

19. Ronald W. Walters, *The Price of Racial Reconciliation* (Ann Arbor: University of Michigan Press, 2008), 74–76.

20. Desmond Tutu in Martha Minow, *Between Vengeance and Forgiveness* (Boston: Beacon, 1998), 81.

21. Ibid., 93.

22. Walters, *The Price of Racial Reconciliation*, 136.

23. Ibid., 58. After the final government report was issued in 2003, the South African government did pay R 30,000 to approximately sixteen thousand victims. However, a study reported that the

payments made little difference in their socioeconomic status. Moreover, the government opposed reparations lawsuits against large corporations complicit in apartheid. Some believe the new South African government is more sympathetic to the TRC recommendations. See "Reparations—Traces of Truth—the South African TRC," accessed July 26, 2011 at http://truth.wwl.ac.za/cat_descr.php?cat=4.

24. Walters, *The Price of Racial Reconciliation*, 129.

25. Mahmood Mamdani in Walters, *The Price of Racial Reconciliation*, 48.

26. Wole Soyinka, *The Burden of Memory, The Muse of Forgiveness* (New York: Oxford University Press, 1999), 31.

27. Ibid., 36.

28. Constitution of the Republic of South Africa, 1996, especially the Preamble and Bill of Rights, Sections 30 and 31, accessed July 23, 2011 at http://www.info.gov.za/documents/constitution/1996/96cons2.htm#9.

29. Iris Marion Young, "Equality of Whom?" *Journal of Political Philosophy* 9, 1 (2001): 2.

30. Ibid., 16. A recent study by the Pew Research Center indicates that the wealth gap between whites and minorities is widening. From 2005 to 2009, the net median household worth of Hispanics declined 66 percent, African Americans' declined 53 percent, while whites' fell just 16 percent. See "Study Says Recession Hit Hispanics Homes Harder," *New York Times*, July 26, 2011, A1, A12.

31. Eric K. Yamamoto, *Interracial Justice* (New York: New York University Press, 1999), 117–19.

32. Iris Marion Young, *Justice and the Politics of Difference* (Princeton: Princeton University Press, 1990), 164–65.

33. James Baldwin quoted in Scott L. Malcomson, *One Drop of Blood* (New York: Farrar, Straus & Giroux, 2000), 12.

34. "Texas Conservatives Win Curriculum Change," *New York Times*, March 12, 2010, accessed July 22, 2011 at http://www.nytimes.com/2010/03/education/13texashtml.

35. "Arizona Bill Targeting Ethnic Studies Signed into Law," *Los Angeles Times*, May 12, 2010, accessed July 22, 2011 at http://articles.com/com/2010/amy12/antion-la-na-ethnic-studies-20100510.

36. Jill Nelson, "The New Confederacy," *Ebony*, February 2011, 103.

37. "Teaching the Civil War: Debate Still Alive," *Washington Post*, April

8, 2010, accessed July 22, 2011 at http://voices.washingtonpost. com/answer-shett/history/the-debate-over-how-to-teach-t.html.

38. "Bachmann Does Damage Control over Slavery Quote in 'Marriage Vow,'" *The Atlantic Wire*, July 10, 2011, accessed July 22, 2011 at http://www.theatlanticwire.com/politics/2011/07/Bachmann-does-damage-control-over-slavery-reference-marriage-vow/39772/.

39. Ibid.

40. Jon Perr, "Everything I Know about the Founding Fathers I Learned from Republicans," accessed July 22, 2011 at http://crooksandliars.com/taxonomy/term/4803,22142,8409.

41. Elazar Barkan, "Restitution and Amending Historical Injustice," in *Politics and the Past*, ed. John Torpey (Lanham, MD: Rowman & Littlefield, 2003), 102.

42. Torpey, *Politics and the Past*, 83.

43. Ibid., 56.

44. Minow, *Between Vengeance and Forgiveness*, 110.

45. Young, *Justice and the Politics of Difference*, 168.

46. Will Kymlicka, *Multicultural Citizenship* (Oxford, UK: Clarendon, 1997), 188–89.

47. Young, *Justice and the Politics of Difference*, 174.

48. Walters, *The Price of Racial Reconciliation*, 188.

Part VII

15

Civil Rights and the First Black President

Barack Obama and the Politics of Racial Equality

RONALD W. WALTERS

with the assistance of ROBERT C. SMITH

In the 1940s, the great civil rights advocate and diplomat Ralph Bunche wrote that it was inconceivable that an African American could ever be elected president: a governor, a senator, a general, or a cabinet officer perhaps, but never president.[1] In 2008 the seemingly impossible happened. Newspapers across the country reported that Barack Obama's election was a momentous achievement—a historic occasion for African Americans and the nation as a whole. The *Chicago Tribune* summed up the sentiments held by many when it described Obama's election as the "crowning achievement of the Civil Rights Movement, the triumph of a black candidate in a nation with a history of slavery and segregation."[2] After hundreds of years of racial subjugation Obama's election came to embody the Reverend Dr. Martin Luther King Jr.'s dream that one day in America, even in an election for president, individuals would be judged by the content of their character rather than the color of their skin. For many African Americans the election represented something more. Valerie Grimm, chair of Indiana University's African American Studies Department, reflected on this something else:

> I have parents who are still living who are very enthusiastic about Obama. They live in Mississippi. For a time my parents

couldn't vote, and when they could, their only choice was a
white person. This means more than just seeing a black person on the ticket. It represents things they had been denied.
It's being able to see the unbelievable, that the impossible
might be possible. It represents for them a new day.[3]

Yet, the very same *Chicago Tribune* article that hailed the election as the crowning achievement of the civil rights movement
told of another side to the story. It revealed that conservative activists were using Obama's victory as an argument to scale back the
enforcement of civil rights, including affirmative action and the
Voting Rights Act. Such efforts began almost immediately after election day. On November 11, 2008, for example, Abigail and Stephan
Thernstrom, longtime opponents of affirmative action, wrote in the
Wall Street Journal that the Voting Rights Act could now be loosened.
The "doors of electoral opportunity in America are now open to
all," they argued. "The aggressive federal interference in state and
local districting decisions enshrined in the Voting Rights Act should
therefore be reconsidered."[4] Given the long sordid history of denying African Americans the right to vote, talk of reconsidering the
Voting Rights Act evoked deep concerns that black disenfranchisement might actually worsen in the wake of Obama's victory.

Such arguments point to a curious paradox arising from the 2008
election. While for the African American community the election of
Obama represents a historic win in their ongoing struggle for equality, it also has the potential to represent a loss in that struggle. By creating the mistaken perception that the doors of equal opportunity
are now open to all, when in reality institutionalized discrimination
remains an irrefutable fact of modern American life, Obama's victory might have the effect of dampening the long-term effort to remedy the effects of centuries of racial discrimination. In other words,
winning while losing—or at least not gaining—may be the outcome
of the election of the first black president.

Multiple Dimensions of Civil Rights in the Obama Era

To understand this proposition, we must first correct a common perception about the meaning of civil rights in American history and

politics. At least since the New Deal the civil rights movement has had a dual agenda, focusing on both citizenship rights and social welfare. Yet this dual agenda has been obscured by a narrow understanding that, in the popular imagination at least, equates civil rights only with political rights. In large part, such public perceptions have been trapped by a distorted historical memory stemming from the iconography of the civil rights movement of the 1960s. The movement is remembered primarily for its public protests, when in fact there was a much wider range of strategies and tactics used to advance racial equality. Similarly, historical memory generally distorts the movement's agenda by narrowly defining its goals as merely involving political rights, like the right to vote and run for office, rather than including the much broader spectrum of human rights and social justice that motivated civil rights activists both at the time and since.

The 1960s civil rights movement has thus been badly misinterpreted as having been devoted only to the acquisition of equal access to citizenship rights such as made possible by the 1965 Voting Rights Act. However, human rights that related to what *one could do* with citizenship rights were the core of the 1964 Civil Rights Act—in equalizing access to public accommodations and athletics, as well as nondiscrimination in the use of federal funds—and the Fair Housing Act of 1968. The goal of expanding opportunities as well as protecting citizenship rights were likewise integral to Lyndon Johnson's Great Society Program, which focused on civic participation, community development, job training, and poverty elimination. So, too, has affirmative action been premised upon breaking down lingering barriers to economic and educational opportunity for disadvantaged groups. Such broad social objectives were both central to the welfare rights movement and to Dr. Martin Luther King Jr. at the time of his death.

Moreover, both civil rights and welfare rights have been enshrined in the Constitution for generations. The Fourteenth Amendment created *citizenship rights* for African Americans by theoretically extending equal citizenship to all Americans, allowing them "due process" of law and "equal protection of the laws." Furthermore, that the status of any citizen should also allow them access to *human rights* has long been understood to be one of the basic purposes of government. In fact, the Preamble to the Constitution says that the American government was formed, in part, to "promote the general welfare," an objective that was included in Article 1, Section 8, directing Congress to "provide for. . . . The general welfare."

Thus, although citizenship rights and welfare rights are often viewed separately, in fact they are joined. There is some support for this in the thinking of Supreme Court Justice Thurgood Marshall, who identified three elements in an interwoven pattern of rights.[5] First, there was the civil element of society, comprised of the rights necessary for individual freedom, such as those protected by the Bill of Rights: liberty of person; freedom of speech, thought, and faith; the right to own property, to conclude valid contracts, and assert one's rights on an equal basis to all others. Second, there were political rights, or those that gave citizens participatory access to engage in making government decisions through the vote and their representative power. And finally there were social rights, including the right to economic welfare and security, to live life according to the prevailing social standards.

The civil rights movement of the twenty-first century and especially in the era of Barack Obama will continue to struggle to close gaps in all three interwoven categories of rights: civil, political, and social. The task will be to protect and advance these rights at a time of contradictory reactions to Obama's victory. While many in the black community have heightened expectations of empowerment generated by the election of a black president, public policies that advance civil rights or that appear to "favor" African Americans are likely to be resisted by others who believe Obama's victory signals the endpoint, rather than merely a way station, along the road to racial equality.

Citizenship Rights

As the *Chicago Tribune* article quoted at the beginning of this essay reveals, the election of Obama reinforced the impression among some that laws protecting citizenship rights are no longer needed. This, of course, is a matter of perspective, inasmuch as civil rights laws that passed in the 1960s restrained whites who dominated the political systems of the South and in other regions from prohibiting blacks from enjoying integrated education, public accommodations, voting, higher education, fair housing, and other privileges of citizenship. Blacks, on the other hand, still continue to experience racial prohibitions today. While admittedly far less than in the 1960s, racism not only continues to limit black access to the old privileges but has erected new limitations.

One sign of the lingering challenges facing African Americans may be found in a 2004 summary report on the attention to civil rights by the Bush administration.[6] Composed by the U.S. Civil Rights Commission, the report found egregious lapses in attention to civil rights enforcement by the Justice Department. It asserted that President Bush:

> Seldom speaks about civil rights; implemented policies that have retreated from long-established civil rights promises; did not provide leadership to ensure timely and swift implementation of the Help America Vote Act . . . ; has not exhibited leadership on Affirmative Action, but instead promotes "race-neutral" remedies that do not account for past discrimination; [and his requests] for six major civil rights agency funds amount to a loss of spending power for 2004 and 2005.[7]

This strongly suggests that the civil rights of African Americans are not a settled affair, even if the new limitations stem less from individual manifestations of racism than from institutional racism. That such challenges continue in the era of Barack Obama are revealed in the field of voting rights. In two Supreme Court cases in 2009, for example, the conservative majority on the Supreme Court narrowed the reach of the Voting Rights Act by interpreting the law, in the words of law professor Richard Hasen, "in even stingier ways."[8]

Human Rights

Of greater concern, the broader spectrum of human rights—including the alleviation of poverty and promotion of the general welfare of citizens—remains a paramount concern and one that needs to address openly the racialized dimensions of poverty and opportunity in America. The Great Recession that started during 2008 had devastating effects on the well-being of the American people, increasing enormously human suffering. The loss of aggregate household wealth from both private and public investments has been estimated conservatively by a consensus of economists at 9 percent or $5 trillion in the last three months of 2008—double that for the entire year.[9] This loss was disproportionately devastating to African Americans whose ratio of wealth to whites was 10 to 1 before the economic crisis. This loss was made even harder by the disproportionate loss of employment, such that it affected income mobility to the point that although the movement of whites from the bottom to the top quartile in income was 10.2 percent in 2008, it was only 4.2 percent for blacks.[10]

The black middle class has experienced a substantial degree of immobility relative to the growth of the white middle class for nearly two decades, a position held by researchers in hearings before the U.S. Civil Rights Commission in 2005. Black middle-class incomes between 1980 and 2003 grew from 29 percent to about 40 percent but were unable to close a substantial gap with whites. The top quintile has grown by 66 percent, but the lower 10 percent has remained stagnant at twice the proportion of whites for the past forty-five years.[11] The lack of growth by the black middle class relative to the rest of the economy made this group especially vulnerable to making debt with the instruments that were marketed in the housing field. Small wonder, then, that the black community is disproportionately represented in the home foreclosure crisis.[12]

While there is some evidence that the comparative lack of educational access and performance is a critical variable, it is also important to note that black mobility has been constrained by the lack of attention by previous administrations to human investment policies. The weakening of affirmative action in higher education, the lack of vigorous K–12 education financing, higher education financing changes that privilege loans instead of grants, and the retrenchment of minority business contracting have done much to restrain the opportunities available to African Americans.

Most important, the lack of economic progress by the black middle class is related to the failure to curb intransigent poverty, creating community pressures that continued to fuel the drug trade in poor black neighborhoods, which in turn exacerbates the massive incarceration rate of blacks and the growth of female-headed households. The impact of this problem on the black community was vested in the 1994 Crime Control Act, passed under Bill Clinton but with the strong wind of the conservative Gingrich revolution at his back. Today, half (48%) of everyone incarcerated in the United States is black. Professor Bruce Western of Harvard's Kennedy School concludes that: "Growing rates of incarceration mean that, in the experience of African Americans in poor neighborhoods, the advancement of voting rights, school desegregation, and protection from discrimination was substantially halted. Mass incarceration undermined the project for full African American citizenship and revealed the obstacles to political equality presented by acute social disparity."[13] The interaction among factors such as incarceration, poverty, and unemployment was important in shaping a rationale for increased voting by blacks in 2008, together with the equally alluring fact that an African American could be a credible candidate for president, yet it remains to be seen whether Obama will enact policies that remediate these conditions.[14]

The Obama Victory and the Civil Rights Agendas

In the immediate aftermath of the 2008 election, some commentators suggested that that it may have constituted a classic, realigning election, one that reconfigured the electoral landscape and turned the page on the conservative era in American politics. Such speculation may have been premature. Obama's election appears to have signified not so much the advent of a new liberal age but a referendum on the last eight years of Republican rule and George W. Bush. The electorate wanted change, and Obama was the change candidate. This made for an ideal climate for Obama or any Democrat to win. Throughout 2008 the Democrats maintained a double-digit lead on the generic ballot, which asks voters which party they would like to see win the presidency. As the general election approached, 90 percent of the population thought the country was headed in the wrong direction; the nation faced rising gas prices, two unpopular wars, a collapse in the housing market, a massive budget deficit, rising unemployment, and an incumbent president whose popularity was in the low thirties. Finally, a month before the election the stock market dramatically declined and the credit markets collapsed, requiring a $700 billion bailout from the federal treasury. Newspaper headlines and television newscasts raised the specter of another Great Depression. *Time,* for example, in its cover story of October 13, under the caption "The New Hard Times," showed men in long, Depression-era soup lines.

In this dismal strategic situation Obama should have won in a landslide. That he did not, many scholars attribute to "Ballot Box Racism." For example, Michael Lewis-Beck in his initial forecasting model predicted a victory for the Democratic nominee of 56.58 percent, but after including variables taking account of Obama's race, the margin dropped to a razor-thin 50.7 percent.[15] Ultimately, on Election Day Obama won by a margin of 53 percent to John McCain's 46 percent (the remainder was won by minor party candidates). He carried 28 states and the District of Columbia with 364 electoral votes to McCain's 163. Obama's "minority-majority" coalition resembled the typical Democratic presidential coalition since the 1960s; 95 percent of the black vote, 67 percent of Latinos, 86 percent of Jews, 66 percent of Asian Americans, and 70 percent of gays and lesbians.[16]

Although Obama lost the white vote to McCain 43 to 55 percent, his margin was slightly better than John Kerry's 41 percent in 2004. Yet as Alan Abramowitz writes: "Obama's 12 point deficit among white voters was identical to Al Gore's in 2000. However, the fact that white voters favored the Republican candidate by a double-digit margin in 2008 despite the poor conditions of the economy and the unpopularity of the incumbent Republican President suggests racial prejudice did affect the level of white voter support for the Democratic candidate."[17] In other words, Obama won in spite of his race, and he did not win as decisively as he should have because of it.

Nevertheless, Obama's candidacy mobilized the black community in an unprecedented way. More so than even the Jesse Jackson campaigns, blacks participated in the process to a greater extent than whites. Forty-eight percent of blacks compared to 46 percent of whites reported following the election "closely," 31 percent reported making campaign contributions (compared to 21 percent of whites), and twice as many blacks (14%) reported working in the campaign. This is extraordinary, given that whites have always participated in presidential elections more than blacks.

Obama received a higher proportion of the black vote than any previous Democratic nominee, 95 percent compared to Lyndon

Johnson's 94 percent in 1964. While the number of non-Hispanic white voters remained the same as in 2004, in 2008 2 million more blacks turned out. Moreover, in 2008, for the first time the percentage of blacks who voted nearly equaled that of whites at 65 percent (versus 66% for whites).[18] In several states—Maryland, Mississippi, Missouri, Nevada, Ohio, and South Carolina—turnout among blacks surpassed 70 percent. Among young people and women, blacks voted at a higher rate than whites.[19]

This heightened participation gave rise to empowerment expectations in the black community: expectations that the first black president would take their civil rights concerns into consideration in policymaking. However, Obama received this extraordinary outpouring of black support on the basis of racial identification and solidarity rather than because he addressed issues of specific concern to blacks. During the campaign, he avoided frank discussion of the particular challenges facing African Americans, framing his policies and proposals instead as ones that advanced human and welfare rights for all.

Of course, the danger of embedding human rights resources designed to achieve the viability of a racial group into broad social policy aims is that they may fall into the naïveté of the view that "a rising tide lifts all boats." This has seldom been the case for African Americans. Indeed, the most authoritative student of race and poverty, Harvard professor William Julius Wilson, noted that the issue of race should not be buried in public discourse but brought out into the open.[20] In a 2009 book synthesizing two decades of sociological research, Wilson convincingly documented the ways in which underlying structural issues—the historical legacy of slavery and discrimination, together with imbalanced public policies—served to create and sustain systematic poverty in the black community. Impoverished urban ghettos, for example, were themselves the products of government policies that segregated neighborhoods, denied mortgages to inner-city neighborhoods, reduced drastically federal aid to cities, focused transportation resources on suburban over urban areas, and other policies that encouraged the middle class to flee the cities for the suburbs, leaving ghetto residents effectively cut off from mainstream society. Accordingly, Wilson suggested, measures designed to affect solutions for disadvantaged African Americans should be highlighted and dealt with openly so that the American people understand the gravity of its dimensions. Only an aggressive public policy response that addressed both cultural and structural contributions to economic inequality could begin to break the cycle of poverty for African Americans.

Professor Wilson took his cue from a speech on race that Obama delivered in response to the racially incendiary remarks of his former pastor, the Reverend Jeremiah Wright, during the 2008 primary campaign. In that speech, Obama framed the problem of race in both structural and cultural terms. "We do need to remind ourselves," he said, "that so many of the disparities that exist between the African-American community and the larger American community today can be traced directly to inequalities passed on from an earlier generation that suffered under the brutal legacy of slavery and Jim Crow." Obama cited such things as segregated schools, legalized discrimination, a lack of economic opportunity for black men, and the lack of basic services in urban black neighborhoods as perpetuating economic disparities between blacks and whites. Yet he also addressed cultural issues within the black community that keep "us from squarely facing our own complicity in our condition," and he spoke of "taking full responsibility for our own lives." Although Obama identified specific policies and grievances that created the wealth and income gap between blacks and whites, he advocated what sounded like a race-neutral approach to remedying the situation. He urged African Americans to bind "our particular grievances—for better health care and better schools and better jobs—to the larger aspirations of all Americans." He implied that he would improve the condition of the African American community not so much by addressing its specific needs but by improving health care, education, and the economy for all.[21]

When subsequent speeches more strongly emphasized personal responsibility to the detriment of corrective public policy that would address structural problems, Obama drew criticism from the Reverend Jesse Jackson Sr. and others. So, inasmuch as he has continued as president to emphasize personal responsibility to achieve social viability on the part of African Americans and others, the great anticipation is what public policies will be constructed to make the acceptance of such responsibility practical based on access to human resources that may be provided by the federal government.

The Obama Presidency and the Civil Rights Agenda

Obama continued to emphasize this broad human rights approach to civil rights during the first two years of his presidency, consistently and persistently saying that as president he was required to subordinate race-specific needs to the broader human rights dimensions. In his hundredth-day press conference he was asked by the correspondent for Black Entertainment Television (BET) what specific policies would he propose to deal with the huge racial disparities in unemployment between blacks and whites (the rate for blacks was twice that of whites). The president responded by saying that his "general approach is that if the economy is strong, that will lift all boats as long as it is also supported by, for example, strategies around college affordability and job training; tax cuts for working families as opposed to the wealthiest, that level the playing the field and ensure bottom-up growth."[22] Later, the president told April Ryan of American Urban Radio, "The only thing I cannot do is, by law I can't pass laws that say that I'm just helping black folks. I am president of the entire United States."[23] Responding to mounting criticisms among some black political and intellectual leaders, Obama cited the enactment of health care reform as emblematic of his approach to race. He argued that since blacks were disproportionately without health insurance, they would benefit the most from health care reform.[24]

Although the Obama administration and its African American attorney general did in its first year increase funding and enforcement of citizenship rights, reversing the Bush administration policy of neglect,[25] it addressed the issue of civil rights indirectly and without race-specific focus.

"A Racial Pass?"

There are several contradictions at the heart of the first black president's policies on race. First, if it is a mistake to think about ethnic segments of the country in his governance, then why did the president sign an executive order mandating the increased participation of Asian and Pacific Islanders in federal programs or say in a speech to the Hispanic Caucus that when their unemployment number reached over 10 percent that was not just a problem for Hispanics, it was a problem for the whole nation? No such statement was made by the first black president about the 15.7 percent rate of official black unemployment. Thus, a black president feels free to address the ethnic-specific concerns of Latinos and Asian Americans but not the more pressing needs of his own people.

During the campaign Obama and his staff were aware of polls showing that as much as half of whites thought he would favor blacks if he became president. Of that number only 32 percent said they would vote for him.[26] And during his first year in office there was a three-fold increase in the percentage of whites who believed his policies favored blacks, up from 11 to 13 percent in October 2008 to 37 percent in August 2009.[27] Thus, the first black president was acutely aware that he had to avoid any appearance of favoring blacks. To do otherwise would put at risk his presidency and his prospects for reelection.

So, where does this leave the black community, winners or losers? Many African Americans think they are winners. Public opinion polls during Obama's first two years show that his approval rating among African Americans rarely fell below 90 percent. "African Americans" the *Washington Afro* concluded, "have given President Obama a racial pass."[28] One reason for this "pass," said the capital's black weekly, was that

> many believe the president is sensitive to Black issues and dedicated to solving them—albeit in his own way and his own time given the deluge of problems—recession, foreclosures, health care reform, two wars, etc.—he has to tackle. . . . That political maturity also recognizes that should Obama display even the suggestion of favoritism toward blacks, he would get a backlash from Congress and the public and would feed the conservative talk show machine for months.[29]

It appears, then, for most blacks the mere fact that this talented, handsome, charismatic, and *liberal, progressive* black man defied history and won the presidency is a win, win. But the final contradiction at the heart of the Obama presidency is that if he does little to address both the citizenship and human rights dimensions of the civil rights agenda, his election will be a loss. Blacks have a right to demand a useful product from the political system in exchange for their participation and to evaluate the worthiness of politics on that basis. That is, it is valid for them to ask what difference it makes to the satisfaction of their interests that a black is elected president. To give him a pass is to ask for a loss. Because if a black president can ignore those interests, little can be expected from his white successors.

Notes

1. Ralph Bunche, *A Brief and Tentative Analysis of Negro Leadership*, ed. Jonathan Holloway (New York: New York University Press, 2005), 36.
2. Peter Wallsten and David G. Savage, "Voting Rights Act Opponents Point to Barack Obama's Election as Reason to Scale Back Civil Rights Laws," *Chicago Tribune*, March 15, 2009.
3. Quoted in Darryl Fears, "Black Community Increasingly Protective of Obama," *Washington Post*, May 10, 2008.
4. Abigail Thernstrom and Stephan Thernstrom, "Racial Gerrymandering is Unnecessary," *Wall Street Journal*, November 11, 2008.
5. Adam Seligman, *Civil Society* (New York: The Free Press/Macmillan, 1992): 113–14.
6. U.S. Commission on Civil Rights, Office of Civil Rights Evaluation, "Redefining Rights in America: The Civil Rights Record of the George W. Bush Administration, 2001–2004," September 2004.
7. On the slow-down in enforcement of civil rights laws during the Bush administration, see also "Enforcement of Civil Rights Laws Declined Since 1999, Study Finds," *New York Times*, November 11, 2004; Dan Eggen, "Civil Rights Focus Shift Roils Staff," *Washington Post*, November 13, 2005.
8. Robert Barnes, "Supreme Court Restricts Voting Rights Act's Scope," *Washington Post*, March 10, 2009; David G. Savage, "Supreme Court Narrows but Preserves Voting Rights Act," *Los Angeles Times*, June 23, 2009.
9. Vikas Bajaj, "Household Wealth Falls by Trillions," *New York Times*, March 13, 2009.
10. Lawrence Mishel, Heidi Shierholz, and Jared Bernstein, "The State of Working America," Annual Report of the Economic

Policy Institute, Washington, D.C. 2009, Table 2.4, "Income Mobility for white and black families . . . "

11. U.S. Commission on Civil Rights, Briefing Report, "The Economic Stagnation of the Black Middle Class,", July 15 2005, http://www.usccr.gov/pubs/122805_BlackAmericaStagnation.pdf.

12. Ruby Mendenhall, "The Political Economy of Black Housing: From the Housing Crisis of the Great Migration to the Subprime Mortgage Crisis," *The Black Scholar* 40 (2010): 20–37. As an example of the institutional racism referenced earlier, this article reports, "black communities are now experiencing reverse redlining as minority neighborhoods are often the target of subprime lenders. In neighborhoods where at least 80 percent of the population is black, those obtaining refinance loans were 22 times more likely to get a subprime loan than the national average. More striking is the fact that upper income borrowers living in predominantly black communities receive subprime loans at twice the rate of low income white borrowers" (31).

13. Bruce Western, "Reentry: Reversing Mass Imprisonment," *Boston Review*, July/August 2008. http://bostonreview.net/BR33.4/western.php.

14. For a succinct overview of the social and economic well-being of the black community at the time of Obama's election, see the special issue of *The Black Scholar*: "The Political Economy and the Deteriorating Condition of African America in the Age of Obama," edited by Sundiata Keita Cha-Jua, 40 (Spring 2010).

15. Michael Lewis-Beck, Charles Tien, and Richard Nadeau, "Obama's Missed Landslide: A Racial Loss?" Paper prepared for presentation at the annual meeting of the Southern Political Science Association, New Orleans, January 7–11, 2009.

16. These data are from the 2008 general election exit polls as accessed from http://www.cnn.comELECTION/2008/results/polls.main.

17. Alan Abramowitz, *The Disappearing Center: Engaged Citizens, Polarization and American Democracy* (New Haven: Yale University Press, 2010), 115.

18. Tasha Philpot, Daron Shaw, and Ernest McGowan, "Winning the Race: Black Turnout in the 2008 Election," *Public Opinion Quarterly* 73 (2009): 995–1022.

19. Ibid.
20. William Julius Wilson, *More Than Just Race* (New York: W. W. Norton and Co. 2009), 141–44.
21. Transcript of Barack Obama speech, "A More Perfect Union," March 18, 2008, http://www.npr.org/templates/story/story.php?storyId=88478467.
22. Presidential Press Conference, Transcript, *New York Times*, April 30, 2009.
23. Howard Kurz, "Color of Change," *Washington Post*, December 23, 2009.
24. Sheldon Albert, "Obama Rejects Charges He's Ignoring Black People," Canada.com, December 22, 2009, http://www.canada.com/business/story.html?id=237/1848.
25. Charlie Savage, "Justice Department to Recharge Civil Rights Enforcement," *New York Times*, September 1, 2009.
26. Lewis-Beck, Tien, and Nadeau, "Obama's Missed Landslide," 14–15.
27. Michael Tesler and David Sears, *Obama's Race: The 2008 Election and the Dream of A Post-Racial America* (Chicago: University of Chicago Press, 2010), 144, 182.
28. Zenitha Prince, "Muffled Black Criticisms Reflect Racial Pride, Pragmatism," *Washington Afro*, March 18, 2010.
29. Ibid.

Afterword

ROBERT C. SMITH

The purpose of this volume is to assess the impact and influence of Ronald Walters' work on black politics, thought, and leadership; to provide a critical assessment of the life and career of one of the most consequential political scientists in the history of the discipline. We also prepared this volume to preserve Walters' legacy for the next generations of students, scholars, activists, leaders, and public intellectuals. Over the years, Walters trained many students—two generations are represented in this volume—but for the future this book may serve as an introduction to his work as well as a study in the sociology of knowledge. Similarly, over the years Walters counseled, advised, and strategized with two generations of black leaders and activists of all ideological stripes. Many of those leaders and activists have passed or are passing away and are being replaced by new generations of leaders and activists unfamiliar with Walters' work and the struggles out of which it emerged.[1] Thus, another purpose of this volume is to make available to future generations of activists and leaders the broad outlines of the work of a man who in the past half century contributed much to the understanding, evolution, and development of black power in the United States.[2]

In a small way this volume is a substitute for the memoir Walters did not get around to and anticipates biographies that might yet be written.

When Walters begin his career there were perhaps sixty-five black PhD-trained political scientists in the United States,[3] and concerns about race were marginal to the discipline. In 2010 the American Political Science Association estimated that African Americans constituted 5 percent of the nearly ten thousand PhD-trained political scientists in the United States.[4] And "The historical devaluation of Afro-American politics as a subject worthy of study is no longer the norm in the discipline."[5] On the contrary, "During the past thirty years, the status and recognition given to scholarship on race, racism and Afro-American politics has gradually improved . . . culminat[ing] in a virtual explosion of scholarship on race, racism and Afro-American politics during the last twenty-five years."[6]

When Walters entered the profession, probably no more than a half dozen books by political scientists on race had been published in the United States; Walters published as many during his career. Thus, when he died there was long-overdue receptivity to work by scholars on race. Yet, much of this scholarship tends to be divorced from activism, divorced from empowering the black community in its continuing struggle for a racially just society.

In 2007 Wilbur Rich edited a collection of essays, *African American Perspectives on Political Science.* In his chapter he wrote political science as a discipline "does not reward scholars who are activist. . . . Indeed, being perceived as being too close to politics is frowned upon."[7] The emergent "perestroika" movement has challenged this apolitical, irrelevant political science.[8] But the norm prevails, and Rich writes that the "lure of academic heaven" (an appointment at an elite university) prevents many black political scientists from engaging in the kind of activism that characterized the work of Walters.[9] Mack Jones, the founding president of NCOBPS and the founding chair of Atlanta University's PhD program in political science, was with Walters a key figure in the development of an activist-oriented black science of politics during the 1970s.[10] In an address in 1989 commemorating NCOBPS' twentieth anniversary, Jones concluded that black political scientists appeared to have succumbed to the "seductions of the mainstream."[11] Rich contends that the lure of academic heaven even "serves to discipline the behavior and research of professors at lesser known universities."[12]

The black political science of a Walters, a Jones, or a Hanes Walton did not emerge in a vacuum. Political thought never does. As Bertrand Russell wrote in his great history of Western philosophy, "philosophy [is] an integral part of social and political life, not the isolated speculations of remarkable individuals, but as both an effect and cause of the character of the various communities in which different systems flourished."[13] Walters was a remarkable individual, but he also came of age in a most remarkable period of African American history—the tumultuous, rebellious black 1960s. This era of revolt was effect and cause of his work. Likewise, the conservative ascendancy in American politics since the 1960s, in addition to the lure of academic heaven, is effect and cause of the behavior of many black political scientists in the late twentieth and early twenty-first centuries.[14]

I cannot conclude this last word on Walters' work without coming to his defense, and engaging in argument. Perhaps the major criticism of Walters' work relates to his unqualified, unapologetic defense of the integrity of the black community, its culture and its collective interests. The essays by Tate, Gillespie, Campbell, and Errol Henderson in this volume challenge in different ways this major premise of his work, and it has been challenged directly or indirectly, implicitly or explicitly by numerous other scholars.[15]

At the outset I should observe that it is self-evident to me, as it was to Walters, that there is a black community in the United States,[16] a historically constructed community of shared history and memory, psychologically and culturally bounded, with relatively distinctive economic and political interests and with a geographic or spatial anchor in the nation's major urban centers and the heavily populated black belt counties of the rural South. This community is characterized by relatively autonomous religious, fraternal, educational, and media institutions. There is also a remarkably homogeneous view of the community's interests insofar as claims on the state are concerned. Again, to us this is self-evident.

This self-evident black nationalist principle of community is challenged by scholars who contend that because of increased class differentiation in the post–civil rights era among blacks the idea of a black community is a myth.[17] Often this is qualified to say that the idea of a "monolithic" black community is a myth. While I am willing to be influenced on this issue by empirical studies that show a weakening of community among blacks in the last quarter century—and there are some, although more to the contrary—at present this argument is advanced more as an ideological assertion by integrationist, assimilationist conservatives or radicals committed to the doctrines of liberal individualism or class solidarity. Virtually all of the empirical studies of opinion in the black community show remarkably little class heterogeneity.[18]

The African American community in the early twenty-first century is for sure marked by more class differentiation than at any point in its history, but there has always been class divisions in the community, and as Gaines, among others, has noted these class differences resulted in class (and gender) tensions within what he calls "the uplift" tradition.[19] However, Gaines concedes that these class differences and tensions did not destroy the sense of legitimate community among blacks of all classes.

The post–civil rights era black community, like any developed or developing one, is divided by class, culture, region, and gender, and these divisions may result in differences in ethos, interests, and lifestyles. But, the fact of these differences are not—should not—be in and of themselves sufficient to destroy a sense of community, any more than similar divisions undermine the idea of the American community, despite its deep racial divisions. Divisions by race in the United States are certainly deeper than any divisions within black America. Yet, both blacks and whites share a sense of American community.

Related to this problem with community is the contention that in the "post-segregation era" there are no black interests and therefore there can be no black agenda. Indeed, Adolph Reed Jr. writes "that there are, or can be, authentic or automatically discernible community interests . . . is now the greatest single intellectual impediment to the construction of left equalitarian black politics."[20]

Again, it seems to me (and Walters) self-evident that the core interest of blacks in the United States is to achieve a *racially equalitarian* society. At the outset of the post–civil rights era Matthew Holden conceptualized this interest as "integration," which he defined as a society where "race would not predict the distribution of either material benefits or psyche esteem in any significant degree."[21] More recently Tommie Shelby conceptualized this interest as a "soft black nationalism," which is the kind of politics Walters was talking about when he referred to himself as a black nationalist. With respect to the interests of the black community, Shelby's soft nationalism is anchored by two interrelated propositions: 1) "what holds blacks together as a unified people with shared political interests is the fact of their racial subordination and their collective resolve to triumph over it," and 2) "the only interests that blacks share on account of their being black and that can serve as a stable and legitimate basis for political unity are race-related ones—fighting racism, promoting racial equality, eliminating racialized poverty, and reducing racial antagonism."[22]

Reed appears to reject both of these propositions, writing that this approach "perpetuates the practice of defining black interests in terms of an exclusively racial agenda—even though many of the most pressing socioeconomic concerns of a great many black Americans are not purely or most immediately racial."[23] And the idea of racial equality or parity, he writes, is a "modest ideal of equalitarianism or social justice," because "[i]f black and white unemployment rates were equally high, for example, it is not clear that there would be no objective black interest in reducing unemployment."[24]

Undoubtedly some blacks—perhaps a majority—would be satisfied with the attainment of this "modest ideal." Others would not be satisfied and would work for a more thoroughgoing transformation of capitalist relations. This would, however, take them beyond the realm of black politics into class politics. However, in understanding the really existing situation of black politics this class-based leftism is immature and premature.

A more telling problem of a premature class politics is that a successful effort by blacks to achieve their race interests is likely to require thoroughgoing transformations of the society and economy. In other words, the pursuit of racial equality is likely to result in more equalitarianism generally.[25] This was certainly Walters' view, and it was the fear of neoconservatives in the late 1960s and 1970s, who argued against policies to achieve racial equality precisely because they argued it would inevitably result in further demands for equality and thereby undermine capitalist relations and state legitimacy generally.[26]

Bayard Rustin identified this relationship between black politics, black interests, and class politics in his famous 1965 essay, "From Protest to Politics: The Future of the Civil Rights Movement." Rustin wrote, "while most Negroes in their hearts—unquestionably seek only to enjoy the fruits of American society as it now exists, their quest cannot be *objectively* satisfied within the framework of existing political and economic relations." Rather, Rustin wrote that adding up the costs of a full employment program and a program of ghetto reconstruction "we can conclude that we are talking about a refashioning of our political economy."[27] In other words—and this has been historically the case—when blacks fight for their interests, the interests of all Americans are served. Herbert Aptheker sums up this historical really existing condition nicely: "The Negro people have fought like tigers for freedom; and in doing so have enhanced the freedom struggles of all other peoples."[28]

Notes

1. On this new generation of black leaders, see Andra Gillespie, ed., *Whose Black Politics? Cases in Postracial Black Leadership* (New York: Routledge, 2010) and Gillespie, *The New Black Politician: Cory Booker, Newark and Postracial America* (New York: New York University Press, 2012).
2. In April 2011 Howard University announced the establishment of the Ronald Walters Leadership and Public Policy Center. The university president said, "Through this Center, his name, his spirit and his work will live on as we prepare others to follow his footsteps and impact the world as he did." See "Howard University to Establish Walters Center," http://www.howard.edu/newsroom/releases/2011/20110415howard.
3. Maurice Woodard and Michael Preston, "The Rise and Decline of Black Political Scientists," *PS* 17 (1984): 789–92.
4. American Political Science Association, *Political Science in the 21st Century: Report of the Task Force on Political Science in the 21st Century*, October 2011, www.apsanet.org/content60076.
5. Jerry Watts, "Political Science Confronts Afro-America: A Reconsideration," in *African American Perspectives in Political Science*, ed. Wilbur Reed (Philadelphia: Temple University Press, 2007), 399.
6. Ibid.
7. Wilbur Rich, "African American Political Scientists in Academic Wonderland," in *African American Perspectives in Political Science*, 49. See also Andrew Stark, "Why Political Scientists Aren't Public Intellectuals," *PS* 35 (2002): 578–87.
8. Kirsten Renwick Monroe, *Perestroika: The Raucous Rebellion in Political Science* (New Haven: Yale University Press, 2005). See

also the symposium "Pracademics: Mixing an Academic Career with Practical Politics," ed. Michael McDonald and Christopher Money, *PS* 44 (2010): 253–92.

9. Rich, "African American Political Scientists in Academic Wonderland," 46.

10. Adolph Reed, Jr., "Reflections on Atlanta University Political Science," *National Political Science Review* 9 (2003): 236–45.

11. Mack Jones, "NCOBPS: Twenty Years Later," in Jones, *Knowledge, Power, and Black Politics: Collected Essays* (Albany: State University of New York Press, 2014).

12. Rich, "African American Political Scientists in Academic Wonderland," 46.

13. Bertrand Russell, *A History of Western Philosophy* (New York: Simon and Schuster, 1965), ix.

14. Straying from the academic norm and becoming an activist may also impact the careers of those African Americans who have already ascended to academic heaven. Cornel West is generally recognized as one of the most creative and original contemporary American philosophers. West is also an activist in the Marxian-Du Boisian-Waltersian traditions. Because of his activism Harvard's president Lawrence Summers (hardly a disengaged scholar himself, having served as an advisor to President Bill Clinton and as secretary of the treasury) criticized West for his activism and public intellectual work and contemptuously dismissed his scholarship as "not serious." West subsequently left Harvard and accepted an appointment at Princeton. Later he left Princeton to teach at Union Theological Seminary. West's most important philosophical treatise is *The American Evasion of Philosophy: A Genealogy of Pragmatism* (Madison: University of Wisconsin Press, 1989). On his work as an activist intellectual, see Mack Jones, "Cornel West, the Insurgent Intellectual, *Race Matters*: A Critical Comment," in Jones, *Knowledge, Power, and Black Politics*, 277–90.

15. Watts, "Political Science Confronts Afro-America," 419–20; Adolph Reed Jr., *Stirring in the Jug: Black Politics in the Post-Segregation Era* (Minneapolis: University of Minnesota Press, 1999); Cedric Johnson, *Revolutionaries to Race Leaders: Black Power and the Making of African American Politics* (Minneapolis: University of Minnesota Press, 2007); Orlando Patterson, *The Ordeal*

of Integration (Washington, DC: Civitas/Counterpoint, 1997); Richard Payne, *Getting Beyond Race: The Changing American Culture* (Boulder, CO: Westview Press, 1998); and Shelby Steele, *The Dream Deferred* (New York: HarperCollins, 1998).

16. We briefly lay out our case for this proposition in our jointly authored conclusion in Ronald W. Walters and Robert C. Smith, *African American Leadership* (Albany: State University of New York Press, 1999). See also, Ronald W. Walters, "Barack Obama and the Politics of Blackness," *Journal of Black Studies* 38 (2007):15–27, and his chapter "The Integrity of Black Interests," in *White Nationalism, Black Interests: Conservative Public Policy and the Black Community* (Detroit: Wayne State University Press, 2003), 249–74.

17. A popular version of this argument is Eugene Robinson, *Disintegration: The Splintering of Black America* (New York: Doubleday, 2010).

18. Norman Nie, Sidney Verba, and John Petrocik, *The Changing American Voter* (Cambridge: Harvard University Press, 1976); Robert C. Smith and Richard Seltzer, *Race, Class, and Culture: A Study in Afro-American Mass Opinion* (Albany: State University of New York Press, 1992); Michael Dawson, *Behind the Mule: Race and Class in American Politics* (Princeton: Princeton University Press, 1994); Jennifer Hochschild, *Facing Up to the American Dream: Race, Class and the Soul of the Nation* (Princeton: Princeton University Press, 1995); and Katherine Tate, *What's Going On? Political Incorporation and the Transformation of Black Public Opinion* (Washington: Georgetown University Press, 2010).

19. Kevin Gaines, *Uplifting the Race: Black Leadership, Politics and Culture in the Twentieth Century* (Chapel Hill: University of North Carolina Press, 1996).

20. Reed, *Stirring in the Jug,* 15.

21. Matthew Holden, Jr., *The Politics of the Black Nation* (New York: Chandler, 1973), 137.

22. Tommie Shelby, *And We Who Are Dark: The Philosophical Foundations of Black Solidarity* (Cambridge: Harvard, 2005).

23. Reed, *Stirring in the Jug,* 42.

24. Ibid.

25. Lani Guinier and Gerald Torres, *The Miner's Canary: Enlisting Race, Resisting Power and Transforming Democracy* (Cambridge: Harvard University Press, 2002).

26. Irving Kristol, *Two Cheers for Capitalism* (New York: Basic Books, 1978); and Aaron Wildavsky, "Government and the People," *Commentary* (August 1973): 25–37.

27. Bayard Rustin, "From Protest to Politics," in *Down the Line: The Collected Writings* (Chicago: Quadrangle Books, 1971), 117–18.

28. Herbert Aptheker, *A Documentary History of the Negro People in United States*, vol. 1 (New York: Citadel Press, 1967), i.

Editors and Contributors

Editors

ROBERT C. SMITH is professor of political science at San Francisco State University. A former student of Walters, he coauthored with him *African American Leadership*. In addition he is the author of the *Encyclopedia of African American Politics* and ten other books, including most recently *Conservatism and Racism and Why in America They Are the Same* and *John F. Kennedy, Barack Obama and the Politics of Ethnic Incorporation and Avoidance*.

CEDRIC JOHNSON is associate professor of political science at the University of Illinois, Chicago. A former student of Walters, he coauthored with him *Bibliography of African American Leadership: An Annotated Guide*; Johnson is the author of *Revolutionaries to Race Leaders: Black Power and the Making of African American Politics* and is editor of *The Neoliberal Deluge: Hurricane Katrina, Late Capitalism and the Remaking of New Orleans* (University of Minnesota Press, 2011).

ROBERT G. NEWBY, a lifelong friend of Walters, is emeritus professor of sociology at Central Michigan University. His articles on racism, inequality, and the civil rights movement have appeared in leading journals of sociology.

Contributors

ADOLPHUS G. BELK JR., a former student of Walters, is assistant professor of political science and African American studies at Winthrop University. He is currently working on a book dealing with mass incarceration and the prison industrial complex.

HORACE CAMPBELL is professor of political science and African American Studies at Syracuse University. He has published widely in scholarly journals and edited volumes and is the author of four books, including most recently *Barack Obama and 21st-Century Politics: A Revolutionary Moment in the USA.*

COREY COOK is associate professor of political science and director of the Leo T. McCarthy Center for Public Service and the Common Good at the University of San Francisco. His research has been published in the *Du Bois Review, American Politics Research,* and *Presidential Studies Quarterly.*

ANDRA GILLESPIE is associate professor of political science at Emory University. Her current research focuses on the political leadership of the post–civil rights era generation. She is the editor of *Whose Black Politics? Cases in Postracial Black Leadership* and *The New Black Politician: Cory Booker, Newark, and Postracial America.*

ERROL HENDERSON is associate professor of political science and African American studies at Penn State University. He is the author of *Afrocentrism and World Politics: Toward a New Paradigm* and *Democracy and War: The End of an Illusion.*

LENNEAL J. HENDERSON is Distinguished Professor of Government and Public Administration and senior fellow at the William Donald Schafer Center for Public Policy at the University of Maryland, Baltimore. An internationally recognized authority on urban politics and policy, he has written extensively on District of Columbia politics.

CHARLES P. HENRY is the Emeritus H. Michael and Jeanne Williams Chair of African American Studies at the University of California, Berkeley. He is the author of more than eighty articles and reviews and seven books, including *Ralph Bunche: Model Negro or American Other?* and *Long Overdue: The Politics of Racial Reparations.* He is coeditor of *The Obama Phenomenon: Toward Multiracial Democracy in America,* and from 1986 to 1988 he was chair of the Board of Directors of Amnesty International, USA.

ALDON MORRIS is the Leon Forrest Professor of Sociology and African American Studies at Northwestern University. His *The Origins of the Civil Rights Movement: Black Communities Organizing for Change* is a seminal contribution to the literature of the civil rights movement. He is currently writing a book on the role of W.E.B. Du Bois in the founding of American sociology.

KARIN L. STANFORD is professor Pan African studies at California State University, Northridge. A former student of Walters, she is coeditor of *Black Political Organizations in the Post–Civil Rights Era* and author of *Beyond the Boundaries: Reverend Jesse Jackson in International Affairs*. She is a former Congressional Black Caucus Fellow and director of the Washington bureau of the Rainbow/PUSH Coalition.

KATHERINE TATE is professor of political science and African American studies at Brown University. She is the author of the award-winning *From Protest to Politics: The New Black Voter in American Elections*, *Black Faces in the Mirror: African Americans and Their Representatives in Congress*, *What's Going On? Political Incorporation and the Transformation of Black Public Opinion*, and *Concordance: Black Lawmaking in the U.S. Congress from Carter to Obama*.

HANES WALTON JR. (1941–2013) at the time of his death was the foremost scholar of African American politics in the United States. The first person to earn a PhD in political science from Howard University, professor of political science at Savannah State University and the University of Michigan, he authored twenty-six books and scores of articles, essays, and reviews. His *Black Politics: A Theoretical and Structural Analysis* and *Invisible Politics: Black Political Behavior* are foundational texts in the study of African American politics.

Index